ANDRÉ
PREVIN

ALSO BY MICHAEL FREEDLAND

Jolie: The Story of Al Jolson
A Salute to Irving Berlin
James Cagney
Fred Astaire
Sophie: The Story of Sophie Tucker
Jerome Kern
Errol Flynn (In America: The Two Lives of Errol Flynn)
Gregory Peck
Maurice Chevalier
Peter O'Toole
The Warner Brothers
So Let's Hear The Applause – The Story of the Jewish Entertainer
Dino: The Dean Martin Story
Jack Lemmon
Katharine Hepburn
The Secret Life of Danny Kaye
Shirley MacLaine
The Goldwyn Touch: A Biography of Sam Goldwyn
Leonard Bernstein
Jane Fonda
Liza With a "Z"
Dustin – A Biography of Dustin Hoffman
Kenneth Williams

With Morecambe and Wise – There's No Answer To That

With Walter Scharf – Composed and Conducted by Walter Scharf

ANDRÉ PREVIN

MICHAEL FREEDLAND

CENTURY

LONDON   SYDNEY   AUCKLAND   JOHANNESBURG

Published in 1991 by Century
Random Century Ltd
20 Vauxhall Bridge Road, London SW1V 2SA

Random Century Australia (Pty) Ltd
20 Alfred Street, Milsons Point, Sydney, NSW 2061, Australia

Random Century New Zealand Ltd
9-11 Rothwell Avenue, Albany, Auckland 10, New Zealand

Random Century South Africa (Pty) Ltd
PO Box 337, Bergvlei 2012, South Africa

Michael Freedland's right to be identified as the author of
this work has been asserted by him in accordance with the
Copyright, Designs and Patents Act, 1988.

Typeset in Linotronic Sabon by
SX Composing Ltd, Rayleigh, Essex

Printed and bound in U.K. by
Mackays of Chatham, Chatham, Kent

A catalogue record for this book is available from the British Library.

ISBN 0-7126-3503-3

Contents

FOR FIONA AND ROBIN

The evidence of a father's love and admiration

Acknowledgements

It's frequently a difficult job to know where to begin in thanking the people involved in a task such as this. Not so on this occasion. Some three years ago, I approached André Previn and suggested this book. He accepted my invitation knowing that it was going to mean hour upon hour of talking to me. In the event, the hours were numbered in the hundreds. We began speaking to each other in his then home in the Surrey countryside outside London, followed it through to his house in California and supplemented it by further interviews in Vienna and in a whole series of hotel suites on both sides of the Atlantic. His work with me was very much beyond the call of anyone's definition of duty and certainly more than I could have hoped for. When the writing was all over, he not only read the manuscript, but also the final proofs to which he added his own comments, now incorporated in the text. So to him, above all, my gratitude.

I am also intensely in the debt of his charming wife, Heather, who not only consented to André's spending so much time with me – and a constantly-touring conductor has very little of that commodity – but also gave me her own insights into her husband.

The list of others who agreed to talk to me about my subject is a lengthy one, but I couldn't have proceeded with this task without the help of:

George Anderson, Vladmir Ashkenazy, Arlene Auger, Camille Avellano, Emmanuel Ax, Dame Janet Baker, Franz Bartholomey, Irving Bush, Schuyler Chapin, Saul Chaplin, Cyd Charisse, Alexander (Sandy) Courage, Carl Cohn, Robert Crone, Harold Diktorow, Maurice Diktorow, Blake Edwards, Sumner Erikson, Paul Furst, Anne Giles, Clive Gillinson, Alan Goodman, Brigitta Grabner, the late Johnny Green, John Harbison, Boyd Hood, Michael Kaye, Gene Kelly, Rheiner Kuochl, Michael Kidd, Lorin Levee, Mrs. Betty Lowe, Linda Marks, Rob Roy McGregor, James Mallison, the late Johnny Mercer, the late Eric Morecambe, Heiichero Ohyama, Jasper Parrott,

Itzhak Perlman, Mel Powell, Jack Renner, David Raksin, Joel Roteman, Danny Rothmuiler, Albert Sendry, Walter Scharf, Keith Shelly, Harold Smolier, Isaac Stern, Tom Stoppard, Al Woodbury, Billy Wilder, Ronald Wilford, John Williams and Ernie Wise.

There are numerous other people to thank — my editors at Century, my agent Desmond Elliott who sparked off my happy association with my publishers, and above all to my wife Sara who, as always, patiently experienced the years of gestation at my side.

Michael Freedland
Elstree, 1991

ONE

Berlin was where André Previn was born and it was from Berlin a year before World War Two that he and his family fled. He didn't go back until 1968. It was a year that became very important in his career. He was made conductor of the London Symphony Orchestra. If that was the fulfilment of dreams – and it was – it was going to Berlin for the first time in thirty years that gave him an unrepeatable, special, emotional tug.

He retraced the footsteps he had trudged in his childhood – to the park where he had played every day, to the house on the Innsbruck-erstrasse where his family had lived, all round the neighbourhood of the city from which they had had to escape when the Nazis made life impossible.

Near the family house was a cinema, the Royale. He remembered it affectionately because that was where he was allowed to go on Saturday mornings. He wondered what they were showing that week and saw the very pillars on which, he remembered, the theatre would advertise its programmes. It was a snowy day and the pillars were covered. So, with his gloved hand, he wiped away the snow and hoped it would show the title of the film of the week. It didn't. Instead, a poster read: 'Berlin Philharmonic Orchestra. Brahms. Conducted by André Previn.'

If his manager, Ronald Wilford, hadn't been with him, it would have been one of those stories that no one would have believed. He himself says of the 'find': 'I put it to you – if Frank Capra in his wildest moments had put that in one of his films, you'd have wanted to retch and run up the aisle.' He also admits: 'I've tried to do it again for years since then on my many visits to Berlin, but I have to say that whenever I look for a poster on a pillar advertising one of my concerts, I can never find one.'

1

But since this was the city where it had all begun, the symbolism of the 1968 find couldn't have escaped the attention of anyone with a modicum of intelligence or emotion. André may not have felt he had come home, but he had to realise he had made it – and in a very satisfying way. Jack Previn would have been proud.

TWO

Everything had gone right for Jack Prewin*. He was a handsome man with a charming, witty wife and three attractive children.

Stefan was the eldest and Leonora, whom everyone knew as Lolo, the second. Perhaps the greatest pleasure of all came from his youngest child, André Ludwig†, who was born on 6 April 1929. His first name was undoubtedly the choice of Charlotte, or Lotte, his mother. Even though German was her native tongue, she came from Alsace (which, since the Versailles Treaty, had been part of France for the first time since the Franco-Prussian War of 1870). The second name left no doubt about the parents' sense of German affiliation.

Jack Prewin may have been born in Poland and Lotte's maiden name may have been Epstein, but they had long felt themselves emancipated and part of the very fabric of the Germany they loved. How else could Jack spend part of his time sitting on the judicial bench?

André was plainly a very clever child, an attraction in itself to his father, although after the boy's earliest years he would rarely admit it. There are, however, stories of how Jack would like to boast of André's abilities to friends, and not only in music. He was proud of how he could read anything placed in front of him, including the most adult books in the house.

Even more important to Jack, André was the one who, from the very first time he had been shown a piano, had realised that by placing his fingers on the keys, he could make music. Even more significantly, he could enjoy making it. The other children thumped and made a noise which they considered no more attractive than did any

* The family name until it was changed by Jack, see p.34.
† When André arrived in America his middle name became George.

3

of their casual listeners. But from his first introduction to the instrument, André produced sounds that were as sweet as they were competent.

Jack himself was an accomplished pianist – 'a very fine amateur pianist' is how his son now remembers him, and indeed the family friends who heard him play would have testified to that fact. He, however, had never considered that part of his life as any more than a diversion.

Jack and his friends would gather for musical soirées. André can also remember, as a tiny child, sitting under the piano while his brother and sister pounded away with their father on four-handed pieces, although these were intended more for their education than mere casual entertainment.

Charlotte was not a musical participant, but, like the rest of the family, enjoyed the levity and relaxation that music brought to her elegant flat. She liked hearing music on the radio and when her husband took her to concerts, she enjoyed them too. Jack would even tease her with posers about the origin of particular tunes, which he was convinced she would never recognise. Sometimes, just sometimes, she would prove him wrong.

André's first piano lesson came on his fifth birthday. Other youngsters in 1934 – or at any other time for that matter – might have regarded it as more a penance than a present. But to the bright-eyed André Ludwig Prewin it was a revelation, a gift not so much from his parents as from heaven.

In fact, the child had been asking for the lessons for months. It is one memory that André has deeply engrained into his psyche. 'I think,' he told me, 'I was fascinated by the piano as a sort of large toy, just as any kid is when he has one at his disposal.'

His father could only agree. It was the kind of toy he wanted for the boy. Jack knew the cost of the lessons would be money well spent. He had believed that since the day he took André into the family music room, played the scale for his young son and named the notes on the piano for him.

'What note was that?' he asked his son.

'B flat,' André replied.

'How do you know?' his father pondered.

'Because you told me.'

There was little to say after that.

Ten minutes later, André got his wish – the promise of the piano lessons, and more.

He did so well – and so much better than either Stefan or Lolo –

that the two older siblings decided immediately to have no more lessons themselves. They wouldn't undergo the frustration and humiliation of constantly being compared so unfavourably with their
younger brother. So they announced the end of their own lessons.
That was a reasonably brave step to take. Their father accepted the
joint decision and didn't press the point.

Jack himself had a brilliant brain which, in his mid-forties, had
taken him to the very top of the German Bar (a fact also proved by
the time he spent serving as a judge). The result was that he commanded both high respect and even higher fees. The Prewins lacked
for little.

As her love of concerts showed, Lotte was a woman of culture as
well as of wealth. She was widely travelled and had a large circle of
friends. As her son now says: 'I remember her going on what seemed
to me to be a great many trips with her friends, including several
world cruises. There were great long periods when I never saw her.'

André describes his father as being 'an imposing presence'.

'He was not at home all that much, so he was a bit scary. I didn't
have with him what, for instance, my son has with me. Go into my
room to see if I was awake? Forget it.'

But in André's earliest childhood there were also kindnesses and
joys that he still remembers with a smile. 'He did tell me stories and
was sometimes terrific, especially when we went for occasional walks
together.'

His very German nanny, Ida, would take André to the zoo. Sometimes just the two of them went, but often, when she wasn't travelling to the end of the earth, Lotte accompanied them, keeping a
watchful eye on both her child and the way he was being supervised.
Despite the fear, the happiest moments were the ones when, quite un-
expectedly, Jack joined them. The signal for his approach was the
sound of what the Prewins regarded as the 'family whistle', Jack's
warbling of the opening bars of Beethoven's Eighth Symphony.

The prosperity of the Prewins was a direct result of his advice and
advocacy and was obvious to anyone granted the privilege of a visit
to the Innsbrukerstrasse apartment. There were very dark rugs on the
floor. The furniture was heavy and equally dark. The house was full
of books, with shelves in practically every room, 'which made it look
very nice indeed', André remembers now.

Only once was André taken to court by his father. All he remembers of the occasion is being bored to death by the drab proceedings
he had imagined in his mind would be grand, ceremonial and perhaps, had he been able to think in those terms then, Kafkaesque.

It was obvious at that stage that André Prewin was not going to be a lawyer. In the child's earliest years, when already the first signs were apparent of just how clever he was, Jack might have wished for nothing more than that André walk in his own powerful footsteps. After all, he would have been entering that most respected of professions and he was more than bright enough to do so.

If it hadn't been for the elections that brought Adolf Hitler to power in Germany in 1933, the Prewins' lives would have changed little, except that Jack would have become even more successful and quite possibly ended his days as a judge of the high court.

Hitler, though, changed all that – and in the process, the family's background, which hitherto had been nothing more than an occasional inconvenience, become paramount. The Prewins were Jewish, but until the Nazis let them know it was more important than they had ever imagined, it meant nothing to them.

Jack was much, much more concerned with music, which was why he taught André sight-reading. Naturally enough, he did it better than nine out of ten other children plodding their way through first books of nursery rhymes. The reading and the instrument on which he demonstrated his new-found abilities became his priorities. As his father had hoped, they took precedence over any notions of becoming a lawyer, and over the threat of Hitler.

Those scores were meant to be studied and used. In addition to the special, four-hand piano arrangements of the Beethoven and Brahms symphonies that Jack bought, there were editions of those by Mozart and Haydn, too. There were overtures and even string quartets, arranged for piano 'so that people could stumble through them at home'.

Jack expected André to do more than stumble through them. Now that Stefan and Lolo no longer played, it was André who was expected to play duets with his father – and to play them excellently, at that. The child didn't object. Not because he thought he was showing off, not even because he particularly wanted to please his father, but simply because he enjoyed it. The fact that he did it well pleased him, but as in other matters in his life since, that in itself was no triumph. He expected to do so.

The boy had to play at the correct speed and then adapt to the problems with which he was faced. 'If you get lost,' said Jack, 'catch up. If you make a mistake, keep going.'

It was, André now realises, 'my first introduction to the symphonic repertoire and it left such a mark that even now I can describe the covers of that music. I know, for instance, that the 'Pastoral' was dark green with gold lettering and had a kind of stain at the bottom of the right lower corner.

'Even though at the time I must have felt hassled if I didn't know a certain piece of music and I am sure there must have been the occasional tear, it must have done me a phenomenal amount of good, and by a kind of osmosis I learnt all that music.'

It was the way religious Jewish boys learnt their Torah and Talmud, from books that became even more holy because of their very familiarity.

Apart from lip service to a Passover Seder – 'That's enough,' Jack would say barely before five minutes of the recounting of the story of the departure of the Children of Israel from Egypt had got under way, 'let's eat' – there were no trappings of Judaism in their lives. André now recalls: 'He only tried to have the festival once in my childhood. He just didn't know. That one time, he tried it but didn't know what to do and gave up.' The bound music scores occupied the same places of honour and were treated with the same reverence which religious families divested their Hebrew books. For the Prewins there could be no dilution in their spiritual activities. Music was there on top of the pedestal and nothing, and certainly not Judaism, could be allowed to knock it down.

'My parents were absolutely disinterested in the religious aspects of being Jewish,' André now says. It was a disinterest that he inherited.

'I am the bane, for instance, of Itzhak Perlman's life. I never know when the holidays are, or if I find out when they are, what they are. I've never learned about them or cared. It's the same with Vladimir Ashkenazy. We say, "Is that the one when you can't eat?" and Itzhak goes mad.'

He was taken to his first concert soon after that fifth birthday awakening with the piano lessons. He has never forgotten the experience.

It came hot on the heels of his being given his own gramophone – a little black portable, just big enough to take ten-inch 78s but capable of dealing with the twelve-inch discs that André played, providing he was careful not to knock the black shellac platters as they overhung the turntable. There is something about one's first record player. The images of the machine and the smell of the records as they are first taken from their brown cardboard envelopes are inclined to linger like the memory of a banquet to a gourmet.

André's first collection of records might have sounded scratchy as they vibrated through the acoustic soundbox of the wind-up machine, but he was overcome by the sound just the same. Leopold Stokowski and the Philadelphia Orchestra playing the second of the *Nocturnes* of Debussy – *Fêtes* – at his own command was something to be relished. The sound of the trumpets getting closer and closer left an impression that was more than just indelible. Had it been physically carved into his brain and then actually labelled, that sound couldn't have made a deeper impression.

As a result, the adult André Previn will never cease being grateful to Stokowski. So much so that he told me: 'I was so whacked out about that piece that I played it until the record almost fell apart.'

He knew every moment of the piece and exactly where the records had to be turned over. 'I got very expert at that, until it took seconds instead of the casual minutes most people took.'

If the records were fairly worn out by being played over and over again and the needles blunted into useless shafts of metal, his own love of the sound of music – and particularly the sound of that one piece of music – was only being sharpened in the process. 'I tried to play it on the piano and wanted to go and hear it if I knew it was being played.'

An ear less attuned to music and how it should be played might have related it always to the records – certain bars might have been associated always with where the needle had stuck, or with where the disc had had to be turned over. André passed that stage very quickly. The recorded *Nocturne* was replaced in his subconscious by the live performances he heard subsequently.

He now tells about casually hearing that Stokowski recording again thirty years later. 'It was really quite amazingly eccentric and broke all the rules. It is very interesting that I could have loved it so, as my first record.'

That being so, he still didn't spend the hours and hours listening to his classical records on that old wind-up gramophone that a later generation would devote to pop music. It was never more than a substitute for the real thing. He wanted to play music himself and to listen to it in the one place where Jack had told him it should be heard, the concert hall.

Since the gramophone gift was followed so soon afterwards by that first experience of a live concert, it turned out to be quite a realistic proposition for him.

To Jack, taking André to a concert was a natural progression from all that he had been doing, musically, up to then. His father assumed it would also answer the nagging question of whether it was the music or the possession of the gramophone and all it could do that had impressed his young son so much. After that evening, when the little six-year-old, who was never very big for his age, had to stand on tiptoe to try to see what was going on on stage, there were no doubts. It was the music.

Wilhelm Furtwängler was conducting an all-Brahms programme, ending with the Third Symphony. Now André says, 'That's about the worst thing you could possibly take a child to hear – and typical of my father.'

The concert was by the Berlin Philharmonic, the very orchestra that would play an important part in his own professional life. That day in 1934, he stood and he listened and for the length of the concert he was enthralled, in the way other boys of his age became ecstatic at seeing a clown in baggy trousers and red nose or at watching a movie comedy. It was a world that he could never have imagined to exist. Instantly, he wanted to be part of it. Leaving the concert hall and on the way home, the intensity of the experience only increased.

Looking back now, he agrees it is impossible to divorce the theatricality of the occasion from the music that it produced – and to know which it was that made the bigger impression. 'All I know is that I was just mad for the experience. I suppose that if I were crouched over a dreadful old portable phonograph, which I had to wind up, and enjoyed that, then the sound of one hundred-plus people really playing would have been an eye-opener, or an ear-opener or a brain-opener. I just loved it.'

He arrived home in a daze and had to be put to bed. So overcome was he by the experience that he was almost ill.

He remembers the concert as clearly as most children remember their first day at school, which in some ways this almost was for him. He doesn't actually recall the effect it had on him from first-hand knowledge. But he is perfectly happy to accept the family story. A few years later, he was told that he reacted much as if he had just been struck by a virus. He actually had a fever. 'It was just so unbelievable for me.' He certainly remembers it all very much better than he recalls the first concert at which he actually *played*. That is a total blank for him, swallowed up in all that has happened professionally since then.

Soon afterwards he was taken to an opera. Again, it was his father's idea. 'He was very methodical, or perhaps it was just very Germanic of him you know, "The boy has seen a concert and will now see an opera."'

Unfortunately, Jack used absolute logic in his selection of a suitable vehicle for his son's opera education. He knew that most examples of the opera repertoire were just too long for a child to accept. Jack looked in the papers and selected the only one-act opera that was being presented that season.

The choice was Strauss's *Salome*. It was a selection even more eccentric than the concert choice. The boy whose every movement was subjected to such intense parental scrutiny, was being encouraged to watch the dance of the seven veils. But that wasn't why André now considers it a strange choice. 'It was just so difficult to understand, musically.

'It's like saying to a child, "I'm going to show you your first drawings" – and then showing him Aubrey Beardsley. It's madness, just madness. I didn't know what the hell was going on on the stage. Somebody running around with a head on a plate. But, again, it was theatrical and I did enjoy that.'

The one-and-a-half-hour opera was part of a double bill – Berlin audiences demanded value for their money in those days. The companion piece was 'inexplicably' the ballet, *Coppelia*. 'And that bored me to tears, even though it took place surrounded by toys. I thought it was rubbish.'

It also left him with a sense of bewilderment. 'I always believed that John the Baptist lost his head in a toyshop.' Which was more than he ever knew about the Old Testament.

He was also, if he was good, allowed less intellectual or artistic pursuits – like going to the Royale. Courtesy of Shirley Temple and her film, *Wee Willie Winkie*, André discovered the movies.

It took considerable pressure by André to be allowed to break the film barrier. His parents were seemingly not that keen. But he was constantly being recommended to give the cinema a try. 'I kept hearing from my elder brother and sister how terrific it was to go to the movies. And finally, finally I went to see it. It was a last-minute decision by my parents to allow me to go and I was taken to a newsreel theatre.'

There was one hour of news, which André dismissed as 'not very exciting'. It was an experience not at all like his first visit to a concert. What was more, a fair time would elapse before he would go to see a film again – 'because I just didn't want to go. To me, watching a film was seeing the news.'

But then he was taken to *Wee Willie Winkie* and the cinema and all its glories were opened to him. He liked it – very much. In fact, he couldn't wait to go again. André even remembers the second picture to which he was taken, a German movie based on the *Turandot* legend. Thereafter, the movies would be a treat. He could not know that within a decade, they would gain a place of more than a little importance in his life.

On Saturday mornings, there was the two-blocks rush to the nearest advertising pillar to discover what the Royale was showing. If he came back with the title of a film to which his parents couldn't object, he and the Royale were in partnership.

Jack and Lotte had no reason to fear for either his moral or his physical safety. That was not to last. It was when the Nazis came to power, and started to exercise that power, that it all changed, and the family's Jewish background started to have a relevance to their lives they would never have imagined.

At first, Prewin was no longer allowed to sit as a judge. Then his private legal practice suddenly shrank. Ultimately, the time came when Jews were not permitted legal representation of any kind, but Jack and Lotte started worrying before that.

Under Jack's feet the ground had turned to quicksand. But once he realised that André was the one who looked set to become a pianist, he was unrelenting. It was as though he thought there had to be some means of rescuing his pride from all that was tumbling around him and André was his chosen instrument.

Not that he needed to lay down an iron hand. As André has since said, 'The moment I saw that piano I fell in love with it.' But there was nightly piano practice when he came home from school. He could be depended upon to be playing at the precise time his father came home from his office. Yet, whether he was playing loud or soft, there was no mistaking the arrival of the senior Prewin. It was, he now says, 'an extremely vivid memory' for him.

The Prewin family's apartment was at the very top of the building. As André now remembers, Jack announced his arrival the very moment that he opened the front door. He didn't simply turn the latch. Once in the flat, he threw down his keys on to a brass grille, the one which covered the central heating pipes in the floor of the entrance hall. 'The sound would ring throughout the house.' He would then come to the door of the room where the child was practising, listening out for the first mistake. 'I would continue practising with the sweat now falling all over my face because I knew he was listening outside the door.'

'My father would then listen until I did something wrong, open the door and scream the word, "falsch" ("wrong") into the room, close the door and leave.

'And until I heard him leave and go upstairs, I couldn't breathe or continue practising in any form. Now that was an interesting test of

11

daily discipline! Jesus, I remember the sound of those keys being slammed down on the floor!'

It certainly served to scare the teacher, one Alfred Mayzel, who before long left to become an officer in the Polish Cavalry. 'So I wouldn't like to give you much money on the chance that he was still alive for very long.'

Mayzel had been the one charged with teaching André what would happen if he put certain fingers on certain keys – 'although,' he says now, 'I had already worked that one out for myself. By the time he came I was playing little tunes that I had worked out myself with very little trouble.'

Mayzel didn't leave his pupil, however, before asking to see Jack. When they did meet, it was for him to tell André's father, 'I don't really think I should be teaching him. I think he ought to have someone who knows much more and with whom he could get on much more quickly.' It was, André now concedes, 'an act of amazing generosity on his part'.

André was so good that he had already been admitted to the Berliner Hochschule für Musik, a conservatory under the guidance of one of its most eminent teachers, Professor Breithaupt. There were no concessions to André's age or lack of experience. As an audition piece he was handed the music for Beethoven's E Major Piano Sonata and told to play it. Jack's insistence on sight-reading ability had paid off.

The news of André's passing his audition gave Herr Prewin one of his few reasons to smile in those days. Old Professor Breithaupt – he was an octogenarian – pronounced himself satisfied with André's progress and helped the youngster, now about seven years old, graduate to ever more complicated pieces.

'You were taught by *him*?' the conductor George Szell was to ask him. 'Even if you were only a little child in those days, he must have been absolutely ancient.' As André told him, he was.

Now Jack, who had so firmly abandoned any ambition for his youngest son to follow him into the law, had no doubt at all what André *would* do – he was going to be a professional musician.

Despite the apparent strictness his father represented and all the sweat he brought, André is today more than just sanguine about his father's influence. 'He did things for me which, in retrospect, did as much for me musically as anyone has ever done. He was determined that I would not just grow up to be a piano player but a real musician.'

He wasn't the only one at this stage who had marked out the boy's career. 'I don't think there was any doubt in *my* mind either that it was going to be my career.' He remembers wanting to do that when he was five, and wanting it more and more when he became six and seven.

There was everything about the way his young son took to both the sound and practice of music which told Jack that any other profession would be a waste of a talent which, had he been religious, he might have assessed as God-given. Every talk he had ever had with André's teachers indicated that he was one of those very few students they would identify as being totally cut out for a life in which music would be the governing force.

The conservatory did no spoiling of him, however. He may have been very young, but André went there every evening to subject himself to an experience so tortuous he either had to have a total personal commitment to its curriculum or to have a parent who was committed for him. André had both. He learned and when he did so he knew he had to conform to standards of conduct that were, to say the least, not usual in primary schools.

Thinking of the Hochschule today, André says: 'They were disciplinarians – but I learned quite a bit.'

It wasn't usual for a child to do what André was doing, but again it was part of Jack's search for perfection and his determination to find it. The choice was either the Hochschule or a private piano teacher who might or might not go off to join the Polish Cavalry. 'He probably didn't know anywhere between those two extremes of teaching,' his son says now.

No one would tell André so, but he was clearly a child prodigy. No one told him, either, that all that concentration on music would affect his school work, so it didn't – although he says now, 'I remember almost nothing about going to school.' And he adds: 'Whether it's blocked or I genuinely don't remember, I'm now too old to pursue in daily analysis.'

When he wasn't working at his piano, André was having to do the same lessons as every other boy of his age in Germany. He didn't go to a state school, but to the private Zickelschule, close to the Innsbrukerstrasse, and if the discipline was going to be tough – Jack for one wouldn't have wanted it any other way – there was a degree of protection for a boy like he at that sort of institution. He wasn't very good at arithmetic, but then he never would be. It didn't have anything to do with the time he spent playing the piano.

When he was about seven years old, his brother Stefan was no longer at home. As he now explains it: 'My parents didn't like the idea of him spending his young manhood in Germany, bearing in mind all that was going on there.'

An intricate game had had to proceed to get him out of the country. The Nazis at that stage were not stopping many people from leaving, but in order to go to America, as the Prewins wanted their son to do, Stefan would first have to have an invitation from an American citizen.

There was a second cousin, named Charles Previn, whom they later discovered was the head of the music department at Hollywood's Universal Studios, whom they could approach, but decided to go a different route. The family had become very friendly with the eminent violinist Jascha Heifetz and had entertained him in their home along with his agent, Rudolph Polk. They had got on so well that Lotte had started a correspondence with Heifetz and it still continued. At first, they just talked about music and the arts and family gossip. Now, though, with the international situation as bad as it was, there were more serious things to write about, if only obliquely, in the face of the Nazi censors.

Would Heifetz issue the invitation to Stefan? He did and Stefan, at Charles Previn's suggestion, became Steve, and stayed with Rudolph Polk.

So in those early, formative years, André was deprived of his elder brother's company. He knew of no reason why he should have left so suddenly, but reasoned that he was off on some adventure somewhere. Meanwhile, he had Lolo to play with and they got on very well indeed.

That Jack and Lotte had plans for their other two children as well as for themselves was not at the time revealed to André. How could it be? No matter how many times a child is told a secret that has to stay a secret, the temptation to break it is so strong, the risk cannot bear contemplation. So André didn't know that Jack was seeking ways of winding up his practice and taking the family away from Germany. His father's hope was that it would happen very soon. If they could also get to the United States, a country riddled with quota restrictions, the family's problems would all be over.

Yet Jack knew those problems would never be over. His practice did still exist and did still bring in some money, although there was nothing like the old prosperity. Certainly on the surface, it seemed that he did still have the wherewithal to make a journey that others couldn't possibly have contemplated. He wasn't short of the odd Mark, was he? No, he certainly was not, and if he could sell up, he and the family would be able to live in great comfort for the rest of their lives.

That was the theory. The practice was very different. It is one of the great paradoxes of totalitarian regimes that those they wish to persecute and excoriate for being so unwelcome among them are the ones they prevent from leaving. There was a need for an exit visa, which would have been given to more people than were actually able to take advantage of the 'privilege'.

But just suppose the Prewins did manage to get away – there were laws about taking money with them. Those who did leave Germany were expected to do so with the contents of a couple of suitcases and an amount of money varying between nothing and ten dollars per person.

Somehow, they planned to go nevertheless. If the children weren't to be told, life had to be made to proceed as normal.

André continued to go to school during the day and to the Hochschule every evening. But it was the conservatory that was the more important part of his education. 'My schooling tailed off into all the absolute necessities, so that I got permission to avoid all the things that might have been thought of as extraneous and fun. From there, I would go straight to the conservatory.'

He and his friends were surprisingly unrestricted in some of their social activities. All that would change, however, after the day that André and his best pal went on a picnic to the Grunewald and lingered in the streets on the way home – in time to be caught up in a torchlight procession of stormtroopers so beloved of Hitler and his henchmen.

They had had a pleasant enough day, these two boys for whom politics didn't exist. They took the tram home and were let off with about a fifteen- to twenty-minute walk to go – his friend lived on Innsbrukerstrasse, too – until they saw the stormtroopers.

André said to his friend, 'Hey, let's just stand and watch this for a while.' As he now recalls it: 'We stopped and we watched and we watched. They came by with the polished boots and the torchlight and the signs and we thought it was amazing.'

Indeed, there was nothing more sinister to it all, as far as they could work out, than a parade of Salvationists – and even they knew this was a much better show.

Neither child was aware of any particular risk, other than the possible danger of inadvertently being crushed in the crowd, and there was a basic instinct for dealing with such things – you just tried to keep out of the way. All they knew was that they were caught up in the most exciting thing they had ever known.

Suddenly, though, they realised that it was getting very late and it was more than about time they got home. They anticipated shouts if not beatings. They did not know why, on this evening, being late was causing more concern than usual.

For two hours neither André's nor his friend's family knew what had been going on and worried all the more. The other boy's parents had gathered at the Prewin's apartment and, long before the boys turned up, were fearing a dreadful worst.

When André and his friend finally did make their appearances, they realised something of the anxiety they had caused. 'We found both parents in total hysterics, knowing that the Nazis were going round smashing the glass in store fronts and hitting old people.'

Today, André isn't precisely certain that it was this event which persuaded his parents to wait no longer and get out by whatever means was at their disposal, but it most certainly must have influenced them to do so very soon afterwards.

There was also another reason: André was told to bring his father to the Hochschule. Jack went to see the professor. The door of the old man's office was closed and the situation was explained carefully, perhaps even kindly. There was no way the professor could afford to keep a Jewish boy in his academy, particularly one who was so obviously talented. The Nazis did not like to hear that so frequently expressed and not always totally accurate statement that the most talented and clever children were usually the Jewish ones.

It had to be one of the most complicated trips ever devised. As we have seen and as hundreds of thousands in their position knew only too well, it couldn't just be organised by means of a visit to a travel agent – although in their case that happened too.

First, there had to be the invitations issued. They had gone through all the procedures long before. Jack wanted to do it legally, to have the correct exit visa, the necessary papers that indicated there was an invitation waiting for them, too, in the United States, where they could join Stefan. That way, they could go with a reasonably clear mind and with at least some of their most treasured possessions.

'Then,' as André remembers, 'all that was happening triggered my father into thinking, "Let's move now."'

There was no news from the States, none at all from the exit visa office in Berlin, so some other means of leaving Germany had to be found. It was then that Jack came out with the idea that was very much second best for them, but which at least offered some hope of saving their lives, even if it meant not saving their money, their books, their paintings or any of their other most valuable belongings. Jack's answer was that they would go first to Paris.

How they were permitted by the German Government to go to Paris and not directly to New York is another one of the quirks of the Nazi bureaucratic system. Going to New York, if they could possibly have got there, would have looked like what it was – running away – and they would never have been able to come back. Taking a trip to Paris could be seen to be a weekend away – and they could just have come back if they, as a last resort, needed to do so. So go to Paris was what the Prewins did. They planned a weekend away and took a flight from Berlin's Tempelhof airfield to the French capital.

It was a mark of the desperation they felt. Even in 1938, there were few German Jewish families who were that desperate. André knew just before the drive to the airport that he and the family were leaving Berlin. He also knew that he wasn't allowed to tell anyone about it. No one should even suspect that there was anything afoot.

They left at just two hours' notice. Nothing was altered in the apartment. It was locked up no differently than it would have been had the family gone to a concert or the opera. Not only was the furniture left, but so was the china, and in the drawers of the sideboards, all the family silver cutlery. The piano remained standing in the music room as it always had. The music scores in the black and green leather covers stayed where they were. None of them would ever be seen again by members of the Prewin family. The house was to be destroyed in an Allied bombing raid.

They took just one suitcase with them. All André himself remembers thinking was that this was going to be great fun. Going to a new city. And getting there by aeroplane!

It was desperation indeed. Even on the journey to the airport they must have wondered whether it might not be sensible just to sit and wait. If the invitation to the United Sates would come – and with it the immigration visa for which they were in the middle of an agonisingly long queue that seemed, and probably was, endless – they could take some of those precious belongings.

The family's flight lasted for just a couple of hours, but for those hours they didn't dare speak, didn't dare hope. All they could do was worry that they were about to be sent back.

Indeed, it frequently seemed that they would be. On an otherwise fairly quick scheduled flight – by 1938 standards and even all these years and scientific developments later, it still seems that way – the Lufthansa plane made a distinctly unscheduled stop.

All the passengers, and not just the Prewins, expected the police to come into the aircraft, examine papers – and take them back again. But they never did. The plane just stopped and without any explanation took off again. If hearts could ever be said to be in people's mouths, the Prewins were all but physically choking with theirs. The sense of relief when they landed in France and *were* seen by police who carried guns and did look at their papers was palpable.

Even then, they couldn't really be sure that they had reached Paris and that this was not yet another unscheduled stop inside Germany. 'When the people came on board, the customs men, and we could see they were French, the feelings of my parents were unbelievable.'

The normally unemotional Prewins were at this moment anything but that. Finally, they were able to breathe – and then to contemplate what they had done. They had taken nothing with them. In truth, they were dead broke. But it is a credit to them that they were not also broken.

'It was "broke" in the sense that there was absolutely nothing,' André now says. Jack had no more money on him than he could be expected to need for a weekend. What was more, there was no prospect of ever getting any more. That being so, how could they even contemplate going to America?

André today can only guess at what all this really meant to his parents, particularly to his mother, who had never had to work for a pampered way of life that had always been hers as if by right. 'I can guess that she treated it all,' he says, 'with a mixture of relief at having got out, while still feeling terribly sad at having to leave a lifestyle that she would have had no reason to believe was going to end so catastrophically, and so frightened of the trip itself and of everything else. But she had enormous courage and was really quite indomitable and I don't think it ever occurred to her that this was going to get her down.' In the midst of a problem that really was so immense, she decided that she had to deal with it with a kind of courage few had known she possessed.

It was not in Jack Prewin's character to neglect any fine detail in his plans. Indeed, he had arranged his family's future with the precision of a military operation – bearing in mind that one's estimation of the future in military terms must always be dependent on the moves of the enemy. He had assessed the enemy's response like a grand master in a chess tournament and come to a conclusion. He knew what he must do.

There was no apparent reason why he couldn't use his office in Berlin to salvage at least *something* for himself and his family. But making that particular move was, in itself, as complicated as anything that had gone before it.

He contacted the office via Switzerland. A friend who had gone to the country managed to phone Jack's secretary and pass on a message that was almost as bizarre as it was urgent. He told her to use some of the money tied up in the office and in Germany to buy the family tickets for the ocean voyage to America. That would still have been legal and raised not too many suspicions among the Nazis. As far as they were concerned, Prewin was in Paris on business and was due to come back.

More than that, once having decided that he was able to book passages to America for the whole family – as soon as the invitations to the States had been processed and finalised – he was determined to get the best cabins and berths his money could buy. After all, it couldn't be used for anything else.

That, however, did pose a question for which André Previn, now in his early sixties, has still no definitive answer: if the money could be used to buy steamship tickets, why couldn't he take out more cash so that he could use it to set up in this new life?

I suggested an answer that could be the root of the whole matter: Jack Prewin was always, first and foremost, a pedantic German who had to do things in an orderly fashion. Second, he was also a lawyer who had been trained to uphold the law, whether he agreed with it or not. Even a viciously cruel Nazi law was not going to be flouted by someone like him. The *law* decreed that no one should take money out of the country and he accepted it.

'He absolutely refused to try to smuggle anything out,' André recalls, 'and he absolutely refused to allow my mother to smuggle anything out either.'

They stayed in Paris for five months, living what he would subsequently call 'really hand-to-mouth'.

For them, it was the first sample of the changed life they were all about to lead. No luxury hotel suites. No meals at the finest restaurants. When they moved from place to place, they travelled by bus or by the Metro.

But they were not alone in the city. Lotte's brother, Georges, was living there and some financial provision had been made for their arrival. Georges arranged the basics of life for them, like the modest hotel rooms where they would live, and the children's schooling. The hotel was more modest than the family could have imagined would ever come their way. 'It was a family hotel but one which I'm fairly sure sold rooms by the hour.'

That establishment close to the Madeleine would for ever after create an image of Paris for André Previn not detailed in any of the guidebooks. 'Lenny Bruce once told me,' he says now, 'about a place he had stayed at in Paris that instantly took me back to that hotel. It was, he said, an hotel where the pillows smelt like the rug. It was one of the most loathsome descriptions I have ever heard, but I didn't care at that time.'

They were traumatic months. While they waited for their visa to come through, they also had to wait for the ship booking to be finalised. 'I think my father also hoped that while waiting he might be able to rescue something of his money, but it never happened.' And then there was the constant flow of news from Germany, all of it getting worse. To Jack, nothing was more ominous – although it made him even more certain that he had taken the right step the day that he booked that flight to Paris – than when he heard that all the Jewish lawyers in Berlin had been not only forced out of practice but rounded up and taken . . . at the time no one knew where.

It took a long time before that strange mixture of relief and total despair would wear off. It was true, he and his family were free – poor but free. But Jack had to resign himself possibly to never seeing his home or his office again. He had lost his personal war with Adolf Hitler and it hurt much more deeply than his children could possibly have realised at the time.

Yet because of it, in that time, André learned French. He went to school, and before long, thanks to Uncle Georges, to the Paris music conservatoire. Georges Epstein knew someone at the conservatoire and arranged an audition for his nephew. He passed with flying red, white and blue colours. Fortunately, it didn't cost anything. The child prodigy was going to be able to use his talents in ways that certainly would have been barred to him in Berlin.

If it was through Georges that he gained access to the academy, it was his own talent that kept him there, under the watchful and firm guidance of the man who, besides being one of the finest musicians in the country, was also the organist at Notre Dame, Marcel Dupré.

Dupré was a task master of the old school. Dupré taught form. 'He was a throwback to earlier days. He was able not only to improvise, but to improvise fugues and in the absolutely accredited full-of-rules way.'

It was very much his father's idea that the months in Paris should not only not be wasted but used as effectively, to say nothing of as ambitiously, as possible.

André now is somewhat modest about the achievement the mere entry to the establishment undoubtedly represented. 'I couldn't play yet. I mean not really.' But he adds: 'Much more than actual accomplishment, I am told that the strides I took were extremely quick and that it took me no time at all to learn those little pieces and that it took me no time to memorise them and that it took me no time to embellish them and make up stuff. I suppose that part of it was not so usual and my father thought he would nurture it.'

With the benefit of hindsight and the quite remarkable amount of success that has come his way since those childhood lessons, he is also ready to admit: 'I think a lot of it came *too* easily.' He also didn't put in the required amount of practising. Now that is a strange admission, since the one thing Jack undoubtedly insisted upon was practice. 'I mean by that, I may have put in the required number of hours in a day, but there wasn't enough selfless sitting there, getting one run honed to perfection at age eight and nine; I didn't do it. I didn't do it because I knew I could get by.'

As he told me, it wasn't until much later in life that he developed the kind of self-discipline which he says is 'much harder than any kind of inflicted discipline could possibly have been'. In fact, it has only been in the last sixteen or seventeen years that he has agonised for months over one particular piece to the point that it is 'pretty well locked in to my subconscious'.

Work at the conservatoire involved as much listening as playing and theory. Being in France was an ideal setting for André's musical education as his own young, immature mind would have seen it. Ever since hearing those Debussy *Nocturnes* on his first wind-up gramophone, he had become enamoured of French music. 'I was absolutely wild over Debussy, particularly the *Nocturnes* – I thought they and things like *Après-midi* and *La mer* were absolutely the last word in exotic, interesting things.'

He also heard a lot of Mozart, which he liked, and a lot of Beethoven, which he did not. 'I liked the melodic Brahms, but not the stormy one.' The mature Previn would rectify that. At the age of nine and ten, André Prewin was already developing a sophisticated taste in music far beyond his years, although he sees it as fairly typical of the child music student. 'I think the only unusual thing for me as a child was my predilection for French music, which tends to be a little difficult for children – a lot of notes to take in. But I liked all that great wash of sound.'

André was learning the French language all the time as well as the French music.

'When you are that age and are suddenly surrounded by French, you are all right in those couple of weeks, whereas now it could take years. At eight or nine you just assimilate it with the air.'

By any definition, it was a tough regimen, possibly not made any easier by the precarious financial state of his parents. But he knew nothing of that. All that he did know was that the harder the music instruction got, the more he liked it, was delighted by it, thrived on it.

It was all, he now says, reminiscent of the English public school system in a way that even the Hochschule never was. There was, for instance, the orchestration teacher who would appear like a gust of wind through the corridors of the conservatoire, his academic gown flapping in the breeze of his own making.

Spotting a cowering victim like young Master Prewin, he would stop and pounce. 'The lowest possible trill of an oboe?' If the boy didn't know the answer, the teacher would move away as though propelled by rocket power. But not before saying, 'Trop tard' – too late. As that cowering pupil admits today: 'It scared the crap out of everybody, but you did look it up in case he did it again.'

In André's case, it all seemed worthwhile the day he set himself the task of writing a fugue for a Hollywood movie. 'Somebody, for a reason I can't remember, had to write what pretended to be a fugue for a picture. It wasn't my picture, but I went back to my office to see if I could do one. I sat down and managed to write a perfectly correct, perfectly lousy fugue. But the point was, I could still do it. The sort of drilling I had at that conservatory doesn't leave you.'

Nor did some of the other things he picked up in Paris – the preliminaries of how to write for the various instruments in the orchestra. He went to classes which were specially set up for children, not of any particular age but with very particular gifts.

Even so, it was a regimen that to him was little different than for another child being taught and nurtured to play tennis. And it was no more irksome. 'I didn't think it wasn't a normal childhood. I just assumed that everyone had to practise music for eight or nine hours a day.'

It all came to an end when the news finally arrived from the United States that the immigration procedures had been completed and that there was no reason why the Prewin family could not sail for America and be welcomed there.

The day for departure arrived. The Prewins took a train from Paris to Le Havre and from there, on to the SS *Manhattan*. As Jack had arranged, they would travel first class. If it were going to be a last fling, it would be done in style.

THREE

They were were travelling on the SS *Manhattan* in all the splendour not just of first class, but of the very finest first class accommodation the money they no longer had could buy. Everything they were enjoying had been paid for by themselves using wealth that quite legitimately was theirs – and yet they knew there was absolutely nothing to back them up when they docked. There were four members of the Prewin family on board, enjoying the finest of meals, dining and lunching with the finest of company, treated and spoilt by the crew as though they were the clan of an Eastern potentate. Yet between them, they had precisely . . . twenty dollars.

'It was the most surreal voyage you could imagine,' André now says.

Whether or not his parents could gather any sense of enjoyment out of the luxury at their disposal has long ago gone into the realm of conjecture.

'He must have had the following train of thought,' says André about his father now: 'Why leave anything for the Nazis? And when we finally get to our destination we are not going to get a can of beans, so why not enjoy it now?'

It was all totally contrary to the normal way of thinking of the Jack Prewin who clearly was as prudent as he was methodical. In the normal course of events the very Germanic nature of his personality would have rebelled against doing anything so rash. As it was, because the events were not in the least bit normal, there was no feeling of being rash either.

'But there we were on the SS *Manhattan* for the long journey to New York and then on another ship through the Panama Canal to California, with no money at all and no prospects, and yet we were living it up like the last of the big spenders.'

23

Surreal indeed it was.

It is possible that the Prewins, particularly Lotte, who had done so much travelling, managed to convince themselves to take it all for granted. This was, after all, the way they always went anywhere and how they were used to living. Paris had been an aberration that they were now anxious to forget.

It was the most wonderful and exciting adventure. André had plenty of opportunities to demonstrate his musical prowess. Jack didn't want him to get out of practice and arranged for the child to have the use of a piano in one of the elegant lounges.

It was towards the end of the voyage that the reality of the financial situation in which the family now found themselves became totally apparent. They may have been able to 'enjoy' all the facilities of the voyage with everything paid for in advance, but there was one thing on board for which they needed instant money that they did not have – tips for the steward and other people who were employed to make their lives comfortable and pleasant and very first class.

'Lotte, are you crazy?' Jack asked her when she first raised the matter of the tips. But a woman who had spent a lifetime travelling that way was not easily assuaged. To Jack, the notion of having to use the tiny amount of cash they carried to pay to men who, at that moment, had more money than they did or could possibly hope to get, was ridiculous. Lotte, on the other hand, who was worldly-wise on such matters, thought differently.

'We can't just go away without tipping,' she said. The very idea offended her sense of dignity as well as of what was correct.

She would no more have left a ship – or a restaurant or a taxi, things which for five months had become so unwillingly and so totally foreign to them – without tipping than she would have tried to swim ashore. There was an element of *noblesse oblige* in travelling first class and she was determined to honour that.

The question was how? The answer came just before the *Manhattan* docked at New York and is in the best tradition of a Somerset Maugham or O. Henry short story.

Lotte knew she had to do something. For her the answer was to put her $5 on the ship's pool – the competition to see who among the passengers could get closest to guessing the time of the ship's arrival. Here her experience as a traveller paid off handsomely. She won. Every cent of the $100 she picked up went to the crew members. Jack thought she was mad – and that was in his kinder, more indulgent moments. She felt altogether much better.

'I always thought that was something extremely stylish,' her son now says. Even though the $100 would have been more than merely useful to a family of four people with just $5 each in their pockets, particularly at 1938 economic standards. All that Lotte carried as she got off the ship was her own $5.

André now remembers: 'Later, when I asked her how she could have done that to all of us, she told me, "I'm sorry. I felt, we're now just ending a very large chapter in our lives and I'm going to go out the way I came in and I'm going to start all over again. I don't mind anything that's going to happen now, but I'm going to get off this boat right." You can either think that was hateful or it was sensational. I am inclined to think the latter – although my father was absolutely beside himself.'

There was a short period in a New York apartment with another family, a base from which André walked open-mouthed around Times Square and other notable parts of Manhattan. He even saw a movie, although he couldn't understand what anyone was saying. He had fewer problems with two other absolutely irresistible staples of American life, a strawberry ice-cream soda and a hot dog.

Their temporary New York home had been found for them by their sponsor to the United States, Rudolph Polk, who had earlier been responsible for bringing Stefan over. Polk and his wife entertained the family frequently and tried to make their stay as reasonable as it could possibly be.

Then they were off again on another ship, in which once more they travelled first class, the proceeds of Jack's decision to use his money for the one cause left for him, temporary but highly tangible comfort. By now, after suffering the rigours of Paris and the discomfort of New York, few people would have argued with him.

On the SS *City of Newport News*, they began a voyage almost as long as the previous one, from the Atlantic to the Pacific through the Panama Canal until finally they docked at Los Angeles, which at the time, even more than now, seemed to justify its reputation as a collection of suburbs in search of a centre.

They found themselves an apartment off Hollywood Boulevard, which was not at all the kind of place to which the urbane Prewins had been used. But this was not the only culture shock. They were absolutely and immediately faced with a reality that would have been totally unacceptable had they not had the sense to realise how much worse things would have been had they stayed at home. It was a situation in which the minuses mounted and in which it seemed that once they accepted they were lucky just to be alive, there were no other plusses. Jack had no job and, like his children, no English. His wife, the elegant sophisticated Charlotte, had only the social skills and none of the practical ones.

It all came alarmingly to the fore on their first night in their American home. Jack turned to his wife and said, 'Lotte, what is for dinner?'

This was a moment of truth and shock for them all. Lotte had no idea what was for dinner. And if she did know, she couldn't do anything about it. Equally, she had no idea how to cook it.

As André says, 'I don't think she had ever cooked in her life – although I suppose at school she may have learned how to make truffles, but cooking an ordinary meal was beyond her. Suddenly to have to go into a kitchen and then see about a stew and cook dinner was impossible.'

But she tried – and failed miserably. The woman who had a cook to make everything they required was as unable to deal with the reality of the situation as her family feared. 'It was as close to inedible as anything I have ever had,' says André now. 'But by God, we chewed it down.' They also chewed on the words that they knew that they had to offer. 'Oh wonderful,' they all said, but were kidding no one.

André now realises how hard it all was for his parents, particularly a mother 'who had been trained for absolutely nothing and consequently was now working *only* a twenty-hour day'.

But it was a situation that would change. The woman who was so conscious of her responsibilities in life that she would spend what was virtually her last dollar on tipping the crew of a luxury liner was not going to be beaten. 'Typically enough, within a few months, she had become a very good cook indeed.'

André himself went to school in the neighbourhood, happy and content to be with children of his own age. It was a grammar school, which in America meant that it gave him a basic primary education. That wasn't much of an achievement for most American kids, all of whom had that. The difference between them and him was that André still couldn't speak English – 'not a single word'.

Lotte was more disturbed about that than anyone, but Jack was insistent. It provoked an argument between them, the like of which had probably not been heard since Frau Prewin decided she was obliged to 'blow' those winnings.

'You can't do this,' she pleaded with her husband. 'I mean, the child can't speak a word. He's got to have tutoring in English first.' But Jack remained adamant. 'No,' he said, 'he's young, he's clever and he'll pick it up infinitely more quickly with other children than

he would with a private tutor saying, "This is how you say, 'Hello'."
The fact that he could never have afforded a private tutor was not
allowed to cloud the situation. André himself didn't worry about the
new language with which he was faced. He was convinced he could
cope with that before long – his experience with French during the
stay in Paris had assured him of that. He was not, however, immediately prepared for the first consequences of going to an
American school.

They became obvious on his very first day. Like all the other children, he brought a lunch-time snack with him, gathered together
with all the love that Lotte could command, which meant that it was
all the boy could do to carry it. He put the package on the desk to
which he had been assigned and sat up straight and angelic-looking,
the way he had been told to behave back in Berlin. He also smiled,
for that was the polite thing to do.

The teacher then announced that all lunch packages had to be
taken to the back of the classroom. André smiled. The teacher repeated her instruction. André smiled again and looked politely and
pleasantly in the teacher's direction. This time, the teacher was not
smiling. She was not whispering either. 'We put our lunches at the
back of the room,' she declaimed.

It was only when one of André's classmates – most of whom, up
till that time, had been thoroughly enjoying his discomfort for there
is nothing quite so horrible yet quite so natural as teasing a child –
decided to explain the situation, that matters were eased. This boy
couldn't understand English, the sympathetic child revealed. The
teacher's tone changed and André Prewin, not quite ten years old,
relaxed.

The question remains to be asked how this young foreigner with
absolutely no command of the basic means of communication in an
American grammar school was allowed anywhere near a classroom.
All that André can today surmise is that he was 'something of a curio.
And it wasn't all that taxing. After all, you can add up a column of
figures in any language'.

At the end of a month, he had a smattering of English. By the end
of three months, he knew enough to cope with everyday life both at
school and outside it. At the completion of six months, he understood practically all there was to understand and spoke English
fluently. At the end of the year, he was using it as his first language.
His father was right in insisting that his child should not have private
tutoring, although André has noted that his English was perhaps a
little slangier than it might otherwise have been. In a way, it has re-

mained so. At the age of sixty-two-plus he colours an English that is both elegant and articulate with the kind of language that might make a sailor blush.

But he has always been fascinated with words and with grammar and syntax and studied it much as he studied music – making words talk to him, so that, as it were, he liked talking to them too. Any subject a child does from love is going to be learned that much more easily.

The German influences would, of course, remain. There's an old legend that says you can always discover the first language of people by studying the way they count. André wasn't aware of that when I asked him which language he used, fifty years later, to count. 'German,' he said in 1989. He mentally does the alphabet in German, too.

Jack had more serious problems with the language. The principal one was simply that, as things were, he couldn't earn a living – at least not in the way he had in Germany.

The one thing that had to be recognised straight away was that he had to forget, from the moment he landed on American soil, any thoughts of picking up his old profession in California. Now that is hard enough for any man who, by his fifties, has spent almost his entire life doing one job at which he was reasonably proficient. For Jack Prewin, a judge of the Berlin bench, to realise suddenly that there was nothing he could do in his chosen profession was like hearing one of those life sentences he had witnessed so often inside court pronounced over himself.

There was nothing he could do about changing that situation. He was not an American citizen. His command of English was halting – he barely knew any of the language at all when he first came to the country – and the California Bar was very different from the one in Germany which Hitler had prostituted. It had several Spanish influences that were totally foreign. To practise law in California would have entailed detailed studying and eventual examination passing. It was beyond even his own brilliant academic brain. More significantly, it would have taken time.

As his son now puts it: 'It wouldn't have mattered if he had been Clarence Darrow, he would still have had to do that studying and it was not something he could consider. He would still have had to start right over.

'The exigencies of the situation were that he didn't have that luxury of spending so long studying. He needed to make a living NOW. Nobody else was. I was little and my mother and my sister couldn't.'

He, therefore, had to use his German sense of practicality and offer his services in the one other field at which he excelled and which he loved – music.

The trouble with that was that although he was a very fine amateur pianist, he was not a professional. He wasn't up to playing with an orchestra, and certainly not to appearing as a soloist. With all these thoughts in mind, Jack advertised his services as a piano teacher.

He was no fool when it came to picking that occupation. Quite quickly, he found himself in demand in the Los Angeles suburb where the family had established their home. Neighbours decided that there was some social cachet in having a German Herr Professor who spoke with the kind of accent Hollywood movies loved their screen musicians to have, especially when a degree of *gravitas* was called for.

The lack of English and the accent suddenly changed from being a huge handicap to being a great advantage. As André himself says, 'It added to the patina.'

All their social needs were taken care of by Herr Professor Previn – on the advice of his second cousin Charlie, Jack had changed the spelling of his name; the risk of being called Professor Pruin was too much of a risk to his dignity.

He earned a miniscule income but a bounty of flattery, none of which he could declare on the tax forms which he still filled out with the assiduity and conscientiousness of a philanthropic millionaire. His son remembers seeing his father spending days completing forms, which always ended up with a big fat zero.

André also remembers the seriousness with which Jack took his work. Students would come to the small Previn house and play on the piano that Jack had bought as almost his first priority. Most of them made a sound that might have pleased the neighbourhood cats but which left anyone with the slightest musical ear holding on tightly to the wall. Jack, on the other hand, was totally unfazed.

He had sliding doors installed to separate the dining room from the living room, where the piano was housed. André occasionally had the temerity, 'when the hacking noise from inside suddenly stopped', to slide open the doors and see if his father was ready for dinner.

'This artist is almost finished,' Jack would announce, walking slowly and ceremoniously from one part of the room to the next, sliding the doors behind him.

'He knew it sounded absolutely terrible,' says André, 'but there was nothing he could do about it.'

The humiliation that the senior Previn must have felt was totally lost at the time on André, who just set about becoming as American and having as good a time as he could. Today, he says that he recognises what his father probably suffered. 'I knew what a tough existence it must have been for them, but mentally I didn't realise how tough it must have been for them both until way later. I've always been sorry about that, for I must have been as blithely cruel as only kids can be.'

In moments when he feels more kindly about Jack's attitude than at others, André will say: 'Really, he was wonderful. He was just unable to pay a total flat-out compliment.'

On the other hand, I just went off to school and had a good time while he was having to teach some monumentally ungifted kids who hacked their way through a piece. I never gave any consideration to the fact that between lessons my father must have thought about how he used to live – and not only on how he used to live but on what he had been planning to provide for his children, which he could no longer do. That was terribly tough.'

All that André was aware of at the time was that the stiffness and formality that Jack had practised in Berlin as part of his natural personality was only exaggerated in California.

The disagreements between Jack and André, on the whole, did not come from music. André played and studied and practised and Jack could only be impressed, occasionally, perhaps, marvelling at his son's progress, although always insisting on more and better and never giving much of a hint about how satisfied he really was. The arguments about music in detail, particularly with regard to the directions André's music appeared to be taking, would come later.

What would also come much later was the realisation of what Jack Previn's new career was doing to him psychologically. 'He was able to keep everybody afloat. What it did for his insides must have been cataclysmic. I didn't know at the time and if I had known, I wouldn't have known how to cope. But he didn't whine. He just got on with it. I am sure he must have wondered what the first forty years of his life had been about.'

Now André has no doubt that his father was something of a tragic figure and his relationship with him at times resembled one which might have existed between characters from an Arthur Miller play script. But the tragedy was the more pronounced sensation. 'Having been at the top of a specific profession and all of a sudden being penniless and in an alien country, not having the language and doing something, which had only been a charming hobby, for a living and keeping the family going: that's heroism on the level of climbing Everest to me now. But then, what did I know?'

There was also the question of status that had to be considered. It may have been more than acceptable to someone for whom music rated so highly to give master classes, but to have to keep thundering at talentless kids saying, 'No, no, that's an F sharp' was hardly in the same league. 'That sort of teacher really hadn't been within his ken. He just didn't know about such a person.'

He had never taught André himself. 'He was much too smart for that,' his son now says. 'He supervised and he was obviously vitally interested. And I have a lot of childhood remembrances of being set down very hard by my father, but now with the luxury of age, I think he was right. The relationship between teacher and pupil has to be one that is in no way encroached on by personal feelings. You have also to be something of a disciplinarian.

'I owe my father a lot for my earliest lessons and for stressing the importance of sight-reading and so on. But technically, his knowledge was slight. As indeed, why wouldn't it be?'

The first of the real problems between father and son came when André himself realised that his knowledge was already greater than Jack's. 'Then it became impossible for me to say anything – and yet I knew it and he knew it and I knew that he knew it etc., etc., etc.'

There was no music conservatory in Los Angeles, so Jack decided he had no choice. He had to engage private music teachers for his younger son, something he wouldn't have entertained at that level in Berlin, despite his wife's entreaties. But the tutors *were* of the highest calibre, men who chose to go to Hollywood because there were studio music chiefs willing to pay them a fortune to provide playing hands for stars who themselves had only used pianos as shelves for family pictures. André's first teacher, Max Rabinowitsch, had a regular job in the studios because he had hands that looked good on the screen and made sounds that were perfect on the soundtrack. But he had a bigger claim to fame. He had been the accompanist of the Russian bass Fyodor Chaliapin. Another of his teachers was the violinist, Joseph Achron, whose work on counterpoint is still regarded as a standard textbook. Achron had been recommended to Jack by Heifetz. His musical knowledge was impeccable. His style of teaching recalled the days at the conservatories, but writ large. When André was twelve, Achron began to teach him orchestration, form and the analysis of scores.

'My God, he was a tough customer,' says André now. 'I used to go there after school and I remember very well he wanted me to write an absolutely, strict-style fugue, which was very, very difficult.'

André brought it to the man following a week 'working like a beaver'.

Achron was impressed. He looked it over and couldn't understand it. 'I can't believe that. There's not a single mistake,' he told his pupil. The fact gave him no pleasure whatsoever. So he said he was going to look it over again. He looked it over again and said, 'It's not possible. There's not a single mistake. I will look it over again.' For a third time, the teacher studied André's fugue – all this had taken quite half an hour – and still couldn't find anything wrong. Until suddenly he spotted the error he had been so convinced would be there. 'Ah,' he said, jumping with a great whoop of satisfaction, 'hidden octaves!' It was a sin for which there was just one possible punishment: he tore up the paper. And André was told to do it again. 'You don't forget that in a hurry,' he told me. 'I could have cheerfully killed him.' Instead the twelve-year-old very uncheerfully did what he was told to do and produced another version of the fugue. Jack probably approved.

There was, though, one music teacher whom André did like and admire. He was Mario Castelnuovo-Tedesco, an elderly Italian composer who had a reputation for 'teaching everybody'.

Being taught by him was an altogether happier experience for André and a no less rewarding one. If Tedesco taught everybody, he also composed for everybody. Heifetz and Toscanini were among the many who played his work. He learned from him and respected him. It was the perfect pedagogue-pupil relationship.

As he says: 'He liked me and I liked him and on lesson days, he would give me a cup of insanely strong coffee and a piece of raisin cake or occasionally a glass of wine and he sat around and told stories. He was absolutely wonderful. I wish to God I'd worked a little harder. But it came easily to me and I coasted for a while. But I did learn a tremendous amount from him.'

The lessons were part of a life that was constantly rosy for André, as rosy and bright as it was mournful and dark for his father. As far as André was concerned, he himself couldn't have been happier. He played the piano and he played tennis, although Achron was as disgusted at the risk to which the boy was exposing his hands as he was thrilled at finding a hidden octave.

Achron plainly was not André's kind of teacher engaging in his kind of teaching. Neither was the kind of lesson taught in music periods in American schools. Music appreciation was almost guaranteed to make children do anything but appreciate music. 'All that often consists of is playing records to a lot of bored kids.'

Educationalists had been aware of that for a long time, which was why a lot of teachers indulged in trying to persuade their children that every piece of music told a story. 'It's very harmful to tell kids, for instance, "This is where Beethoven goes for a walk in the woods." I had my own ideas about what the music is about.'

Once, he deliberately failed a music exam to make his point that no one could possibly know what was going on in the mind of a composer when he wrote a symphony.

Somehow, that was a point that others hadn't thought about, or, if they had thought about it, had swallowed whole the legends which, in music appreciation as in other things, had been going around long enough to achieve the status of facts. If teachers had always taught that Beethoven was thinking about walking in those woods when he composed such-and-such a piece, who were those of the early 1940s to question it?

It was one of the hazards as well as one of the advantages of going to a so-called 'normal' school. André had to suffer his unappreciation of music appreciation, but he was gathering up information for later years when his views on education would count.

'Music is a joke in schools,' he says now, scathingly. He himself was, however, helped by having a music teacher at school to whom, remarkably, he could relate as well as he could to his private tutor. Her name was Mrs Moore, and he looks back upon her now nothing but kindly.

Music should be treated in the same way as languages are taught. 'It is not possible to go to school without learning the rudiments of some language,' he says now, somewhat hopefully, I thought.

But as he explained: 'It seems to me that if, for the sake of an overall education which they can then elect to forget or remember, children are taught irregular French verbs, then the very, very basic rudiments of music should be taught, too. I am not saying that it would turn on the majority of them, but it would turn on untold thousands of children. It not only doesn't exist, it's getting worse and worse.

'In the same way, if you learned to read music, you would be able to play at least something, like a one-handed piano or a recorder or a flute, I don't care. The avenues then are non-ending. If you can play something badly, then it will lead you to want to hear someone play that thing well, concerts or records or whatever. That would mean people would want to have some music to read, which would make people want to compose music. It would unlock such a lot.'

Records alone are not the solution. It is not enough for people to have 'at the touch of a fingertip, the world's greatest artists'. As he told me: 'I don't like that anyway. It's a wonderful thing, but the fact that you can put on the *B Minor Mass* during lunch is odd.'

But if children learnt music at school, and as a result found out how to read it, they would know more about a piece than they would from hearing it 150 times. 'So much of music is personal predilection anyway. They should not be told that something is great music. They may not think so, for many years anyway. Also, I think that if someone said to a teacher that *Carmen* was the most sublime piece of music he or she had ever heard, it would be nice if that teacher didn't laugh.'

He thought it would help them to appreciate music fully – and quotes Aaron Copland to prove his point. 'Copland said that most people sit in an orchestral concert like they sit in a hot bath.'

But these are pipe dreams. If things were bad in the war years, they are are much worse now – on both sides of the Atlantic. 'No music is taught in normal schools any more. And music at home is a lost art.'

By the time he himself was fully into his stride in the High School, recapturing an art that was very much not lost, André was sitting on top of a world that seemed to offer him everything. Already, as a very young teenager, he had left behind most of the shyness, seriousness and inhibitions. They had vanished at about the same time as the German accent. He was very close to his sister who, at the various Los Angeles galleries, had introduced him to art – the first paintings he had seen since the ones that were left behind in the Innsbruker-strasse house. Together, they discussed literature, which ever after would be an abiding passion not so far distant from his love of music.

He had realised that California was a place in which to enjoy living. It was also the land of the all-American boy and if he never had any ambition to be President – the one door that would forever be closed to any immigrant to the country – André had felt he was that the moment he took his first paper round.

In America, it was not yet wartime, but there was a spirit of patriotism in the air. Even so, André knew where he drew the line on his new allegiances. 'I was never a Fourth of July American.' But for years, he wouldn't think of his home being anywhere else and wasn't even going to contemplate going back to Europe until he was, at the very youngest, sixteen. 'I certainly never thought of going back to Germany, but I did think that I would eventually be in Europe at least part of the time. But I didn't want to be anywhere else specifically. People didn't think of going to Europe in those days a great deal at all. I can't say I yearned for it.'

A lot was going to happen before he did start yearning, if only the simple matter of doing what most others of his age did and liking it.

'I enjoyed school,' he told me, 'in a very straightforward way. I just had a good time.'

In the fairly distant background seemed to be hovering the presence of Uncle Charlie Previn. Charlie may have been Jack's second cousin, but, as André points out, 'Since you can't say, "Hello, Father's Second Cousin Charlie", he became Uncle Charlie.'

Charles Previn is frequently spoken of as a) the great influence in his 'nephew's' career and b) the man who sponsored the German branch of his family, allowing them to come over. He was neither of these things, but he was there and at a time when the Previns seemed to be lonely and destitute, he was kind to them.

He was a highly accomplished musician – 'one of the best of that kind,' says André, not intending to be patronising. It was simply that as head of a studio orchestra – and the music department at Universal – there was a limit as to what he had to produce musically.

Charlie had been born in Brooklyn and went to Hollywood after a serious music education. He never married but kept a comfortable home to which Jack, Lotte and their children were regularly invited. 'He was the successful relative and although I don't think he helped my parents financially at all, he was there – and very nice.'

He was very fond of André and, in the days when that was useful to a student who was then still very young, spoke to him often about music.

The big treat for André was to be taken to the studio to watch Uncle Charlie at work. 'I picked up a lot of things from him. I used to ask him some very nuts and bolts things, like if you have a very slow six – how do you beat that? And he'd always show me.'

Later on, when he could analyse such things, he realised he was 'an innately very good conductor. He was very much at ease in front of an orchestra and could elicit very good performances from them. But it was very limited, playing for films up to and including Gershwin.'

André was twelve years old when the Japanese struck Pearl Harbor and America entered the war, also fighting what had been his old country, even though its Government, given half the chance, would have sent him and his family to the gas chambers.

He was intelligent enough to read the papers he dropped on to people's lawns and to cheer the same victories everyone else cheered – when, after the early defeats, they started to come.

Most of his emotions were centred around his brother Steve, who quite some time before had become an American citizen and had now gone into the Army. He didn't want anything to happen to him. Already a cousin of whom André had been particularly fond had been killed as a fighter pilot. It was an event that disturbed André tremendously.

But he gave no more thought to what would subsequently be called the Holocaust than anyone else. He knew what Nazis did – sent people away from their homes, deprived them of jobs and marched around town in shiny jackboots. No one was talking about those gas chambers yet.

Hollywood, just down the road from where the Previns lived, was fully into the spirit of fighting the good fight, but you didn't have to be terribly sophisticated to know that the goodies were always going to win and that there was no question of a good German being anything but a dead German, a sentiment in the Nazi context with which no one could disagree. There was little to learn that way. Children didn't need to be taught that their country was usually right. Before long, André, too, was a citizen and knew as much about American history as anyone else on the block.

Basic education was left to school. At thirteen, he was attending Beverly Hills High, scene of probably more than 100 movies because more than 100 movie stars, starlets and writers went there, too.

André liked Beverly High School, as it was best known, as much as he had liked his grammar school. They seem to have liked him as well. Today, he is in the institution's Hall of Fame. 'I try not to let that go to my head,' he told me, 'because I've heard that June Haver is in there as well.'

At fifteen, he heard for the first time the Bartók Concerto for Orchestra. He was so overcome by it that he ran home to tell his father about this new revelation. Strangely, Jack was not totally dismissive of his son's pleasure. When the work was next performed, André persuaded Jack to go with him to hear it, too. André retained his enthusiasm, to say the least.'I went absolutely crazy. I thought it was the best thing I had every heard in my life.'

When the concert by the Los Angeles Philharmonic was over, he could barely contain himself. 'Well,' he asked his father, hardly able to get the words out, 'what did you think of it?'

Jack was somewhat less impressed. Looking at his son in a way not totally different from how he would have confronted a witness, he said in very measured terms: 'Well, it's not the "Eroica".'

As André now says: 'When you are a fourteen- or fifteen-year-old you can't always get out the right words. What I wanted to say was, "It isn't meant to be. It's a new, different piece." But for him the

"Eroica" was the yardstick, and whenever he heard a new piece, he would say, "Well, it's not the 'Eroica'." I was very sorry.'

Each time he was put down, André says he would walk away 'and grind my teeth'. Then, a month or so later, he would tell Jack about his latest activities. '"Guess what I'm doing now, Papa ..." You never stop trying.'

There is possibly an explanation for all this. It is also likely that Jack quite genuinely believed that his son would only do well if he was constantly pressed to do better. André accepts this: 'What was at the back of it was parental educational thinking.' But that did have to be coupled with the emotions of a man who had been such a success, heading a huge number of employees, who now had 'to sit on a kind of clapped-out sofa listening to neighbourhood kids hacking away at something. The bitterness that must have been somewhere, although it was hidden, must have been considerable.' And then there was something else, something very important which André does appreciate: 'I never heard him complain. Not once.'

Instead, he used opportunities whenever they presented themselves to criticise his son. That was his demonstration of distaste, to say nothing of his bitterness.

André, meanwhile, was finding ways of simultaneously earning a living, extending his musical experience and making Jack less happy – in about equal proportions. He formed his own dance band.

Now this was enough to drive any of his teachers, let alone his parents, to distraction. The very notion of a serious musician playing anything – to them – so unmusical as, say, 'Perfidia', and 'Moonlight Serenade' was nothing less than a prostitution of their art. But to André it was no worse than a talented carpenter going out to neighbours' homes to supplement his income by putting up shelves.

'And it was great fun,' he says now. Such great fun that he enjoyed watching the various proceedings before him. It did, however, have one considerable disadvantage. It would be years before he had any chance to learn to dance himself. 'How could I?' he says. 'I was playing piano while all the other kids were engaging in their legalised foreplay – and before my eyes!'

He is quick to point out that there was nothing special about anything he did. 'I didn't lead any particularly sheltered teenage life. I had a great time. I was as much a hooligan as anybody. I had lots of friends. There was nothing to separate me from the others.'

But there was a whole series of other piano-playing jobs. 'I played anywhere that I was needed or where there was work. Not as a solo pianist, but where someone wanted a pianist to play chamber music or to accompany a singer. Anything I could do after school.'

It was a demonstration of industry and enterprise that even Jack had to admire, to say nothing of its being a means of extricating himself, as well as the family in general, from the mire.

There were the times when he played just for the sheer enjoyment of it, occasions like the one that came happily flooding back to him in 1989 when, as musical director of the Los Angeles Philharmonic, he was called on to audition a 'very, very good young violinist' named Franklyn D'Antonio, who was so 'sensational' that he was hired right away.

The young man wanted to play some chamber music for André and chose the Richard Strauss Sonata, 'which was fantastic'. Then he said he wanted to play the César Franck Sonata. André wondered about that. As he told me: 'It's a wonderful piece, but it's played a lot and I was surprised that that was the first piece he mentioned.'

Somewhat less enthusiastically, André agreed to the youngster's choice. And then it all clicked for him. 'Suddenly, it all came out as to why. I remember it very well. When I was in high school, aged between fifteen and sixteen, I played the César Franck Sonata at a recital at the Wilshire Ebell Theatre in Los Angeles with his mother.

'Well, we played it, but suddenly I wondered if I was ready to play the same piece with her son, who was now a member of the fiddle section of the Los Angeles Philharmonic. I met her again after that. She had changed remarkably little and we laughed at it. She was pleased that I remembered it so well. Now I'm trying to find out whether Frank has kids and how old they are and wonder if I can make it three generations of the family with the César Franck Sonata.

Memories like that tend to linger. He wishes that his own first concert was equally vivid – or even just vague. But as he says, there was an 'endless' – one of his favourite words but it describes precisely what he achieved – run of work after school, playing for a ballet class or a dance school. (It is perhaps interesting to contemplate the possibility of aging matrons who, as children, were forced by ambitious mothers to go to those places and who have no idea that the little boy at the upright was André Previn.) He played in a vaudeville theatre and in the pit for another show in the neighbourhood. He also played in jazz clubs. When someone wanted piano parts written, André Previn would supply them.

'It was kind of odd. I'd be at school all day, then go to a dancing school and at two o'clock in the morning wind up in some jazz club.'

He seemed content. 'It was a colourful life for a sixteen-year-old.'

He doesn't know whether Jack was worried about his prodigy of a son diluting his talents. By then, they didn't talk much about it. The change that had come about in Jack's life had taken its toll. 'Here was this man who had been a roaring success, who had run an office with staff and was now an old man without a profession, having trouble with the language. He must have thought that his children didn't think of him as a success. It was not true, but I can understand why he thought it.'

The effect of all this was considerable and would have been recognised by any psychologist. Jack retreated into a shell that was anything but of his own making.

'He had become quiet and didn't think of interfering in what I was doing, because I was working so hard. I am sure that privately he wished that circumstances were such that I could have been in music school, analysing the first movement of whatever, without having to work in the commercial field. But that was not to be. I had to work.'

André is not sure if Jack realised what was happening as a result of his first hearing jazz and his first sessions in the late-late-night jazz clubs. He was captivated by listening to Art Tatum on a record bought for him 'by some kind soul' when he was thirteen or fourteen. The young, German-born boy, who had been taught that Beethoven, Brahms and Mozart wrote the sort of music he should emulate, was suddenly captivated by 'Sweet Lorraine'.

It was something that his father couldn't have begun to understand, but it opened new vistas for André, who by now was seeing new sights and hearing new sounds all the time. Few of them were like the Tatum experience, however. And yet, André's reaction to hearing it was to demonstrate a capacity for musical theory that, even though totally out of place, would have pleased Jack very much indeed and made him think that his emphasis on study of written scores was far from wasted.

'I did something totally irrational,' he now recalls. 'I listened over and over again to the Tatum record and copied it down note for bloody note – until I was ready to play it exactly, as I thought, the way he had played it. I copied it totally, every hemi-, semi-, demi-quaver of it.'

It was, he agrees, totally due to his 'orderly student mind', which owed not a little to his European, particularly German, background. 'It did nevertheless show me certain kinds of harmonic, technical themes. It was not that bad a way of unlocking a door.'

He saved up, 'and begged and borrowed' the little money that he could raise to buy Tatum records and those of another two heroes of the day, Teddy Wilson and Mel Powell. He copied them slavishly, too, 'until I could play very pale imitations of what they did'. He developed a technique. 'But I didn't know what to do with it.'

That was, of course, a total negation of what jazz really was, a music form that had to be improvisation or nothing. 'I never did it again,' he now says. However, the influence of Tatum would remain. From then on, André Previn was also a jazz pianist and one who would become more and more proficient in an art for which he would always have tremendous respect.

For a while, he missed not being able to go to university 'because of the romanticised aspect of it'. But in retrospect he doesn't worry about it. As he says, he knows a lot of very talented and very smart people who went to university, but he also knows a lot of very talented and very smart people who didn't.

The competitive life, in any case, had no great pull for him. He once entered a piano competition – only once. He came second. 'Now I have my own theory about that. I think it is perfectly marvellous to come in first and perfectly all right to come fiftieth. But second is terrible. It means you're . . . just not very good, right?'

But there was a consolation to it all. 'I might add with loathsome happiness that the boy who won has never been heard of since.'

Quite seriously, he says that competitions have no real value. They don't do what they set out to do. 'It's not necessary and there are people now who are professional competition players and that's wrong. It puts emphasis on the success of the moment. That's not the way to find talent.'

Whether he won competitions or not, as a teenager, André was more than content. He was getting more professional experience than his paper route and the dancing lessons and dance band seem to have allowed him. He was also playing piano on radio programmes, some of them quite distinguished for the American broadcasting scene of the 1940s. He had made his debut on the popular show, *Music Depreciation Hour*, hosted by Frank De Vol.

If he didn't meet girls by dancing with them, there were other opportunities for him to do so, and he took advantage of them happily. His chances were considerably enhanced by another part-time job which he accepted with a certain degree of enthusiasm. It would be one that would form the root of his career for the next fifteen years. André Previn was going again to work in a film studio. This time, he was really noticed.

FOUR

He didn't expect to make Hollywood his career. Indeed, if he had ever mentioned the idea, Jack would have wanted to show him the door and formally initiate the proceedings for the thing that came closest to secular excommunication. But frankly, nothing was really further from André Previn's mind either.

He was still no more than fifteen and had as much intention himself of embarking on what might have seemed to be a conventional classical music career as his father had for him. But matters were about to get out of hand, if that was the way you saw them.

Word had got out that André was a gifted youngster who was pretty anxious to make a few dollars in his spare time and MGM just happened to need an odd job done. It was nothing very exciting in film studio terms.

The studio was making one of its famous Esther Williams swimming pool musicals. As a concession to culture, the studio thought it wise to bring in a professional pianist to sit poolside and play for their star in the wet bathing suit.

It was now a familiar role for José Iturbi, a then highly popular and gifted Spanish musician with an international reputation as a concert pianist. He had quite suddenly found life a lot more convivial as a film star, playing kindly uncles who just happened to be close to a white, mirrored piano whenever there was a camera turning. The bonus was having Esther Williams to show that famous red-lipsticked smile of hers as she raised her gold lamé bathing cap from the pool. Iturbi may not quite have been a Horowitz, but he had played Mozart with Toscanini. Now he was faced with a problem that had never come his way before – or Toscanini's, for that matter.

In the film *Holiday in Mexico*, Iturbi was supposed to demonstrate just how easy it was to play boogie-woogie. It was something that he

41

actually found quite impossible. He may have played at Carnegie Hall, but give him two bars of music to improvise and he was lost.

The film script called for Iturbi to demonstrate his non-existent dexterity by playing 'Three Blind Mice' in jazz. Since he couldn't do it, someone had to be found who could – to write the jazz variations on the nursery rhyme, which Iturbi could then play.

As André knew after his Tatum experiment, by its very nature, jazz was something that couldn't be written down and then sight-read from a piano score. But the celebrated pianist didn't mind. The musical director George Stoll didn't mind. Neither did the producer, Joseph Pasternak. As for the director, George Sidney, any solution to the problem was welcome.

Would André like to do it? It was a question that he felt like answering with a whoop of joy, like a child being offered a huge ice-cream sundae.

No one was more thrilled by all this than Uncle Charlie Previn, who by now had retired and gone back to live in New York. But when he heard that it was his cousin who had answered the SOS for 'Three Blind Mice', he could only be a little tickled.

How André came to be even thought about is something of a mystery. Certainly, Uncle Charlie had nothing to do with it. He was, after all, a whole continent away, and an important thing one learns about the Hollywood studio system is that once an executive retires, the last thing any successor is going to do is to ring him up for advice. Besides, in this case, Charlie had been at a different studio.

Nevertheless, someone had heard André on one of his radio programmes and decided that here was a kid who could do the job for peanuts and think he's getting a big break. That was precisely what happened.

André, for his part, tried to remain as calm as any fifteen-year-old could be reasonably expected to be when told to report at Hollywood's most prestigious studio, and got on with the work. This pleased the bosses sufficiently for them to offer him a hundred or so dollars, which they figured would buy enough ice-cream sundaes to keep him happy. They didn't know that it was all going to help the family income. As far as they were concerned, a good job had been done with a piece that would now slot comfortably into their ideas for an orchestrated interlude.

What happened next is perhaps a perfect example of that much-used but little understood word, 'chutzpah'. It is sometimes trans-lated as 'cheek'. André Previn at fifteen provided a definition that deserves to be printed in some new edition of the *Dictionary of*

Common Usage.

André was told that his work was perfectly usable and to go and pick up his money, and if they had that sort of work again, they would let him know. Meanwhile, the next step was clear: Would he now take it to the man who was going to arrange it for the orchestra? He muttered something about not having any profound, principled objection to doing that, but that he thought he might have another suggestion. What he actually said was: 'Fine. But I'd just as soon write the orchestration myself.'

The orchestration was not for some little group working at the side of the lot. It was a Big Band – in days when the capital letters were wholly justified. There were eight brass, five saxes, four rhythm and a reasonable string section. 'Whatever it was,' says André now – not marvelling at the chutzpah himself, but minimising the operation in hand – 'it was not Richard Strauss.'

He is convinced that the MGM men were operating on the premise that there was no harm in letting the boy have a try. On the other hand, this was, after all, a too finely-tuned organisation to want to take risks that no one could be sure would pay off.

He also says now: 'I presume it was humiliatingly bad. But at that time, and in the framework of that time, it can't have been all that bad, or they would not have used it.'

If that now seems like a twist on the old *Forty-Second Street* routine of unknown stepping into the breach, then another cliché is called for. In this instance, truth was really stranger than fiction. It proved to be the start of his Hollywood career, even though he continued to go to school in the daytime, take lessons in the evening and go off and play piano for dancing schools or in rehearsal rooms.

It was 'kind of odd', he says now. Getting the commission wasn't quite as simple as it now seems. He was, in fact, auditioned by people in the music department and put through paces that would have seemed hard even for a place at the nearby headquarters of the Los Angeles Philharmonic.

'But it wasn't really that hard to convince us,' the late John Green, who was to be head of the MGM music department, told me. 'I remember sitting there and being convinced I was in at the beginning of what was going to be a brilliant career.' Now André dismisses such comments as typical of the kind of hyperbole in which Green frequently wrapped himself, but that could be modesty on his part. A fifteen-year-old would not have been given that sort of assignment by that sort of studio, even in 1945 when a large section of able-bodied men were still in the armed forces, working for military organisations or even playing in uniformed bands. They were pretty certain that the kid knew what he was doing.

'Knew what he was doing?' countered Green. 'This little wonder was amazing to watch. It was the legendary experience of having one's goosebumps getting goosebumps.'

Every day, André would get the bus from school to the studio, pick up various bits of arranging or other musical legwork that the MGM people had for him, and then take the bus back home, where he would do it straight after finishing his school homework.

It was all on piecework. But then someone decided it might be in their interest to put him on some kind of a retainer. As a result of those goosebumps which people like John Green still claimed to feel, André was taken on as a supernumerary member of the music department, earning a flat $125 a week.

His was a job that wasn't covered by any of the musicians' union regulations, so they could get away with what they still considered to be peanuts – but which André thought was more money than there was in the world.

He immediately proved himself to be fully reliable. So much so that the next occasion that Esther Williams put on a swimsuit for an MGM movie, André was in demand again. George Stoll would greet the youngster as soon as he got back from school and tell him that Miss Williams needed three minutes of music to which she could crawl or do the breaststroke and would he oblige?

No one was asking him to write the music for the most memorable works of the cinematographer's art, but he was proving himself adept indeed at whatever arranging was needed. Once having succeeded, and then twice having beaten the problems with which he was faced, the name André Previn seemed a fairly safe bet for those little odd jobs around the MGM house.

André did whatever was wanted of him – playing for a dancer here, copying some sheet music there. 'And I was always writing out piano parts and trying to write the occasional arrangement.

He spent part of his time as a rehearsal pianist, then one of the lowliest of jobs in a studio music department, occupied either by youngsters or – and this was the most usual situation – by elderly musicians who couldn't get any other kind of work.

Even so, the rehearsal job was very much a step up. There were choreographers on the lot, men of the calibre of Michael Kidd or Gower Champion, who got to hear about him and offered jobs at a moment's notice. 'Hey, kid, they want a pianist in rehearsal room A', 'rehearsal room B' or 'rehearsal room C.' It was one of the rewards or penalties of being good or available. He heard the offers all the time. He never felt he was demeaning himself. He was having fun and knew it was just a start.

His name was also down as a 'casual'. Someone wanted a pianist out of the studio for a morning. Did he want the job? He would say yes. Always.

'Some dancer would come up to me and say, "I'm in a class in the Valley. Do you want to go and play there?" and I'd say yes. I don't think I did it for very laudable reasons. But I didn't have much to do, except study, and there was money and it was around that kind of world, the theatrical world.

André saw the ups and downs of the rehearsal room regimen very early on. 'I could see you could be a good rehearsal pianist or a lousy one,' he says now, looking back on the cavernous bleak halls with the bar and the mirror to one side. 'But I tell you there were some outstandingly good rehearsal pianists. As long as you didn't look at it as, "This is what I am doing to do, full stop," it was a very good start in the music business.'

As it was, the rooms were filled with those elderly men, people who provoked the thought in him: 'How many hours of endless dreaming went into that?' The Hollywood films of the time portrayed the rehearsal pianist totally accurately. Many of the genre really did sit at their instrument, a burned-out cigarette dripping from their lips and a hat perched at the back of their heads.

If someone wanted a pianist, André would go. 'I didn't know if I were going to play *Swan Lake* or *Blueberry Hill*. I didn't care. And it didn't make much difference. It is the most faceless part of the music business that there is. You play whatever's wanted. But I didn't do all that much of it and I kept my eyes open.'

He could have become a full-time member of the MGM team, but for one requirement – it would have meant his giving up Beverly Hills High School for good. No matter how indulgent both Jack and Lotte Previn had been about the way their son earned the so-valuable extra money he was bringing in, they would not have allowed him to leave the school.

There was, of course, a school on the lot – that was essential to keep the law of the state of California happy – but every time magazine photographers visited the classroom, the studious looks on the faces of people like Margaret O'Brien, Elizabeth Taylor and Roddy McDowell represented some of the best acting that they ever did. Whatever these youngsters learned at MGM, it wasn't trigonometry, American history or ancient Greek. The Previns demanded something very much more for André and they were right. He was the first to agree.

When an MGM executive actually posed the question: 'Say, why don't you go to school here? We have a very nice schoolhouse,' he felt obliged to reply: 'I just can't see it.' As he told me: 'It was an attractive thought but I wouldn't have learned a damn thing, even if it *was* a little unreal going to school during the day and working at the studio in the evening.' But really this was just another conservatory for him. He was doing again what he had done in Berlin and Paris.

By the age of sixteen, though, he no longer had to please his parents, MGM or the law of the state. It wasn't just the film studios who had heard about him. A number of universities were ready, able and extraordinarily willing to offer him a music scholarship, that he wasn't interested in accepting. He just wanted to get to work. What was more, André Previn was finally free to become a staff member of MGM, clocking in at nine-thirty in the morning and not expected to leave until six-thirty – at which time he had to ring up and get permission to go home.

This period was to make him some good contacts. He got to know the choreographers and when those choreographers needed music written for them or heard musical directors say they wanted some music, they could see there was this youngster called André Previn who would be able to provide it.

Keeping his eyes open helped him take advantage of them to the full. 'When it was for a good choreographer I would watch, see how he got round it, what relation it had to the music at hand and what the people who then came in to write the music took down. So I was trying to learn something.'

The money he was paid every time he walked into MGM with a bunch of manuscript paper was for him a not so small fortune. No one told him that he was the closest a Hollywood studio had yet come to employing cheap, if not slave, labour, but it didn't matter. He was as happy as not just a sandboy but a boy let loose and dropped down on a kind of fantasy land.

There had always been child stars, like Roddy McDowell (who would become his friend forty-five years later) and there were always the messenger boys and girl typists, but for most youngsters of his age, getting inside a Hollywood studio was a Walter Mitty-like dream.

There were other similar dreams being realised almost at the same time. In November 1945, he had made his first records on what in grandiloquent terms could be described as an independent label, Sunset.

A young man had put himself into the record business – 'Where he pressed them I don't know; in somebody's garage, perhaps' – and sold the discs only in specialist jazz shops. He had heard André playing in one of the jazz clubs that helped both boost his income and excite his emotions and asked one of those questions that were becoming almost routine but never lost the thrill they conveyed: 'Would you like to make a record?' The answer always had to be, 'Of course'. A bass and a guitar were assembled and all three of them met in a hall and recorded the tracks. He didn't think anything would come of the discs, but that didn't matter. It was just marvellous to have the completed 78 in his hands. That was a pessimistic view. As he now remembers, 'They made a little noise. For I was only sixteen, and they weren't totally reprehensible.'

He was telling people he was still in the grip of Art Tatum fever, although now Nat Cole was showing his influence, too, in the way André was playing his jazz piano. MGM were pleased to note that they were not the only ones to recognise his talents. He was particularly happy to do an album of Duke Ellington's compositions. Not so happy – as it turned out in the late 1980s, forty years after they were made – to see a series of records for a transcription service for use in elevators and in the reception rooms of dentists' offices. They were André's interpretations of the music of Fats Waller. 'And they were lousy then. They were never meant to be sold.'

It was early Muzak, if jazz style, and once recorded soon forgotten – until in 1989 they turned up on a compact disc with a contemporary picture of Previn on its cover. André was not impressed and neither were his lawyers. As they pointed out, the recordings were never made for commercial use. To add insult to injury, the discs – for which he obviously received not a cent – included tracks recorded by someone else entirely.

But it was just the beginning of the André Previn recording story. Even those first records he made, the ones pressed in the garage, would turn up again in the late 1980s on some fly-by-night label which had pirated the originals made by the young man who, alas, had soon after gone out of business.

Nobody would ever have contemplated such a thing in 1945 or 1946, a time when records were made of highly brittle shellac that revolved at 78 rpm. Those were the days when, tiny outfits like Sunset apart, records were only made by huge organisations, the music industry equivalents of the major studios. RCA, Decca and Columbia had most of the output sewn up for themselves.

But they knew what was going on in the shops and monitored what the tiny outfits like André's producers were doing. Someone at RCA heard his discs and came to him with yet another of those who-can-resist-it proposals. They invited him to make an album for *them*. Very few professional musicians without record contracts could possibly resist such an opportunity. No teenager with the slightest degree of intelligence could do anything but virtually grovel an acceptance.

'Oh, boy!' said André. 'Oh boy!' said RCA when they heard the jazz playing of their discovery. 'Oh boy!' said the record industry. Within days of its release, it became the number one non-classical album – in those days they really were albums; 78s packed together in books, the ancestors of the single-disc compilations on LP and then CD.

RCA were so thrilled with the result that they wheeled André back into the studio as fast as they could get more shellac into the factories. They thought they had a very hot property indeed on their hands. André Previn immediately made more albums. 'But it never happened again. We never even came close.'

Yet it was a superb achievement for one so young, and every time André drove into the studio with another day's work ahead of him, there was more than that glow of satisfaction. He was doing incredibly mature work and still having a great time.

Neither was he forgetting what Jack might have thought were his roots. He may have been told to think Esther Williams while being paid by MGM, but when his time was his own, he could and would go back to the classics.

And, then, despite what he would later say about competitions, he entered another – and won. This was not for his piano playing, but for his own composition. He had already taken the sort of composition he had done for Joseph Achron seriously, although he would say he hadn't yet done a great deal with it. But there had already been one André Previn clarinet sonata, a string quartet and a clutch of classical songs. On the other hand, his jazz output was getting more notable results – the sort of jazz that could be put on paper that is.

What he might not have realised any more than he understood about the poor money he was earning at MGM – even though the MCA organisation were now representing him – was just how unusual it all was from the studio's point of view, too. It took about a year – a time when the boy with the serious look in the double-breasted business suit was proving himself to be so useful that he was no longer a freak – for the studio's publicity department to cotton on to the find they had in their midst.

Why it had taken so long to decide that this was a story with an intense news value is perhaps not too difficult to work out. If they made André out to be so important to them, Metro could be forced to look at the cash they were paying the fellow now being spoken of, and not always too kindly, as the 'boy genius'.

But when the story did get out, the studio treated it with enthusiasm. André was to say that it all made him wonder somewhat, which is possibly a polite word for his reaction. 'I was made out to be a combination of Mozart and Jackie Cooper.' Whether he objected to being seen by hard-nosed executives as either of those people, let alone both of them, is a matter for conjecture.

Nevertheless, the studio enthusiasm was picked up with equal devotion by the press who did listen. *Metronome* magazine's Barry Ulanov, in April 1946, was suitably impressed. André played 'How High the Moon' and 'Where or When' for Ulanov. He wrote: 'Here, then, is André Previn at sixteen, with more achieved than most of his colleagues in the music business at twice his age. He's come to jazz from traditional music, but hasn't turned his back on his origins, maintaining a vigorous discipline in both musical fields that should be the envy of the longhairs who talk so patronisingly about jazz but do nothing about it, and of jazz men who talk so longingly about the classics but remain unpractised in them.'

There was one prescient comment that deserves to be repeated. 'You're going,' said the writer, 'to read a great deal about him in these pages and others from now on. The nice thing about what you read of André Previn is that the encomiums, the eulogies, the superlatives will be as much for his humility and his catholicity of taste as they will be for his technical skill.'

He was using that technical skill, working on films like the Frank Sinatra musical *It Happened in Brooklyn*. This is now well remembered by fans of the genre as the picture in which Sinatra is eclipsed not so much the then pretty boy, Peter Lawford, but by the distinctly unpretty Jimmy Durante. André played accompaniment, off-camera, for Kathryn Grayson.

If that could have been thought to be all in a day's work for a youngster like Previn, providing the musical 'voice' for Ricardo Montalban in the movie *Fiesta* was more ridiculous than sublime. Aaron Copland agreed that one of his compositions, the orchestral piece, *El salon Mexico*, should be adapted for a piano concerto. Johnny Green did the adaptation and André recorded it.

'That was throwing the kid into the deep end if anything was,'

Green told me. 'It was complicated enough to start with, but by the time I had turned it into a concerto, you needed a combination of art, brain and tremendous vigour to attempt it. André attempted it and, of course, came through.' André now says, 'It was not particularly difficult, not very long, and certainly not as good as the original.'

Whether it was something which it was all worth coming through is an entirely different matter. It was the story of a young Mexican (Montalban, naturally enough) who wanted to be a musician, fighting his father who wanted him to be a bullfighter.

'An extremely boring idea of a musical which at best is a tedious time-passer,' said Leslie Halliwell in his *Film Guide*. André certainly wouldn't have argued about that.

If Florenz Ziegfeld had once had the legend, 'Through these portals have walked the most beautiful girls in the world' inscribed above his office door, the men at MGM would have been just as entitled to the inscription. It would have epitomised the excitement and glamour that was Hollywood.

Now André was in their midst, caught up in all the atmosphere of the place while, at the same time, practising his music as his profession. At the age of sixteen he had achieved what other people spend lifetimes trying to reach. Now he was two years older and the glamour was only intensified.

André and the film stars laughed, ate and sometimes dated together. What they didn't do was pool their work. The strict demarcation lines that dictated André did not try to play director applied equally to the actors and actresses. It was understood, they did not influence the music to which they danced or sang.

'I worked with people like Debbie Reynolds and Cyd Charisse because they did musicals,' he told me. 'They went and rehearsed their numbers. I would come down and listen and look and write the appropriate things and they were always very nice and very co-operative.'

But this wasn't *always* the case. Already André Previn was experiencing life from the other side of the rehearsal piano. As he told me: 'Sometimes you had people who were phenomenally gifted but difficult to work with. Sometimes, you had people who were just hard workers – but delightful to work with.'

He discovered that very early on indeed. One of the first women with whom he worked at MGM was the blonde Jane Powell, who went into the studio so young, she was almost – but not quite – a child star. He says she was the most 'prepared, hard working, sweet natured, charming person I ever had to work with.'

On the other hand, Judy Holliday would before long show herself to be 'terrifying to work with – but so talented that you couldn't believe it.' The actress felt discriminated against by being given the wrong clothes and made to look fat. 'It all made her so defensive, it was very difficult. But she was terrific just the same.'

It was all perfect and nothing looked as if it were going to change – except the constant certainty that one day, he would do something really serious with his music. In 1947, he could only anticipate what was going to come, and couldn't have been happier with the thought.

And there was some socialising, going to parties to which few other teenagers ever went, yet remarkably enough, ones to which he was already a very welcome guest. The fast André Previn wit was beginning to show itself. He was also very useful – every Hollywood party needed someone to play the piano.

He had been 'used' in that way almost from the moment he first walked on to a sound stage. At the age of fifteen, he was playing for Frank Sinatra parties. The then young songwriter Saul Chaplin was at one of those. The significance of the kid Previn playing at the home of a man who was already a superstar – the thousands of young girls who wet their pants when he sang with the Tommy Dorsey orchestra before coming to Hollywood was proof of that, even if the term wasn't used in those days – was not lost on Chaplin.

'I walked into that party and there was this young kid – Oh he must have been fifteen or sixteen at the time – playing the most incredible piano. None of us had ever heard anything like it – and certainly not just from a young kid at that time. And he got around then. He was very quickly known.'

That did not mean that he was spared the gauche awkwardness that was endemic in fifteen-, sixteen- or even seventeen-year-old youths, or that he didn't suffer from its consequences the same way any other young man of his age did after being pushed away the moment he got a hand inside a young girl's brassiere. He had to deal with all the consequences of young love and young rejection that was part of the deal of being a teenager.

Frequently, it was just a matter of knowing the right answers. Being able to sight-read a concerto or to play for Cyd Charisse's dancing practice didn't mean he knew how to deal with all the sophistication around which he moved.

But, away from the parties, there were advantages from seeing the studio from the little room to which he himself had been assigned. He met stars because they were the ones who had, one way or another, to perform the music that he wrote or orchestrated. When he wasn't talking to the actors, singers or dancers he was liaising with the director. He was spared the endless conferences with producers. Executives, as far as he was concerned, stopped before the actors' eyeline, certainly a comfortable distance away from the camera.

But, as he said, 'It became a very insular profession. The boundaries were the musical people I worked with, the arrangers, the composers, the orchestrators, the musicians. They made me feel right at home, right away.'

The most remarkable thing of all, the seemingly boundless talent apart, was the immediate recognition André got as a member of that team. No one seemed to complain about the kid from Berlin walking in and playing at being part of the scenery – which he undoubtedly was.

Now, with the benefit of more than forty years behind him, he is as mystified as he then took it all for granted. Now, he wonders how it did happen quite so easily. As he told me: 'I haven't thought about it until now. Looking back on it, so many could have said, "Well, who does this little snot think he is? We didn't ask him here."'

Of course, that wasn't the immediate reaction. At first there *were*, of course, the usual murmurs. 'They did greet me with suspicion, but once they found out that I almost knew what I was doing, they helped.' From then on, the orchestra members, some of the most brilliant in America, took what he handed to them and played it. 'There were so many very famous arrangers and composers and yet they could not have been nicer. It was terribly decent of them.'

It wasn't, however, an altruistic business. What he was offering was something that the studio needed in order to make their films as good as they could afford to make them, which was, of course, without limit. He, meanwhile, made no more dent in their finances than a couple of girls wheeling the sandwich trolly. As he later said, the music group wasn't considered any more important than the department of fake lawns. That may, of course, have been true at Republic, never at MGM. But one gets the idea.

His father also had a perfect idea of what it all meant. Thinking about it, André knows that Jack couldn't possibly have approved of his work at the studio. 'I think my father was in a terrible quandary. He didn't approve of my work, and yet it was a great help that I was doing it. I think he would have much rather seen me do serious work but was in no position really to set anything up as a shining example. It must have been horrendous for him.' Certainly, Jack was not sorry to note that André did still devote at least some time to what he would have considered to be serious music.

Since the age of sixteen, André had been a member of the California Youth Orchestra, playing piano concertos at the least comfortable locations it was possible to imagine in a state that put a greater premium on comfort than most places in the world. But if there were a draughty building in an outlying town, that's were the orchestra would play. André remembers: 'One time the stage was so cramped that a mirror was placed into the wings so that I could see the conductor while I played!'

There were, however, gifts in exchange for these devotions. Not only was it a chance to play a symphony repertoire with an orchestra that liked to think of itself as 'real', there were also opportunities to work under the batons of leading conductors like Sir John Barbirolli, whose greatest claim to fame was as the conductor of the New York Philharmonic and, in Britain, of his beloved Hallé Orchestra in Manchester. André also played classical music for a series of concerts, mostly joining musicians who were a lot older than himself, held every Monday evening.

They were opportunities to express himself, to satisfy himself that he had benefited from the youth orchestra experience and that he could manage classical music with an outfit of mature instrumentalists as well.

Under the guidance of Lawrence Morton, they didn't concentrate on the best-known works, but provided airings for pieces that were almost never – in many cases really never – played by more established ensembles.

It appealed to the genuine music lovers of Los Angeles and gave opportunities to those who liked to think that other people thought they were music lovers to indulge themselves.

But Monday evenings became serious music nights and he appreciated the chances. It was good for him to be able to talk about doing that sort of work. Jack could only approve. On the other hand, there was no actual advice coming from home, which in itself only had to be gratifying to the young musician. 'The people for whom I worked were kindly disposed towards me, but they didn't advise me.'

Someone who did advise was Joseph Szigeti, whom André describes as 'one of the great, great violinists of the time, if not as great, glittery a violinist as Heifetz, but the people for whom he was a cult thought he was the best there is.'

Szigeti would prove to be one of the big influences on André Previn in these very early formative years. From his home in the small Californian township of Palos Verdes, he gave André lessons that he would never forget, even if instruction wasn't intended to be the order of the day.

Szigeti was a lifetime champion of modern music. It was a reputation that went hand in hand with the admiration he commanded as a violinist and he was constantly being sent reams and reams of manuscript paper, all of which he read with a diligence that was not common.

He also played a great deal of chamber music. He and André came together as a result of that. The marriage broker was Wilem Vandenberg, one of the musicians who did manage to ride two horses in the Los Angeles community. He was both first cellist with the Los Angeles Philharmonic and principal cellist with the MGM studio orchestra, a fact, had it been well known, that would have impressed many of the doubting Thomases who refused to accept that working in Hollywood was a real job for a real musician.

Vandenberg told Szigeti that there was this kid at MGM who not only was a good pianist but who could read what he was playing. In fact, he could sight-read anything. Since what Szigeti was frequently called on to play would have made many a piano player go cross-eyed, that word *anything* had great moment for him.

'Szigeti wanted to know if I wanted to come up and plough through some crazy music and I, well, leapt at it.'

As he put it to me: 'I duly went up there and I duly fought my way through three Bulgarian sonatas with him and it was crazy. Well, I didn't know how good what I did was, but it couldn't have been awful because he said "fine".'

Towards the end of the evening, Szigeti felt sufficiently at ease with André to suggest more work. He asked him if he would like to come back the following week and look at some other pieces he had been sent. Then Szigeti said something which he believed would act as a kind of light refreshment after the heaviness of the operation at hand. 'I tell you what,' he said, 'why don't we play a Beethoven trio to finish?'

To any other musician of André Previn's undoubted capabilities, it was without any shadow of doubt an invitation that could not be lightly turned down. Except, André had a flaw he didn't always enjoy talking about. At the drop of the suggestion, André said, 'Wonderful'. The young man who could play anything wouldn't be put off. If he could play Bulgarian sonatas, Beethoven was tried and true. Except . . . not by him. Szigeti asked him which of the trios he would like to play.

What happened next went precisely like this: ('I can't believe I uttered this sentence,' he says in mature mitigation for the folly of it all.) André told him: 'I don't care. I don't know any of them.' It was not a wise thing to say. 'Well, he looked at me like you look at a specimen under a microscope.'

'What do you mean, you don't know them?' the older man asked, totally incredulous. He just could not believe such a thing.

'I just don't know them,' André replied, seemingly equally incredulous that it should have been such a big deal – which is another reason why he can't believe he uttered such heresies.

'How could you be such a good pianist and not have played the Beethoven Trios?' Szigeti wanted to know.

'I don't know,' André replied, 'I just never have.'

This had to provoke more cross-questioning. Did he play the Schubert Trios or the Brahms Trios? No, André replied, he didn't.

By then, Szigeti had got angry. 'That's an outrage,' he stormed. 'I tell you what you are going to do,' he told André. 'You're going to come back on Monday nights. I am going to give you something to eat and we're going to play and then we can take a break. You can have a glass of wine and a piece of cake and then we can play some more.'

Says André now, not just contrite but extraordinarily grateful, 'That man with his international reputation took me through the chamber music repertoire. Just out of kindness, but he must have been amused by it.'

André went back about six times, in which period they played about three trios together. 'It was amazing. It was the greatest education in chamber music anyone could imagine. Once in a while I had to pay for it by sight-reading, say, the Ives Violin Sonatas – dear God! – but he was wonderful. I read later that he was a difficult man and so on, but I never saw anything but kindness. I owe him plenty because my whole predilection for chamber music comes from that. That it exists comes from the way it was nurtured by those few weeks.'

The morning following those lessons, he was back on the lot, either playing a concerto or an inane theme he was glad soon to forget. It didn't make the slightest difference to him. 'You have no idea how callous a talented kid is. That I was talented would be insane to deny, but I was also callous and I was a kid. So I simply changed gears and went back.'

The studio had every reason for satisfaction that he did. In 1948, aged nineteen, he was given his first film score to write, for a picture starring the most successful movie dog since the days of Rin Tin Tin, Lassie. The picture was called *The Sun Comes Up*. It was also the last movie made by the pre-war queen of musicals, Jeanette MacDonald. But Lassie was the female interest in the picture whom most people went to see, which possibly accounts for it being the last MacDonald film.

For the first time, a movie carried the credit, 'Music by André Previn'. He was excited beyond measure. What his father thought is not on record. But some fifteen years later, André saw the picture again on television. His instant conclusion was that his own sun had deserved to set there and then, and he couldn't understand why it hadn't.

'Like all "Lassie" pictures, there was hardly any dialogue but a lot of barking. I thought it was easy, but it was the most inept score you have ever heard. It was also, inadvertantly, an hilarious film.'

He was indeed a busy young man, a tribute as much to his willingness to work as to his talent.

Once that willingness to go anywhere, do anything, brought him into trouble – and, the law being as it is, someone in some dusty legal department at what serves as the remnant of MGM could still decide to take out a legal summons against him.

For soon after signing his contract with MGM at $125 a week, André took a job outside the studio. Steve had more than a little to do with that. He was now a freelance film cutter working on a David Niven/Barbara Stanwyck picture for the independent outfit, Enterprise, called *The Other Love*.

In that, Miss Stanwyck played a concert pianist at a Swiss sanitorium – what else? – and a musician had, naturally enough, to be hired to play for her. The trouble was that the picture was terrible, even though it had music by one of the most talented men in Hollywood, Miklos Rozsa.

Things were not helped by the total lack of musical knowledge of Miss Stanwyck. Now normally, that wouldn't have mattered. Ever since films had been made with soundtracks, actors and actresses had been photographed at piano keyboards which made no sounds when they touched them or with violins in their hands that produced not even a screech. But this was more difficult. Barbara Stanwyck had been photographed full-length at the piano, using the movements of a Zulu warrior about to drive home his spear. The trouble was that none of the music recorded for the picture could possibly match such wild activity.

It was for this reason that André came on to the scene. It was suggested that the film might do better if the star's movements could be made to match. But Mr Rozsa was adamant he couldn't help. So

Steve mentioned his brother. Would he care to write it? He would remain anonymous, of course, with the emphasis on the word 'remain'. How could the youngster say no? He couldn't and he didn't.

As Steve knew he would, André came up with the music. But it wasn't quite as important a picture in the André Previn story as legend would have it. The story has developed over the years that he, or rather his hands, played a part in the movie, that because the hands of the original pianist photographed in close-up looked nothing like Miss Stanwyck's, the young fingers of André Previn doubled up nicely. That may have been a fact, but it didn't have much to do with the truth of the film. They were not André's hands on screen in the picture.

Had anyone at MGM discovered it at the time, the boy should have been out on his ear. As it was, his misdemeanour was discovered – because Rozsa was mischievous enough to reveal all. But he begged his colleagues at Metro to show leniency for the talented young pianist he kept repeating they were so lucky to have in their midst. Necessity proved more vital to the Culver City studio than principle.

People like him were not in great supply. More to the point, no one came as cheap as he did. But he wasn't any more aware of that fact then than he had ever been before.

There was also the catholicity of work he was doing. He was doing a lot of radio, now still working on the Frank De Vol Show and, more important, the Hoagy Carmichael programme.

André's MGM connection was paying full dividends. He was working on composing pieces now more than he had done before, none of which he would remain proud and some compositions he abandoned soon after starting work on them. He doesn't talk about such pieces now. He would say he was embarrassed by them. They were far too pretentious. But for a teenager, the ambitiousness of it all was quite staggering.

In the white stucco Spanish-style house that the Previns shared with another family – one apartment downstairs, the second, upstairs – Jack contemplated his son's early success and didn't quite know what to think.

His mother, on the other hand, heard everything André did and thought it was wonderful. 'If I had gone out and had a total lapse of memory and started playing the yo-yo, she still would have said it was better than Horowitz.'

Was André himself just a little bit priggish at that time? Probably, and perhaps it would have been difficult for him to be anything else.

When a boy of his age – and his youth was an extraordinarily important factor in the André Previn story at this stage – had achieved so much, people like the *Metronome* writer only seemed to flatter.

Mr Ulanov wanted to know what he thought about contemporary instrumentalists. 'King Cole is one, two and three among pianists for me,' he told him. 'Tatum and Mel Powell – fine.'

He wouldn't know that before very long the highly talented Mr Powell would become one of his closest friends. André had, however, gone off Fats Waller. He knew his jazz so intimately that he could rattle off his favourite arrangers the way others of his age would talk about baseball players. He had no doubt that Eddie Sauter and George Handy were on a list along with Duke Ellington.

The way he listed his favourite classical music might just have seemed even more pretentious in 1945. Mozart was his favourite composer, 'above everyone'. Then there was Ravel and Debussy, which confirmed his affection for and near devotion to the French composers. He went on: 'Stravinsky of twenty years ago. Prokofiev is the best of the living moderns. Brahms the most fun to play. Rachmaninov for getting a big kick out of playing with an orchestra – great big juicy things.' André now says, 'In other words I was a pretentious, opinionated, loathsome kid!'

André couldn't wait to get his first opportunity to play big juicy things himself in big juicy auditoria with big juicy orchestras. The ambition burned even more now that he had left school and when he walked through the security gates at the MGM studios at Culver City.

FIVE

He was caught up in the glamour of it all just as much as some child star who suddenly realised that when he was given a haircut, a million other kids of his age would want to copy it. André Previn may have been what in other industries would have been known as a back-room boy, but he was at the back of the most exciting business in the world and he loved it.

'When you're sixteen, seventeen, or eighteen, the best kind of glamour is tawdry. I mean, there's nothing better than that. You can't resist it. I couldn't.'

As soon as he was old enough to get a driving licence, André bought himself an open car. He prayed for evenings cold enough to allow him to wear the new suede coat which was considered *de rigueur* for a man of his status. 'The whole thing was wonderful.'

He also had his own flat. Jack, meanwhile, looked on it all with constant bewilderment, but still said nothing. It was a world of which he knew nothing and wanted to know nothing. 'He was very sweet. I am sure he felt I had made a Faustian bargain somewhere.' But he kept it to himself.

He, of course, didn't know all the things André was asked to do by his bosses. When they met and André handed over the contributions he was still making to the family, he might have boasted about the orchestrations he was being asked to make and the promises that he was constantly being offered, like, 'It won't be long, son, before you write a major film score.' But he didn't reveal everything that he did. Certainly, he didn't talk about his ghost writing.

The musical director Herbert Stothart gave him a few chords to work on. André had been told he could put all he wanted into the work, use as many instruments, bring in a chorus, anything. The only requirement was that it be written on proper paper and that André would be around to hear how it sounded.

André put all his ambitious pretentions into this work. He then sat on the podium, close to the feet of the conductor, waiting to answer any question a musician might have. Apart from the music copyists, the only people who realised that the alleged composer had nothing to do with the finished piece were the members of the orchestra. André says, 'The theme was composed, in its entirety, by Mr Stothart – what I did was elaborate on it.'

'The boys in the orchestra knew very well, because you couldn't ask the men on the rostrum a question.' And that was precisely why, when Stothart was ready to play *his* new theme, André had to be there to deal with the questions.

He turned up, as requested, as the piece was being readied for playing. Stothart gave the downbeat, and heard the massive chorus that had been handed to him. He turned to his young colleague: 'Did I write *that*?' The white-maned Stothart gave every impression of being no more fazed than had he heard a violinist cough. The film came and went and is so well remembered it isn't listed in Leslie Halliwell's *Film Guide*. But nobody blamed the music. On the contrary, the reaction Stothart got from his orchestra members and then from the MGM hierarchy seems to confirm that the theme, overpowering though it might have been, was almost the best thing about the whole movie.

He wasn't the only one for whom André had become a ghost writer in the business, although occasionally now the Previn name was appearing on sheet music in its own right.

'In those days we really did have people around who couldn't write anything. I mean, they really couldn't, even though they were employed as composers. There were throwbacks to the days of when sound first came in.

'People were hired who had written operettas for Broadway or had conducted orchestras in the pit at the Winter Garden or somewhere and they had hung on. They played golf and made friends in the right places or they had great charm or were very clever.'

It was a game played as assiduously and as seriously as any other, certainly as assiduously and seriously as their golf. People like André were their caddies. The studio didn't know what was going on, 'not in so many words, anyway'.

But because these were important, respected people they needed to be pampered by the studios. They provided them with helpers. What did the studios care about the way their star music people were being helped? Or if they did, they kept quiet about it. This was another part of the vicious circle of Hollywood politics, like taking time to issue a press release about André Previn. If the studio bosses started finding out that some of their prize music men couldn't *write* music, it wouldn't say much for their own capabilities in hiring them in the first place.

This work of fiction was in train throughout the lot, with people kidding other people and frequently kidding themselves. How this worked was described for me by Albert Sendry, a contemporary and fellow 'ghost' of André's at this time. 'Stoll or Stothart would go to the piano and play the C major chord – maybe a D sometimes – to show us round about what he had in mind and we would go away and write it.'

Stoll himself had won an Oscar for the music in the 1945 film *Anchors Aweigh*. 'But we were happy to do it, even though we knew the man's reputation. After all, we were well paid.'

The eminent Joe Pasternak produced *The Unfinished Dance*. Sendry remembers him saying: 'I know you boys wrote this, I know you did this, but Georgie (Stoll) is my boy and he's the musical director.'

And as Sendry now adds: 'You couldn't argue with Stoll. After all he handed out the work in those days.' And for teenagers who clocked in on the lot at MGM, being handed out the work was all they could hope for. So there was no reason not to play ball. Indeed, André was more than happy to go along with it. Most of the men for whom he wrote were very nice to him – and not simply because he helped to maintain them in business and, what is more, kept quiet about it.

At André's age, he was only too delighted to hear music that he wrote played by an orchestra the way he wanted to hear it played.

'One man – an Academy Award winner – had a history from the early '30s on, of not actually ever writing anything. But the path of really talented people who had gone through his office was really impressive. He had a kind of a cunning, shrewd, genius talent for getting the right people to write the right thing for the right sequence, so that the end result, which was all that anybody cared about, was not a bad score.'

The man won his Academy Award by using just such a process. 'But,' as André now says, 'what saved him was that he was a very sweet man. In those days in Hollywood, that he never hurt anyone was points for ever.'

Needless to say, it was not just the music men who were less than knowledgeable about this basic requirement of practically every film ever turned out in Hollywood. For one production, which had a scene where the romantic couple starring in the film attend a chamber music concert, the producer turned to André and asked him to provide 'something with a piano'. André suggested that a piano quintet would be nice. The producer said he thought that was a nice idea and added slightly quizzically, 'Now a quintet is a harp and what else?'

André convinced him that the Schumann Quintet would be perfect. And it was. The producer said it sounded very pretty. And so it should – André had used five of the finest of MGM's own symphony for the piece. But he said it wasn't enough. If the Quintet sounded so good with five, it would sound even better with a full orchestra. 'Do it,' he commanded. André probably muttered something about the bones of Herr Schumann not liking that idea too much, and said that it couldn't be done. André says, 'I won that round, it remained a quintet.'

For him, it was simply a question of assessing one's values and the real importance attached to them. If you followed the system and just *knew* you were going to get out before long and do your own thing, there was little else to worry about. The musical director would actually tell the orchestra: 'Didn't So-and-So write this very well?' Yet, of course, his was the name up there on the screen among the credits. It was a music department variation on the theme of Bob Hope's joke factory.

'But the people who wrote the really great scores would never have farmed them out. You would never find a Miklos Rozsa, an Alex North or a David Raksin doing that. The really memorable scores were written by the composers themselves. Who really cared about who wrote the other drivel? These people were in the shoe business. If this fits, right . . . Next!'

Nevertheless, the Norths and the Raksins and the Rozsas did occasionally also have help in orchestrating. They, too, had arrangers, whose task was precisely that, to arrange; certainly not to ghost write. 'But that,' André recalls, 'was only because they weren't given enough time to do it themselves.'

They made what were known as 'short scores' – usually six staves one on top of each other, divided into strings, wind, brass, exotica and what other instruments were likely to be used. 'They were usually so detailed that really, in a way, you could just hand it straight away to a copyist. I've always had the theory that if you're doing a film or anything you have to hand over to an orchestrator because there really isn't the time to do it yourself, that's fair. But if you give out one chord because you don't know how to do it, that's not on.'

In years to come, when André himself was composing film music, he was also to use the occasional arranger. 'But that *was* because I just didn't have the time to do everything myself.' And he was just one of a whole group of people in the same boat. So much so, that they formed themselves into a society of arrangers comprising men who wrote for other people, with or without credits.

'My big heroes were in that lot,' he now remembers affectionately. Once a month, they gathered for dinner at a café at the intersection of La Brea and Sunset Boulevards. 'People would get quite drunk and tell funny stories and it was quite wonderful. It was the sort of camaraderie that I suppose exists in a platoon in the Army or in prison.'

He was a child among those veterans, 'the lowliest of the low', but he was welcomed as a soul brother and he respected them for the respect they showed him. 'They were a group of arrangers and orchestrators who could make any sound in the world, and overnight. I couldn't do that, but I was learning to, and they were all amazingly nice to me.'

He enjoyed the shop talk at these gatherings. Sometimes, he received personal compliments that boosted his ego even when he liked to pretend that it was all in a day's work. 'Once in a while someone would say to me, "Hey, did you do the arrangement for Nat Cole in that new musical?" and when I said "Yes", they added, "Well, that was very good," it was all I wanted to hear.' In fact, he admits he is not totally averse to hearing it now.

By the time André reached the age of eighteen, the seduction of Hollywood as a whole was complete.

He looks back on those days with great love: 'I think it is not possible to be eighteen finally and debate on which chorus girl to take out tomorrow and not be carried away. To turn that down, it's not possible. It takes a while.'

At the age of thirty he would decide that it was all nonsense to him. But until then, he was going to enjoy it all to the full and, as he says, 'I'm still not strong enough to resent it or regret doing it. I had a wonderful time.'

I asked him what his definition of a 'wonderful time' was. 'A good time was the absence of responsibilities. I contributed to my family's welfare. I had no worries, no wives, no school fees, no mortgages and no payments.'

It was the time of life when anyone over the age of forty seemed to be tottering over the edge into senility. 'At that stage, you have no intimations of mortality. When that's coupled with enough money to have a nice time and enough talent to know that you are not going to be stuck with doing that which you are doing for long, it's wonderful. It was great fun and I was doing a lot of musical work that I wasn't totally displeased with.'

He was using his spare time – and there was quite a bit of that – to study more serious music than he was working on at the studio. He played 'endless' chamber music and he conducted a rehearsal orchestra which wouldn't have sounded at all bad if it had had the name 'symphony' attached to its title.

He wasn't making any fortunes, but the $100-plus the MGM cashiers were handing out every Thursday was more than most youngsters of his age were getting.

The studio were still delighted to have him. Money was certainly no object to them. After all, it was an age when it was an unknown phenomenon for a motion picture to flop, least of all the 'Lassie' pictures which could virtually guarantee a captive audience in all the little girls who would line up outside a movie theatre for the chance to see their four-legged heroine doing wondrous things. Ask them the story and the stars and the supporting actors and actresses and they would have been able to reel off the lot. The one thing they would never have remembered was the music, but music there had to be and Mr Louis B. Mayer and his staff were happy enough to let the young Mr Previn provide it.

Since it *was* an impossibility for a film to lose money – the studios controlled chains of theatres and had to provide the products to fill them; in addition, they had watertight contracts with smaller cinema groups which ensured that bad films would be taken along with the good – anyone doing their jobs satisfactorily was sure of continued employment. After all, the big studios would boast of making a film a week.

Now, that was the general rule. It was also true that André's talent was recognised. The press releases still spoke of him as a new genius who enjoyed having lunch in the same commissary as their exciting child star, Elizabeth Taylor; but they also did know that they could back their words with his deeds. So it was a mutually beneficial arrangement. 'The ferocity with which they needed music,' recalls André now, 'was like the earliest days of television. Anyone with some technical knowledge who could write quickly, was wanted.'

There was the time George Stoll threw André instructions for a piece he wanted orchestrated. He went through the rough theme on the piano, playing the keys using nothing more than his thumb, and said that the part that was an octave above high C should be played by trumpets.

'Trumpets?' André asked. 'Trumpets?' 'Trumpets,' said Mr Stoll determinedly. But André pointed out, trumpets can't reach that register. 'They don't play up there.' To which the 'composer' came up with what to him seemed a reasoned, if not reasonable, riposte: 'Well,' he said over his shoulder as he left André's office, 'try it.' As he now tells it, that was an exhilarating moment: 'That's wonderful. Really wonderful. It's like saying, "Open the window and try flying." It can't be done. It's not like saying, it's high or it's very high. It was just impossible. I was, like, seventeen or eighteen and I didn't know what to do.' But he found out. The young man who had been stopped in the corridors of the Paris music conservatoire and asked for the highest note of the oboe couldn't allow himself even to appear to go along with such a heresy.

So he wrote the theme for trumpets 'in the normal register and put a kind of militant sound upstairs above them'. There was piccolos playing as a kind of cover. Mr Stoll never noticed. That may, however, just have shown how subtle the whole operation really was. 'Either he didn't know they weren't playing up there or he didn't care.'

Soon, as if to prove how useful he was to MGM, his income went up – to $250 a week. He may only have been a teenager, but he was composing scores for pictures that had to be important because they were making more money than many of the other things that MGM were producing.

But he didn't have to be terribly philosophical about it all. 'When you're nineteen or twenty or so and earning $250 a week – and let's not forget what years those were, 1948 to '49 – it's great, particularly before the dawn of the era of responsibility. I was totally on my tod, so I didn't care.'

What they had to play may not have been the finest music ever written, but the skills they had at their disposal certainly were as good as any found in the world's greatest symphony orchestras.

'Every studio had a contracted orchestra of say sixty players who would come in every single day, not knowing whether they would be doing either a score of Bernard Herrmann's or one for a Tom and Jerry film or doubling for the Tommy Dorsey band or whatever was going – a piece by Copland or a Debbie Reynolds dance, you name it.'

It is not true, though, that every one of the musicians enjoyed their participation in the Hollywood scene as much as if they were playing constantly with Toscanini.

'I think,' André now recalls, 'there were always people in those orchestras who knew better, who had come from the great symphony orchestras and from the great chamber music ensembles in the world, and some of them were ashamed. But being very professional, they never intimated that they were doing you a favour by playing. We had one guy like that – and he didn't last long. Most of them were doing their level best. Whether they went home at the end of the day and hit the wall with their fists I don't know. But you would not have known by their demeanour.

'I really think that if somebody plays the cello in one of the great symphony orchestras and he's not going to be a principal and he's not going to be a soloist and the touring, which is fun for a while, becomes a very hard graft; and if he's sitting in the anonymity of a section, and then he hears that for ten times the money and a tenth of the personal work involved he could be sitting in one place, buy a house and keep his family in the sunshine, I think that is a very great seduction.'

But there *were* different disciplines involved. 'Don't forget they never got to practise what they played professionally. What they practised was their instrument or whatever they were playing as part of their outside activities. But no one ever practised an Alfred Newman score. How could they? Where would they get the score from? The ink was still wet.

'Certainly, there was no denying that they had to be chameleons. They were all capable of reading and playing phenomenally well and learning very, very quickly. And the jobs were considered great. They got paid very well and they stayed put. Some of the greatest instrumentalists in the world worked there.'

It was an apprenticeship that he never stops saying was better than anything he could have had in any other job in music. As he says over and over again – lest anyone suggest that his subsequent departure from the world of film for that of the classical orchestra platform could be seen as implying a denegration of the art of the film musician – he maintains the respect he learned to hold for them.

'Those were all virtuosos in those days. If you wanted the easy life without musical responsibility. It was one of the most sought after jobs in the world. People who had sat in Toscanini's orchestra, in the Philadelphia and all the way down to the great dance bands, they all came – and traded the hard life for all those soft clothes.'

The standard of musicianship was evident simply from the classification the studios gave their ensembles. They were *symphony* orchestras and there was not a single practitioner of the art of music who queried that. Their standards and their qualifications had nothing whatever to do with what they were required to play. As he now says, they were first-rate musicians content to play tenth-rate music, but play it all with as much seriousness of intent as they would the *Missa Solemnis*.

'They were fantastic and very sweet, too. I would hear them and watch them record every day of the week throughout my formative years and I learned, psychologically, how far you can push players, how long you can rehearse them, what you can ask of them, what discipline, admonishment, jokes, whatever.'

This wasn't like the apprenticeship of an actor in repertory or summer stock or a journalist on a regional newspaper. This was the very biggest time of all.

More important than the mere experience of being able to see these people at work, there were lessons to be learned and once learned taken to heart, not just during his years in the film capital but afterwards, when he had left movies behind.

'It gave me,' he says, 'a rehearsal technique which has stood me in good stead ever since, because I also played in the orchestra a great deal as a keyboard player and I learned so much from the other side that I have never forgotten.'

One of the things he never forgot was that the accuracy they tried to bring to the music he played and orchestrated was not always also put into the details of the story. He still remembers with shocked amusement a film being made at MGM while he was working on the lot.

It was called *Rhapsody* and starred Elizabeth Taylor and Vittorio Gassman, based on a music conservatory and the effect a wealthy woman had on the lives of two musicians.

'They got it so wrong,' André recalls, 'that one of my favourite lines in all of filmdom is in that movie. Elizabeth Taylor sinks down in the café and says, "Boy, that Sibelius Piano Concerto is really murder to learn." And nobody checked to discover that Sibelius never wrote one. And yet they went to the trouble of getting the piano tracks recorded by Claudio Arrau and the violin tracks made by Michael Rabin.

If nothing else, those lessons were the things that André remembers with gratitude. He learned how far he could go pushing an orchestra to play music for which they might have no respect.

'There is a moment when stoicism turns to active dislike,' was how he put it to me. 'I found all that watching people record nonsense. The bassoon player, for instance, has to work technically just as hard playing for a film star as for Beethoven. The sitting there is just as hard – and he also has no personal involvement at all. It becomes a real slog.'

Speed was part of the Hollywood game. The music department was, as he told me, 'at the end of the line'. This was the scenario with which a musical director could be faced: 'If a film was a little late coming off the shooting stage and therefore a little late in the editing and further behind in the sound effects and therefore even later in the special effects, so that all the available time had been eaten up piece-meal by all the departments that had their hands on it, music, being the last, had no safety edge on the calendar. We got it last but it had to be done. Of course, artistically it's the kiss of death, but as far as the work discipline is concerned, it was wonderful.

'If, when I was eighteen or nineteen and someone had said, "Here's a musical with Kathryn Grayson and Jane Powell and we need a lot of music in it," who's kidding who? As long as it was nicely done, you didn't really have to be inspired to do it. But, nevertheless, it was endless hours and if they wanted it done, you had to sit there till four in the morning if necessary in order to get that done. No one is in-flicting that discipline on you except yourself, so for that eighteen- or nineteen-year-old, it's not bad.'

It's a lesson he has learned and uses even now with composition commissions. If, in 1991, he has to get a new song cycle completed in time to be able to move on to a violin sonata and sits in his basement room from early morning until late at night until he is finished, then he puts it all down to his early days in Hollywood. 'I still think that that comes from having to be sure that Cyd Charisse has something to dance to.'

None of that means, he will insist until all the music publishers in the world come home, he didn't do his best work after driving through the Culver City gates. 'Yes, but so does a headline writer on the *Sun*.' As I pointed out, the fallacy of that argument is that there is a very distinct art in writing headlines, which is as different from writing poetry as Hollywood scores *ipso facto* have to be different from Tchaikovsky symphonies. Being different doesn't have to be inferior.

'Oh yes,' he agrees, 'if I managed to write a couple of minutes of something that I really thought was attractive or inventive or even in-novative, then I was terribly pleased. But if you do hack work with-out trying, that must be like drowning. Whilst doing the hack work, if you do try to do some work that is good – even if you know that no one is going to say it was a nice way to use the woodwinds in the middle of a chase, but if I know it, it's a good feeling.'

He was doing those chase sequences from his earliest days. In 1947, he wrote one for the Frank Sinatra film about early California, *The Kissing Bandit*. He soon graduated to his more significant work.

In later years, he was to show how important a part it was of the serious music business, too. Hollywood, he says now, 'taught me to work very quickly. Basically, an orchestra just want to go home. If you waste time, they get to go home later. So just get on with it.'

He learnt an art that has never left him – how to treat the music at hand very seriously indeed, but to use the time between actually conducting that music as light-heartedly as possible. 'I've never believed in great poses of, "I'm communing with Beethoven now."'

More than that, he learnt how to be with people – 'with people I admired and with people I couldn't stand. I learned how to be respectful without being servile, be slightly dominant in other situations. All that stuff that other conductors are supposed to learn by osmosis or at a conservatory. It was much better actually to get up in front of people.'

And he added: 'I've conducted dreadful music many times a week for years in front of a great orchestra. You could say that I would have been better working with a provincial opera house, at least spending my time with great music. Now there's a lot of truth in that. But at the same time, the kind of nuts and bolts that I learnt every day is invaluable. If you're at a conservatory and show your music to the master and he says, "If you do that with a clarinet it won't sound very good," you nod. But I wonder if it isn't a lot more graphic to write it wrong and then hear it played – within days or even hours of having put it down. So I would sit all those years with my score, saying, "This sounds very nice and this sounds bloody awful. This is a mistake. This would be better if you did this, and don't ever do it again." At the end, I had learnt reams, without it being so awful that it was unusable.'

By the age of nineteen, André was a professional orchestrator and arranger, to say nothing of composing scores for MGM movies and conducting the orchestra. For that nineteenth birthday, Jack gave him a present that was received with less than total joy and appreciation: a book on orchestration. A beginner's book, no less.

'It was a demeaning gesture. I don't think he meant it as that. At least I cling to the hope that he didn't, but I had been a professional for a few years and was making my living at it.'

The book, by Berlioz, was a treatise written in 1843 which emphasises the love that the composer had for the power of the *en-masse* orchestra and the emotions engendered by its individual instruments. A nineteen-year-old who had every reason to consider himself a more than competent professional, might be expected to bristle at the suggestions he thought were implicit in the gesture of this gift. And undoubtedly, he still does. 'It would be nice to think that he gave it to me as a fascinating treatise which everyone studies. As such, it was a very wonderful present. If, on the other hand, he meant it as, "It's time you learned to orchestrate," it would have been neatly forgetting what I had been doing for years.'

With that thought in mind, André wouldn't mind having it as a gift today. 'I would certainly like to be given it in a brand new spanking copy so that I could look at it again – but not necessarily with an eye to learning what the range of a clarinet is, no.'

If Jack really thought his son had sold his soul to the devil for joining the Hollywood gravy train, there were other aspects of André's work that should have pleased him more. *Should* have pleased him more – like the time the teenager was invited to play the Rachmaninov Paganini Variations with the Los Angeles Philharmonic. Jack would plainly have wanted to go to the concert, but he was ill and so could not make it. After the first half of the concert, André was in a glow. He thought he had played very well. 'I had a typical, I-did-well ambition to tell him. So I rang him during the interval from the concert. I told him it had gone very well.'

Instead of muttering words of encouragement, excitement or even a simple, 'Well done,' Jack posed André a question: 'When are you playing the Schumann in San Francisco?' André told him it would be in two weeks, but wasn't sure why the older man had asked. 'You'll never get it practised in time,' Jack said.

His son was crestfallen, dumbstruck and every other cliché that came to mind at a moment so damning as this. 'What?' he asked.

'You'll never get it practised in time,' Jack repeated. 'I suggest you really get to it.'

André knows that what he really wanted to say was, 'Look, I played the last chord of a totally different piece five minutes ago,' but he merely replied: 'Yeh, I know.'

It spoiled his evening. 'Now I know,' he says, 'he didn't mean to do it. He was the most kind-hearted man and, of course, he loved me and all that. But he couldn't say it.'

It was a situation that would never change. There would always be something more that André should have done, not just another rung of the ladder to climb, but a totally different set of steps on which to move.

'I think that fifty per cent of our generation have similar parental memories and if you allow those reminiscences to get out of hand, it's going to cost you a hundred grand in analysis.'

Alexander Courage – 'Sandy' to his intimates – who became one of the most respected film music arrangers, remembers the arguments the early-teenaged André had with his father. He disliked Bach and didn't enjoy Beethoven – two further cardinal sins in the Jack Previn book. He told Courage that he didn't like Beethoven 'because he writes all those rumbly bass parts for the piano' and he hated that sort of stuff. In future years, he would, of course, change that view and some of the best reviews for his work have been for his interpretation of Beethoven symphonies.

Certainly, he didn't allow his prejudices to cloud his early attempts at conducting scratch orchestras made up from the Hollywood ensembles with whom he worked. Today, he will say he was terrible in those early forays on to the podium, but they were all part of the useful apprenticeship these early days in Hollywood comprised.

There were no audiences, so for every terrible *fortissimo*, there was another lesson learned. It taught him conducting technique, but also opportunities to play Brahm's Second Symphony, not at all the sort of thing usually heard in one of the darkened rooms on the lot where musicians would play in front of a giant screen.

To him, it was worth all the problems that arose, like never knowing who was going to show up for these *ad hoc* concerts. Sometimes, there would be seven flutes and one clarinet player. The next night, six clarinets and four flutes. 'But those players were always wonderful and there was always, but always, something for us to play.' The orchestra members appreciated it as much as he did and so did André's friends, who occasionally would sneak in to watch and to listen.

Steve, after a period as a film editor, was being marked out for executive positions in the studios. Lolo was embarking on a different life entirely. She was the Previn with the social conscience. While André was living it up at the studios and with the girls from the chorus, she was working among the deprived people of Los Angeles.

'We were quite close,' he told me, 'but not at all alike. She was doing a great deal of social work and I, with the selfishness of a talented youngster, had no time for that. But I admired it.'

There was a great deal of opposition to her work, too, from Jack – and from Lotte. They told her: 'Those are awful neighbourhoods and you shouldn't be out there at night.' But as André now says, 'She took no notice and just went ahead and always did it. She was an absolutely marvellous young woman.'

There was also another 'paternal' figure in André's life, even though he himself would never have regarded him as such. But Louis B. Mayer – 'LB' to the gang of yes-men who surrounded him like worker bees around the queen – liked to think of himself as a father to the youngsters who were being hired by his studio. At the very least, he hoped they would think of him as an uncle.

At the age of seventeen, André had come face to face with this archetypal Hollywood mogul when he was summoned for the first time to Mayer's office. It was the most intimidating place he had ever seen – as indeed it was intended to be. The room was reputed to be the biggest private office anywhere in the world and resembled a scene from a Fred Astaire/Ginger Rogers movie. It was entirely white, from the desk to the carpet, from the ceiling to the walls. 'It would have made Freud incredibly happy,' André now chuckles.

Intimidated he undoubtedly was. He says, however, that he was not particularly scared by the encounter. 'After all, I hadn't done anything yet that would have made me afraid. I hadn't invested my time, my abilities or my ambition into my career yet to make me afraid of being fired. If he had sacked me, I'd have just gone somewhere else.' But he admits that the whole thing was strange – 'that sudden creepy interest'.

But Mayer regarded André as he did the prodigious trainee director Stanley Donen, as important an investment for the future as his young stars.

Before very long, André learned a basic philosophy to follow when in the company of Louis B. Mayer: 'You have to agree to sit by his side and say nothing and appear to be a fool.' That way you were unlikely to earn the wrath of the man who knew that he was always right in any case.

André came face to face with the necessity for such action the day that he was walking along the MGM lot and was stopped by the chauffeur of a gleeming black limousine that silently crept up alongside him. Inside the car was Mayer, who beckoned the young Previn to join him.

How could André refuse? This was Olympus and Mayer was one of the gods. Or as he puts it himself: 'Apollo was riding in his chariot.'

They sat in silence for what seemed like the length of an entire movement of a Beethoven symphony when finally Mayer spoke – it would have been foolish to initiate a discussion, just as in the presence of another kind of royalty, it would have been regarded as a breach of protocol. He asked André, 'Were you at the Bowl last night?'

To André, it seemed a marvellous ice breaker. Jascha Heifetz had played at the Hollywood Bowl, the open-air arena which the film colony regarded as their principal gift to American culture, and André had been suitably impressed by the performance. 'Yeh,' he told Mayer, 'I sure was there.'

More silence followed until Mayer ventured a further philosophy: 'You know, that man [Heifetz] will never be a success . . . ' Before he could finish his sentence completely André's mind began to boggle. Mayer was talking about one of the world's greatest and patently most successful musicians. But the old man went on, totally oblivious to the look of incredulity that was plain on his employee's face. 'That man will never be a success because he doesn't play things that people know.' ('Holy shit,' André now remembers thinking, 'the Sibelius Concerto?')

After that, André agreed that sitting and looking like a fool was the safest course to take.

It was plainly a workable philosophy. If it hadn't been, people like Mayer would have lost not just their mystique but also a great deal of their power. Become approachable and their authority disappeared.

André, for his own part, had other things to keep moving, particularly that non-stop career of his, even if he was still being paid the equivalent of a packet of peanuts sold from a pushcart outside one of the MGM sound stages.

SIX

André Previn was fast establishing himself as one of the more notable Hollywood musicians, which is not far short of damning him with faint praise.

At MGM, his leaning towards what they would have described as 'serious' music never ceased to surprise the people who rarely thought of him as anyone other than an arranger of fairly indifferent scores by people they knew couldn't write a single note. His earliest conducting had been with the youth symphony orchestra, which he now says could not have been too wonderful for the musicians.

Johnny Green had no such doubts about the man he described as 'the only authentic genius at the studio'. Shortly before his death, Green confessed, however, that he did at that time have profound doubts about his ability to deal with more complicated pieces of music.

Green knew that André was going to play with Franz Waxman, one of the better Hollywood composers, who used to organise a series of concerts at Los Angeles' Royce Hall. He knew because it had been up to him whether André would be allowed to play there or not. As head of the music department at MGM, the name Johnny Green had to appear at the bottom of any document granting permission to a member of his staff to do any outside engagements.

André was asked if he would like to take part in one of the concerts. When he agreed, Waxman gave him his assignment – to play Richard Strauss's *Burleske*.

Green, when he heard, was suitably impressed. 'It was a piece I had never seen as a score and asked André to take a look at it. He said that he didn't yet have one. In fact, he had never seen a score either. He had never played it. That worried me a little – it was a notoriously difficult work.'

For weeks, every time they met – and that was usually daily –

Green would ask him: 'Have you learned the score yet?' He always got a veiled answer which amounted to no. 'I kept at him about it and every time, he said, "Next week".'

He maintains he got that answer right up to the night of the concert itself. Green was one of the first in his seat at Royce Hall – not a stance usually adopted by one who prided himself on being a local celebrity, but this time he wanted to be able to look at his surroundings, which amounted to seeing how prepared or ill prepared the young Mr Previn looked.

'I couldn't see anything at first, but then came the break, the point at which they move the piano on. I kept watching for them to put the music on the stand. But there was no music. I was quite astounded. I was certain that he was a prodigious sight-reader, but I didn't think he could possibly have memorised it. But there was not only no music, but no music rack on the piano.'

'Then, on came Waxman with André and no music. I thought I'd die a thousand deaths. I grabbed my wife's hand.'

Reassuring thoughts ran through his mind – alongside the worries and the doubts. The pianist obviously intended to lay his music down flat. 'But not André. He actually *had* memorised it. He played it brilliantly. And got great reviews from the critics.'

It was, by general consensus, no more than was justified. Of course, it is easy now all these years later to see the whole story in perspective, but the memories of contemporaries appear to be strong on the issue of the Talent of André Previn. The composer David Raksin, for instance – he was to be best known for writing the music for the movie *Laura*, which has the reputation for being the one of the very few themes to be more famous than the picture from which it comes – has little doubt about him. 'I thought he was a kind of walking miracle, a whiz kid who was sufficiently street smart to know what was being done. He wasn't, after all one of those who suffered for his work. By now he had the best cars and the best women. But he never let any of it get in the way of his work.'

As Raksin also says: 'We were very privileged. We were thought to be a little arrogant, but we did all that we wanted to do.'

There are those who even to this day say that there is an arrogance about André Previn. If it is true, it is based on a belief that what he demands of himself in terms of workload, he will demand equally of others. He makes few concessions to lack of talent in others. He doesn't like carrying passengers along with his baggage, but occasionally suffers them rather as he would tolerate a parcel someone asked him to deliver.

The concert Green remembered was just one of a whole series organised by Waxman in which André took part. He began mostly playing the piano. It gave him a perfect opportunity to stretch his musical limbs, to play what was clearly 'real music' to him.

'Franz used to take advantage of the fact that I was willing to learn almost anything and I was a good reader and all that, so I played a lot of very strange things for him. Pieces by Bernstein, by André Jolivet, by Rolf Lieberman, all kinds of people. They were all completed and how good they were, I leave it to others to judge.'

André was about nineteen when Raksin first became aware of what the young musician could do. He was introduced by his brother Steve, with whom Raksin had been working. Raksin says he hated André at first sight, a judgment not to be taken too literally.

Friends were what André had in abundance. He seemed to collect them the way he collected music scores. There were always plenty around, many of whom he cherished, even if sometimes they may have felt, like the scores, they were being put on the shelf from time to time. Even today, since André has never been a hug-and-kiss type of man, there are those who consider him cold and unemotional.

One of his dearest friendships dates back to those days in the late 1940s when he was working at MGM. Mel Powell, now a Pulitzer Prizewinner and head of the music department at the California Institute of the Arts, remembers André at his coldest, but he was certainly anything but unemotional.

He was twenty years old and Mel six years his senior, both luxuriating in the splendour of being able to give Culver City as their work addresses. Because they liked each other, they decided that the time had come to go away for a weekend; Mel and his wife, the film actress Martha Scott, and André.

It was the depths of winter, a time of year that always makes André yearn for snow and ice, a possible relic of his time in Germany. It is certainly no time to spend in Los Angeles. So Mel and André decided to make for the skiing country just beyond Lake Arrowhead, a spot which at that time of year resembles Alaska on a coolish day.

It was the one time that proved beyond any shadow of doubt that when technical things go wrong, it would be fairly wise not to call on André Previn. He may have known his way around a sheet of music like a child in his own living room, he undoubtedly could make the keys of a piano sing. But show André a screwdriver and he will not only wonder which side is which, but will quite seriously question what it does. The weekend in Arrowhead demonstrated perfectly that practicality is not an asset he possesses to any degree. That might have been all right, if it didn't say exactly the same thing about Mr Powell.

The proof – and the resulting trouble – came when they looked around the picturesque log cabin they had hired for the weekend and decided to start a fire.

What happened thereafter would perhaps not have featured very suitably in an MGM film but would have been made-to-measure had Laurel and Hardy still been in business.

'I don't know who is less practical, Mel or I,' André says, just to complete the picture of both men going to search for logs outside their cabin. They were soaking wet as they lunged them all into the gaping fireplace. Well, as is not difficult to imagine, they were too wet to do more than fizzle and put out the matches as well as fail to catch.

That was the point at which André spotted a bottle that he soon wished he had never seen. It was labelled 'Coal Oil'. The quart bottle seemed to answer their needs. André poured half the bottle on the logs. 'That should be enough,' he decided. But Mel wasn't satisfied. 'You've got to have more than that. The logs are just sodden.' So André took his friend's advice and emptied an additional amount on to the wood, which was now soaking more from the oil than from the water that had originally saturated it. Powell still wasn't satisfied. So the bottle was emptied.

'Some providence and cowardice made Mel and I throw a lighted match from what we thought was a safe distance.' As he added in a somewhat low-key reminiscence: 'To say that it lit is really, I suppose, an understatement. The flames went right up the wall. We opened the door, threw snow at it, yelled and screamed. Eventually, we got the fire out – but the wall was no longer the same.'

It was quite an eventful holiday as holidays go.

The fire out and no particular adventures obviously in store for them, the two men grew restive, particularly since they were still in the cabin and, four-engine blazes apart, still hadn't learned how to light a fire safely. It was at that point that André remembered seeing an old upright piano in a nearby shed. 'We both felt the need for music,' he now remembers. The solution to their understandable frustration, born of rhythmic starvation, was to bring the piano to the cabin. 'After all, we couldn't play it in the shed. It was just too crowded in there.'

Simple? Not quite. Moving an upright piano 200 yards in deep snow is not a good idea.

As Mel Powell picked up the story, the true poignance of the scene became even more apparent. 'All around us people were out skiing, while we tried to push this piano. It would have been difficult for anyone but neither André nor I are exactly sterling athletes.

'We decided that the best way was to *drag* the piano back. Well, we couldn't even do that successfully. So now there was the piano sitting in the midst of the snow bank.

In the midst of their combined despair and complete hilarity, André turned to his friend and asked: 'Do you remember any of the four-hand stuff we used to play?'

Mel said yes he did. So in the midst of the snow bank, both men wearing gloves, they directed their fingers to the keyboard and played Haydn.

What else would anyone do in that situation? 'We were freezing our behinds off, playing four-hand stuff.'

Then they started pushing it once more. They stopped to rest – and the piano rolled back down again. Meanwhile, people heard them play and one actually walked back to the cabin with them in time to light a fire for them.

So one lesson Mel Powell – who had begun his career working as Benny Goodman's pianist, had gone on to being a member of Glenn Miller's Army Air Force Band before moving to highly successful serious music and academic fields – learned was to treat practical advice from André Previn with care.

There were other suggestions from André that Mel had good reason to accept. Powell had gone to MGM to earn more money than he had ever seen in his life, but without being given a great deal of work that would stretch his intellectual and musical prowess. It was on André's advice that he himself made the trek from east to west. 'He wanted me out there because I could play jazz. He told me about the money and I had to yield to temptation.'

For Powell and for a lot of musicians who weren't content to be merely members of a band, there were other advantages. Musicians could only be called if they were given two days' notice that they would be required. Frequently, the notice was not given and Powell could spend his time writing music of his own.

Days and weeks went by before he was called to the studio to sit down for serious work. 'They set me up in an hotel but they never saw me, other than to send me a cheque. They didn't call me to work. All I got were the cheques for some ridiculously high amount, something like $500 a week. I thought that for that I would be expected to play both Liszt Piano Concerti. I rented a piano and practised. I don't think I had ever been in better technical shape.'

Finally, the call came. Would he, in two days, report to the sound stage where the music for a new MGM film was being recorded? Not really the sort of movie that he might have been hoping for, although it was an important part of the Metro stable's output. It was a . . . Tom and Jerry cartoon.

He realised it wasn't terribly demanding work with which he was now being entrusted, but it was important nevertheless. Mel's task was to provide the music for the scene where the mouse runs up the clock, just as in the nursery rhymes.

André entered the room, accompanied by the pianist-wit Oscar Levant, just as the recording was in full swing. For reasons that had absolutely nothing to do with Mr Powell, one take followed another.

It was the moment that André felt a good turn was called for. He tapped his friend on the shoulder. 'Don't hurt your fingers by doing that over and over again,' he told him. Try doing it with a comb.' Mel took the comb out of his pocket, ran it along the keys, and everyone was satisfied. But Powell felt guilty for trying an easy way out. 'Listen, André,' he told him, 'at this level of salary, I'll bleed a little.'

It was a favour Mel was never to forget, even if it didn't do a great deal for his obvious musical prowess. It was also the start of a long friendship between them. In recent years, Mel Powell has become seriously ill but André and he still have occasions to laugh about their past. 'His wit has all the power of a professional stand-up comic,' Powell told me. 'In fact, he is the only man who literally has made me pee in my pants. That's how funny he is.'

Right from those early days, they developed a kind of code between them. 'We only had to mention a name and we'd giggle like schoolkids.'

The parallels in their mutual, eclectic approach to music produced a relationship that both treasure. 'Sometimes a wink is enough to communicate in a way that I couldn't with, say Itzhak Perlman.'

Right from the start, there was an admiration for each other's work, with André trying but never succeeding in playing 'The World Is Waiting For The Sunrise' just as Powell managed to do. 'But he has always been a freaky marvellous player without doing so.'

Certainly, the ability to laugh was always a factor that made André Previn popular in Hollywood.

André didn't contemplate a whole lifetime spent in California. He was beginning to be certain that one day he would go to live in Europe again, although he had no doubt it would not be in Germany, but he wanted nothing more than to spend that life surrounded by music.

André, meanwhile, was building up a roster of some very impressive work on what were some rather less than impressive films. After *The Sun Comes Up*, at the age of twenty, he wrote the score for *Scene of the Crime*.

It was not until André was in his early twenties and working on still more important pictures that he got a phone call from Lou Wasserman, then the head of the MCA organisation. 'I've just heard kid,' he told him, they're only paying you $250 a week. That's impossible,' he spat. (He tended to talk a little like Sylvester the cat in the cartoon series.) 'I've got you a raise. From tomorrow, you'll be getting $1,000 a week.'

It was a fortune for one so young – and for the vast majority of people twice his age, too – but considering his responsibilities and his position at the studio, the rise had come none too soon. 'I worked for so little money. By then I was orchestrating and conducting and getting a separate card [his name and his position as musical director alone on the screen and not shared in the credits with anyone else] and yet getting the same money as I would for being a rehearsal pianist.'

André had more than proved himself to be part of the team. People like Sandy Courage, who had known him since reading the first of a whole library of *Time* magazine stories about André and was to work on sixteen pictures with him, told me about the impact he made on Hollywood at the time. 'There really hadn't been anyone here quite like him. We had plenty of extremely good musicians, but none like André. After all, he could memorise everything he did – even the page numbers.'

He had also shown that he relished the sweet life which had been his ever since he discovered that 'Three Blind Mice' could be more than a nursery rhyme. Besides the work on the lot, he was still playing in concerts and, every week, he was featured on the Frank Sinatra radio show, playing and arranging.

But $1,000? And every week? He couldn't believe his luck.

The call came in the middle of an all-night jazz recording session in a warehouse in Los Angeles' Melrose Place. He was playing with guitarist Barney Kessel, Benny Carter on alto sax and a host of names considered to be legendary in a world totally different from any other in which he moved, but one for which he had as much respect as any.

André couldn't believe the increase in his salary. From $250?' he asked incredulously, no feigned attempt at saying something like, 'I should think so, too. What took you so long?' He was as delighted as he was surprised.

'Sure,' splattered Wasserman. 'They've been taking advantage of you for years.' And he hung up. As André now remembers: 'It was quite a moment.' A moment for Wasserman to flex a muscle or two, but quite a moment for André. The head of an agency as important as MCA to go to the trouble of ringing him in person? Incredible.

There were other 'perks' of the job, like having his own office. More than that, it was an office in the music department, which enabled him to build on the cameraderie such departments engendered. They were a lot more civilised than most people's definition of that word 'office' – a series of bungalows, divided by a single partition into two rooms. André shared one of those buildings with Saul Chaplin, the music man who had been so enamoured of the young piano player at Frank Sinatra's parties.

'We became very friendly,' Chaplin told me, 'because we had the same sort of sense of humour.' So the friendship between Previn and Chaplin was cemented behind the flimsy walls of their bungalow and via the pianos they both had in their rooms.

'We had all kinds of musical jokes together,' Chaplin recalled. 'He knew, for instance, that I was crazy about Richard Strauss. So that if he wanted me, all he had to do was play a few bars of *Don Juan* and I'd go running in.'

And, of course, they would socialise. Chaplin had two pianos at his home, and they would play duets. 'He was far, far better than I was. There was no comparison. I had no pretence at being a concert pianist, but he was one.'

He also had the retentive memory of the professional musician, to which he was more than content to bring that sense of humour – an ability which, for one night in 1949, Saul Chaplin was perhaps a little less happy to consider a quality.

It was the time he was working on the Judy Garland/Gene Kelly film, *Summer Stock*, the first picture in which Miss Garland had shown herself to be as genuinely sick as she was temperamental. Nothing seemed to be going right with the picture, including the songs. Saul had been brought in to write three or four extra tunes for Judy and Gene to sing in the movie. The complete score was supposedly to have been written by Mack Gordon and Harry Warren. But because Judy's various illnesses had altered all the schedules, they had had to bow out, which was how Saul Chaplin came into the picture.

André heard one particular song on which Saul had been working. He came into his office and asked about it. The song was "All For You". André liked it and joined him in playing the number four-handed. 'We played it all morning,' recalled Chaplin.

That night, the songwriter followed the hallowed Hollywood tradition and went to a cocktail party. Behind him, he heard a man whistling – the tune of the very song he had just finished writing. It was a moment to be compared with an author suddenly discovering that someone else had actually just *published* a story identical to one on which he himself had been labouring. It's an invitation to either show strength or to take an overdose of sleeping tablets.

'I tried to see who was whistling it, but I couldn't tell. There were just too many people. So I decided I must have imagined it. But then I heard it again.' Finally, he found the whistler – Arthur Jacobs, later to be a Hollywood producer responsible for films like *Dr Dolittle* and *The Planet of the Apes*. At the time, he was a publicity man.

Saul asked him what he had been whistling. He said he wasn't sure. 'Can you whistle it again?' he asked shaking like a leaf of film script printed on airmail paper. 'I don't know,' Jacobs said. 'You mean this?' And he whistled it again. Finally, Jacobs said he had probably heard it on the radio. 'All I do know,' he added, 'is that I didn't write it.'

'Well, I as sure as hell think I did,' Saul replied. He was depressed to the extent that he skipped dinner and spent the entire night trying to work on a new song. Kelly and Garland were coming in the next morning to start rehearsing. He couldn't offer them the tune he had so unwittingly plagiarised.

He got to his office at seven o'clock the following morning to try to work on a new song. 'But nothing jelled. Nothing was as good as the thing I had written the day before.'

It was as this jaded figure was poised over his piano that André walked in on the dot of ten o'clock. Saul told him the long, sad story. André burst out laughing – 'which infuriated me . . . '.

It was then that the truth had to come out. Arthur Jacobs and André were good friends. He knew that Jacobs was going to the same cocktail party as Chaplin and decided it would be a good joke if he taught him the song to whistle. Chaplin would be surprised, he said. They both knew just how surprised.

'He said it infuriated him because it took the whole afternoon to teach it to Jacobs, who was tone deaf. He couldn't believe it had worked so well.'

Says Chaplin now: 'I didn't know whether to kick him or kiss him. It worked brilliantly. I was about to hit him because of the sleepless night I'd had, but I was so glad to get my song back.'

Glad enough to want to work with him again, if more wary now about that sense of humour. In 1950, the opportunity came for them to make a film together, a movie which on the surface suited Saul Chaplin like a dusty old Tin Pan Alley piano and André like a . . . a straightjacket?

Three Little Words starred Fred Astaire and Red Skelton – strange casting for these men to play a pair of songwriters. They were just the sort of people Chaplin had seemed to have imbibed along with his first glass of beer. But for André Previn? The score was by the men whose story was supposedly being told, Bert Kalmar and Harry Ruby, who between them wrote the title song. They also banged out between them pieces like 'I Wanna Be Loved By You', 'Nevertheless' and Groucho Marx's theme tune 'Hooray for Captain Spalding'. Perhaps their biggest success was 'Who's Sorry Now'.

When Saul Chaplin sat down at his upright, he could virtually smell the fumes of the old trucks which trundled up and down the imaginary thoroughfare he thought of so nostalgically. As vocal coach and the piano player – neither Astaire nor Skelton could play in the rinka-tink-tink style of the songwriter, so a real professional had to be brought in – he was happier on this film than he had been on anything for years.

André, on the other hand, was not being asked to do any of the things for which he had built up that reputation of his. The music wasn't jazz and it certainly wasn't classical. There would be no spectacular numbers to compose. But he was being given the best job he had had in Hollywood to date. In this picture, the credit read, 'Musical Director, André Previn'. He was barely twenty-one years old. When it is realised that he was actually having to be the musical director for one of the greatest musical performers in the history of Hollywood – and that Fred Astaire didn't object to his occupying that role – the true magnitude of the task becomes even more apparent.

Red Skelton was entirely out of his element. He was, after all, a clown made to look serious as well as a music man. Fred only had one dance number in the entire picture, but André's role was pivotal. 'Fred was unfailingly nice to me,' he remembers now. 'He certainly didn't give me any problems.' Even so, unlike his close friend Gene Kelly, they didn't mix socially. 'He was not the sort you could ring up and say, "What are you doing tonight?"'

There are those who think that André made a great success out of being a young man in a hurry. Albert Sendry, not André's favourite person, a music arranger whose father was a conductor, says he concurs with John Green's description of the young Previn as the 'only authentic genius' on the lot at MGM.

André was the living embodiment of the man who believed he could only work hard if he was also playing equally hard. Not that it was in any way a penance. Hollywood, which was not called the dream factory for nothing, made an industry out of fostering the careers of talented youngsters. But he was still very much the phenomenon of MGM. There had been very few youngsters like he, charismatic, but working behind the scenes.

The days when he was invited to parties simply to provide the music were over. He went to them in his own right as a Hollywood person, and because other Hollywood Persons enjoyed his company. The women detected an obvious sex appeal that went well enough with the wit that was enjoyed equally by his men friends. The friendships continued outside the party circuit.

To be sure, André continued to enjoy the studio life. His success was making life easier for him at home – or rather at his parents' home, when he chose to visit it. Things were considerably easier for the older Previns now. Jack's reputation as the neighbourhood Herr Professor had grown sufficiently for him to be able to extend his circle of pupils, which meant that more money was coming into the house. André's contributions to the family were reduced accordingly, although he did still provide the occasional fillip to the Previns' income.

Perhaps the best example of how things were changing was that Jack now only occasionally made comments about Hollywood and almost never suggested that his son was wasting his time there.

André went into the studio every morning and for him it was no harder than practising on his piano at home. The fact that he was extraordinarily well paid for what he did and that his reputation in the business was constantly expanding were mere bonuses.

He wrote standing at an architect's board and every so often he would go to the piano to put the theory of his writing into the practise of playing. Saul Chaplin saw him at work and says now: 'It never occurred to me that there was anything unusual about that. We just took it for granted that that was the way he wrote. Now, I wonder why he didn't sit down to do it.'

The seriousness of his writing work didn't affect his sense of humour. As Chaplin told me: 'Once I met him in a shoe store. I had one shoe on and one foot was bare, but he said something funny and we both ran out into the street laughing – without my putting on both shoes. In fact, we always seemed to be running out into the street. Once we were playing two pianos and it was so funny, we ended up laughing in the street. Why we went out I've no idea.'

After *Three Little Words*, there was an instant demand for more of the same from André's bosses. There was also a reason for the rise in his already huge popularity among the studio hierarchy. For the movie, he won his first Oscar nomination. But before he heard about it, there was another change to his lifestyle.

SEVEN

It took just three years for André Previn to graduate from writing his arrangement of 'Three Blind Mice' to conducting studio orchestras. They were three hectic years, but also three very instructive ones. If anyone were to ask him today what the real lesson of Hollywood was, he could answer in one word – respect. Respect for the musicians if not the music they were paid to play. He may not have felt the same way about all the visible performers, but as far as he was concerned, the people playing the instruments deserved every consideration.

'They were great musicians. We had two people who played violin and cello for Toscanini and had spent decades of doing that sort of thing, never seeing their family with all their nerve ends exposed and suddenly there they were with a house in a couple of acres, two cars and the doggie and all that. For what? For coming in and using a tenth of their brain power. But they had marvellous talent.'

They were a fine antedote to some of the other people with whom he worked. It hadn't taken him long to realise that the music department at MGM was divided roughly into two sections of people – 'a roster of truly gifted people and a roster of charlatans'.

That he would align himself with the truly gifted cannot ever have been in doubt. He also became very defensive of them, not just to people who still wondered whether you could work among the glamour and the glitter without having sold your soul to the man with the pointed ears and the long tail. Since it was the exceptional film – the *very* exceptional one – when anyone really noticed the sound made by the cymbals or the flutes, there were people on the Culver City lot who tended to agree that the department which made artificial lawns was just as important.

The time André came into conflict with one particular leading lady illustrated this attitude perfectly. The lady was a singer-actress whose reputation was somewhat bigger than her talent. She reported to the sound stage to record a movie's theme song. Barely a few seconds of the first take had elapsed before she fluffed her words. No one bothered. It happened all the time – in fact, the chances of being able to complete anything in one take were fairly remote. She tried again and once more, fluffed her lines. Again, there were no complaints. André gave the downbeat and the music started once more. In the midst of the third take, the actress broke down again.

This time, there *were* shouts and complaints – from the singer, not the conductor or the musicians, who took it all as part of a day's work. She stormed: 'This is impossible. Get me some musicians who can play, and I'll pay for it myself.'

She plainly thought that the offer to foot the bill would absolve her of any responsibility to observe the decencies of life. There was nothing wrong with the musicians, and even if there had been, André would have defended them, because it was his responsibility to make sure that they played properly. It was, on the other hand, quite clear that the woman was at fault. Not only was she not very good, she was also ill-mannered. She was unprepared, too. He couldn't forgive any of those faults.

At this point, the twenty-year-old André Previn, no taller than a hat stand, found authority and height he may not have known he possessed. 'Get the hell off this stage,' he ordered the singer, who had been performing on film for longer than he had been in Hollywood.

He told his musicians, many of whom were at least twice as old as he was and some three times his age, to go home, placed his music under his arms and stormed out to his office. Nobody asked him any questions – they knew what the star was like – and another orchestra was found (whether she got on any better with them is not on the record). In later years, André was to regret somewhat the way he behaved, if not the decision to act at all. 'If I had been more adult myself, I might have seen that she was merely transferring her guilt to someone else.'

With André, the guilt of his own behaviour was usually mixed with more humour than that particular star would have known how to appreciate. There were MGM studio executives who didn't altogether appreciate it either, but then it was frequently their fault. This was particularly true of the ones who allowed their jobs to go to their heads and the bureaucracy to replace any sense of judgment. Musicians and writers were the bane of those bureaucrats' lives. The men who decided that an efficient business or industrial organisation depended on regular time-keeping had no notion that the rules they applied quite justifiably to cleaners, managers of the coffee wagons, even actors could not in the same way be demanded of *everyone* else.

André was not alone in seeing the folly of the rule that decreed that all composers on the MGM lot had to be in their offices at nine o'clock in the morning and stay there until six at night – and could not leave without permission of the accounting department. Not only that, when they did leave, they also had to let the department know where they were going – the addresses of their homes or their girl-friends, or whatever.

Screenwriters and musicians who liked to think that inspiration could not always be confined to office hours – what happened if an idea came at one minute past six after they had announced they were checking out? – wanted to treat such strictures with contempt. But it was the bureaucrats who made the rules. You didn't see indents for 'inspiration' on the annual balance sheets. But André found a way round the bureaucrats.

It was one of the not infrequent occasions when he was forced to stay longer than the six p.m. deadline – a rule easier to flout than the one that said they had to arrive after nine in the morning. In fact, he stayed more than ten hours after he was supposed to leave. At four-fifteen the following morning, after a working session that barely allowed him time to go to the lavatory or munch a snack, he finally completed the rush assignment he had been given. As he stretched, he realised that his obligations to MGM didn't stop at writing the music. He had a rule to obey. Somehow, he had to find a way of let-ting the accounting department know that he was packing up, and that his destination was his own home.

He looked in the internal telephone directory, which listed ex-ecutives' home numbers to be called in an emergency, and decided that such a time had now arrived. He found the home number of the man who had issued the order about reporting in and out and rang him. 'This is André Previn,' he slurred into the telephone mouthpiece. 'It is four-fifteen in the morning and I want to report that I am leav-ing the lot and going home.' He didn't allow the man to reply and put down the receiver. Nothing was said next morning, but the reporting order was quickly rescinded.

The year 1950 was still a time when being given a film of his own to compose and an orchestra to conduct was enough in itself. It wasn't for him to complain about the films to which he was assigned, but he wouldn't have done so even if it had.

In later years, he might not have been too delighted to be assigned the film *Kim*, a version of the old Rudyard Kipling story set in the days of the Raj in India. Errol Flynn starred along with Dean Stock-well as the orphaned son of a British soldier whose adventures with a horseman, who really belongs to the Secret Service, form the main plot of the picture. Paul Lukas was in it, too. The music of *Kim* wasn't as important to anyone as it was to André himself. For him, it was another career move and if he objected it wouldn't have got him anywhere.

The film may have come towards the end of the Errol Flynn era. His 'wicked, wicked ways', to quote the title of his autobiography, were showing their effect and he was beginning to look dissipated. But he was still extremely popular, which meant that millions of people – had they only noticed – would have seen the credit for 'Music by André Previn'. Since he was only twenty-one years old, that was good enough for anyone, André included.

Flouting authority was going to prove more difficult for André thereafter, however. In 1950 he received a letter with a Washington postmark, a note that began with the word, 'Greetings'. The greet-ings were from Uncle Sam, or rather the War Department. André Previn was being called up for Army Service.

There had been a kind of selective conscription to the United States Armed Services since World War Two. Now, there was apparently more justification for it than at any other time for the previous five years. The Korean War had broken out and America was the princi-pal participant in the United Nations forces which had gone to the aid of South Korea after the invasion by the North. The principal asset that a composer-conductor-arranger-piano player could bring to an army wasn't immediately apparent, but there was no denying that the order had been issued and once made, it had to be respected.

There was a lunch party at the MGM commissary the day before André was to go into the service and personally defend his country. A couple of writer friends, a few directors and all of the music depart-ment joined a gaggle of the most beautiful girls in America to wish him Godspeed before he climbed into his convertible and went home to pack. It was still the good life and he was participating in it as though by right for as long as he were able to.

'It was quite a ridiculous situation,' he now remembers without laughing too much. 'One moment I was having a farewell lunch and then twelve hours later I was waiting with a duffle bag in the freight yard of Los Angeles station.'

At four-fifteen the following morning, in fact, he was taking part in the cold, misty overture to what was going to happen to him for the next two years. Plainly, the early hour – which to non-acting Hollywood people was sometimes experienced at the end of the day, almost never at the beginning – was part of the demeaning and depersonalising process of getting a civilian to become a soldier.

'There I was, just wondering what had happened to me.'

He was about to go into basic training, be handed a uniform he would hate to wear and to risk being taunted for the talents that had hitherto brought him nothing but praise and financial reward.

As he told me: 'After a certain time being at MGM it was even harder to believe than it would have been under normal circumstances. It was all completely unreal.'

He was totally depressed. 'I was not so much depressed by what I had to do and the regimentation of what was being expected of us as by the unalterable stop to my career and the waste of time that I thought it was. Normal measurements of patriotism don't work in peacetime. I mean, you're not protecting the nation from fascism.

It was to be a rude awakening and he wasn't really sure how he would cope. In the event, he would do so better than he could ever have thought, but as he waited on that platform, all he could do was ponder and worry – and think of the party and the guests in whose company he had been just a few hours before. Certainly, there would be little wining and dining to come.

Now, there was the rude awakening of being paraded outside the barracks at four-thirty in the morning 'when we were all absolutely frozen stiff'. Alongside the parade went the more than just unpleasant form of a drill sergeant, the like of whom André hadn't known to exist outside one of the war comedy films MGM and all the other studios were still turning out. And there was also a lieutenant who, lowly officer though he was, still believed his duty was to throw his weight around.

André saw that weight being hauled rather than thrown at one of his companion rookies. It just so happened that André was not the only professional musician in this particular intake at Camp Cooke. Also with him was a bass player called Don Bagley, whom André had met in more pleasant circumstances and whose work he admired.

The lieutenant inspected the line, stopped in front of Bagley, who had been used to a totally more relaxed way of life, and told him to have a haircut. André remembers very well what happened next. 'Don looked at the lieutenant and said quite politely, "Yeh, OK."'

The officer was appalled. 'What?' he barked. 'Yeh, fine, OK,' replied the hapless Private Bagley. At which the lieutenant, two shakes ahead of apoplexy, countered, 'Yes, fine, OK what?' which drew the additional response: 'Yes fine, OK, I'll get a haircut.'

This seemed like a test of nerves to which André couldn't be sure whether it was necessary to offer encouragement or keep quiet. The officer had now turned puce and was asking if this new raw recruit was trying to be funny at his expense. 'No man,' replied Bagley, 'you told me to get a haircut and I'm agreeing with you, man, what more do you want?'

'By now,' says André, 'bloody murder had broken out.' Someone whispered, 'Say "Sir".' To which Bagley countered: 'Yeh, right, OK man, I'll get a haircut, *Sir*?' 'That's better,' said the officer and walked away. 'Far out,' said Bagley.

'And that's the only human response possible.'

André did all the things recruits were supposed to do, like assembling guns, which to someone for whom machinery can never be entered under the heading of Success and Dexterity, was a huge problem. But he managed. He learned to shoot – and here the result was quite remarkable. He became very, very good at it – a legacy that has remained with him, which is perhaps something that putative burglars around his home in New York state these days might do well to remember.

He was so good at it that a gunnery instructor named Sainsbury, newly home from the front line in Korea, sidled up to him on the range and on the pretext of saying something, squatted by his side and said: 'Are you crazy? Try missing a few.' As André now says, 'There were talent scouts around, looking for the fellows who got the bull's-eyes. So I took his advice and stopped shooting so well. I knew otherwise I would be sent off to Korea.' The message was taken to heart. Suddenly, his shooting prowess had lost all its magic. It was courageous of the instructor. 'He could have got court-martialled for it, as could I.'

Being court-martialled wouldn't have been pleasant, but nor were all the meetings he had with officers during this time. One meeting, however, was a little more happy.

André was among a detail digging a latrine when a sergeant came to him and ordered him to put down his spade and go to the camp office. He wiped his hands on his denim fatigue outfit, followed the sergeant into the camp office and, coming face to face with his commanding officer, stood to attention and saluted.

'Previn,' said the officer, 'I see you've been nominated for something called the Academy Award.' It was the result of his efforts for *Three Little Words*, a movie that the CO professed to know no more about than he did about the identity of the Oscar. André got as far as muttering something like, 'Thank you, Sir,' and the officer ordered him to work. 'So I went back to digging my shit ditch.' He eventually got permission to go to Los Angeles for the Oscar ceremony, the first in which he had been involved. Friends noticed the different haircut.

He flew to the ceremony but as it turned out, he didn't win. He didn't expect to do so.

Half-way through basic training, André's past caught up with him. The barrack-room tease, who is almost as unpleasant an individual as the Army bully, latched on to the fact that Previn over there had been something of a celebrity in his civilian past. He got hold of a Hollywood fan magazine in which André was shown to be sitting at a night-club table with a very pretty actress wearing an extremely décolleté dress. He then pinned the picture to the pot from which lunch was to be served.

'It was not the most pleasant lunch I've ever spent,' he recalls today.

From Fort Cooke, André was posted to the Canadian border at Fort Lewis, Washington. There, he spent what was also hardly the happiest of New Year's Eves – on guard duty. He was feeling more than a little sorry for himself. Considering the New Year's Eves he had spent in Hollywood, this was depressing, perhaps a little degrading and very, very cold.

'I never knew who I was protecting us from. The Canadians? Were they going to come over and invade? I was feeling more and more sorry for myself. It was *very* cold. It seemed the weirdest way to spend New Year's Eve.'

Things were even worse for him when he could hear the chiming of church bells coming from the nearby town. Self-pity was fast degenerating into outright depression. He looked for the remote chance of finding some company – and then he saw a dog. Dogs always follow Army camps, rather the way rats find their way on to ships. They know that there's a good chance of food cans or odd bones and scraps being thrown across the camp perimeter. He bent down to the dog, to express solidarity with another creature left out alone and cold on a night such as this. The dog looked at him with a longing stare. Brotherhood in adversity? Not quite. André said: 'I thought to myself, "Well here comes a friend. Happy New Year."' Then the mutt expressed its true feelings. 'He pissed on me. I thought that was quite right.'

The basic training went on for a seemingly interminable time. Then there was an equally interminable time waiting for his assignment to the kind of job that he would do for the rest of his time in the service. Unusually for an army – an American Army or any other for that matter – there was one officer who thought it would be a fairly

92

good idea if he could do a job that would be related to his civilian occupation. André would be sent to the military music school in Washington D.C., where he would teach. What was more, he would be instantly made up to an officer. Lieutenant André Previn would get his silver bar on his shoulder without even having to go to officer school.

'I said, "sen-sational". I could live in my own flat, no matter how humble and all that. "That's really great news," I said.'

Unfortunately for him and, as it turned out, for the Army as well, there was one little snag. To get that instant commission, Private Previn, André, would have to agree to sign on for an extra year. 'I said, "No, no, forget it."'

His refusal wasn't exactly warmly received. 'It was a bad move on my part,' he says now. 'The Army treated it as an insult. It was the last I ever heard about a commission.'

About nine months later, the same quirk that had been responsible for offering the teaching job worked once more to attempt to deposit a square peg in a square hole. He was made up to sergeant and sent off to San Francisco, where he was to write music for the Sixth Army band. 'I wrote things that would never be used by anyone, although I also wrote endless marches.' And because someone thought they could also play band concerts – 'They weren't good enough to play concerts' – he also wrote band arrangements for them. 'Absolutely unplayable nonsense like the first movement of Shostakovich's First Symphony.'

He was, meanwhile, also expected to play an instrument himself. So he taught himself to play the flute, 'because it was the lightest instrument to carry. I can't play it, but I played it well enough to fake. It was completely hopeless and, in retrospect, hilarious.'

He is happy enough now to see that, despite it all, there *was* a nicer side to his military career. 'I met some very interesting, very nice people whom I otherwise would not have met and became infinitely more independent.'

Nothing fitted more into André's definition of 'hilarious' activity than the visit he paid while he was stationed at San Francisco. André made his way to Solvang, two-thirds of the journey from Los Angeles to San Francisco. He had a weekend pass, but didn't fancy going home. Instead, he wandered around the town and in the area immediately outside it. There, André stopped at a mission church, which he thought was charming, standing in an equally beautiful rose garden. The church itself was served by monks in brown robes, a church close to the desert, similar to those in various parts of Latin

America and Spain. Strangely, the traditions of this little town itself were very different. One of the requirements laid down in its charter was that you could only open a business there if you were of Danish extraction.

A monk asked André if he would care to look round the chapel building. He said that he would. Inside, the monk noted the sort of visitor he had that day. 'I see you are interested in the organ. Are you a musician?' André said that he was.

This was plainly not a conversation to be ended at that point. The monk said that he would dearly have loved to invite him to mass the following day, but since the choir director was off sick there would be no music, so he wouldn't enjoy it.

That was when André did something of which he says: 'To this day, I haven't the faintest idea what possessed me to say it.' What he said was: 'Listen, if the choir can be got together, I'll rehearse them for you this afternoon and give you a nice Mass.'

The brother couldn't believe his ears any more than André could believe his mouth. 'Would you really?' he asked him. 'But you're on a weekend pass . . .'

'I'm sure he thought I was on a weekend pass from being shot at, but he was pleased with my offer.' They had their rehearsal. The following morning, André did give him the Mass. Outside in the rose garden, the monk was almost embarrassing in his effusion of thanks and praise.

'Please tell me the name of your parish priest,' he said, 'I would like to write to tell him how marvellous it was of you to do this for us.'

At that moment, André says, 'I thought, "Oh God, I bet I've broken some Church law or other that I didn't know about."'

'Well,' he stammered, 'Father, actually, I don't have a parish priest. As a matter of fact, I'm not a Catholic, I'm Jewish.' To which the priest commented: 'Well, I don't suppose it is your fault.'

When he had settled himself, the priest asked André how it could possibly be that he not only could play so well, but knew the Mass so perfectly. What André could not tell him was that shortly before being inducted into the Army, he had been working at MGM on a film with Gregory Peck (who was a Catholic) and Ava Gardner, called *The Great Sinner*. It contained a long sequence containing the Mass and all the responses, which André had had to learn. As usual, he did not forget it.

André used the time in San Francisco well. He thought more than at any time since going to Hollywood of the kind of music that would have pleased Jack, for one, a great deal more than what he had been producing in the studio. He carried with him almost all the time in his uniform, pocket scores of the symphonies, books that he would study whenever there wasn't anything of a more military nature, or at least of the kind for which he was being paid, to do.

'So I got to know quite a lot of the standard symphonic repertoire instead of just lying around on my bunk doing nothing.' He thought that was a recipe for ceaseless teasing from Army mates, a group not known collectively for their thirst for culture. 'Oh, but you see, I wasn't reclusive about it. I wasn't funny about it. They didn't care. I still went out for beers with them or went to the movies.'

It had all come about when Leonard Bernstein came to San Francisco, a musician with whom André might have been thought already to have a great deal in common.

André had played the solo at the West Coast première of his Second Symphony, 'The Age of Anxiety', conducted by Franz Waxman, which he enjoyed.

Whenever there was a concert to which André could go while he was in San Francisco, he went. The night in 1951 that he heard Bernstein conduct the Israel Philharmonic in the city was to become one of the most important in his life.

The young Bernstein – he was thirty-three at the time – 'absolutely bowled over' the even younger André. He had never seen him at work before and realised what he had missed. The Friday evening concert wasn't enough for him. The following night, he heard Bernstein again at Stanford University, on the Sunday he followed the orchestra across the bay to Oakland. Each time, his reaction was the same.

He and the man everyone called simply 'Lenny' met after the third concert. Bernstein commiserated with him over having to be in the Army, but said there was, of course, a consolation. 'You're very lucky because you have Monteux here in town.'

Pierre Monteux, conductor of the San Francisco Symphony, was one of the most respected conductors then working in the United States and one of the greatest conductors in the world. 'Yes,' said André, 'but I've never met him.'

Bernstein said, 'Oh you must meet Monteux. How long are you going to be here?'

'I don't know,' said Previn. 'Perhaps another year.'

'Well,' replied Bernstein forcibly, 'you must meet him. I will set it up.' And, unlike so many pious promises in circumstances like these, he did.

He was also told about the classes Monteux ran for particularly advanced students. Monteux, like many conductors, enjoyed extending his activities to teaching – after all, that is essentially what a conductor is, a teacher as well as an intepreter of the music he is playing; the musicians have to learn to play pieces the way he believes they should be played.

'Monteux was an absolutely walking encyclopaedia,' he now recalls. 'You don't have to be a musicologist to work out how much he knew. You just had to look at his list of world premières. He was the first to conduct *The Rite of Spring, The Afternoon of a Faun, Daphnis and Chloé,* unbelievable. Things that you wouldn't think anyone could have done the world premières of any more.

'He was just terribly nice to me and gave me pointers that I have remembered all my life and that still come back to me.' As with all the lessons he had ever had in his life, André was a quick student. Sometimes, as far as Monteux was concerned, too quick.

Once, he took to acrobatics on the podium that Monteux did not think at all suitable. 'Did you see Mr Bernstein last night?' he asked. André said that he did. 'I thought so,' said the old man, who suggested that André adopt a style more natural and more suited to his own temperament.

Bernstein did everything very naturally and resented the label of 'showman' that I myself had once, in all innocence, foisted on him. André has told me: 'When Lenny jumps four feet in the air for a *fortissimo* or goes to his knees in a *pianissimo* or dances a pirouette, it is the most natural thing in the world for him and it is endearing.' In André Previn, it was not so endearing and he never did it again.

Nor did he adopt again a practice Monteux noticed when André conducted a Haydn symphony, 'one that has one of those last movements that just frolics away'. He was allowed to conduct it uninterrupted. But when it was all over, Monteux looked at him closely, 'Tell me, in that last movement, did you think that the orchestra played quite well?'

He thought that it sounded like a trick question. Finally, after wondering what he would say, if anything, André got up his courage. 'Actually, *maître,*' he stammered, 'yes, I did. I thought they played very well.'

'Yes, so did I,' said the conductor. 'They played very well. Next time, don't interfere.'

That, André concedes, was sage advice indeed and a message he has remembered ever since. 'When it's going well, don't interfere; they don't need you. You have to be experienced enough to know when the next dangerous corner is coming up, when they'll be looking to you. But when it's really going along, leave it alone.'

There was another thing he heard Monteux say – to another pupil, it must be said: 'Now, that was very impressive. But before you try to impress the ladies in the balcony, make sure that the horns come in.' As André says: 'That was very nice. And always said with a smile.'

On another occasion, a student conductor called to the string section: 'Don't give me one of those revolting Stokowski slides.'

From the auditorium came the hand clapping of the master. This time he was not so easy-going. 'You are in no position,' he cried in an accent that became more like Maurice Chevalier's with every intonation, 'to criticise one of the most distinguished conductors in the world and someone you should look up to. I will not have you saying such demeaning things. You are nothing . . . '

Says André: 'He went on and on. Years later, I reminded him of that. I said, "*Maitre*, I did not know that you admired Stokowski." He said, "I didn't, but that's not the point."'

André had thought of extending his repertoire and taking up conducting serious music before meeting Monteux, but it was in the studying with him that the notion came to him that this could be his career, a life away from the studios and the tenth-rate material he and other first-rate musicians were paid to produce.

During the time he was with Monteux, rumours were rife at André's base that he and several others of his unit were going to have to find other jobs than merely teaching pupils at the military school. The story was that he would be shipped soon to Tokyo, which at this time was never more than a way-station for the Korean battle front. When he told Monteux the news, the Frenchman said 'I fell for that once,' he said. 'The Tokyo orchestra, it is terrible.' He had no conception of the possibility that Previn could be sent away for purely military purposes that would have absolutely nothing to do with the local symphony orchestra.

Also, it is fair to assume that Monteux had no knowledge of André's other musical activities while in San Francisco, or at least no conception of what they involved. He was playing more jazz than he had ever performed before, going to smoke-filled clubs at weekends and on evenings when it was safe to leave barracks. He was doing it not only more frequently, but in a more committed way than he had before.

He was still able to find young women who were ready to open more romantic doors for him, including the lady who helped him cook a steak by remote control. He was hungry and fantasising about what he would do if he could get a piece of red meat on the grill of his tiny, one-roomed flat. It was after one time in his life when he could afford to go into a restaurant to buy one, and before the next. So he rang the girl, who provided him with the basic instruction by phone on what to do with the steak he had just bought. Having told him the ingredients and the sort of dish he would have to use for the task, she added that she thought it ought to be grilled for nine minutes each side. That was fine, except that he remembered that his watch was being repaired. But a music man doesn't give up that easily. He also remembered that he had a record of Berlioz's *Roman Carnival* which was precisely nine minutes long. He played the record twice, once for each side of the steak, and the meat was perfect. It was perhaps the most successful culinary exercise of his life. Playing music was always very much easier. Jazz certainly was infinitely simpler than cooking.

Quite suddenly, his Army days had enabled him to find what he calls his own 'voice'. In the barrack room he had been introduced to the records of Charlie Parker, Theolonious Monk, Dizzie Gillespie and others of their ilk. 'I really couldn't believe it and used my technical prowess to emulate that kind of playing.' After sitting in at the jazz clubs, he gradually realised that he was no longer a pale imitation of other jazz men but was, as he puts it, 'beginning to sound like myself'.

Others liked that sort of sound, including a certain jazz singer called Betty Bennett.

She was performing at what was then the Fack's Club on Market Street, which was a popular haunt of most people around town who liked to hear the kind of modern jazz in which the place specialised. Betty was the principal attraction there.

She told me: 'There was a disc jockey in town who worked not just for local radio stations but also donated some time to working with the Army. He asked me if I knew that André Previn was in town and then added that he would bring him along to the club.'

She didn't know much about the 'authentic genius' of MGM. 'I thought he was a British piano player who played too many notes' (a jazz illusion to more serious music. As André was told by one eminent practitioner in the field, the real art of jazz was to know what to leave out.)

He came, heard her sing her own individual interpretations of numbers like 'Over the Rainbow' and 'It Could Happen To You', was introduced and, as she now unblushingly concedes, 'I think it was love at first sight.' They sat up the whole night, talking.

The next day, she had promised to go out by ferry to an incoming troop ship, bringing soldiers back from the Korean battle front.

André was free and offered to play for her.

Soon, they were dating regularly, with André borrowing $30 from another sergeant to pay for dinner and two tickets for the current hit show, *Guys and Dolls*. She admits, 'He took me to see *Guys and Dolls*, but really we didn't see *Guys and Dolls* at all.' In the end, he had to borrow another $30 from the sergeant to pay for another date.

'There was something about him,' Betty told me. 'He was so bright and interesting and funny and if you meet him, you're his.'

The romance ran strong and, on the whole, smoothly. But it helped his jazz progress, too. Through Betty he met outstanding jazz personalities like Shelly Manne, Shorty Rogers and Zoot Sims. He began working with them. The Army gave André time to think as well as to study. In a way it changed him.

'It was the final and absolute alienation from my parents because I never went back home to live, even for a short time, and I didn't relax quite so much because I thought I had lost two years of my life, which indeed I had. In retrospect, though, I had no reason to resent it. Other people go into the Army and get shot at. I didn't. It was uncomfortable and a bit pointless. But it was ten years before Vietnam. If you were called, you went in.'

He had done nothing to be ashamed of while in the Army. 'I led a coward's life there and did what I was supposed to do. All I can say is that I did it without bitching. I just put in my time and got on with it.'

The day that it was all over, in 1952, André was faced with a reality that he decided had to be met with some degree of ceremony. Demobilisation involved more than just saluting, picking up his final packet of Army pay and being told he was a civilian again. There was a great deal of bureaucracy involved.

Papers had to be filled out and he had to be signed off in numerous places to which he had never been in all the two years he had served his Uncle Sam. The motor pool, the mess sergeant, the weapons sergeant and the supply sergeant all had to sign him out. Sometimes, the right man couldn't be found in the right place and the procedure that could have taken minutes or at the most hours, spread into days.

Finally, he had all the signatures on all the pieces of paper that he needed. He picked up the small suitcase that he had ready, went to the end of the camp and at the gate, asked a guard: 'Does this really mean that I'm no longer a soldier?' The soldier confirmed that it really did. Sergeant Previn was now a civilian.

This being the case, he thought to himself, what the hell was he doing still wearing a uniform? There, in the middle of the desert, with just a lone car driving past, he changed.

But he decided not to go straight back to Los Angeles. He wanted to have a break, to get to know San Francisco, which would provide him with a good opportunity to get down to some serious music study.

'I decided not to go back right away because I wanted to study, to stay with Monteux. I was having a good time. I saw no particular reason to rush back to the studios when I was studying and really learning something and also trying to find my way through some jazz at the same time.'

He also had Betty there with him, although that would not have stopped his leaving the city had he wanted to do so. They had talked about marriage and she would have gone where he went. But there was also the continuing pull of the jazz clubs. He played more and more with people like Shelly Manne and Shorty Rogers. 'Betty was, to a very great extent, a help to my listening to important people and being able to play with them. She introduced me to them and vouched for me.'

With the experience behind him of playing the clubs while in the Army, he admits to having been in 'vague demand' on a more permanent basis now that he was out of the service than he had been before. The clubs discovered he was available and took advantage of the fact. Very much a two-way traffic with demand being satisfied with ability and willingness.

It was much more than a mere relaxing diversion. He says he had always treated jazz with the utmost respect – and the musicians along with it – and not as simply something to do when he wanted to rest his brain. But now, in those San Francisco clubs, he was treating it as seriously as he had his lessons with Monteux. Certainly, the disciplines were different but disciplines there were. Undoubtedly, the people were different, but he liked them tremendously.

Not all the friendships he made at this time were strictly with jazz people, although many had jazz connections – like the comedian Lenny Bruce, who was perhaps the most outrageous man to stand before an audience and make them laugh. His wry sense of humour, mixing expletives and sexual innuendo with stories about the top names in the news at that time, made him a sell-out draw wherever he played. All over America, there were attempts to ban him. But in San Francisco, the still young Bruce was in his element – an element he would before long ruin. He was deported from Britain for indecency, for taking the drugs that would get him a suspended jail sentence in California and eventually kill him.

'He is now a cult hero,' André says on reflection, 'but at that time he was just a struggling comedian with most of his friends in the jazz business. Yes, he was a junkie, yes, he was probably known to every vice in the world. But he was a very sweet man and a darling friend. I knew him and I liked him and he liked me.'

They were both now working at the Fack's club. Bruce would go on while the musicians were taking a rest. Every night virtually, there was a different show, with André standing in the wings along with other resident or guest jazz men who had either been on or were waiting to perform.

'I would stand in the wings for two weeks while he did the most horrendous things.'

Very little that he did, however, could have been more horrendous or more loving than the offstage experience of the afternoon walk they took together through Sucher Street in the heart of San Francisco. They passed Books Incorporated – a name that will for ever be indelibly implanted on the Previn brain – and in the window saw the three-volume edition of the *Mozart Letters*, translated by Emily Anderson. It was a set André desperately wanted to have and he told Bruce that. But the price for a now impecunious jazz man newly out of the Army was prohibitive – $25. 'It would be like $2,000 now. One simply didn't spend $25 on books in 1952.' But he did talk about how great it would have been to have it.

From Books Incorporated, they walked to a nearby coffee house. 'I'll be right back,' Lenny said after their joint orders had been placed. He returned with a package – the three Mozart books.

André was stunned. 'Lenny,' he said, 'you can't do that. You don't have $25 to buy books any more than I do.'

'Don't be ridiculous,' he replied. 'I didn't buy them. I stole them for you.'

At this, André Previn looked furtively around the shop, expecting either uniformed cops or detectives in soiled fawn overcoats to swoop in. Between those looks, André managed to stammer his protests to his friend. 'I can't do that, Lenny,' he said. 'I can't accept that. You mustn't steal for me.' André was outraged, but not quite as outraged as Mr Bruce.

'He got angry,' Previn now recalls. 'But the point that is impressive about that is that he got seriously angry.'

'Listen,' he said, eyeing his friend, 'you're a good friend and you've done me lots of favours and I want to make you a present. Now, if I had $25, it wouldn't be much of a present. But to *steal* a book and risk getting busted and possibly going to jail for it, that's a big present.' As André says: 'The philosophy of that so blew my mind that I didn't know quite how to answer it. For that could be an argument of enormous length.'

This was a battle that could not be won. The receiver of stolen property then decided to show his gratitude and asked the bestower of this largesse to sign his gift for him.

On the fly leaf, Bruce crossed out the $25 price and substituted $19.95. Then he wrote $19.00 and crossed that out and a series of other prices until he got to 50 cents. At which point, he added: 'Take it shmock, nobody's looking. Love, Lenny.' He now says: 'So I have the only copy in the world of the *Mozart Letters* signed by Lenny Bruce.'

Of course, the Bruce style of humour went down particularly well in the jazz clubs. In a way, his performance was a kind of jazz in itself, an improvised adaptation of known facts, just as jazz was an improvisation on known notes.

There were other outrageous things he did *inside* the jazz club that affected André. At the time, he might well have preferred to have been left alone, but the memory gets more and more precious as the years go by. Like the time Lenny approached two girls at a ringside table. He had a small hand mike. He directed his jokes at the girls and then got personal. 'What are you two doing after the show?' he asked, to which he received an answer that was a mere flood of giggles.

'Come on, come on, come on,' he responded in the rhythm of a machine gun. 'Do you want to come out with me after?'

Eventually, one of the girls managed to offer the not irrelevant information that there were two of them. To which Bruce turned to Previn in the wings and through the packed club shouted: 'Hey André. Want to get laid later?'

André took off as far as the leather soles on his shoes would carry him. But not far enough away not to hear Bruce adding: 'No, guaranteed. Well, how about it you two?'

One of them replied: 'Well, really . . . '

'Oh come on, honey, don't crap around – yes or no?'

'No,' came the answer.

Later André stopped him as he left the stage. 'Jesus,' he said, 'you've got some nerve!'

'Why?' Bruce asked. 'I wasn't hurt when they said no.'

André stayed in San Francisco for about six to eight months and then the call of MGM became strong. He returned to Los Angeles and Betty went with him.

EIGHT

Going back to Los Angeles was important to André, and for Betty. His job at MGM was waiting for him and the studio had a number of projects begging his attention.

Before he thought about fixing a date for the wedding, he had time to reassess his future. The presence of his parents so near was no longer an inhibiting factor. Lotte was always the epitome of encouragement in whatever he did. Jack couldn't appreciate that good music could still come from behind a cinema screen and understood jazz even less.

Nevertheless, the senior Previn had cause to appreciate some of the things his son was doing. Back in Hollywood, André was not only not going to ignore the jazz that had become so important to him, the experience with Monteux had been vital and was to frame his future. That much he knew. How long it would be before he was totally overwhelmed by it, he couldn't yet say. What he was sure of was that it would happen, just as he remained certain he would one day go to live in Europe again. But before that, he had to sign his new contract with MGM's music department and plan his wedding.

Most of his classical work involved chamber music for which he now had a love bordering on devotion, a feeling which he has never lost. He was part of a permanent trio. They played a great many concerts, particularly at the two local universities, UCLA (University of California at Los Angeles) and USC (University of Southern California). In addition, there were Lawrence Morton's Monday evening concerts, which continued to emphasise new or neglected music. André became more and more involved in them, because he was always prepared to spend time learning something rare, like the Hindemith Piano Sonatas and an evening of Roussel's piano music. 'I must have been crazy. Not because it's difficult, but because you'd

103

never get to play it again.'

Then there was the time he and Lukas Foss played the Mozart Sonata for Piano Duet in D Major – at two days' notice. Morton told André that it would be easily enough done, even though André had never played it or seen it in a score. Foss knew it intimately.

The next day the two men met to play, with André calling on Foss's assistance. 'That's funny,' said the other musician, who was one of André's closest friends, 'I've never played it either. We've been in the oldest con. game in the world.' But the concert went ahead. The next night, they played the piece together. During the performance we were trying to hiss at each other, "Are we making these repeats?" We had no idea. But it wasn't bad.'

The next day, the *Los Angeles Times* commended them for 'preparing this piece with such diligence and care, musically and musicologically researched so precisely as the performance by Mr Previn and Mr Foss'. 'And', said André, 'we didn't even know which page we were on. But those were all very nice and very carefree days. We weren't weighed down by having to care what this concert was going to do for our careers. We just played.'

That could have been marked down for some future use as André Previn's epitaph, but he almost never 'just played'. He had, of course, already won her. As soon as they were ensconced in Los Angeles, a wedding was arranged. Before that would happen, they were still getting to know each other.

What André already knew about Betty – or 'Betsy' as she was more affectionately called – was that she was somewhat sensitive about her age. She knew that she was a year or so older than André but there wasn't too much of an age difference to worry her unduly.

In April 1952, she and Lotte Previn were in the kitchen of Lotte's and Jack's house talking about André's coming birthday. They were planning the presents they were about to buy. Inevitably, they talked about his age. 'Well,' began Betty, 'since he is going to be twenty-seven . . .'

'No,' interrupted Lotte, 'he's going to be twenty-three.'

'No. No. No,' Betty persisted, until she rationalised that no one could possibly know more about a man's age than his mother.

Betty was, to use her own word to me, 'devastated'. Here was this sophisticated man of the world, the Oscar nominee, the pride of Hollywood, who was just about the best jazz pianist she had ever heard, and he was . . . twenty-three! Instantly, she felt as if she was about to be arrested for cradle snatching. Meanwhile, she felt for herself that she was 'retarded . . . I should have been singing better, I should have got further, I should have been paid more . . .'

The car journey back to where Betty was living in Los Angeles was not the easiest either she or he had ever spent. It was also a long one, which gave them plenty of time to thrash out this matter.

'You have such a hang-up about your age,' André told her, 'that I was afraid to tell you.'

'Well, you miserable bastard,' she replied, 'it's too late. I'm in love.'

The wedding was held four months later, on 24 August 1952.

The ceremony was held in the large mock-English home of Johnny Green on North Bedford Drive in the heart of the Beverly Hills film executive belt. Green, as his position as head of the music department at MGM decreed, had turned the elegant house into a combination of home and recording studio. In the days when most people's idea of playing recorded music at home was still either an upright radiogram or a box that played the new-fangled long-playing records, Green had what would now be called state-of-the-art stereo, putting out taped music at a rate of decibels that could have damaged the foundations. But it was a very small occasion. Altogether, no more than about fifteen people were present. By normal Hollywood standards, very, very private.

Best man was Saul Chaplin. He was more than thrilled to do the honours at the ceremony. 'Betty was a wonderful singer and a wonderful girl. When he played and she sang, it was something very special.'

After the wedding, the Previns set up home at Doheny Drive, close to where Saul Chaplin lived. 'I lived on the west side and he lived three blocks south of me on the east side,' Saul remembers. 'When we would play two pianos, he would make a U-turn and park outside my house.' So far so good. But André Previn didn't have any better sense of direction in 1952 than he would have almost forty years later. 'Almost every time he left the house, he would make another U-turn and go in the wrong direction. He had no sense of direction whatever.'

Not quite true. He may have been geographically off-compass, but his sense of direction about his career was always spot on, as if he had it marked on a score and planned it to the very note.

He was taking jazz more and more seriously and wanting to be a part of its world, while at the same time working at the studios and flying up to San Francisco at weekends for more conducting lessons from Monteux.

When there was time, he joined the Jazz At The Philharmonic All-

Stars – an offshoot of the famous series held in conjunction with the Los Angeles Philharmonic – and went on all-night playing binges with them, travelling from city to city in buses whose lack of comfort was matched only by the excitement they generated. To him, then, it was the jazz equivalent of being invited to conduct the Vienna Philharmonic – and if *that* was a dream, it was in the far distance, towards the back of the score.

He heard some of the other great piano players of the day, most notably Nat 'King' Cole, whom he admired tremendously and whom he now wishes was as well remembered for his keyboard work as he is for that gentle, velvet voice. There would be others in the years to come. Most of his concentration had to be devoted to the studio.

It was once more a familiar world to him. He was, however, no longer being asked to arrange other people's music; he was now devoting his time exclusively to conducting the studio orchestra and writing his own compositions. He was also earning more money than he had seen for some time, but, according to Betty, he was by no means rich.

'His salary had been down to nothing while he was in the Army, but the studio did keep paying an allowance to his parents. When he returned after the Army service, they made him give the damn thing back. They took it out of his salary, so we had no money to speak of.'

Betty found it harder than André to take the Hollywood life for granted. 'I think the difficult part for me,' she told me 'was suddenly to be dumped among the George Burnses, the Jack Bennys, the June Allysons, the Dick Powells. There were all those high-powered people. I always felt like a frump. There was no way I could dress the way those people did.'

There was another problem, too. Suddenly becoming Mrs André Previn denuded her of her own self-esteem. It would have been difficult for anything else to have happened. But it was hard for her. 'I really thought to myself that I was as good a singer as André was a piano player, but all they thought of me was as André's little wife – so all the insecurities began to surface.'

There was no question of jealousy. 'With every advancement for André, of course it was better for me, but I did think there was more to me than I was being given the chance to prove.'

Entertaining was never a real problem for either of them. André was then, as now, always the life and soul of his and everyone else's parties. Having jazz men over for an evening was just a reprise, in new and slightly plusher circumstances, of what she had been doing for years. When she gave dinner parties it was for people like Betty

Comden and Adolph Green, who were close friends and made the life of most hostesses easy enough. They were the writers of a dozen musicals. Most notably up to then, they had updated for Hollywood Bernstein's *On The Town*.

Later, they were to make a couple of albums together and the results indicate a pair of musicians who quite clearly had got their act comfortably together.

There was another point of their relationship. She knew jazz people who were now in Los Angeles just as she had in San Francisco and, as then, introduced them to her husband, who took mental notes of their performances. He had never been so certain that he wanted to play more and more jazz, although never at the expense of classical music.

Soon, they had moved from their apartment to another one and then to a house on Mulholland Drive, high in the Hollywood Hills.

Now his name appeared on credits that gave him considerable pride. One of the first movies on which he worked on his return to the Culver City lot earned him his second Academy Award nomination. The movie was *Kiss Me Kate*, a musical adaptation by Cole Porter, of the *Taming of the Shrew* story, and starred Howard Keel and Kathryn Grayson, with Ann Miller in evidence most of the time. The music was provided – along with the lyrics – by Porter, but it was André as musical director, together with Saul Chaplin, who made it work for the screen. The film was one of the first to be made in the short era of 3-D, and it was replete with objects being thrown at the audience. That André and Chaplin only had plaudits thrown *their* way said a lot for their contributions to the movie.

He and Chaplin followed this with a less exciting picture called *Give A Girl A Break*, which was produced by Jack Cummings as a vehicle for Marge and Gower Champion. The story was old hat, about show girls auditioning for a new Broadway musical, and the movie was not terribly successful either commercially or critically.

The following year, 1955, André did his most ambitious film work to date. It was the score for part of the ballet film, *Invitation to the Dance*, starring the man who more and more was becoming a close friend, Gene Kelly. For him, he wrote a forty-five minute ballet, called *Ring Around the Rosy*.

Now, writing a ballet can be difficult at the best of times. This one presented problems more complex than any that had ever faced Tchaikovsky. It was the first – and possibly the only – ballet ever written the same way as any other piece of film music: the sound had to be laid on to the existing action. In other words, the dance had been filmed before the music had been written. Actually, it wasn't precisely like that. There *had* been music written for the episode – it was one of three which comprised the picture, this one based on the famous *La Ronde* story, a chain reaction of romance in which a girl goes to a boy who goes to another girl who goes to another . . .

The film was shot in England at the MGM studios, Boreham Wood. Music had already been supplied by the eminent British composer, Malcolm Arnold, but Gene Kelly didn't like it and asked André to come up with a new score.

Kelly briefed André about what he wanted. What he didn't tell him were the precise details of the task – mainly that the dance had already been shot. When he first saw the footage, he was able to hear some of Malcolm Arnold's music and some counting off-camera from Carol Haney and Jeannie Coyne, who were Kelly's assistant choreographers. Their task was generally to make sure that Gene did the steps he said he was going to do, things he couldn't see for himself while he was actually performing.

But most of the film he was shown was entirely silent, which gave an eerie kind of feel to the whole thing, as though he had suddenly been transported to the pre-talkie era and a scene from King Vidor's *The Crowd*, when girls danced and viewers tried to convince themselves they almost heard the music.

It was a daunting task, 'a jigsaw puzzle, a nightmare'. For three weeks from early in the morning, he sat with Carol Haney in a booth with lots of knobs and switches which he could turn to freeze frames, make them go faster or slower.

What he could not do was ask Gene Kelly to give an additional step which could provide a grace note or another beat which he might have thought necessary. Instead, for three weeks he and Miss Haney sat in the booth while he tried to build up some kind of musical framework for what he had in mind. But she had to keep telling him what tempi Kelly wanted.

Kelly was impressed with the result. So was the Screen Composers' Association. They were so struck by André's work above and beyond the normal call of Hollywood duty that they made him a special award.

He tried to say that it really was all in a day's work, but whichever way anyone looked at it, it was a pretty impressive job. It pleased Gene Kelly and cemented their friendship still further.

'I remember saying to André that I couldn't understand how he could come up with his music so quickly,' Gene Kelly told me. 'It seemed so effortless. For a dancer, working on routines for a film took so long.'

More than that, he wondered how he could manage to work as hard as he did, frequently on so many things at once, and still get to sleep nights. 'I found it very, very difficult to take the dance routines and the music out of my mind. I found it impossible to sleep.'

He couldn't get over the fact that André told him he never used sleeping pills. 'I've since discovered that about other musicians. They can do so much more without affecting their sleep than can dancers.'

André himself recognised the time and effort that Kelly took with his work, even if it weren't apparent to everyone. On one occasion, he walked into the rehearsal room and found Gene lying on the top of an upright piano, his coat supporting his head like a pillow, looking up at the ceiling. André crept across the room, sat in a corner, took out some work he was doing and started writing. He continued for forty-five minutes, while Kelly remained on top of the piano. After those forty-five minutes, Gene was shocked to notice him. 'My God, André, I didn't see you there.' To which Previn replied: 'Well I could see you were working there so I didn't want to disturb you.' 'You knew that? You didn't think I was asleep. Well, you're a good man.'

It was true, he did realise. But artists have often had difficulty in convincing outsiders that labour doesn't have to include sitting by a desk or standing with a shovel. It was James Thurber who said that his greatest problem was convincing his wife that when he looked out of the window he was working. André knew that Gene Kelly was 'in labour', reaching the end of a gestation period for a new dance number. In his line of work, it was the birth process of the actual dancing through a New York street, past store windows in and around water hydrants that was done in public.

His principal work with Kelly followed on the dancer's biggest of all successes, *Singin' In The Rain*, a triumph which neither he nor anyone else for that matter would ever be able to repeat. It is now regarded as the archetypal Hollywood musical. So, by the time André was working with Kelly on *Invitation to the Dance*, the dancer couldn't have been held in higher esteem, both by the public in general and by him in particular.

'I was very, very close to him,' André remembered. The open house that he held every Saturday night to which nobody was invited but everyone who knew him was always welcome – gatecrashers would be spotted immediately and were shoved out – underscored their relationship. It got to the point that whenever a light was on in the house at Rodeo Drive, people would pop in. The door was never locked.

André once decided to take advantage of that fact when he and the director, Stanley Donen, called at the house on an afternoon when no one was in - even though the door was open. The days when that could happen are long gone, of course. Burglar alarms are attached to cups and saucers now!

But in those days Kelly trusted everybody. He was trusting to the point of carelessness, which is strange considering the effort he put into his work, the demands he made on people who worked for and with him. Yet he even had his valuable art collection exposed to whoever chose to walk through his front door. It was that collection that Previn and Donen decided to make the butt of their own practical joke. They unhooked all the pictures and loaded them into Stanley's car. Somehow they thought it amusing that Gene would believe he had been burgled. The dancer was, however, cleverer than they thought. He immediately worked out what had happened, phoned André and asked him to bring the pictures back. Rarely had a joke backfired so quickly.

But the work he put in would have strained to beyond breaking point many another relationship. Compared with Astaire, with whom André had never been anything like so close, Gene was, he says 'a much more inventive choreographer, in terms of cinematic complexity. And he was wonderfully indefatigable. After all, he changed the movies. God, he worked long hours.' And not just lying on top of his piano.

He was also, he says, 'terribly nice'. But he *could* appear to be otherwise. He was a man of 'blatant prejudices'. He liked people who had talent, had no respect for those who didn't. 'If you were talented, he not only liked you, he gave you a great deal of leeway. But if you didn't, he had no time.' That became clear at his open-house parties, which were, in effect, nothing of the kind. He was inclined to take the same attitude about girls brought by his friends – if they were pretty and decorated the house, they were welcome. But if they didn't and had little to add to the conversation, it was made clear that they were not encouraged to come again.

André concedes: 'That was unforgiveable in a way. His friends were those who had something to offer. If you were just *nice*, he wasn't interested.' André admits, perhaps reluctantly, that he understands that. 'It's a failing. Of course, it's a failing. But it exists more than you might think. After all, are you friends with your dentist? Many artistic people shy away from those who just go into an office every morning.'

André met, to quote the cliché that is always invoked in such discussions, the great and the near great at those parties that Gene Kelly and his then wife, Betsy Blair, gave – the Chaplins, Noël Coward, Maurice Chevalier. He had a very impressive group at those parties, not just stars and musicians, but politicians or writers like Norman Mailer.

Since Previn *was* talented, the relationship between him and Gene Kelly was close. 'He taught me a great deal about movie musicals. He taught me a tremendous amount about writing for a dancer and all that.'

There was also a lot of fun. André recalls, 'many good times and laughs', but never at the expense of sheer grind and hard work. 'You had to work until you fell down. Gene thought nothing of twelve-hour days. But I was young, I enjoyed it.'

He enjoyed indulging his own personal predilections. Sandy Courage recalled the days when André had taken over the office that once belonged to the head of the music department. 'He would sit there, with its big piano, and have great fun. We would play English music together. He was batty about English music.'

It's a 'battiness' that has survived the years. He admired the English, he told Courage.

As we have seen, Saul Chaplin remembered those sessions on the studio piano too. 'We played symphonies together. Why he indulged me I don't know. He knew so much more about music than I ever would and played a thousand times better.' And yet when the playing was over, with Beethoven running through both their brains, André would take an Oscar Peterson record and put it on his player.

'That was a wonderful example of André's musical abilities, the result of his education and all that he had done with it.'

André would say that was all part of the discipline of working in a major studio, making major films of all kinds. Almost as important was the speed with which he had to work. 'There was a lot in that saying that producers did not want things good, they wanted them Tuesday.'

There was also a spirit of co-operation and support from above. Other people in the film business complained about being frustrated by the moguls and their minions. At MGM, Louis B. Mayer had already gone, prompting local wags to note that 'the old Grey Mayer ain't what he used to be', and had been replaced by Dore Schary, who kept his own lion eyes on what was going on around the lot. But the musicals were left alone for two reasons – simply because the studio was still Making Great Musicals and because there was one man in charge of them.

Arthur Freed headed a unit that was having more success than practically anything else in Hollywood. The golden age may have been coming to an end and there were some who, in later years, said they had predicted it, but the enthusiasm was greater than ever.

André was right in saying that Gene Kelly changed the movies, but it was under the guidance of Arthur Freed that the genre of the musical really altered. He saw it as a medium made to measure for the new wide screens, the improved colour and, most important of all, the coming use of stereo sound. Musicals became no-expense-spared plays with scenery that seemed real and in which you couldn't see the joins. He had been a songwriter himself – the score of *Singin' In The Rain* had been entirely made up of the lyrics he wrote to the music of Nacio Herb Brown (although the song 'Make 'Em Laugh' bore an uncanny resemblance to 'Be A Clown', Cole Porter's song from the recent MGM Gene Kelly/Judy Garland picture, *The Pirate*).

Freed ran a unit that was practically self-governing. He took to it the experience he had had in the years before moving to Hollywood, which was quite considerable. He was a former vaudevillian who became a producer – via Army shows in World War One – on Broadway. In a world in which nothing ever manages to succeed like success, he was highly successful.

'His unit was a very, very good thing to be in on,' André recalls, 'because they were the élite. He made some of the best musicals ever and he surrounded himself with all those people whose work he liked and to whom he was unceasingly loyal.'

Unlike almost anyone else in Hollywood, he didn't take as his maxim that a man (or woman) was only as good as the last picture. 'With him it was win some, lose some. You could come off the biggest flop in the world and move to something that was just as big a deal because he thought, well, you'd do it this time.'

He also allowed people to make what he, in the normal course of events, would have regarded as mistakes. Like the time André was put on a new Mario Lanza film which, as far as Previn was concerned, was the equivalent of being given a free trip to Siberia.

Freed didn't have anything in his department for André to do, so the Lanza film, produced at another unit, was his next assignment. But the days when he happily wrote tail-wagging music for Lassie were thankfully over.

He had no respect for Lanza, which was a negative factor that did not bode well for either of them, let alone the picture. He was an invention of Louis B. Mayer,' says André. The flesh (and there was a very great deal of that) and bones were moulded by Mayer and his publicity team into the big new star of the early 1950s.

Lanza might have had a huge success with *The Great Caruso* at the studio, which made him potent box office material. Indeed, he might even have had a voice which Previn thinks could have been trained into something musical. ('Let's give him a compliment first. He had a remarkable, untrained voice which could have been moulded, probably, into a first-rate tenor, but he was content to just scream.') But he was not the sort of person he enjoyed working with. 'He was a very vulgar man – in every sense of the term. Added to which, I thought he made some terrible movies.'

André said no. He was not going to work on a Lanza picture. Once the no had registered with the studio's big brass, he was sent formal notice that he was under suspension. Now, being suspended was a fairly hallowed Hollywood tradition. Some of the biggest names in the business had spent months on suspension. At Warner Bros., Bette Davis practically made a profession out of being suspended – but it remained a powerful weapon. Artists who were suspended had their pay stopped. Not only that, the length of time they spent not drawing a salary was added on to the period of their contract and to ensure that nobody used it as a means of getting out of an agreement, they were banned from working anywhere else. Eventually, that would be ruled unconstitutional, but it was one of the traditions of the studio system.

Saying no was not what the people who assigned senior staff to jobs at the studio expected to hear. André only did it after working with Lanza for one afternoon.

'I don't want to do this picture,' he told them.

'You will do it,' they told him.

'Give me a break, fellas,' Previn replied. 'I've not done too badly here and I really don't feel like doing this. Besides we won't get on and he won't want to work with me either.'

The suspension was imposed with immediate effect. But the next day, André returned to the studio to collect his things. He was walking out to the parking lot – if he wasn't working any more, he wasn't able to park his car there either – when he bumped into Arthur Freed.

'Are you really doing the Lanza film?' Freed asked him.

'No, Arthur,' André replied. 'I am not.' And he told him the whole sad story.

Freed roared with laughter, a perfect imitation of the studio's Leo the lion in action. 'Do you need rescuing?' he asked André, who was not in the least bit reluctant to agree that a rescue seemed very tempting indeed. 'Why, do you have anything for me?'

Freed conceded that he didn't. 'Well,' said André, 'think of something mythical.'

The producer said that he would allow his imagination to run ... 'But don't worry, I'll make up something.'

The very next day he was put on full salary to advise on the possibility of a film based on the musical show *Carnival* being made in the unit. 'Of course, it never happened. But we were only fooling about until something else came up.'

Michael Kidd was one of the stars of *It's Always Fair Weather*, the next Gene Kelly film on which André worked. Kidd was joint choreographer of the film with Kelly. He was used to this role. Unusually for him, on this 1955 picture about the reunion of three ex-Army buddies ten years after their demob, he danced on-screen along with Kelly and Dan Dailey. Kelly directed the picture with Stanley Donen.

André was musical director, but most important and significant for him, the score included the songs sung by the actors – with lyrics supplied by Betty Comden and Adolph Green, who also wrote the screenplay.

It was another milestone in Previn's career, a career that has always seemed dotted with milestones like markings on a road. He had never before written songs for a movie. Two that remained in the finished film seemed as if they might take off: 'The Time Has Come For Parting' and 'I Like Myself'. They didn't make the charts, but as bitter-sweet pieces of honest nostalgia mixed with pure melody, they served their purpose.

Comden and Green liked 'I Like Myself' so much that they thought they could persuade Frank Sinatra to record it. They hoped that Sinatra would be in the film too, but he shied away from it.

One number in the film written for Michael Kidd was cut out after being shot. 'Gene Kelly elected not to use it because I think it was too good,' Kidd told me. 'André did a marvellous job with that, probably too good.'

Previn confirmed the story for me. 'The greatest of performers do like to think that they are shown to come out best of all,' he said. 'It is human nature.'

But Gene Kelly's nature was perhaps more human than most and it made André's visits to the house at Rodeo Drive less frequent. What he describes as Gene's 'competitive streak' precluded the having of fun and made him himself feel uncomfortable. And it was a time to have fun. Hollywood was still the big, best place. 'We didn't know we were all sitting on the *Titanic* while the band played, "Nearer My

God To Thee".'

It's Always Fair Weather had enough to commend it to make it seem unlikely that that sort of thing couldn't go on for ever. It was a splendid, highly polished piece of work which, unfortunately, did badly at the box office. People may have related to the notion of three old soldiers having a reunion and then finding that they have nothing in common. But they probably found it too close to the heart. It pricked consciences of some, for others it was too close to a war that they didn't want to be reminded about.

Comden and Green had first come up with the idea of the picture. They saw it as a kind of sequel to *On the Town*, which had been about three sailors having a day off in war-time New York.

The problems involved in making the picture did not, on the whole, concern André, although he almost shared Michael Kidd's disappointment at losing the big musical solo. Michael is still nursing a wound that has never completely healed.

'Michael was one of the real shining lights of choreography, but he also now had a chance to sing. They all – Gene, Dan and now Michael – had big numbers of their own. Michael's was very ambitious, about Jack and the Beanstalk, all done with enormous humour, very wild and very complicated.

'I spent a lot of time on it and we recorded it and we filmed it. And it was sen-sational. But it was a little too sensational and Gene took it out.'

Kelly decided, so he said, that the film was too long. 'And Michael never got over it.'

To Kidd, he was being robbed of a chance to shine and be given public exposure he had not been allowed before. To André, it was merely another good piece of scoring and there had been plenty of those in the past and it was likely there would be many more to come.

As far as Gene Kelly was concerned, says André thirty-five years later, 'It was an immovable thing. Gene who was brilliant himself was in charge. There was him and there was Fred Astaire at the very top of Hollywood musicals. In this film, Gene was in charge. If he said it was out, it was out.'

There was an abundance of technical problems, not least of all the part the speed of the music played in governing the movement of cameras.

They wouldn't work together again at MGM. It was Kelly's last work for the Freed unit. André would, however, continue. Meanwhile, he and Comden and Green were all nominated for Oscars, which none of them actually received.

As far as his MGM work was concerned, he moved from musical to straight drama with the sort of consummate ease some people could have thought was a substitute for hard work. To be fair, he was doing so much and so quickly, it seemed as though he only had to take up a sheet of paper and it would be ready. The agonies, the biting of pencils, the cramp as he stood by his architect's drawing board were not for public consumption.

There was very little that was wrong with *Bad Day At Black Rock*, the Spencer Tracy film for which André provided some of the most evocative screen music since *High Noon*.

It was the story of a one-armed man, played by Spencer Tracy, who gets off the train in a hick town and tries to work out what the big secret in the place is. It was a haunting piece of cinema for which André's score only heightened the drama.

Not all his spare time was occupied with the musical scene. There was a Hollywood influence with another of his pastimes. André had discovered fencing. He not only enjoyed it, he was quite good at it. His style, however, as he was the first to admit, was hardly classical.

He was trained by one of the Hollywood fencing aces, the man who, reputation had it, had taught Basil Rathbone for his role as the Sheriff in *The Adventures of Robin Hood*. Such qualifications were not to be sniffed at. He liked Previn more than he liked his style, but he did acknowledge that he could wield a powerful sword when minded to do so. After one lesson, the coach burst into what was seemingly genuinely uncontrollable laughter. 'You know, André,' he said, 'you have no class whatever. But you're a klutz who kills.'

But this was a mere diversion in the ever more busy life of André Previn. He, meanwhile, had become more involved in a production than ever before. A different kind of production than any he had ever experienced. In 1954, at the age of twenty-five, he became a father. Betty gave birth to a daughter whom they called Claudia.

NINE

Betty told me: 'Through André I got to know about Ravel and Richard Strauss and Stravinsky. I thank him forever for that. On the other hand, although he had been playing jazz for a long time, until he met me he didn't know who the really good rhythm sections in town were.'

So Betty set about changing that just as André himself had broadened her classical education. 'I introduced him to Shorty Rogers and Shelly Manne. I'd known Shelly since 1941 (I obviously knew him when I was in my cradle) and I think it was through me that he stopped playing with people who, on the whole, were quite inferior to himself.'

It was in their love of jazz that they were really as one. André had totally outgrown the inhibitions he felt after hearing people like Bud Powell, Charlie Parker and Dizzie Gillespie play. For a time, after being exposed to them, he had been so confused by it all that he couldn't play any more. He just listened. Now, though, that voice of his own had been found. 'It changed my way of thinking, my way of playing, my way of keeping time for ever.'

There would be tours, visits to jazz festivals, college dates – the college audiences were the real jazz fanatics, the people who followed that kind of music the way students today go for rock or pop.

The trio played some of the best-known jazz clubs in America, particularly those that had come to specialise in his kind of business – in piano trios. Brubeck, Shearing, Peterson and himself followed each other into one club after the other. Some were the kind of places jazzmen liked; clean, not too noisy.

Oscar Peterson preceded André into one club and delighted in regaling André with his experience on checking in there for the first time. Nothing was right about the place and he complained to the manager, who grew more and more incensed by the minute. Peterson was particularly angry about the piano. Unlike violinists there is no way a pianist can cart his own piano with him, date to date, so is very much in the hands of the owners of the venues where he plays.

When he pointed out the virtually unplayable piano, the manager looked at Peterson and declared: 'You've got a lot of nerve. I just had it painted.' André was advised to get that matter sorted out before he went there.

For a man still in his twenties, these were not matters to complain about. 'They were seedy, and interesting and tawdry and glamorous places all at once.'

He would go to work there late at night and at two or three o'clock in the morning, he and his fellow musicians would go out to eat. 'I don't think I could do it any more, I'm sure I couldn't.'

There is a theory of André's jazz musician friend, Ray Brown, that since many of his colleagues had died before the age of thirty, any who managed to pass that milestone would go on at least until they were ninety.

One Christmas, André and his trio were playing in the lounge of a Las Vegas hotel. It wasn't most people's idea of festive surroundings for the festive season. No number of girls in short costumes dressed as Santa Claus in the middle of a heatwave can really compensate for the traditional Yuletide. Yet here he was surrounded by walls without windows, decorations without clocks and everywhere the slot machines.

The trio had been there for the best part of a month – 'which was quite hilarious because almost nobody listened; it was something they were just not geared up for.

'It is terribly funny to think I am now engaged in preparing Beethoven seasons at Salzburg and there I was walking through the lounge of this Las Vegas hotel, at midnight, in order to go to work.'

But it was another chance for the jazz men's cameraderie, a unique freemasonry with its own signs and its own language, and if its members don't spout brotherly love, most would jump to a fellow jazz man's defence should *anyone* dare cross them. Also in town at the same time were Nat King Cole, George Shearing and Woody Herman. 'We all had a very nice time,' André recalled for me. 'But nobody was listening. We didn't care because we enjoyed it thoroughly.

'In a way it was quite wonderful because it heightened the insanity of it all.'

In the space of a single morning, as though a button had been pressed at some secret control point, the town where there are no clocks suddenly realised it was Christmas and time to put out the decorations. Casinos in one movement discovered crèches with three wise men and the Virgin Mary statues, which had to elbow in for room with the roulette tables and the slot machines.

André was asked if he had any thoughts about improving what he tongue-in-cheek described as the 'stunning' decorations. The decision to offer his reaction was a mistake. He had forgotten that most of the desert city's gambling joints were operated by branches of the Mafia and that *ipso facto*, most of the members of the gang were extremely religious.

'I suggested that because of the holiday season, maybe it would be a good idea if the slot machines could pay off on three crucifixes. There was an insane silence. The man then said: "I don't think that was funny in the least."' At which, André's bass player sidled up to him and whispered from the corner of his mouth: 'May we go out please?' When they did go out, the musician nervously looked in André's eyes to see if he were totally conscious. 'You must be joking. You can't make a joke like that to a gangster. Are you crazy?' Recalling that time now, André says, 'that man who was almost a parody of the archetypal underworld type made me terminate my stay there as quickly as possible.'

He quite enjoyed the jazz club scene. 'What I didn't like was when we had to have rehearsals in the day and they'd open up specially for us and there was all that smoke and the stale smell. But what I liked most was that whatever city we were in, the local jazz people would come and hear us. We got on so well. It is the popular misconception that jazz people were only interested in that kind of music. It may have been true in the old Eddie Condon Dixieland days, but it's not true with modern jazz players and they genuinely liked to have someone to whom they could talk who knew something about Bach and Stravinsky.'

There were more basic, more personal reasons for enjoying the company of the people involved in the scene. 'The jazz players don't predicate their friendship on proximity,' he says. 'If you don't see them for a while it doesn't mean that they have forgotten you or are not pleased to see you.'

Even now, he can have coffee and talk with a pair of trumpet players he hasn't seen for thirty years and the atmosphere is as if they had been together the night before. 'Certain of those people were really as close to me as anyone can be, and continued to be so long after I stopped being an active jazz player.'

There is a trademark about the professional jazz player that can't be escaped and which the Previn mind appreciates still – the kind of laid-back cynicism which interweaves with kindness.

Thirty-five years later he still says about jazz: 'It is not only a source of admiration for me as an art form, but I probably have as much or more fondness for the purveyors of it than anybody else. In their own way today, guitarists like Joe Pass are just as good as Perlman is as a violinist – even if, because of the art form, it is in a more limited way.'

Also, it was something to be taken very seriously indeed. Right up to the 1990s, he holds a perhaps too strong a resentment against musicians who say they intend to take a little time off and play some jazz – as though it were going to be a hobby for them or at best a sabbatical. To him, playing jazz was a job to be taken no less seriously than the prospect of an unseen Mozart piano concerto.

Recently, he heard of a famous classical pianist saying that no, he didn't play jazz, but he thought that next season he would take some time off and start playing it. 'I can't tell you how many Anglo-Saxon words I used to describe my reaction to that. But that is the way many very fine musicians think. And I don't understand that attitude. I'm certainly against it.

'I have an absolute horror of people who think of jazz as a hobby. I have always taken it quite seriously. I don't want to say, "This doesn't count, it's only jazz." But taking it seriously does not preclude me from having fun.'

For that reason, he needed to organise himself. If he were going to play properly, he needed to play with others who were, as Betty had indicated, also the best – and people who could guarantee to be present and not find that they had another gig that evening.

That is why he formed the André Previn Trio, with the best. Shelly Manne and Leroy Vinnegar were a team – the best whom he paid to be certain that they would be there when they were needed.

Shelly Manne became one of André's closest friends, a business association cementing what had always been a good relationship, since Manne himself first came to Hollywood.

André never once considered giving up his film work to play jazz – he couldn't have afforded it. But neither did he think of abandoning his classical music. He couldn't have afforded to do that, either, but for totally different reasons. He was practising jazz in a highly professional way. Classical music was his greatest love, but it was something he could only do much less frequently and with very much less public exposure. But he never even for a moment considered abandoning it for the jazz at which he was becoming so renowned.

Even when he was on a jazz tour, there was always a selection of classical scores in his case to study, just as there had been when he was in the Army.

Jazz was easier, because there were no scores to study, no rehearsal, apart from what he describes as the 'bare bones of some sort of organisation, but nothing to really, really work on.' The sheer ease of that sort of regimen made jazz a relaxation that classical music could never be. After all, even when he was planning a jazz concert, he didn't have a great deal of practising to do. But, as those scores testified, it was that very classical music that was still bubbling within.

It was, of course, modern jazz in which he excelled. What had once been known as beebop and then merely bop was to the musician simply modern jazz, the kind that sometimes seemed to bear no resemblance whatever to the melody of the original piece. Like a painting seen from a distance it could, detached, be identified – and, like the painting, it was the interpretation of the artist that was to be analysed under a metaphorical microscope.

He went on making records. They got better, but as he admits, they sold less and less. The fluke of his teenage years when his first RCA album, 'Andre Previn', became the best seller in the country, was not repeated.

He then moved to Columbia Records and made albums for them. At the same time, he recorded some classical pieces for the label, too. But his most satisfying output was for a tiny Los Angeles firm called Contemporary, which was run by Lester Koenig, who had once worked in the movie business as William Wyler's assistant. Falling foul of the UnAmerican Activities Committee, Koenig decided to devote his time to his hobby and passion, jazz.

The records were highly successful, although he, too, never really cared very much for sales. All he wanted to do was break even, which they always managed to do. He set up his microphones and his recording system in the garage where he also packed the discs. The acoustics were perfect.

The André Previn Trio was sometimes called something else. The leader of the group – and there had to be a leader – was paid as much as $100 more than the other two members. So they decided that they should alternate the name they gave themselves.

It was as Shelly Manne and Friends that the three of them – Shelly, André and Leroy Vinnegar – assembled at the garage at Melrose Avenue in the summer of 1956 without knowing precisely what they were going to record. That was the spirit in which jazz records were made. The inspirational improvisation of jazz permeated the sheer mechanics of the operation. It was Koenig who had the best inspiration of all. 'You know,' he said, 'that amazingly successful show, *My Fair Lady* is on the cover of *Time* and *Look* and everybody is talking about it.'

In particular, everyone was talking about two tunes from what was fast becoming the most successful Broadway show to date, 'On The Street Where You Live' and 'I've Become Accustomed To Her Face'. On the other side of the Atlantic, Julie Andrews dreaming of having danced all night was played constantly on BBC record request programmes. Why don't you guys record the score?' In those days, it had never been done. Jazz groups only played single songs.

A great idea, of course. Except, as André said, 'Who knows all those tunes? I certainly don't.'

But there was an all-night record store open at the nearby corner of Sunset and Vine, perhaps the best known junction in California. So they sent for the cast album. They heard the score, tune by tune, and played it the way it came to them – with the microphones turned on. Nothing in the history of jazz or popular music has ever come to anybody so successfully or seemingly so easily. 'We did it any way we wanted to.' André or one of the others would listen to a song and suggest how he thought it needed to be performed, slow or fast, and once his idea had jelled in his own mind he would add: 'Here let's try this. What if we make the middle bit Latin and there we'll double it?' Of course, there was no intercutting.

They learned the piece harmonically by playing bits of it at various speeds. 'Once we had got a road map, I'd play the tune, then three choruses and Shelly would play an eight-bar break, we would write it down like instructions on how to get to someone's house.' Writing down the instructions ensured that no one came in at the wrong time with the wrong thing. 'That didn't keep us from changing it. If I felt I was doing quite well with a couple of choruses and wanted to go on, I would signal and go on I would.'

Since no one was planning to make a single out of the stuff they were recording – it was due to go on LP – it didn't matter just how long the individual tracks lasted. One went on for ten minutes.

No one had any conception of what had occurred at Lester Koenig's garage that night. 'We were mightily surprised. I thought it was amusing, and I thought it was good natured and I thought some of it was very inventive. By morning it was done.'

It could never have happened with a classical piece, which would have had to be scored and rehearsed over and over again. Even then, no one could guarantee the results. As Previn says: 'In classical music, it is almost always the music that is better than the performance. In jazz, it is nearly always the performance that is better than the music. Charlie Parker, for instance, played the dumbest stuff.'

Conversely, as he once said, if the Girl Scout Symphony played the 'Eroica', you could hear somewhere a little bit of what Beethoven had written. 'They can't completely destroy it. But, in jazz, Bird could blow "Sandman" and make it jazz.'

After the completion of that night's *My Fair Lady* work, André thought he saw the irony of what had been accomplished. 'We have just made the most expensive private recording ever,' he said, 'the most expensive private joke.'

Before any complete score could be recorded, there would have to be the granting of grand rights – the sort of thing anyone who wanted to record a whole opera would have to get. 'Lerner and Loewe are never going to grant them,' said André, who knew a thing or two about matters like that, but knew nothing at all about Lerner and Loewe. He had never met them, but he knew the wholly understandable sensitivities of people who wrote musical shows. As he told his colleagues: 'We've made slow tunes fast and fast tunes slow. All kinds of violence has been done to their tunes.'

But a man who had worked as William Wyler's assistant was not easily going to forego the chance to experiment. Koenig wrote asking for grand rights, sent a tape of the recording – and instantly had a letter of approval from the writers saying 'Go ahead.' It became neither private nor a joke.

The record was made and Lerner and Loewe were sent the first copies almost literally hot off the presses. 'They were absolutely crazy about it,' André now recalls.

They liked it so much that they gave, as Christmas presents, copies of the disc to every member of the Broadway cast – and to numerous other friends and relatives whom they thought would appreciate it. Their own copies were wrapped carefully and installed in the midst of their personal collections.

Somewhat modestly, André now describes it as 'one of those curious milestones of luck'. But that session in Koenig's garage in 1956 made history.

The disc became the first jazz album ever to sell a million copies. It established Contemporary Records as a leading label. Then, as André says, 'true to the code', they asked the trio to make more show albums, sometimes with Red Mitchell in Leroy Vinnegar's role and Frank Capp deputising for Manne. 'And we did. Of course, we did.

But it never happened again.' They did *Pal Joey* and *L'il Abner*.

The worst flop was *Camelot*, which, considering it came from the same Lerner and Loewe stable as *Fair Lady* might have been thought to lend itself to the medium perfectly, but it was found to be totally unsuitable. Previn disliked it as much as the public, who failed in their hundreds of thousands to buy the disc. He partly blames himself. 'I didn't play very well and I was by now getting tired of the whole thing, so there wasn't much to it.' He also partly blames Columbia, who commissioned this one. 'In those days, I had absolutely no control over record covers. In this one, they had me dressed in armour.'

It was, needless to say, an artist's impression. André's impression was pretty predictable.

Other jazz groups played show tunes, too – 'almost anything, you know, "Dizzie Gillespie Plays *The Student Prince*".' Not really, but practically everything else. The Previn Trio carried on in their own footsteps. They were to record altogether six further show albums after *My Fair Lady*.

In the commercial world of the record business, Previn and the other two members of his trio had created a new art form. He himself today looks on it all a great deal less charitably – and with thirty-seven years behind him, he can afford to be fairly dispassionate. 'It wasn't a new art form. I just created a gimmick for selling records.'

The closest they came to the *My Fair Lady* success was *West Side Story*. And Leonard Bernstein loved it as much as Lerner and Loewe had appreciated *Fair Lady*. 'But we never got a *My Fair Lady* again – and neither we should. Some of the shows just never lent themselves to that sort of treatment. But it led to the most loathesome craze of people doing what they liked with show music.'

André's trio decided to call it a day after *Bells Are Ringing* and *Gigi*. 'That was that. I had wrung that one dry.'

The truth was that *My Fair Lady* succeeded on the back of the immense success of the show itself, in addition to the response to the record's quality too. 'It was an outrageous idea and jazz was very popular in those days. The fact that somebody took those tunes and turned them inside out was an attractive thought. And it was new. There was a new image for André Previn and, as it turned out, a wholly new audience for him. It could not have sold as well as it did just to those for whom jazz was a passion.

The people who bought the disc were not all the usual jazz *aficionados*, but, in the main, youngsters who had heard about something quite different entering the lives of friends. The word of mouth travelled faster than the record revolved on turntables. Some people bought it simply because it was the fashionable thing to do. It was a response André had never had to his work in the studios. Certainly, he had had nothing like it from classical music audiences, let alone the habitués of the jazz clubs.

He may have wrung out the show options, but he did continue to make jazz albums, one of them with Betty. There were more with Shelly Manne, too. He played the piano on a Manne record and Shelly himself also made more André Previn Trio discs. The same people were playing, they just changed the names. And people continued to buy them. He had found a way of doing what he thoroughly enjoyed, being totally in charge of the operations and making not an insignificant amount of money at the same time – for him and his fellow artists as well as for the record companies.

André was to do a solo album, appropriately called 'André Previn All Alone'. He was not only all alone in the record studio but all alone in his tastes. Just as on the *My Fair Lady* date, he had no idea what he wanted to record. He simply went into a music shop, let his fingers do the walking through a pile of sheet music and when a tune caught his fancy, bought it, took it to the RCA studios and improvised it there and then. Each of the final tracks were the ones he played just once at that recording session.

André and Shelly Manne linked up with pianist Russ Freeman to make a record called 'Double Play', an album of nothing but baseball songs. 'Take Me Out To The Ballgame' had never sounded so vibrant since the day Teddy Roosevelt left the White House.

The audience for Previn and jazz grew. Television was taking off in a big way – one of the few writings on the wall that the film studios were noting, but refusing to do very much about. They introduced wide screens, but didn't widen the appeal of their movies. Instead of fighting TV head on, they hit it on what they thought was their home ground on which no one else was allowed to tread. For years, Hollywood studios refused to allow a TV set to appear in any of their movies.

André stayed away from the fray but not from the new medium. When he was invited to appear on television, playing jazz, he did so and because he was good at TV, he was asked back, again and again. There were no clauses in his MGM contract that prevented his doing so.

He went on making his television appearances, without realising they were presaging a new Previn career. For the moment, he was delighted to play while Marge and Gower Champion danced or while Ella Fitzgerald sang. He also appeared on the Benny Goodman television show.

Goodman was still one of the giants of jazz, even though his brand of the art was still dubbed 'swing'.

He had heard André's trio playing at a jazz club in New York. Frank Capp looked ahead into the smoke and told André about the guest who had slid in while they were playing. 'I think that's Benny Goodman over there,' he said. It was. They went over to him when they finished playing the set and Goodman invited them to sit down and have a drink. Then, he asked the question that many jazz men at the time made the subject of their wildest dreams: 'You guys want to make an album with me?'

Even for a much lauded and now highly sought-after group like theirs, an invitation to play with Benny Goodman was not one to be taken lightly. As André put it to me: 'In the old days, in the big band days when Benny Goodman sent you a telegram telling you to join his band, well, it was like getting knighted!

'Even though it had long been past-history when Goodman was at the top, it was still an offer no one wanted to refuse. When he asked us to come along, I said, "Sure, Benny."'

They accepted with the same sort of alacrity they would have shown as small boys being offered a huge box of chocolates. 'Benny was good-natured and I liked him and he was very nice to me, but he was very strange.'

So strange that he insisted that they come to his house the very next day to do it. And he added: 'I want to make an early start. Can you get there by nine? You guys got a car?'

That was not a sound question to ask of a jazz man, for whom nine o'clock frequently isn't even the middle of the night; it's the beginning.

André told him that that didn't sound a totally marvellous idea. 'Wait a minute, Benny,' he said. 'We don't get through here until four o'clock in the morning and without knowing exactly how to get to your house, it's going to be a two-and-a-half-hour drive.'

Goodman's answer to that was: 'Well, you'd better go straight home after the gig then.'

'Sure,' said André.

'Then I'll give you instructions about how to get there.'

When they got to Goodman's sprawling mansion in Connecticut to go through the material they would cover, the trio were shown down to the huge studio room he maintained in his basement. Everything about it was fine. The acoustics were superb, the furnishings of the best, the library stunning. What wasn't so good was the installation of radiators, or lack of them.

'It was the middle of winter,' André recalled, 'and it was cold. So cold, in fact, that you could see your breath.' He decided to take it upon himself to do something. 'Hey, Benny,' he said, with a combination of due deference to the importance of his host and the friendliness that was as much a part of the professional world of jazz as the ability to play an instrument. 'It's really terribly cold here, you know, so cold, in fact, that it's very difficult to play.'

Goodman pondered that. He was very good at pondering. 'Gee,' he said, 'that's right.' And he went upstairs and came down again, wearing a warmer sweater.

'That's what I mean about strange. He was absolutely unbelievable. He would do that sort of thing all the time.'

Goodman was not the most generous of people at the best of times. Four or five years after the incident of the basement recording, he asked André to do some arrangements for him that he could take to play at the Brussels World Fair.

He played them and recorded them. But it was many years later that André – 'at a time when I no longer cared and I no longer needed the money' – plucked up the courage to remind him of the assignment. 'You know, Benny, you never paid me for those.'

'Oh, didn't I?' he replied. 'That's terrible. I thought I did. I liked those things. I'll pay you for them.'

'Do that,' said André. Before long, a cheque did arrive – for $125. 'Now the correct fee at that time would have been something like, I don't know, between $1,000 and $2,000. But I didn't say anything. I don't know how he arrived at that figure.'

The jazz world is a cause for reflection from him. 'Now I find that I have the same heroes that I had as a youth. The people who helped form you as a jazz musician are the ones who remain your heroes all your life. Dizzie Gillespie and Charlie Parker and Horace Silver. People do have long, kind and flattering memories. But people still write to me about them, come up to me backstage and talk about them.'

He has reason to be grateful for what he describes, somewhat modestly, as a 'curious form of flattery'. In some parts of the world, in the United States and in Japan, for instance, those records have never gone out of the catalogues. The tunes that enthusiasts heard on the first, heavy LPs are now readily purchasable on shiny, silvery compact discs in Tokyo and Osaka.

One should not, however, be under the impression that only flattering things happened to André Previn and his fellow jazz men at this time. Occasionally, they were faced with the unpleasant reality of all their human frailties. Mel Powell and he, for instance, would continue their commitment to the total belief that brilliance in music allowed them a complete dispensation from more worldly matters. Their triumphs with orchestras and jazz combos rightly had to be matched with a thorough ineptitude in matters practical.

'I can't think of anyone in our time,' says André, 'whose musical life has been richer than Mel Powell's. Jazz pianist, serious pianist, arranger, teacher, academician, musicologist, composer. All on the highest order, all successful, always influential. His fund of knowledge is frightening, his tastes catholic, his musicianship impeccable. His vocabulary rivals that of Isaiah Berlin, he's a good painter, he can play stride piano and he's probably capable of finding cabs in the rain.' André, who might not know where cabs go in the summer either, possibly admires the last most.

The Previn's home in Mulholland Drive had one of the most spectacular views of Hollywood and both enjoyed it when there was neither work at the studio nor a jazz engagement to fill. Occasionally, just occasionally, he allowed himself to be concerned with the domestic arrangements at home, which was perfectly fine when it didn't require him to use any of his gifts for practicality that he plainly did not have. One Sunday morning, however, he decided he did have the answer to a wholly practical problem.

The beautiful grass at the Mulholland Drive house was hardly benefiting from a plague of gophers, the moles who sometimes seemed to form as big a slice of the local population as film stars.

They would burrow under the grass, leaving piles of earth and numerous holes in the lawn. So André decided it was a perfect reason to demonstrate his prowess. He crouched down on the ground with a shovel, lying there seemingly for hours. When Betty went looking for him, she saw him in the prone position.

'I'm going to get that little son of a bitch,' he declared. And he did. André Previn was not going to be deflected from one of the important purposes of life.

TEN

Hollywood was entering one of its unhappiest times. Not many realised it was seeing the decline of the whole studio system. Just as André had said, they were all standing on the deck of the *Titanic*. Now the band played, but they couldn't see the water rushing in or the bows slowly rising in the air.

The film capital was under ever-increasing attack from Senator Joe McCarthy and his henchmen and some of the city's finest writers and directors had failed to answer one question to the senator's satisfaction: 'Are you a Communist?'

There were people André knew who were anything but Reds but who felt they were having rights infringed by the mere asking of the question. One man actually appeared before the tribunal and refused to answer and then found the contents of his desk waiting for him as he drove into the lot. The locks on his office had already been changed.

By any definition of the term, André was no Communist, had nothing to fear from any investigation. But his name did come up for discussion in the midst of the mass hysteria which threatened to destroy the careers of dozens; writers like Dalton Trumbo and Carl Foreman, who not only couldn't write, but were also prevented from directing and producing in Hollywood for two decades; actors like Larry Parks, musicians like Larry Adler.

But Previn's name did crop up, if only obliquely, in one of the trade papers' gossip columns of the day. Since everybody in the film industry read the papers - known as the 'trades' — anything published in them could be calculated to make or break careers, especially at a time when none of the major studios was prepared to do anything that would earn McCarthy's opprobrium.

In this article, the writer was determined to nail guilt by association. 'I wonder if André Previn knows that André Previn's orchestra has several pinkos in it,' he asked.

It was very easy to be a gossip columnist in America in those days. No research was needed. Nothing was written in depth. Just short paragraphs like that were enough to cause heads to roll in a world in which too many people were prepared to believe that there was a fire because someone told them that someone else had said he thought – but couldn't be sure – he could smell the smoke that a fourth person had assured him was rising.

The charge of being near 'pinkos' – people who couldn't actually be proved to be Communist, but you knew the way they leaned, nudge, nudge, because once upon a time they had said hello to a man who had once said he enjoyed a plate of borscht – in the climate of the early to mid-1950s was perceived as a dangerous one and André was called to see Sam Goldwyn and explain.

'Seen this?' Goldwyn asked. André said he had. 'I'm sure you know who they are,' he was told, 'so you've got to get rid of them.'

That was the point when the Previn foot went down heavily, far more heavily than it ever was put on the pedal of his piano. 'I can't get rid of them,' he said. 'A, because I don't know who they are, B, because if I did know who they were, I wouldn't get rid of them because in the recording period that we are given to produce music for a film, they don't have time to make speeches or hand out pamphlets, C, because they can play the cello very well.'

There was a summons almost immediately afterwards from the head of the studio himself, Dore Schary. 'Have it your own way,' Schary told him, 'but if one of these guys gets into trouble, I have never spoken to you.'

Curiously, very soon after this, a very fine cellist at MGM, Ed Lustgarten, was fired because he had been one of those who wouldn't confirm on oath that he had never been a Communist. He wasn't one, but he didn't think it was anyone's business. André had no knowledge that he was even being implicated when he spoke about cello players.

André himself did receive one other summons. He had to appear before the editor of a magazine which had been set up as a self-censoring journal that would ease out Communists from under the Hollywoodwork. Its aim was to find people whom McCarthy and his predecessors had failed to get.

The man asked André into his office, spoke pleasantly – and then thrust in his dagger. He shuffled through some papers and said: 'You contributed money to the Abraham Lincoln Brigade!'

André suddenly felt very much more comfortable. 'Do you mean,' he asked, 'during the Spanish Civil War?'

'You know perfectly well when I mean,' the editor countered.

'Date it for me,' André threw back at him.

'You know perfectly well,' he replied. '1936.'

To which Previn answered: 'You know I've been called precocious in my time, but in 1936, I was in Berlin, Germany, I was six years old and therefore very unlikely to contribute money to the Civil War in Spain.'

At which, the man got up from behind his desk, smiled, offered André his hand and said, 'No harm in trying!' Previn again muttered, 'Jesus Christ!' and stormed out. The editor later went to jail for blackmail.

His concert work continued apace as though it was his life blood. He would have liked to have conducted symphony concerts, but for the moment, he was having to content himself with being the soloist – and a very well-paid one at that.

At the Wilshire Ebell Theatre, he was soloist for a programme of modern music, playing Samuel Barber's *Four Excursions*. The *Los Angeles Times*'s critic wrote: 'To meet the composer's requirements for this work presupposes intimate acquaintance with various kinds of popular music, such as boogie, blues, folksong and jazz, all of which Mr Previn was able to set forth in the good taste which behooves it when it finds its way into basically classical forms.' He also played the Hindemith Sonata Number Three and work by Ravel and his own teacher, Mario Castelnuovo Tedesco.

Betty remembers a friend telling her: 'I think André's problem is that he worries about having been a child prodigy. If he had been one, then he is always afraid that he won't be able to live up to it.' That, of course, was never anything for serious worry.

In addition to his work, he loved fatherhood. The natural role of a father, which has become so natural to him in recent years, was already very much a part of him, but it wasn't his priority. Music still offered too many challenges, promised too many opportunities that he hadn't yet fully grasped.

His humour was infectious. He had the effect on people with him to get in there and want to join in as Previn witticism followed anecdote. Some tried to compete, some to top him, some just to want to be part of the scene.

Betty says that she didn't try to be part of the witty set. 'After all, we were talking about some very big people. But I had the reputation for being witty even though I kept quiet most of the time. But when I did say something, I seemed to come in with the right stuff.'

Betty was pregnant again. At the end of the third month of her pregnancy, he left.

Her second baby was another girl, whom she called Alicia.

All André himself will now say of the broken marriage was, as he put it to me, 'I was too young. Just stupid.'

The time of the split with Betty coincided roughly with what was undoubtedly the more complicated of his two films with Fred Astaire. In *Silk Stockings*, the remake of the classic Garbo picture *Ninotchka* with Cyd Charisse in the title role, the notion that part of his Hollywood music training was to ensure that Cyd Charisse had something to dance to was never more true.

Now, he had to arrange and conduct the score while at the same time finishing off *Invitation to the Dance*. He was also doing a similar job for the not too successful screen version of *Kismet*, the Broadway 'Arabian Nights' show that adapted the score of a Russian composer intended for something very different – or as *Time* magazine was to call it, 'A borrowed din from Borodin'. The composer's Polovtsian Dances were turned into tunes like 'Stranger in Paradise' and 'Baubles, Bangles and Beads'. The music sounded good enough and made about the only impact anything achieved in the production.

He worked for six months on *Kismet*. It was not a film he would have suggested doing any more than he would have personally volunteered for a Mario Lanza movie. 'You have to understand the role of the Hollywood composer. Unless you were an Irving Berlin or a Cole Porter, you wouldn't suggest an idea for a movie.

'By the same token, it didn't matter if you had ideas, you just don't do that. It was not your position. You wouldn't think of it.'

Not even an André Previn with an enviable track record always showed up for work at a film studio at nine o'clock in the morning, raring to go on something that excited him. 'I made more than fifty movies in my time, and more lousy films than almost anyone else. Sometimes, even great big movies which were fun to do but . . . *Kismet*? That was unbelievable. But then the next one was going to be nice.'

Silk Stockings had been a reasonable Broadway success, but the real reason for bringing it to the screen was the immense nostalgia that the story held for so many people. Garbo was already a legend who rested on the laurels of being legendary. She hadn't made a film for the best part of fifteen years and few had seen even photographs in the newspapers of her since. But there were still millions who remembered her and most of them had seen *Ninotchka*, the story of a Soviet commissar sent off to decadent Paris to bring back three of her countrymen who had gone to the French capital to see the Imperial Crown Jewels but who, along with the three other Russians, is tempted by the evil capitalist ways of the West. Garbo looked good even in her old crumpled raincoat, stunning when she finally gave way to the finery offered her by the playboy, Melvyn Douglas.

Silk Stockings was basically the same tale, except this time the lady was ordered to bring back a Russian composer who was off to Hollywood to write the score for a lavish new musical – hence the 'Stereophonic Sound' number. Cyd Charisse was the perfect replacement for Garbo. Not only did she have the most stunning legs in the business – she was given plenty of opportunities to wear the sheerest and longest tights, the silk stockings of the title.

But the change of story gave sufficient excuses to bring in Fred Astaire, as a scheming Hollywood producer conveniently in Paris at the right time, and André the opportunity to work once more with a fellow perfectionist.

As André says, the relationship he had with him was never as close as that with Gene Kelly, but they got on very well together and Previn appreciated the help the older man gave him – as much as Astaire was pleased to accept his advice, too.

It was to be the last of Astaire's sophisticated musicals, but it was released within four months of his brilliantly successful *Funny Face*, so that even Fred seemed to be still at the peak of his career. He was, as Hollywood folklore decreed, not the easiest person to work with. Anyone who could make his dancing partner go through so many takes that her feet bled, as he did with Ginger Rogers, couldn't have been an easy touch.

'But he never gave me any problems,' André asserts. 'Either my work pleased him or it was bland enough not to displease him, I don't know, but he never said, "This is not what I want." Not once.

On the set of *Silk Stockings*, he asked André to conspire with him in his determination not to follow one of Arthur Freed's ideas for the film. He asked him to come down to the rehearsal hall. 'They're going to give you a whole thing about this being a big number,' he told him when they met to look over a potential new routine. 'They'll give you a big thing,' he said, 'that this is going to be a big number. But I want it to be just a rhythm section, just piano, bass and drums. Do you think it would work?'

André looked at the music, its place in the film and what was expected of him. Astaire then danced it the way he thought it should be done. The musical director could only agree with the dancer. 'I think it's going to be great,' he told him, to which Fred replied: 'They'll say that sort of music is just for a rehearsal number, but this is how I want to do it.'

Looking back on it thirty-four years later, André says: 'I wrote it and he was absolutely right.'

Arthur Freed heard the music and said, 'When does the band come in?' André told him: 'It doesn't.' 'Yes, it does,' said the producer. 'No it doesn't,' said André. 'Go and see Fred.'

They went to see Fred and there was no band in the number, just the rhythm section.

'He had the perfect eye and ear for what he was responsible for. What he wanted musically was very often cliché, but perfect for what he was doing. Anything else would have been dead wrong. Obviously, unquestionably, the greatest musical entertainer on films ever. I would rather see him walk into a room than anyone else do a twenty-minute number. There was nobody like him.'

Other people were to say much the same thing. One man told me that Fred even chewed gum in time. But the big thing was the way that he could dominate a film set, just by moving in it. Stories abound of how, in rehearsal, technicians would stare open-mouthed at the gorgeous Cyd Charisse, but after only a few minutes no one wanted to watch anyone but Fred. As André puts it: 'Sometimes, you have to remind yourself that anyone else is there. He was just the best.'

He was also very different from Gene Kelly, his only rival to that 'Best' title. Kelly worked more cinemagraphically, planning a routine with the film built around it, designing it for the movie camera. He, of course, directed a number of his own films. 'That took a little more preparation. Fred, with the exception of a few trick numbers, really designed terrific dance numbers which were then photographed.'

In one regard, however, Astaire and Kelly were as one. Neither of them could teach André to do a time step. The young man so consumed with music that it occupied, even if he were only humming to himself, every waking moment of his day, was totally unable to grasp the essentials of being able to move his feet in time with his own rhythms.

'I have been told,' he says, 'that one of the true plusses I have as a musician is a very sophisticated sense of rhythm. But the following story is rather weird.'

The 'following story' being that when he told Fred he couldn't do a time step, Astaire answered: 'Don't be silly. I could teach my dog to do a time step.'

They were about to start a week in the rehearsal room together and Fred promised that during that time he would teach him – to master what came under the generic heading, 'time step'. 'I thought, "How many people have had Fred Astaire to teach them?"'

He tried, but didn't succeed.

'He didn't lose his temper the first day, but on the second day after we had been at it for another forty-five minutes or so, he said, "How is it possible for someone to be so unrhythmic? It's just not possible! Jesus!"'

A year later, he put the question to Gene Kelly. Again, it was the same story. He couldn't master it. After a fairly long time at the exercise, Kelly admitted defeat. He fell about laughing. 'Has anyone *ever* tried to teach you a time step before?'

'No,' said André. 'Just you and Fred Astaire.'

Fred Astaire had once also tried to teach André something about horse racing, too.

If anything rivalled dancing and singing songs – 'with that impeccable sense of phrasing,' as Irving Berlin once put it to me – it had to be the race track. He had horses of his own and one, Triplicate, looked set to break all kinds of records. He would escape to the track at Santa Anita whenever the occasion arose.

He asked André if he ever backed the horses. 'No, never,' Previn told him. So he gave him a tip. 'This horse,' he said, 'is as close to a cert as anything I could possibly give you. This horse will win. The odds on it are terrific.' As André now says: 'He more or less bullied me, lots of giggling and all that. I agreed to put $100 on it. The money meant a great deal more to me than it did to him – the equivalent of several thousand dollars today. Well, the horse is still running.'

After the race and the lost dollars, Fred apologised. But he was more concerned than he appeared to let on. Soon afterwards, he told him: 'Listen, I'm going to make it up to you. This horse I'm going to give you now really will win.' André replied: 'Sure', determined *never* to be caught again. He kept his money in his wallet. The horse romped home at thirty-three to one. He says now: 'That's the equivalent of people saying they could almost have bought a cheap Picasso.'

There was little that was cheap about MGM, particularly when it came to the Freed unit. They were the ones who knew about musicals. Freed's unit was different from any other MGM department.

'He had a genius for finding the right people for the right jobs.'

'But the fascinating thing is that none of us, not Fred, not Gene,

135

not Vincente Minnelli, certainly not I, thought we were doing work to be remembered. We were just working on another musical. Nobody ever said – not even with *Singin' In The Rain* – "Oh Boy, this is going to go into the time vault." No. Just another movie. *Singin' In The Rain* didn't even win any awards at the time. It wasn't until people started writing that other people started taking any notice. But we worked very hard and got a lot of money for it. That's what we thought. Nobody believed it was going to be someone's PhD thesis. That would have seemed madness.'

It may not have been a close buddy-buddy type relationship, but André and Astaire didn't just talk business on the set and leave it at that. They laughed and joked and they drank. As a memento of the work he did with him, André has one of Fred Astaire's walking sticks – with a small piece filed down so that Astaire could sign it for him. 'It's the only bit of fan memorabilia I ever fell for.'

Astaire wasn't the only actor he enjoyed working with on *Silk Stockings*. One of the Russians in Paris was played by Peter Lorre, born in Hungary but adept at playing Germans – and it was in Germany where he began his movie career. Just before work began, walking through the lot with Fred, Cyd Charisse and the director Rouben Mamoulian, the diminutive Lorre reached up to André's shoulder and spoke to him in German. 'Tell me, Previn,' he asked 'is this film a piece of shit?'

André replied: 'Yes, probably.'

'OK,' said Lorre, 'let's do it.'

As André now recalls: 'Everyone else smiled and hadn't the faintest idea what we were talking about.'

André was the musical director of *Silk Stockings*, but he didn't do all the orchestrations himself. It was the perfect example of when people like him had to delegate. Unlike Mr Stothart, however, he allowed the others full credit. One of those orchestrators was Al Woodbury.

For someone as meticulous a musician as André, his instructions to Woodbury before they started recording the *Silk Stockings* score was simple in the extreme. All he said to him was, 'Make it stringy.' And André says that that was referring to only one of the numbers.

They had met when André was conducting one of the first Academy Awards television shows in 1954. It was an annual event which Woodbury had for some time been orchestrating. After this first venture, they were to work on about twenty films together, an example of Previn's sense of loyalty as well as of his satisfaction with a much older man's skills.

'If you know what he wants, and you do it, you're buddies. He's the easiest of them all. A lot of people in our field are not nearly as obliging. He's my favourite composer.'

It was very much a mutually satisfactory arrangement. André knew what Woodbury could do and he was sufficiently confident both in the arranger's abilities and of his own to be fairly sure it would work.

'He's basically a very simple composer,' Al told me, 'His style of writing in the broad true sense is straightforward and not complicated. Yet people say, "I wish I could write that way." He would write certain sequences of just strings, that's all – he won't sneak in trombones or anything like that. He'll put down music on a page and it looks as though there's nothing there – but it's everything I want. I don't really *arrange* anything, in the sense of alterations. What he put down, I gave to him. On the other hand, if he gave me something by someone else, he'd say, "Here, you handle this." That required a bit more.'

Woodbury's convinced that André's being one of the boys helped in his relationship with the studio musicians. His jazz playing and his piano recordings, to say nothing of the concerts he still gave on Monday evenings, earned him, said Al, the respect of the orchestra members.

They loved the way he 'didn't play boss'. As Woodbury put it to me: 'He wasn't one to issue instructions. He'd say, "How about if we try it this way?" Well, they just loved him for that.

'He had the great advantage in that, unlike most other musical directors, he had such a strong musical background, conductor and composer. He always had so many styles churning in the back of his head when it came to film music. That was thanks to his training in the music conservatory. He always have the work done a week to ten days ahead of time.'

What Al Woodbury and others appreciated was that sense that André Previn didn't consider himself above people like him or above having a good time. He told him once: 'Why don't we do something really crazy sometime?'

There were those who thought it pretty crazy that people who knew nothing about music should make decisions about the musical content of films. But executives usually did think they knew something about music, too. Dore Schary, for instance, told André what he wanted – illustrating his point with what looked like a trombone-playing movement, pushing and pulling an imaginary slide.

'That's what I want,' he told André. 'Lots of French horns.'

But André was to be able to counter this kind of philistinism with a certain dereliction of duty – if for entirely innocent reasons.

He was by now a one-man musical assembly line, working on spectaculars one moment, dramas the next and a sophisticated comedy sandwiched somewhere in between. That was what *Designing Woman* with Gregory Peck and Lauren Bacall was described as being, a sophisticated comedy. The tale about a sports reporter marrying a designer of dresses was not always terribly funny and seemed to work hard at being sophisticated. In fact, the most sophisticated thing about the whole movie was André's music, although, really, it had little right to be so.

The film was one of a number of which Dore Schary took personal control as producer. It turned out to be the perfect demonstration of how the last people to be consulted were the music department. They – in the shape of the composer/musical director, André Previn – were brought in only when everything else had been done (a distinct improvement on what frequently happens today when films are edited *after* the addition of the music and a sharp cut in the action can result in the music being equally chopped, sometimes in the middle of a bar).

On this occasion, Schary invited André, along with other executives involved in the production of *Designing Woman*, to his house. They were given a sumptuous dinner accompanied by the best and heaviest wines. It was after the food had been allowed to digest, the cigars smoked and the coffee and liqueurs enjoyed that the assembled company were invited into Schary's personal screening room – the trademark of the mogul and senior studio departmental head – to watch the film.

André slunk down into a huge, leather, club chair, the comfort of which, combined with the dinner and drinks, had the effect of a general anaesthetic. From the moment that the big painting on the wall disappeared into the ceiling, to be replaced by the screen that had been hidden somewhere in the roof, and the lights went out, André fell fast asleep. He didn't wake until those lights came on again.

It is fortunate that André didn't also snore, because he regained consciousness just in time for questions. Other executives were paying the required number of compliments. That, after all, was only becoming of people to whom simple courtesy decreed they had to be nice to their host. Mr Schary had not just produced the movie to which they had all been entertained, he also paid their salaries.

Dore Schary was delighted and so was his director Vincente Minnelli, for praise for Schary had to be praise for him, too. As André tells it: 'There were about ten people there in that room and they were all trading compliments.'

Previn joined in dutifully in the general paeans of praise. Then came the question: 'Well, André – what do you think?'

He had been hoping that that question wouldn't come up just yet. In his mind - that thinking-on-his-feet policy of his had got to work – he had planned to go into the studio the next morning, go to see the film editor, get a copy of *Designing Woman* re-shown to him privately and then draw up his ideas for the background score.

But Schary pre-empted him. He pressed for an instant thought if not an instant answer. Could André Previn risk prevaricating? Plainly, if you worked in a major Hollywood studio and it was the head of that studio who wanted an answer, you had to be ready to give it – instantly, at once, NOW.

How, though, did he cope with that question when he hadn't seen a single frame of the picture between the opening roar of Leo the lion and the switching on of the lights?

'Well,' André muttered, 'I think I'll write this for just string orchestra.'

'Really,' said Schary, 'for *this* film?'

As he now tells the story, one thought ran through his mind: 'Oh Christ, what's it all about?'

'Yes,' Previn replied, 'Trust me.' Well, André was certainly there to be trusted.

It was time to thank his track record, although his boss did wonder and metaphorically scratch his head and then allow himself to add a quizzical note. 'Had you said, just for a dance band, I'd have understood that,' he told André. 'But strings?'

'Well,' André countered. 'Just leave it to me.'

André left the house, feeling as if he had been granted a temporary reprieve. But he couldn't help wondering whether, after all, he *had* been rumbled.

Very early the following morning, André got into the studio and called the film editor. 'Benny,' he asked, trying to sound calm, 'could you run *Designing Woman* for me?'

'What?' the editor asked, knowing it had been shown to the distinguished company the night before. 'Are you really such a glutton for punishment? Didn't you see it last night?'

'Well, actually,' he admitted, 'I didn't.'

The film was re-run for him at nine o'clock. By eleven, he knew what he was up against. 'And of all the pictures in the world *not* to do with strings, this was the one.'

But he had to stand by what he had said. 'There I was stuck, but more than that, I began to realise that I had set myself an interesting little trap.'

That, as Rudyard Kipling might have said to his 'best beloved' in one of his *Just So Stories* was how *Designing Woman* had a score played entirely by strings. 'And it was very nice. But if I had stayed awake . . . it would never have happened.'

As he might also have added, apart from the people in his business and mostly those in his part of the business, nobody would have noticed. André had predicted as much long before when he realised that people watching a chase weren't going to comment on the splendid sound made by the trombones.

As he also says: 'The good directors always appreciated the music. The hacks didn't care. Some people consulted the musical director before a camera turned. Some, not until the film was shot. Sometimes, in the middle of shooting – when there was thought likely to be a music problem, and you have to have the guy who's going to do it to discuss it with him. Certain absolutely straightforward, dramatic films are completely finished and then they get a composer and say "Here you are" and then you write something and they hear it.

'Musicals, of course, are a huge amount of work before a camera starts. It depended entirely on the director. In my day the whole *auteur* thing hadn't happened. They were just making a movie.'

But how much was asked of the composer and the musical director was partly down to the house style. André remembers: 'At Warners, they wanted the music to be overpowering. At Fox they wanted it to be very prominent. At MGM, they wanted the music to be inaudible – always. It was famous for that. MGM very rarely won the music award – for dramatic pictures, not musicals – because you couldn't hear it. When I first left MGM and went to a studio where they wanted to hear the music, I thought I had gone to heaven.'

As for that particular incident with *Designing Woman*, 'I never let Schary in on that one. He was a nice man.'

There were no secrets about *Gigi*. For the writers, Lerner and Loewe, it was a natural progression from their *My Fair Lady* score. The old Colette story about a young girl's sudden maturity as she avoids the fate of the courtesan, first filmed in France in 1948, was tailor-made for their style of music – indeed, one of their *Fair Lady* songs, 'Say A Prayer For Me Tonight' was used in the movie.

It had so much going for it. Maurice Chevalier starring as the old observer of life in the Bois de Boulogne, being glad that he was not

young any more, along with the current French heart-throb Louis
Jourdan and Leslie Caron as the girl. Hermione Gingold as her aunt
who arranges the liaison with M. Jourdan, the score by Lerner and
Loewe, Vincente Minnelli directing, Arthur Freed producing – on
location in Paris with all the freedom that MGM could give him. And
André as musical director.

It was a superb combination of talents used in the most productive
way, which produced the perfect results – artistically, commercially
and simply as entertainment. The fact that André was to win his first
Oscar from the film said a great deal for the achievement it was. He
was not alone. Academy Awards also went to Freed for best picture,
Vincente Minnelli, Joseph Ruttenberg, the director of photography,
Cecil Beaton for costumes and production design, Alan Jay Lerner
for writing and lyrics and Adrienne Fazan for editing, Preston Ames
and Keogh Gleason, art directors; Lerner and Loewe for the title
song and a special award for Chevalier.

It is something of an understatement that André wasn't the greatest admirer of Chevalier. It wasn't just that he didn't like the Frenchman's style of singing – 'I dislike entertainers who say to audiences,
"I'm going to make you love me until I die." Personally, I'd prefer to
sit and watch paint dry.' Chevalier, Jolson et al were not for him.

He disliked him as a man, He was so mean, I couldn't stand him.
That is quite unforgivable in a rich man.'

And Chevalier was very rich indeed.

It has to be said that he performed his role as Louis Jourdan's uncle
so well that the part was one of those which one cannot now imagine
ever being played by anyone else. As he stood in the Bois de Boulogne
thanking his maker for also providing so many charming little girls,
he was the perfect jolly *ancien boulevardier*.

Alan Jay Lerner told me that when he was making the picture,
Maurice asked him whether his accent was good enough.

'Sure,' said Lerner, 'we can all understand you perfectly.'

'No,' said Maurice, 'is there enough accent?'

If that suggested a degree of fraud on Chevalier's part, André is
convinced that he saw too much of the real loathesomeness of the
man's character. This was especially so when he went to his house,
La Louque (called after the nickname of the mother to whom the
singer was devoted) and was amazed by the number of portraits of
Maurice himself, some life-size, that there were around the place.

Most members of the senior echelons of the film team – people like
Lerner and Loewe, Chevalier, André himself, Vincente Minnelli –
drank almost every night at the restaurant, Alexandre. The wine was

glorious and the company mostly French. Somehow, it was also off the tourist route.

'After a time, we got to writing scripts and scenes to try to work out a way to get Chevalier to buy a drink. We never could.'

The problem seemed to get all the larger because of the amount of time they were in each other's company. Arthur Freed, who was producing the picture himself, told André he wanted him in Paris for a week. Adrienne Fazan, the film editor, suggested instead that that might not be quite realistic. 'I've been on these Freed trips before,' she warned, 'I think you ought to pack for a month.'

In the end, he was there for thirteen weeks. Every time he mentioned the idea of going back home, Freed said, 'Yes, but next week, we're doing . . . I think you ought to stay on.'

André was to be described in the opening credits as conducting the orchestra and supervising the music. He was assisted by one of Hollywood's finest arrangers, Conrad Salinger. It can be a delicate role, putting into orchestral form the work of a master composer and songwriter. But that was what he was expected to do.

André took in his hands his relationship with the man on whom he depended so much on his second day in Paris. 'Mr Leowe,' he said politely and deferentially – after all *My Fair Lady* was still doing record business on Broadway – 'would you mind if I occasionally made some changes in a song if I need to make it sit more comfortably in the orchestration?'

Loewe looked at him without betraying any attitudes and certainly no emotions. He had one question that would before long make André wish he had never asked. It had, after all, just been an 'idle moment' which in a matter of minutes Previn would wish had been more gainfully occupied. 'Have you,' Loewe asked him, 'ever been to a conservatory?'

André wondered about that. 'I just couldn't see where it was leading. "Yes," I replied, "I have. Why?"'

Loewe countered the question with another question. 'And did you have to orchestrate the piano pieces of Brahms?'

'OK,' said André, 'I can see where we're travelling now . . .'

As he now says, 'Loewe wasn't cursed with modesty. He had a right to be conceited – his songs were wonderful.'

There was no way he could have pursued that line, although he said: 'It was perfectly ridiculous. Of course, when Brahms wrote his piano parts and they were orchestrated for the first time, they *had* to be altered, if only slightly, to fit the orchestrations.

But he accepted the older man's feelings on the subject and

promised not to change things – at least not so that either Loewe or Alan Jay Lerner would notice. Twice, though, they did notice. 'They thought I got a little too fancy,' is how he puts it.

André admits now that he 'over-wrote' the very long number in which Jourdan and Chevalier, riding in their open coach through the Bois de Boulogne and on through the streets of the Paris of the 1890s, performed 'It's A Bore'. He showed the same over-enthusiasm with the verse of 'Gigi' itself. So much so, in fact, that both Lerner and Loewe joined forces and said, 'Please, do you think we could hear our song now?'

'Of course, they were absolutely right. They were wonderful songs and I did over-write them.' The orchestrations were changed and the numbers – 'It's A Bore' in particular – sounded the way they would have done had Rex Harrison performed them in *My Fair Lady*. They could have had no idea three years earlier just how much of a new genre of performance they had created when Harrison first learned to sing, 'off-pitch'.

The 'over-writing' didn't prevent the two music men, Loewe and Previn, becoming friends before it was all over. They had the co-operation of Minnelli, too, of course. Some directors didn't care about the music. Minnelli was not one of them.

André went home after those thirteen weeks and made a fateful decision for his career. He desperately wanted to do something more with his career, but he was going to stay in the film industry for the moment. It was being so good to him.

One of the reasons it had been so good was due to Arthur Freed. 'Freed was a remarkable man. He wasn't imposing or said clever things, but what he produced was so good, no one interfered with him.'

Yet the mystique remained. It was at a dinner at the Mediterranée Restaurant on the Left Bank that Fritz Loewe posed the question that others had wondered about for so long. Almost all the top names in the film were there, Leslie Caron, who had the title role, with her then husband, the man who would become Sir Peter Hall, Chevalier, Joseph Ruttenberg, the director of photography, Preston Ames, the art director and André himself. 'What is it,' asked Loewe, 'that makes this man Freed such a hot-shot producer?'

Alan Lerner provided the answer: 'It's the fact that we are all here now.' It was a devastatingly simple answer, but it was mostly true. Once more, Freed was to get the results.

Occasionally, however, he did not. One of his less successful ideas was the picture for MGM called *The Subterraneans*.

This was an attempt at combining two of the three worlds of André Previn. 'Arthur Freed asked me to write the first all-out modern jazz film music.' Of it, he says now: 'It was not a success but it was not a bad score.'

The picture was to be brave for its time, the story of the sexual hang-ups of young bohemians living in San Francisco before it became the city of flower power – which gives some idea of just how long ago that was.

André arrived on the scene to find that the leading man was to be a youngster called George Peppard. It was his first role. The original story, by Jack Kerouac, about a beautiful black girl living among the beat generation had caused quite a flurry at the time. Arthur Freed read it and decided it should be one of his very few excursions into straight drama.

When André was approached to do the film, he accepted avidly. Not only could he produce his jazz score, but it was a book he had himself read and enjoyed.

But it was the jazz score idea that he liked best of all. When he was asked if he would like to do it, he replied: 'Oh yes, Arthur, I'd love it.' And he set about hiring the people for it whom he thought would be just right, like Gerry Mulligan, Art Farmer, Art Pepper, Ray Brown and, inevitably, Shelly Manne.

It turned out to be, as he says, 'quite remarkable for its time'. So much so, that the soundtrack album would now be worth a fortune – especially since, at the time, it sank without trace along with the picture.

After hearing about the casting of George Peppard, André was anxious to know more. 'Who's going to play the sensational-looking black girl?' he asked. But there was no immediate answer. A few weeks afterwards, Freed told him: 'Listen kid, I've cast the girl for *Subterraneans*.'

'Is it anyone I know?' he asked.

'Sure,' said Freed, remembering *Gigi*. 'It's Leslie Caron.'

'No,' said André, 'I mean the black girl.'

'Yeh,' answered the producer, 'we're changing all that.'

Leslie Caron it was. Black girls, no matter how sensational they might look, were not considered to be good box office.

'In the end there was no story left. None. It was just a dislikable story about dislikable non-working people in San Francisco. It just went down the drain.' There was, however, one interesting aspect of the movie. In one scene they required two people in the foreground to be playing jazz piano. One was Russ Freeman. And André told me:

'If you look very carefully, you will see that I was the other one. I was visible on film for six seconds.'

Didn't that make him frustrated? 'No. It was a job. Once you think you are making an artistic statement, you're in the wrong business.'

There were, however, more private matters for André to worry about. Lolo, at the age of thirty-two, was stricken with cancer. For a time, André himself was the only one who knew her condition. He wanted to spare his parents the trauma, but it was hard for him. 'It wasn't the most pleasant of situations, I can tell you.'

Leonore, who to her family was always Lolo – or Leah, as friends she had known when she worked on a kibbutz in Israel called her – was dying when in the spring of 1959, André got his Oscar.

He admits that at the time, 'I wanted it very badly indeed.' Since then, he has begun to doubt its importance. But he says, 'It is very difficult to be subjected to all that hyperbole and not to want it very badly indeed when your category is called and that envelope is opened.'

There were reasons for that to be so. As he told me: 'If you win, it is good to know that some work you thought was good was recognised as being so by other people. On the other hand, if you lose, you get angry when something that you consider to be inferior wins instead.'

But he says it was always a transitory feeling. 'After three days of articles in the press and photographs being taken, no one else wants to know about it. And I challenge anyone a year later to say, apart from the actors, who won last year.'

It isn't even the judgment of one's peers. The people who vote are not just those working in the category in which they are balloting. Art directors, dress designers, lighting technicians and cameramen vote too. 'What should I care what Sandra Dee thinks of me?' As Previn also says: 'I never voted outside my category. What do I know about art direction?'

But their votes count and for people in Hollywood, the results of the Oscar selections do matter. 'For practical reasons, they matter because it means you're likely to be worth more money. Certainly, there'll be more offers of work coming your way.'

One thing he did object to, though, was the practice of nominees advertising themselves in the trade press and television. There are those who, even today, resent him for speaking out against this Hollywood tradition, suggesting that he bad-mouthed the film community. As a result of his stand on this matter, he was presented with another award. It was made of plaster of Paris 'and intentionally very, very ugly'. Presented by the Society of Music Arrangers of America, it was awarded to him for being the only nominee who didn't take out an advertisement. 'I liked that.'

He also likes to quote his friend, the director Mike Nichols, who said, 'If you're ever in a situation where you either win or lose, try winning one.' In fact, Previn was to win four Oscars in five years – and was nominated fourteen times. 'So you can say I lost ten times.'

Sometimes André was the other side of the Awards ceremony stage. He was conducting the orchestra when, as a winner, he was asked to go and pose in a photo call. He said he couldn't because he was conducting the band. Ella Fitzgerald was backstage when she heard that. 'Don't be silly, honey,' she said, 'you *must* go on and get your picture taken.'

'OK,' said André, 'but you're on next.'

'Get back into the pit,' she ordered. She meant it. She didn't want anyone else accompanying her.

André has always been ready to put the Award syndrome into perspective, just as he has the films for which the Oscars would be earned. 'I was never like a director who put, say, a year of his life into developing a project and then up to two years making it. Me, if a film I was working on didn't do well, there would be another one coming up.' He is also prepared to admit another factor which is not totally irrelevant: 'No matter how good my music was, there was usually someone else who could have done it just as competently. But if, say, Billy Wilder wasn't there, there would have been no film.'

As for him, 'These days the Academy Award is just a three-dimensional item for my scrapbook. It certainly doesn't mean anything in the life I am living now.' In fact, he not altogether happily recalls the embarrassment when a former leading Hollywood musician asked André to put him on the roster of guest conductors for one of the orchestras with which he was associated. He tried to tell him that it was a very difficult thing to do, since there was so much competition among world-renowned classical conductors. 'Don't they know,' the man countered, 'that I have three Academy Awards?' As André now says: 'I tried to find a kind way of telling him that that didn't mean a thing to a European orchestra. They wouldn't know what an Academy Award is.'

These days, his awards are placed in a little nook off his main living room. They are not quite hidden – 'I think that is as dumb as having a spotlight on them' – but they are in no shrine either. But he knows other film composers who do build special fixtures – 'like grottoes' – to hold them.

The night in April 1958 that André won his first Oscar was his twenty-ninth birthday. But he didn't have very much time to think about either the event or the birthday. Immediately after the show, he had to fly to New York to work on a television special the next day. It was still an unusual thing to do. People he met in the TV studio the next morning couldn't understand how he could be there and yet have been on their small screens the night before.

It was while he was in New York that the telegram arrived telling him that Lolo had died. Her death on 10 April 1959 affected him deeply. Their interests had gone separate ways many years before, but they were emotionally very close and her death was a shock he found more difficult to get over than even he might have thought.

Once he was back in California, he also had to get back to work. But he now had a different place in which to do it. After all those years with MGM, André had decided to go freelance. All that he had said before about being in greater demand because of his Oscar might have been true – except that André Previn's reputation was so great he could have got all the work he wanted without an Academy Award.

Unlike most highly paid people who give up a salaried job to go it alone, there were few risks attached to André's move. He knew that not only could he get all the work he wanted, his fees would be much more than he was getting in his weekly pay cheque.

His freelance engagement was with the Samuel Goldwyn studio. The veteran producer had selected him to be the musical director of what would turn out to be the very last Goldwyn film – *Porgy and Bess*. It was to be a movie that did rather better at the box office – although not brilliantly – than it did with the critics. The music was unquestionably the best part of a film which, even before it went before the cameras, threatened to be called Goldwyn's Folly.

Goldwyn sacked his director, the veteran Rouben Mamoulian, after three months because he didn't care for his stylised approach, and replaced him with the heavy-handed Otto Preminger. The best of the leading players was Sammy Davis Jnr. as Sporting Life, but Sidney Poitier and Dorothy Dandridge in the title roles were not the happiest of choices. André, on the other hand, was in his element – and Goldwyn appreciated it.

He wasn't at all the ignorant dolt that legend has liked to make him. He certainly was responsible for *some* of the Goldwynisms for which he was famous. He definitely did say, 'We've all passed a lot of water since then,' and most certainly was responsible for, 'A verbal contract isn't worth the paper it's written on', but, his son Samuel

Goldwyn Jnr. told me, others were made up by press agents. 'But my father's problem was that his brain raced ahead of his mouth.'

Certainly, his biggest contribution to the film industry was a sense of taste that most of his competitors did not have. Also, he used his own money – a fact which inspired confidence in others in the film business. Confidence was precisely what he felt about André, which accounted for the fact that they got on well.

André's job in *Porgy and Bess* was even more complicated than it had been on *Gigi*, although Fritz Loewe might not have approved of what he felt compelled to do with the Gershwin score.

The great songs – 'arias'? – in *Porgy and Bess* always suffered from the fact that it was sometimes difficult to decide whether they came from a musical or an opera. 'Summertime', 'Bess You Is My Woman Now', 'I've Got Plenty of Nothing', and 'It Ain't Necessarily So' were written for a pit orchestra of a Broadway theatre. To get the sounds to flood out of the stereophonic speakers next to the giant Todd-AO screen, André had to embellish and excite, without losing anything of the original music – or at least make the changes which he thought were necessary to 'fit comfortably'.

The libretto for *Porgy* was provided by the author, Du Bose Heyward. But George Gershwin's brother, Ira, was to say how much he liked what André had done. Certainly, it worked. Previn won the only Academy Award that *Porgy and Bess* received.

Sam Goldwyn was happiest of all. He put his arm around André's shoulder and told him, 'My boy, you'll never work again.' As André told me: 'I think I knew what he meant.'

He still yearned to do more concert work. The St Louis Symphony, one of a string of good orchestras of what could be termed the second division in America, invited him to conduct what they described as a 'beer and pretzels' concert at their Kiel Auditorium. It wasn't enough. Occasionally, he was a guest conductor at the Los Angeles Philharmonic, but, as Johnny Green had observed, he wasn't happy to do just the Gershwin and Rodgers and Hammerstein 'pop' concerts for which he was engaged.

Music critics were, however, noticing him and saying nice things. The writer Joseph Laitin noted in 1959: 'Next to Leonard Bernstein, Previn is perhaps the most versatile man in the world of music ... Now that Bernstein is greying at the temples, the press is reluctantly giving him full adult status, which leaves Previn – at least in the public prints – the oldest boy wonder in the business. His detractors refer to him rather patronisingly as a boy prodigy. His friends refer to him as a giant in the world of music, a conductor, composer and pianist, but more important a man who has successfully bridged the gap between serious music and jazz. Nobody else occupies this position in the musical world, not even Leonard Bernstein.'

The *Los Angeles Times* reported: 'André Previn has become a mature figure in the music consciousness of America.' That had to make him feel somewhat happy. It meant that his efforts to find escapes away from Hollywood were actually bearing some kind of fruit.

There were those who would have liked to have seen what they described as a 'more colourful' Previn, particularly when he did make his excursions into the concert hall. But then, as one MGM music department colleague noted: 'André really doesn't have time to be colourful.'

He still made jazz records. People wrote to Lester Koenig asking for copies of the arrangements he made for *My Fair Lady* and the other show discs. It was no good pointing out that you didn't have arrangements for jazz, people still said they didn't believe it.

'Four To Go' with his friend the bassist Ray Brown, Shelly Manne and Herbie Ellis on guitar was one of his favourites.

He wasn't doing any more show scores, but there were selections from the shows in an album called 'King Size' and he recorded what at the time was called 'mood music'. 'Like Love' was one of those albums, André playing the piano with orchestral backing for a selection of popular romantic songs.

For if all the work he was doing was not enough, he was writing songs, too – with a new collaborator. With his music and her lyrics, they were making a promising partnership. It was also becoming an extremely personal partnership.

ELEVEN

It was another one of Arthur Freed's remarkable insights that led to André meeting Dory Langdon. Unfortunately – for her in particular – he neglected to remember to tell André that he was trying to turn the pair of them into a songwriting partnership. Had he remembered, what could so easily have been a perfect scenario for one of those behind-the-studio movies everyone loved going to see in the 1940s and 1950s might never have happened.

As it was, Dory Langdon put her fear of flying out of her mind – no small achievement considering that she was petrified of leaving the ground – and took the air ticket that had been sent her by MGM for the flight from New York to Los Angeles.

Through that, she met André Previn, but not as she had expected and not straight away.

It was songwriting she most wanted to do and she had already had a modicum of success by the time she wrote to MGM, enclosing some of her work. The letter found its way to Freed, who, always on the lookout for new talent, was impressed. He immediately decided that she could be a perfect collaborator for André. He sent her the ticket, she reported to Freed's office – and waited. And waited. And waited.

She was told that Mr Previn would see her, but that he was quite busy. So busy that she stayed for days outside his office, saw him go in and out of the room, smile at her, but that was all. 'Here was this attractive young woman,' André remembered for me, 'who every time I walked through the hall would pop her head out of a room and say, "Hello", and I'd say, "Hello".'

And that was that – except that André Previn is naturally curious, especially when there were pretty girls popping heads round offices saying 'Hello'.

Eventually, he asked Freed: 'Who's that rather attractive young woman with the red, curly hair?'

'What?' said Freed. 'Who?'

He described her again in some detail.

'That,' he said.

'Oh, she's your new lyricist.'

'She's my lyricist?' André responded. 'You forgot to tell me that, Arthur.' But then she disappeared, or rather he didn't see her popping her head round corners saying 'Hello' any more.

It was a difficult time for him. He was working simultaneously on two movies and there was just no time to arrange a meeting. He determined he would do so – at the end of a week.

'I decided to look her up and make amends, which I did. She then burst into laughter and said, "Great. I just got sacked today." But, knowing that MGM weren't taking her up on their option, she had already decided to move on to other things.

She went to work for a small company making cartoons at just about the time that André went freelance. She also wrote the lyrics for the title song in Joshua Logan's film, *Tall Story*, the first film starring a young girl called Jane Fonda.

But their paths did cross again – largely through David Raksin, who was busy working on a musical show that never happened. It was going to be called *Ernest*, based on *The Importance of Being Earnest*. Raksin had written the music for the show and Dory, the words. The Hollywood jungle drums that had failed to inform André of the appointment made in his name, had let her know about the putative show. She had met Raksin and they agreed to work together.

In the meantime, the composer realised that he needed a really good demonstration record before the investors could be brought in. He asked his old friend André if he would play for them. He needed no persuasion to agree to the favour. It had been years since he had done that sort of thing, but he didn't turn down friends for reasons of pride.

The meeting was in a small recording studio on Melrose Avenue. The demo disc was made, with André playing to Dory's singing along with David Raksin singing, but nothing ever came of the show.

David couldn't be sure at the time how well André and Dory were hitting it off. 'André has always been exceptionally cool. He has this sort of low temperature flame and he appraises people. I always found him terribly endearing, but I couldn't tell how others were going to take him.'

The demo disc did, however, lead to other things. As a result, André read Dory's lyrics and liked them, 'they were unusual and literate.' More than that, they set about writing songs together – and recorded an album. Nobody could be found to sing her words, so she sang them herself, but with André playing accompaniment there were few risks attached to the idea. The album was called 'Leprechauns Are Among Us'. Supposedly, it had nothing to do with Dory's Irish ancestry, but was merely taking a phrase from one of her lyrics.

The record didn't cause any great sensation, and they wrote a number of other songs together that didn't get further than André's piano and manuscript paper, but they enjoyed working together.

Dory straight away told André that she learned a lot from him and all the myriad things in which he was engaged (he had just made a highly successful record with the David Rose orchestra, 'Like Young'.) Her education had been lacking and she knew very little of the sort of life he had lived for more than a decade. Los Angeles wasn't just a continent away from New Jersey, it was a different world, a world where people made films that were huge successes but of which she had never heard.

But was there more to their being together than a mere business partnership? He really started to wonder while he was lying in hospital, suffering from pneumonia. Dory came to visit him, bringing, as she remembered, 'aspirins and kind friendly words'.

Later, he asked her what she was doing for dinner.

In 1959, he and Dory were married in a civil ceremony at Las Vegas performed by a Justice of the Peace, Oscar Bryan. The only other people there were the witnesses, their friends Paul and Monica Richards.

The following Monday, he met Arthur Freed, talking to Vincente Minnelli. 'Have a nice weekend, kid?' asked Freed. 'Yeh,' said André.

'Do anything interesting?'

'Yeh – I got married.'

'Anyone I know?'

'Yeh, remember Dory Langdon?'

'Sure, I remember her,' said Freed. He then gave a nudge to Vincente Minnelli. 'I introduced them,' he said.

These days, André is reluctant to talk about her. 'All the women I married were extremely nice ladies,' he says.

What he did not talk about when they married were her mental problems. She confessed to him that she had had a nervous breakdown. Later, it became clear that the breakdown was rather more serious than that phrase seemed to indicate.

Above: Two
generations of
Previns – Jack with
André, aged 8.

Right: Conducting
on an MGM sound
stage, aged 17. (BFI)

Above: Previn the composer. (BFI)

Left: André with Elizabeth Taylor — both in their way new stars at Culver City. (BFI)

Above: With Audrey Hepburn, star of *My Fair Lady* — the film that won him an oscar. (BFI)

Right: André the songwriter. Dory stands alongside him together with Julie London and Bobby Troup. (Hulton-Deutsch)

With Mia Farrow, rehearsing for the first concert in which they appeared together. He conducted the LSO while she took the title role in Arthur Henegger's *Joan of Arc*. (Associated Press)

Below left: Toasting the Prime Minister. Edward Heath temporarily took over the LSO baton when he conducted the orchestra at a concert in Cologne. The toast is in German beer. (Associated Press)

Below centre: With John Mills at the first night of *The Good Companions* in which the actor starred and for which André wrote the score with Johnny Mercer. (Hulton-Deutsch)

Taking a lesson in comedy from Morecambe & Wise. André says he got a bigger response from that show at his local pub than from any concert at the Festival Hall.

Below right: With Dame Janet Baker.

Previn and Vladimir Ashkenazy were to swap roles at the Royal Philharmonic. André became principal conductor and Ashkenazy music director.

At The House at Leigh. Heather stands next to him while his jazz-man friend Shelley Manne and Manne's wife Flip join them. (Robin Lough)

André Previn in 1986.
(Harrison Parrott Ltd)

The familiar Previn
conducting pose in the
late 1980s.

In one of his favourite settings, Vienna. Heather and André are joined by fellow maestro Lorin Mazel and Mrs Altenberger, wife of one of the Vienna Philharmonic violinists.

André with one of his 'bands' — the Royal Philharmonic. (RPO)

Dory said that she told André about her nervous breakdown and that he didn't make very much of it. She, in turn, was relieved that they didn't have to go into deep discussions about it.

At first, Dory was to write in her own memoir, *Bog Trotter*, she and André wrote together simply for fun, for the experience of working together and the pleasure it brought them. But then, they both started dreaming, she says – of a million seller, of a Broadway show.

Together they wrote a song called 'Yes', which was recorded by Judy Garland. A female chorus sang the lyrics – 'I'll tell him yes . . . I'll tell him yes' – when André recorded the song himself.

Dory dedicated the song to André. It represented her saying 'yes' to André's offer of marriage.

They bought a house in Bel Air, by far the most fashionable part of the world's wealthiest suburb, which David Raksin described to me as 'just wonderful'. Dory certainly thought so. When she saw it for the first time, she asked: 'Are we going to live in this whole house?' As Raksin put it: 'It was good seeing two nice people living in such splendour.'

If Dory turned the ever-moving André Previn career towards new frontiers – in the Kennedy era that was the phrase – together they developed new tastes. Dory had a considerable love of art. With André's money and Dory's own burgeoning success, they were now able to indulge it. John Marin and Georgia O'Keefe were two of the painters whose work they were able to indulge in.

Taste was not the only thing they shared. Professionally, being called Previn was no little help either. The first songs she had written with André were still produced under the name Dory Langdon. After a time, she started using the name Dory Previn. As she would say it opened doors and helped her open charge accounts.

It was particularly helpful because she had faced prejudice – not the kind she believed she had met for being Black Irish, but simply because she was a woman. Three years after first having the name Mrs Previn on her Social Security card, being Dory Previn on a record sleeve proved a good investment.

The name suited her. People in the music business who knew so much about André were more interested in her now than they had been in Dory Langdon. Besides, two Previns on a record looked good – as they themselves looked good together. André seemed even more youthful than his thirty-two years should have allowed. She was pretty, slim and looked superb.

'They seemed very happy together,' David Raksin remembered. It certainly was a good time for André professionally. He took his songwriting as seriously as he took his jazz, which, as we know, he regarded as a very serious operation indeed. But he wasn't forsaking his profession in the film industry for it and even though he knew his days in that business were numbered, he was going to stay there until he could afford to give up everything for the classics. It is a fair bet that on the day he wrote 'Yes' he had a matter of hours earlier been studying Beethoven or Brahms, Mozart or Mendelssohn.

The pair were in newspapers and magazines. They were photographed at home – which is something André never likes having done. When Claudia and Alicia came to stay, as they did quite frequently, Dory was photographed with them, too.

Meanwhile, Mr and Mrs Previn continued to write together with a degree of success – for anyone but Previn, phenomenal success. In 1961, they both worked on the music for the film, *Pépé*, which had no more to say for itself than that it was a vehicle for a small Mexican clown called Cantinflas.

Columbia Pictures believed that Cantinflas, the man who had served as David Niven's faithful sidekick in *Around The World In 80 Days* was just waiting and ready for his own film. In that, Harry Cohn the studio's iron dictator was totally correct. What he wasn't correct about was in assuming that the general public would think the same. They wouldn't. Once more, the music of André Previn – but this time with the addition of the lyrics of Dory Previn – was the only reasonable thing to say about a movie.

The best song in the picture was sung, off-camera, by Judy Garland – 'The Faraway Part of Town'. It was nominated for an Academy Award. That in itself was quite an achievement. That year, there were no fewer than three Previn nominations: for the *Pépé* song; for the score from *Elmer Gantry*, the United Artists film which quite brilliantly demonstrated the effects on America of the religious evangelists of the 1930s, and was one of his most exciting works in Hollywood; and for the Judy Holliday film, *Bells Are Ringing*.

Now that was confusing enough for celebrity watchers. It was made even more so by yet another music nomination for *Pépé* which had Johnny Green's name on it. Green was musical director of that film and wrote the title music (originally with a Dory lyric, too, but this was eventually dropped). None of those nominations won an award.

André said that he had never expected to win on any of his nominations in the first place.

Meanwhile, André's song was seemingly without end, too. Dory certainly went on record to say so. Contemplating her year-plus of marriage she said: 'Life has been full of Christmases and Fourth of Julys and birthday parties.'

Moving from a staff position at MGM had been one of the first calculating career decisions that André was to make, the kind which were to frame his life from then on. He had gone to Metro in the first place because they gave him his big breaks. He stayed because he had made a huge success there. He changed his arrangements only when his contract expired.

When he took the plunge, it was the most sensible thing he could have done. It was as though he had had access to one of the huge computers that were gradually coming into service in the country's giant corporations and the print-out had directed him into the mathematically-calculated future in which he couldn't fail.

His command of both jobs and money was immense. He was able to indulge himself in more modern art – even if sometimes he bought it on hire purchase, making monthly payments to galleries who, when he paid them off, sent him letters suggesting that he re-open the account by looking at their current stocks. He was usually tempted, and so was Dory and she did much to open his eyes to a great many new artists.

Most of the paintings survived a freak fire that consumed a great area of Stone Canyon Road, the Bel Air Street on which the Previns lived. With houses all around their home burning with the ferocity of the London Blitz twenty years before, André and Dory managed to bring out most of their treasures and throw them into the back of their car. (As they escaped down the drive, a TV camera crew asked André to go back and run towards the car again. He says that it took all his strength of will not to run the cameraman over.)

As it turned out, the roof of their house was destroyed along with some bedrooms at the back. Most of the rooms – particularly those containing books and scores – were clear of the flames. One of the people who was glad of that was the author Aldous Huxley, whose own home had been totally destroyed in the fire, along with his library.

They weren't good friends, but certainly they were not strangers. Occasionally, the writer would go to André's Monday night concerts, along with his friend Stravinsky. 'They were sitting in the front row and it was very off-putting to see,' André remembers.

Huxley also knew that over the years, Previn had built up a complete collection of his works, including his pamphlets and introductions to other people's work. As André told me, once you start collecting, you want everything, whether you like a specific title or not.

After the fire, the writer rang André to check that they were all still in place, adding that his own had all gone. André told him he was in a terrible quandary. 'I'm torn between the instinct which says that you must have these books and the instinct that says, "Over my dead body."'

Huxley said that he didn't want them, even over André's fully-breathing body, but was only glad they existed. They got on so well during this conversation that the writer recommended a bookshop. André was glad of the recommendation. The shop where he had first bought his Huxley books is now called 'California's Oldest Yogurt Store'.

The fire meant that André and Dory had nowhere to live for the best part of the year – most builders working in the area were having a very profitable time indeed making good the damage and a waiting list was rapidly building up. They rented an apartment into which they installed most of their necessities, including, of course, a piano. But, if only because there was no room for anything else, it was an upright.

The instrument was an essential part of André's life, almost as though it were an additional limb, at very least an extension of his hands from which he was able only temporarily to remove himself. It also had another purpose, he was to discover during this time – it helped him be friendly to his neighbours.

The Previns' temporary home was so close to the bathroom of the man next door that he could actually hear the neighbour singing when he shaved. That the man happened to be one of the most popular singers of the time, Andy Williams, made this a more interesting situation than listening to the yodelling of a tone-deaf stockbroker.

When André first heard him sing, he hit on a wheeze that would turn into a very well-orchestrated joke indeed. The next day, as Williams started singing, André began playing along with him. But he did it virtually sitting on the floor, with his head and the piano invisible through the open window. Eventually, André realised that every time Williams went into his bathroom – especially when he wasn't going in there to take a bath, have a shave or just wash his hands and clean his teeth – he sang. And every time André heard him sing, he jumped to his piano and started accompanying him.

It took several days before Williams realised not only was he getting a piano in the background with every note he sang, but the direction from which it came. Finally, he called out: 'OK, who's out there?'

André stuck his head out the window and introduced himself.

They soon became friends.

Needless to say, André's work went on. He was now writing scores that not only earned him money and a considerable amount of personal satisfaction. They also gained him considerable critical acclaim. But the best thing to happen in 1962 for the Previn watchers was the nomination that both André and Dory received for their song 'Second Chance', from the film *Two For The Seesaw*. It wasn't enough to please the Academy voters, but it was a recognition, nevertheless, and one that meant more to Dory than it did to André. When it didn't win, it also disturbed her more than it did him.

If anyone who asks André which of all his fifty-odd scores is his favourite, he'll throw into the ring a title that will surprise anyone who knows the very tiniest part about the history of Hollywood in the early 1960s. It was *The Four Horsemen of the Apocalypse*, an almost totally hopeless remake of the picture made exactly forty years earlier which turned a swarthy young fellow known as Rudolph Valentino into a star. This one starred Glenn Ford, Ingrid Thulin and Lee J. Cobb, along with a clutch of soon-to-be superannuated stars like Charles Boyer, Paul Henreid and Paul Lukas.

He says of it: 'It was one of the best scores I ever wrote and for just about one of the worst films I ever did.'

It was, he told me, 'Vincente Minnelli's ideas of wartime'. From the perspective, that is, of a wartime spent entirely in Hollywood. It not only didn't work, it didn't begin to be comprehensible. Nevertheless, André was as delighted as he could reasonably expect himself to be when he completed his score to a picture that he had only seen from the MGM projection room. It was a very long film which was going to have an interval – known in the trade as a 'roadshow' picture. They were very popular in the early 1960s, as films like *Lawrence of Arabia* testified.

It was a very long picture for which he wrote a very long score. But one with which he felt happy enough. Cut now to several years later when he saw the movie in a cinema – the only version ever shown to the general public. The three-and-a-half-hour picture and the three-and-a-half-hour score was cut to two and a half hours.

Exciting, loud crescendos cut suddenly for no apparent reason into soft romantic melodies. Great symbolic sounds were heard echoing through cinemas without anyone knowing why. André knew why. The scissors of the film editors had cut straight across the negative without anyone thinking about what they were doing.

'Well, of course, that really can't be done. Dramatic moments from the film were cut that could not be compensated for. Parts of the score which were intentionally written to accentuate and highlight parts of the story went with it.'

Once more, he decided it was part of the job and he and the other men and women 'below the salt' couldn't allow themselves such frustrations. But you had to think about its effects, nevertheless.

In one scene, on the Pont de Neuf in wartime Paris, Ingrid Thulin, at the time Ingmar Bergmann's favourite leading lady, presses something into the palm of Glenn Ford and says: 'In that case, here's your key' and runs off. 'I went absolutely beserk with the music at this point,' André recalled. 'When the film was released people said, "What key?" And my colleagues asked me: "What the hell are you going on about with that key?" No one had heard anything about a key until then. Oh that was hilarious. The film was full of that. What a horrible film! But it was one of the few complete scores I can still here without cringing.'

These days, he is a lot more good humoured about the whole thing than he was at the time.

In one month in 1960, he gave concerts in the Los Angeles area in both jazz and the classics.

Jazz *aficionados* found it difficult to understand why he shied away from publicity, and couldn't comprehend a man who was so obviously a star who didn't mix with other stars – at least in the restaurants which most stars attended. When he had friends, they were the ones he invited home or whom he visited in their houses and apartments.

He wasn't going to be conventional in star behaviour any more than he was going to be so in the work that he did. More and more these days, he was talking about life after Hollywood. As he said, 'I don't want to reach the age of seventy-five with nothing but sixty or seventy film scores to my name.'

Films remained the main Previn business, however. He made four for Billy Wilder, a man whom he admires in the way a senior schoolboy admires a youngish teacher. It's an admiration that has only increased on André's side – although, as we shall see, Wilder has some reservations – now that the director is an old man and Previn is in his sixties.

The first of his Wilder films was the 1961 movie, *One, Two, Three*, starring James Cagney – about an American businessman in Berlin, trying to sell Coca Cola to the Russians. It was twenty-eight years before the Wall came tumbling down – in fact, a year before it was *built* – but it had the glimmer of prophesy about it.

The second Wilder film was *Irma La Douce*, starring Jack Lemmon and Shirley MacLaine. She played a prostitute, one of the whores made of pure gold that so attracted her and her producers at this stage in her career. He was the 'flic' who was deputed to bring her to court – only to fall for her charms and her favours.

The picture was not an easy job for André. What he was doing was writing an entire score for a non-musical picture based on what had been a musical show. But his score was good enough to win him the 1964 Academy Award – his third. As Jack Lemmon presented the statuette to André, he palmed him a note, rather as though he were handing over a racing tip. 'Like anyone in that situation,' André told me, 'the first thing I did while I walked off the stage was to read the note which Jack had scribbled. It said simply, "Fucking right".'

You don't forget a message like that, especially on one of those evenings when quite suddenly the award you had said you didn't care about became the most important thing in the world.

As for Lemmon himself, 'He's an adorable guy – and not a bad pianist.'

The films themselves he frequently faced with the same determination with which he approached his nominations on Oscar night. When he worked on them, there was nothing more vital to him. He had a job to do and got on with it.

There were, too, the occasional disappointments, like when anticipated success turned into actual nothing. Gower Champion had an idea up his sleeve that both André and Dory could have been forgiven for thinking was right up their Bel Air street – the house had been repaired and they were back in it.

Champion was going to direct a new version of that old Robert Donat classic, *Goodbye Mr Chips*, about the schoolmaster who, thanks to the wife he marries fairly late in life, is as loved by the generations of boys under his care as he loves them.

The former dancer, was going to make it into a big musical that had to be done properly or not at all. For that reason, he was going in big: Terence Rattigan writing the screenplay, Rex Harrison in the title role, Lee Remick or Samantha Eggar as his wife – and music by André Previn, with lyrics provided by Dory.

It looked so good a deal that the Previns got started on their songs. The simple story is that it didn't work out the way it had been planned. The producer Arthur P. Jacobs didn't care for Dory's lyrics – he didn't think she could write for a man. So she was out. Then, thinking about it, André couldn't work on it without Dory. Before long, Gower Champion was off the film too, replaced by Herbert Ross.

The picture was eventually not made until 1969, seven years after the Previns had accepted the job. Peter O'Toole gave a lacklustre performance which totally distorted the lovable Robert Donat character, and his wife was played by Petula Clark. The music and lyrics were by Leslie Bricusse.

André and Dory would have more luck with the song they wrote for another Twentieth Century Fox film whose title began with the word, 'Goodbye'. It was *Goodbye Charlie*, which would be released in 1964. The film, about the reincarnation (as a sexy blonde) of a philandering gangster, starred Debbie Reynolds, Walter Matthau and Tony Curtis. The theme song would actually do better than the film itself – if only because John Lennon was to say that he and his fellow Beatles sang it in India as they meditated on the banks of the Ganges.

Vincente Minnelli directed the picture, which was André's debut at the studio that demanded its music be heard. He also began work on a picture which George Cukor was to direct, but it joined that ever-expanding list of projects that just never happened. The studio also asked him to do a film there which he himself turned down. He didn't think *A Guide For The Married Man* was very funny. Like a reporter working on a sex exposé story, he made his excuses and left.

'Comedies are fun to compose if the music is supposed to have an overall comment on the film, like in Billy Wilder's movies. But when it's the kind of score where the music has to be funny because the action isn't, then it's a pain in the ass to write because it's like a cartoon and I don't want to do it.'

He had no such reservations about an offer to come to Warner Bros. to make his first picture there. *My Fair Lady* was going to be one of the biggest and most important films Hollywood had ever made – and André was to turn some of the most lyrical moments heard on stage anywhere into suitable material for movie audiences.

In a way it was a double sense of *déjà-vu* for André. After all, it was now years after the huge success of the jazz album of the score and five years since he had worked with Lerner and Loewe on *Gigi*. As we have seen, that was in many ways seen as the follow-up to the *Fair Lady* hit. He had come out of both those experiences covered with about as much glory as seemed possible, and the composer and lyricist could be reasonably certain now not to have to ask him again to let them hear *their* tunes. Trust was what they had to have in a musical director at the best of times. Anyone who had played their score in jazz and was now going to have to do it 'for real' had to be trusted.

But for the moment, Jack L. Warner was in charge of production, his favourite film credit. He took André to his heart as well as to his payroll. He was pleased to have him along. Somehow, he thought he added a touch of class to his studio and that was what he wanted for *My Fair Lady*. But he also believed in getting his money's worth. While waiting for filming on *My Fair Lady* to begin, he commissioned André to write the score for a new Bette Davis film he was making, *Dead Ringer*. As things turned out, the effect of making this almost totally forgotten film was to have greater importance in the long run than the movie which would earn André his fourth and last Oscar.

The black-and-white picture was directed by Paul Henreid, who remembered all too clearly the days when he shared a cigarette in the famous lighting-up scene in *Now Voyageur* (he put two in his mouth and gave one to her.) His directing work didn't exactly help a picture which more appropriately had originally been called *Dead Pigeon* – about a woman who shoots her twin sister and then assumes her identity.

Miss Davis and Jack Warner had had a virtual declaration of war in force between them in the 1930s when he successfully sued her for breach of contract in the High Court in London, after she thought she had fairly safely escaped to Britain.

It turned into a *cause célèbre* which eventually would have a profound effect on the studio system and the 'ownership' of stars. *Dead Ringer* would bring her back to her old home territory long after her contract had quite legally expired.

Warner and Previn discussed the script. 'I want music everywhere,' the mogul told André. 'Loud music.'

'Why?' André not unreasonably wanted to know.

'Because it needs the music to cover it up.'

Says André today: 'He was absolutely right.'

In fact, he had accepted the task only because he wanted to work on a film with Davis again.

She told him: 'I'm so pleased you're going to do my picture.'

It was flattering in the extreme, but he wondered why. 'After all,' he reminded her, 'you had that wonderful music by Max Steiner.'

'Yes,' she agreed, 'but did you see *Dark Victory*? That son of a bitch killed me off a reel too soon with that "wonderful music".'

No one was going to be in the business of killing anyone off in *My Fair Lady*, least of all Jack Warner, who wanted everyone to read that the millions he had paid for the rights to the movie were the soundest investment of 1964.

He also wanted importance, which was why he cast Audrey Hepburn in the lead as the flower girl whom Professor Henry Higgins was about to turn into a lady. Who had ever heard of Julie Andrews? The young English girl who had made such a hit on Broadway and then the London stage with the role was, he declared, just not box office. It would be a decision he would later regret – especially when *Mary Poppins*, released practically simultaneously with *My Fair Lady*, turned her into both an Oscar winner and the international star he would have been delighted to have for the role. (He wouldn't have had to employ Marni Nixon to do the singing for her, as he did for Miss Hepburn.)

There was no doubt, however, that Rex Harrison would do a re-run of his stage role. Harrison in some ways had reversed the usual route – he was essentially a screen star making it big on the stage.

With André, too, he had no reason not to be perfectly happy – except when Harrison put the boot in and demanded the services of the man who had stood in the pit conducting him night after night both in New York and London for more than five years. Only Franz Allers knew how to play for him, he said, to get the orchestra performing properly while he did his speech-singing on pitch.

Warner, however, was insistent, after Alan Jay Lerner had convinced him to be so. Lerner was certain that no one was more suited to the job. He really didn't need much in the way of persuasion. The name Previn meant something and the fact that he could get him for his picture spoke for how highly he rated the project.

So André went in and Allers never had a chance. When Harrison's first big number, 'Why Can't The English' was firmly in the can, Warner asked him what he thought of his musical director: 'Very good,' he answered. 'Better than that German bastard.'

Actually, Warner thought that Previn was French. How could anyone of any other nationality be named André? Accordingly, he called him 'Monsewer'. This was only true to form for a man who, when he welcomed the wife of the Chinese leader Chiang Kai-shek to his studio said, 'That reminds me – I have to collect my laundry', and who greeted Albert Einstein with the words, 'Professor, I have a theory about relatives, too. Don't hire 'em!'

Being called 'Monsewer' wasn't funny the first time. 'After about fifty times,' André told me, 'I used to go away and hide.'

In a way, he had an even harder job to do with *Fair Lady* than he had had with *Gigi*. If in the earlier film he had had to turn the totally unknown piano parts handed to him by Fritz Loewe into a complete orchestral work; in *My Fair Lady* he had to adapt an extraordinarily well-known score that people knew from their own record collections into something suitable for a movie. People knew the songs so well that they could hum the introductions to every one of the numbers performed on stage. Keeping the spirit of the original and yet making it work on screen with all those stereophonic speakers dotted around the theatres was harder than most people thought.

He confessed that he understood the magnitude of the task from the moment he first got out the manuscript paper in September 1963. 'The biggest danger I face,' he said then, 'is that many people are waiting to see and hear how the film music compares with the original. It simply MUST be as good as the original.

He was going to use the very best of the men and women of the Warner studio orchestra. Not only that. To their talents he would be able to add all the electronic advances that had been made to sound recording in the previous decade, 'giving it a warmer, richer sound'. In this, he was helped by his old sidekick, Al Woodbury. 'That was some picture,' he told me.

My Fair Lady was all the great success Warner had predicted for himself – even if his desk was about to be emptied and moved. It earned André his fourth Academy Award and Warner one, too. It was one of those unrepeatable ironical moments; it was at the same ceremony that Julie Andrews got her own Oscar for *Mary Poppins*.

But the picture had even greater significance for André.

This was a time when he was reassessing his professional ambitions. Meetings with classical performers like the young Vladimir Ashkenazy a few years earlier had made him yearn to do more serious music. Ashkenazy, soon to defect to the West, had played at a concert in Los Angeles which André attended. After the performance at the Philharmonic Hall in the downtown area, André had gone back to the Russian's dressing room.

Ashkenazy told me. 'It made the FBI very jittery, I can tell you. But André and I got on very well. He was just beginning to make a name for himself as a classical pianist and I knew he had recorded some contemporary American music. I asked him to send me a copy and I gave him my address in Moscow.'

But André never did. 'He told me he was embarrassed because my work was so much better. He's a very modest man.'

André was, in fact, now seriously questioning his stay in Hollywood.

He had already fronted the Cleveland and St Louis orchestras with programmes that included Prokofiev's *Scythian Suite* and Britten's *Peter Grimes*. He had long before decided he had a particular love for English music, but he wasn't deserting America's native composers either.

Then there was his piano work. With his friends Edgar Lustgarten – the man who was the victim of the McCarthy purges – and Israel Baker, he formed the Pacific Arts Trio. More than one hundred concerts were played by them in the area. There were also chamber music concerts with the highly-respected Roth Quartet at UCLA.

'I didn't need the money,' he says now. 'I did it for the sheer musical pleasure of it.'

Most important as far as his recognition as a serious pianist was concerned, he played with the Boston Symphony and the New York Philharmonic in performances of concertos by Beethoven, Rachmaninov and Prokofiev. The concerts began to establish the sort of reputation André wanted.

It was in the midst of all this feverish activity that a visitor had come to the studio to see André conduct the final part of the *Dead Ringer* score. His name was Schuyler Chapin, head of classical music at Columbia Records. As a result of that trip, André Previn decided to change his career totally.

TWELVE

There were people who thought André was mad. At the age of thirty-three he was throwing up one of the most successful and lucrative careers in Hollywood for the unknown. He had decided to become a classical conductor and he couldn't have been happier. Few people could understand why, but it didn't worry him.

He said that he looked in the mirror one morning and told himself that he had been wasting time.

Mad? His friend Blake Edwards told me that there were plenty of people who scratched their heads, although he himself says it seemed like one of the greatest things he had ever heard. 'I thought it was wonderful that someone who had had that marvellous career could stop now, could stop collecting all that money and those Oscars and decide to go elsewhere.'

Of course, cynics could say that he was merely taking an early re-tirement – and that equally naturally, he would be back. He had enough stashed away to afford a sabbatical for a year or two.

Dory didn't object, and he probably wouldn't have listened even if she had done. Certainly, his father thought it was a good idea. It appeared that Jack *couldn't* be pleased with anything he did. 'When I was conducting,' André told me, 'I wasn't playing and when I was playing I wasn't composing etc., etc., etc.'

All this change of direction started with the conversation Schuyler Chapin had with André after his visit to the Warner studios.

As Chapin told me: 'I've had a fair amount of luck in spotting talent and I saw it that day – and how.'

He has some forty years' experience behind him in the performing arts. When he left Columbia Records, he went on to be executive producer of film and TV work for Leonard Bernstein, and then head of the Metropolitan Opera before becoming Dean of the School of

Arts at Columbia University. Now retired, he looks back with a degree of satisfaction at the contribution he was to make to changing the career of André Previn.

Chapin does not immediately strike one as being typical of the music business, least of all, perhaps, of the world of business of any kind. He is tall, fresh-complexioned with the manners and speech of the New Englander he so manifestly is. His own ambition had been to be a composer, until a French refugee teacher told him as a teenager, 'Frankly my dear, you have no talent.' Instead, she told him to go into artist management. Perhaps André Previn has reason to be grateful that she did.

Recalling those times, Schuyler told me that it was while watching him rehearse the *Dead Ringer* score that he contemplated what he could do with a talent such as Previn's. 'I knew that as a pianist he was wonderful, but as a pianist this was not going to be satisfactory to him as a total commitment. I never thought of him as a competitive concert pianist, although God knows he could have entered that field had he wanted to do so.'

It all really started when the producer in charge of popular output working for Columbia in California, Irving Townsend, came on one of his periodic visits to New York.

He asked to see Chapin. There was a man he wanted to talk about. 'You've probably never heard of him,' he said. 'His name's André Previn and he wants to do some classical recording.'

Chapin's reply was, 'Don't be silly. Of course, I've heard of him. His 'My Fair Lady' jazz record is one of my favourite discs . . . '

'Oh you know about him?' he said.

'Yes, I know about him. Just tell Mr Previn we'll think of something. Let's not beat about the bush. I don't know what this is going to be, but we'll find something.'

As a result, Townsend went back to California and signed a contract with Previn, knowing that once a year, in addition to popular works, he would be allowed to record a classical piece.

Three months later, André and Dory were going to be in New York on their way to Europe. They arranged to meet Chapin at the Warwick Hotel. 'I'll always remember that. We went up to his room and had one of the worst hamburgers I'd ever had in my life. That sort of thing sticks in one's mind.' To say nothing of sticking in his throat.

What also sticks in *André*'s mind is his request that he record some chamber music. They immediately agreed on that. It looked as if it would fit very well into the Masterworks catalogue.

166

'I have to tell you that I didn't think of it as a commercial proposition. I ran that department on the philosophic point that commercial considerations shouldn't be the main thought. It was up to the sales department to sell the products, not the other way round. Find me a company that does that today.'

But that was how he believed Previn could fit in – not to make money, but 'as a symbol of faith in what we were doing.'

It was a good time to be making records. Stereo was just coming in and the label already had decided that the time had come to re-record much of its repertoire.

André and Chapin met soon after the Previns' return from Europe and it was in New York that he made his first classical piano records. They worked well enough for more to be commissioned almost immediately afterwards. He did those with the Roth Quartet in Los Angeles, the group André had played with before. But they were now an aging band of musicians who caused a certain number of problems, simply because, to quote Chapin, 'they were getting a little shaky. They were still the original members. But André found a way of circumventing the difficulties.'

The relationship between the two men was such that Chapin was anxious to help him extend his range. When he heard that the eminent conductor George Szell was in Los Angeles, he suggested that he and André meet. They did, in Szell's hotel suite.

André was at a stage in his life when he knew he had few inhibitions about his music, certainly his piano playing. He could talk to serious musicians about serious music. But not always totally satisfactorily. This was one such time. He and Szell met in an hotel in Los Angeles, at Schuyler Chapin's request. Szell asked André if he knew Strauss's *Burleske* – the piece that had so mystified Johnny Green when André demonstrated he could play it from memory. 'Play it for me,' said the conductor. It was an instruction that normally wouldn't have fazed André in the very least, except that there was very good reason for it proving to be hardly the easiest of tasks on the spur of the moment – there was no piano.

'Play it on the table,' Szell ordered, which André did, thumping away at the veneer as though he had a set of ivories in front of him. 'Not fast enough,' said Szell. André, as he admitted, was beginning to feel not a little silly. He either had to proceed with the charade or treat it as a joke. Perhaps not too wisely, he opted for the latter course. 'Yes, Maestro,' he said, 'but you see, I'm not used to this table. On my dining-room table at home, it sounds much better.'

Szell was not impressed. 'I don't consider that funny, young man,' he told him.

Then the two men from Columbia, Chapin and Irving Townsend, hit on the means of serving both their departments, covering both popular and classical music. They arranged for Eileen Farrell, one of the few 'legitimate' sopranos whom they could trust to handle standards, to do an album of popular music, orchestrated and conducted by André.

It worked. 'It was a nice album – not a great one,' is how Chapin describes it. But the important thing was that to firm the matter up, Chapin went to Los Angeles and stayed with André and Dory at their home in Bel Air. They stayed up until two or three o'clock in the morning, talking about music and about plans.

It was then that André suggested that Schuyler go with him to Warner Bros. the next morning. At the Warner studio – 'that remarkable acoustic studio which explained why music in Warner films sounded better than any other; somebody cared enough to get it right' – he saw André conduct for the first time. He saw him rehearse, talk to the orchestra and then record his 'rather complicated score'. As he told me: 'A little shiver ran up and down my spine.'

His old experience as an artists' manager paid off. 'I looked at this guy and said, "My God. He's conducting." I watched him rehearse and decided that only a master, an instinctive master, really knows how to use rehearsal time. You have X amount of time. It is imperative that, if you have clear ideas of what you want from the piece under consideration, you want to be able to express it succinctly to every section of the orchestra. You don't want to waste any time, you want to be able to express it so that after the twenty or thirty minutes, you have what you want.'

Quite suddenly, the man, who as a pianist was 'wonderful', looked as if he could be a conductor.

Chapin said nothing after that session. In fact, he said nothing until dinner that night.

The Scandia Restaurant is on Sunset Strip, half a mile or so from the Beverly Hills border. Then as now, Scandia was an oasis in the desert. Cadillacs and Jaguars are valet-parked by men in red livery. Inside, it is so dark you can have an entire conversation with a complete stranger while your dinner partner sits alone at an adjoining table wondering why you have stood him up. On this occasion, André and Schuyler Chapin went in together and so were spared the embarrassing mistakes.

By now, not only was the Farrell recording under way, but André had, along with his jazz and sweet music output, already recorded

Hindemith's Piano Sonata Number Three along with Frank Martin's Prelude Number Seven. It wasn't exactly best-seller material but it did increase his own repertoire and Columbia were happy to offer him that sop in return for such albums as 'The Theatre Songs of Kurt Weill'.

He also recorded an album called 'Piano Pieces for Children'. More important, were recordings he made of piano pieces by Roussel, Frank Martin, Hindemith and Poulenc. Chapin wanted to see the man to whom he was so committed expand his range. What André didn't do was record with Szell. 'I don't consider him a serious musician,' said the conductor once more. But Schuyler Chapin knew that he was. All he wanted to hear was André say it himself – he wanted to be a serious conductor. And Chapin wanted him to be one.

It wasn't as simple as that, however. He knew that there was something that had to be done – André did have to *make* himself into a classical conductor. There had to be some changes in the way he ran that career of his. 'There has to be a little sorting out,' was how Schuyler put it.

He couldn't, to use the old Jewish phrase, dance at two weddings. He had to decide the one to which he was going – which branch of his career he was going to take up and which he was going to discard. Chapin told him: 'You and Lenny Bernstein are the two people that I have met in the course of my career who are so overpowered with talent that there has to be a little sorting out. In Lenny's case, it's never going to be sorted out. But you are of a different temperament. What are you going to do?'

That was when he said it: 'I want to conduct.'

Chapin still wanted convincing that it was *exactly* what he wanted. 'That's not surprising. Is that what you really want?' Again, André said it was.

Meanwhile, the agreement with Townsend ensured that André now would make his debut as a really serious concert pianist. They had decided to record the Shostakovich First Piano Concerto, with André as soloist to the New York Philharmonic, conducted by Bernstein. It was done, 'and it's still,' says Chapin, 'a wonderful record, the best there is of that piece'.

But the job now was to get him going on a conducting career. It couldn't be rushed. He couldn't move straight away to the podium of the New York Philharmonic conducting Beethoven. They wouldn't have had him – except, perhaps, as a last-minute substitute, as Bernstein himself had been when, in *Forty-Second Street* style, he suddenly stepped into the shoes of a sick Bruno Walter and became a star in one afternoon.

Chapin suggested that André think of following up the success he had already had with one of the orchestras he had conducted for his pops concerts – say, the ensemble he had fronted for those beer and pretzels sessions, the St Louis Symphony.

Schuyler knew William Zalken, the manager of the St Louis orchestra. He was a great friend.

He asked Zalken what he thought of Previn. The superlatives blocked the phone line seemingly for an interminable time. Chapin knew that if he was ever to get André going on the conducting career he apparently so passionately required, it had to be via this route. It was a thought made easier for him when he discovered an unfulfilled contract lying in one of the Columbia filing cabinets. The St Louis Symphony were due to make an album for the label and had not yet done so. No one had been in any hurry to get the orchestra on to a disc. Certainly, Columbia had been happy to let the document lie fallow. The then conductor was considered 'uninteresting, musically' and there was little commercial demand for a disc from the outfit. Hence Chapin's idea. He would record the orchestra and let André conduct it.

But a record alone wouldn't be enough. Chapin put this proposal to Zalken: engage André to conduct one of the orchestra's regular concerts and Columbia would record it. This was an offer that was difficult to refuse – the financial benefit of a recording to an orchestra was fairly profound.

Chapin added for good measure: 'I think the talent of this guy is fabulous. I'd like to take a chance. Let's do it.' Zalken jumped at the opportunity – and so did André.

They agreed that they would mutually decide a programme. It was a gamble, but more of one for Columbia and André than it was for the orchestra, who were being totally covered, as far as their expenses were concerned, by the recording company. Columbia, on the other hand, would have to stand the costs and André was risking the effects all this could have on his career. Make a failure of a concert on which would be focused the eyes of critics and the other people in the music business and this change of career could be killed off before it was really born. If, on the other hand, it all worked, it would be a hundred times more satisfying than receiving another Oscar.

While Chapin and Zalken had to think about the programme, André *knew* what he wanted to do – to record Benjamin Britten's *Sinfonia da Requiem* and Copland's *The Red Pony*. Not at all a usual combination.

Chapin's thoughts on that took a time to formulate. It was an odd choice, even though André loved both pieces – a plus for any conductor, certainly for one who was just starting out. *The Red Pony* was underplayed, so there were perhaps reasons to do something to remedy the situation. As he thought more about it, he came to a final conclusion: 'It's eccentric, but maybe eccentricity would be a useful thing for us.'

The concert went well enough; it didn't cause a huge stir among the music fraternity. Outside St Louis it made hardly any impact at all. When the record was released, however, it was a somewhat different story.

As Chapin remembers: 'The critics seemed to say, "Ho, ho, hum . . . What is this?" Then when they heard it, the *Sinfonia* in particular was extremely well received. I don't suppose it sold 1,500 copies, but that didn't matter. This was André's first moment of appearing as a conductor on a recording.'

But it was sufficiently close to crunch time for decisions to be made. Was he now absolutely serious that he was going to give up the fun and glamour of Hollywood for the uncertainty and grind of the concert circuit? He said that yes, he was *absolutely* serious.

That being so, he had to start making the necessary arrangements. He couldn't organise his own schedules or even his repertoire. It was all a complicated jigsaw puzzle that required a professional player to put in place for him. Schuyler Chapin rang Ronald Wilford, who ran just about the biggest agency of its kind, looking after a whole string of some of the greatest conductors in the world.

The Columbia Artists Management agency – no connection with Chapin's Columbia Records – operated highly appropriately from offices opposite Carnegie Hall, the best known concert venue in America.

Schuyler got Wilford on the phone. He immediately expressed interest, but he, too, was determined that André knew at which wedding he was going to dance. 'Of course, I know of him,' he said, 'but is he serious?'

Chapin informed him that he was certain that André was. 'In which case,' he came back, 'he does have to do this and nothing else.'

Ronald Wilford told me that he talked to Zalken about André, totally independently of Schuyler Chapin. 'We were very good friends. He had told me before that he had engaged Previn, then a jazz pianist – and a very good one – to conduct the St Louis Symphony.

'I didn't think it at all bizarre. Billy Zalken is a man I took very seriously. We had done a lot of business together.'

Wilford sent Zalken a copy of *The Red Pony* disc. He told me that the record 'intrigued' him. 'The next thing I knew was that Schuyler Chapin was on the phone and saying that André Previn's coming to town and would I be interested?'

'I put the two things together. Nobody discovers anybody. One hears of these things.'

They were all good enough friends to be told the truth about a third person. More than if a jazz or film agent had rung Wilford and asked if he would meet one of his artists. 'That would have been a no-no from the start.' A lunch was arranged at the Plaza Hotel, scene of so many big deals in and out of the arts and show business that if the walls of this luxury establishment could talk, they would result in the most revealing memoirs ever published.

Ronald Wilford told me that he was even more 'intrigued' when he met the real André Previn. 'I thought, "My goodness, can I move this image?"'

He answered his own question – yes. But he demanded two things of André. 'You're going to have to give me dates, eighteen months or two years from now.' The concert circuit calendar is so full that it takes all of that time before one can find space for any engagement.

That alone seemed to stump Previn. 'I don't even know what I'm doing tomorrow,' he told the eminent manager, who was not used to being thwarted once an idea was buzzing around in his mind, as this one was now. 'I'm afraid,' he told him, 'you are going to have to, and you're going to have to take it seriously. If you don't take it seriously, I am not going to waste my time with you.'

The second requirement was going to be even harder to fulfil. Wilford told André: 'No films. No jazz. Just a lot of hard work with a lot of lousy orchestras, working in tank towns, while you are looking around. But do as I say, and you'll get the career that you want. I am convinced of it.'

As he says now: 'I guess I was a little rough.' But being a little rough paid off.

Wilford told him, 'This is such a different field that you can't be spread. If you are going to compose movie scores and then you're going to study orchestral repertoire for conducting, it's two different dynamics. You can't do it. Many people have a problem in this area. Conducting is such a difficult thing, rehearsing an orchestra, that either you concentrate or you don't.'

It really couldn't be done without total commitment, he said. Not even Bernstein could do it. 'One of Lenny's big problems was how to have time for conducting and then composing. It's a very difficult thing. The days of Mahler were very different. He would go on a boat for eight days between engagements. The time of Brahms was a whole other day. If you have the pressure of Hollywood and you want to do a film score, the whole booking cycle is so different.'

But there was also a personal element in it for Wilford. As he told me: 'If he was committed to a Hollywood career, why should I go out and build this guy's career and get him engagements and struggle along to make him a classical conductor and then he'd be offered a movie score six months along the line and have to cancel the thing?'

After meeting him, he came to the conclusion André could do it. 'A lot of conducting has to do with a man's intelligence, who he thinks he is, how he could deal with a hundred instruments in front of him. The conductor does not play an instrument; a baton is not an instrument. How does he think of himself? Is there a chip on the shoulder? Is he articulate? Can he *say* what he wants? Can he *show* what he wants?'

He felt André could do it, do all those things, but only if there were that degree of commitment. 'If he were going to say he wanted to straddle Hollywood and this career, the timing was off. There would be no question that the timing was off. There was no question he would be offered a big film score, a lot of money and then these things would be thrown away.'

There would be a few compromises for the first couple of years, while André found his feet.

The St Louis Symphony were impressed with him. They were going to do a deal for more concerts together. Wilford said there had to be performances where he could conduct from the piano, so that it was the concert pianist who was being engaged, but one who could also conduct. It would ease him in to be able to conduct, from the piano, a Mozart work or Mendelssohn's First Piano Concerto.

'I was not surprised how well it went, because Billy had told me how good he was. I heard some of those concerts. He had a lot to learn, but the basic musicianship was always there.' There were the two different timings to get straight – a different timing for playing the piano from the one he would have to adopt as a conductor. It was very much a question of breathing.

'It began to work,' he remembers.

Then Wilford told him: 'Let's now eliminate the playing.'

Wilford did, however, agree to one other temporary compromise – André could do the occasional film until he got himself finally established. It would bring him enough money to keep his home going and keep his hand in the business while he was still not totally certain that it would all work.

As the man who had steered a dozen or more senior conductors' careers told me: 'André was taking an enormous finanical risk. He was changing his life, too. Working in Hollywood meant living in Hollywood. When you conduct, you are on tour all the time. It was a hard discussion we had.'

But it was something that André had always wanted to do and he had enough money to weather the storm for the moment.

The career got under way. 'The orchestras weren't *that* bad. We are blessed in this country by the most extraordinary talent, but they were not the most fashionable ensembles.'

André Previn, classical conductor, started work in places like Minneapolis, Baltimore, Dallas. It was superb experience, Schuyler Chapin remembered.

He knew that his father would be pleased. He told Jack about the success of the concerts and listed them, about seven altogether to date. It was a great thing to be able to do, not just to reel off a catalogue of towns like St Louis, Minneapolis and Detroit, but also to be able to tell Jack things that he thought he would want to hear.

He expected at least a nod of support and congratulations. Needless to say, Lotte was beside herself with pride.

'There was a sort of Pinter pause,' he remembers now with just the hint of a sad smile as he thought of what Jack said next. 'You couldn't get an engagement in Boston, could you?' he asked. André replied with a sharp, 'No' and a walk out from the house.

Jack regarded the Boston Symphony as America's greatest orchestra. The tank town outfits were nothing in his hierarchy of the great music makers in his adopted country. So André shrugged his shoulders and faced the fact that nothing he ever did would please the old man, now in his late seventies.

But ever since then, he says today, the phrase, "They don't want you in Boston" has entered the Previn family vocabulary. 'It has become a household saying ever since. Whenever somebody makes the mistake of saying something grandiloquent or bragging, me or my wife or our children, the answer is "You can't get Boston can you?" It's gone into our private language. But the damning thing is that it still quivers. I've been in Boston countless times, but I'm never backstage in Boston without thinking about it. You know, Arthur Miller's no fool.' The similarity in the relationship of André and his father to the characters created by the writer of *All My Sons* and *Death of a Salesman* seemed particularly apposite to him.

He had to accept his father's comments were just par for the course. They were no more than he could expect. His marriage, however, was turning out to be less than he might have hoped, although even now he won't comment about it or about someone who was once so close to him and for whom he retains respect and affection.

He and Dory were still officially together, but when he travelled on his concert engagements, he went alone. It is tough for the wife of any touring artist.

And then there was another family difficulty. In 1963, just as André's name was being made, his father had a series of heart attacks.

On 16 February 1963, Jack died. He was seventy-six. The brilliantly successful lawyer who became a piano teacher had absolutely nothing to leave in his will.

It was up to André to make the funeral arrangements, a role for which he felt totally unsuited. But Lolo was gone and Steve was out of the country. What he knew was that he was immensely sad, unquestionably the right mood in which to be when such things had to be fixed.

Jack, despite his origins and all the things that Hitler had decreed for people like him, was still no more Jewish than he had ever been, in any traditional sense of the term. So there could be no question of a religious cemetery being chosen for his last resting place.

Instead, André took himself off to the one place that he knew anything about – Forest Lawn. It was a cemetery and the people there seemed efficient. Too efficient, as it turned out. When he introduced himself, he was told, 'Your grief counsellor will be with you directly.'

André felt his grief, perhaps more than he ever imagined he would. But the notion of a grief counsellor had a totally opposite effect on him from the one planned by the people at Forest Lawn, who painted expressions of sympathy and misery on their own faces as successfully as they painted the cadavers after embalming.

'It was so ridiculous,' he recalled for me, 'I just couldn't stop laughing. It was something directly out of Evelyn Waugh.' But not even 'The Loved One' had imagined a grief counsellor. As he told me: 'I didn't need a counsellor for my grief. I wanted to see an official who would get on with the arrangements.' Then he was asked to look at the assortment of coffins, caskets with pure silk linings, lead outer casings to be sure that no worms would get through and do their worst; the finest oak exteriors with gold handles. He declined them all and chose a simple container for his father's remains. The gift counsellor told him he would be sorry. The type of coffin he had just rejected had been used to make comfortable the final journey of Harry Warner, one of the other Warner Brothers.

'When she was very old, my mother told me that my father had been very proud of me,' he now says. 'I said that it would have been nice if he had told me that himself. She said, "You know that he couldn't do that."' It doesn't help to heal wounds to know a father takes such feelings with him to the grave.

André's career was what counted now. But even that could be affected by his moods and his emotions. One night, just as he was about to go out on to the podium to conduct a Brahms symphony, Dory phoned to say she was feeling terrible. André went out and put everything he felt into the concert. He came off the podium, sweating profusely.

'I unleashed all my personal feelings on that Brahms symphony. I was sad, I was embittered, I was angry, I was God knows what. I really felt at the end that this was a truly sensational performance.' But, as André tells the rest of the story, and, as he now says, 'accident will have it,' it was anything but. He painfully learnt the lesson of that evening – and quickly.

Ronald Wilford was waiting in the wings for him. Afterwards, the two men went out to have a drink. It was over that drink that Wilford posed the question André will never forget. 'What the hell was all that about?' he asked.

'Why?' André queried. 'What did you think of it?'

'I thought that was disgraceful. I thought it was absolutely horrible.'

André admits that his own instant reaction was to be ill-mannered. 'I got angry with him and all that.' But a week later, a tape of the performance reached him. He wasn't pleased with what he heard. 'It really was disgusting. I had had the unspeakable nerve and temerity to put my own feelings on a level with, or even superceding Brahms's and that won't do. And I don't think I've ever done it since. Those fellows were a lot better than we are and there's no point in superimposing yourself on them. There is a certain kind of music that needs – not a superimposition – but the addition of a very strong personality; but when people say, "So-and-So's Beethoven" and "So-and-So-and-So's Brahms . . .", how can they do that? Generally speaking, if you do what the little dots say you should do, you're home and dry.'

Most of his other playing, individual though it could be at times, was far more conventional. When he recorded the Shostakovich First Piano Concerto with the New York Philharmonic under Leonard Bernstein, he couldn't have been more at home had he gone into

Lester Koenig's garage with Shelly Manne and Leroy Vinnegar and improvised another show score. The sales and the critical appeal only augmented his own satisfaction. But what he wanted was to do more recordings as a conductor, to be known for what he had now ear-marked his career to be.

Certainly, the big problem was extending André's audience potential. The repertoire was there, but the critics still doubted whether he was serious and even if they hadn't expressed their own uncertainty, there was always the question of a Hollywood composer entering their own world. Even when the critics said he was good, and Previn told me he refuses to take notice of what they say – 'If you decide not to care about the bad notices, the corollary is that you also have totally to ignore the good ones' – they were likely to begin their pieces with the words, 'Hollywood's André Previn'.

Wilford thought that André's record label was partly the problem. He needed exposure with a company that was in the business of exploiting young, comparatively unknown conductors. André wasn't unknown, but that was partly his problem. Perhaps more significantly, André's Columbia image was still, essentially, that of a jazz pianist. A separation was needed.

Schuyler Chapin accepted that. Before long, Irving Townsend accepted it, too, but neither man was empowered to allow André to break a contract that had proved moderately beneficial to them both.

In the end, Goddard Lieberson – the man who had first given Schuyler Chapin the right to do what he liked, even if it didn't necessarily mean making money for the label – said that he would release André. It wasn't known by everyone that Lieberson had a soft spot for Previn. Soon after joining Columbia, André saw some piano music lying around in the studio. He played it and without his knowing, the engineers switched on the machines. They were Goddard's works, among which was one called 'Piano Pieces for Advanced Children or Retarded Adults'. Another was 'Eight Studies In Musicology (Which Will Teach You A Great Deal)'.

The selection was released on the back of works by Mendelssohn, Mussorgsky and Mozart. Lieberson remained grateful to André for it and showed that gratitude by agreeing that Schuyler's protégé could do better elsewhere.

It was not, however, a reckless decision on Wilford's part, made on the spur of the moment. He not only had thought about it very carefully, he already had an outlet label waiting for him. RCA wanted him for their Red Label.

It was further proof that André playing with the Philadelphia

Orchestra had been more than a good idea. Roger Hall had moved from the famous orchestra to take over RCA's classical division and he wanted his former guest to join him. What was more, the label had an orchestra ready waiting for André's attention and a soloist, Leonard Pennario. The only problem was that he would have to go to London for the recording sessions.

What was difficult was that he hated to fly, but Wilford convinced him about the safety techniques now adopted by the Boeing company and that he himself hadn't had an accident yet. So he went to conduct Khachaturian's concerto and Ernest Bloch's *Scherzo Fantastique*. Then there was Rachmaninov's First and his Fourth Concertos. The 1964 recordings at Walthamstow Town Hall – a venue popular with producers because of the amazing acoustics, but hated by musicians who find it one of the most difficult places to get to – went ahead perfectly. The orchestra was the Royal Philharmonic. Two decades later, he would be their music director. But that was far ahead, in concept as well as in time.

For the moment, he just wanted more of the same, and preferably with more orchestras. Later, in 1965, he went back to Walthamstow with RCA, but this time with the London Symphony Orchestra. He recorded more Russian music, the Fifth Symphony of Shostakovich and Tchaikovsky's Symphony Number Two, *The Little Russian* as well as *Eight Russian Folk Songs* by Anatol Liadov.

Coming to London to guest-conduct for the first time was a strange experience, he now recalls. From the moment of his first car journey into the West End and the Savoy Hotel where he was staying, he was struck by the fact that this was going to be something very special for him.

'I had a day off after I arrived and took a walk around London. By the time I got back to the hotel that first night, I was absolutely convinced that I wanted to live in England. Then a few days later, I had a weekend off and I decided that not only would I live in England, but I would live in the countryside. Of course, in those days, it was the impossible dream. But I even saw a house in those days in some little village which was the embodiment of what I wanted.'

Any visit to London – and the odd chance to squeeze in a tour around the surrounding countryside – was worth his while. 'I liked the leisureliness of England, the respect for old things, for tradition. I even liked the politics.'

Now he was guest-conducting concerts in the city, too. People noted them, but still André Previn was being spoken of as The Boy From Hollywood.

The image was going to be a problem for some time. Ronald Wilford was aware of it. A man with a Hollywood background would always be spoken of as being 'light' unless some other angle could be found.

Wilford told me he decided very firmly *not* to fight it. 'I'm not in the business of selling images. Everybody in this field, any orchestra manager, is looking for the new outstanding conductor. I knew that if he played the piano and he conducted and there was a spark there, he would be re-engaged. That was the secret – to get re-engaged. Everybody knew that his conductorial talents were superb, his musical abilities were superb.

'In another sense, it was easier than had he just been a classical pianist. People who are known as classical pianists have always had a difficult time. Rostropovich had a problem going from the cello to conducting. You kind of lose the cello while you are concentrating on being a conductor. Your whole emphasis is switched. Because André had been playing jazz, which was so far away from the classical structure, it was easier for him in this regard.'

Of course, his training had been perfect. His lessons with Monteux had borne fruit. 'I think he had an easier time than most. It just worked like Gangbusters.'

The critics were another matter. They showed the anticipated prejudices – even if only in coupling those words 'Hollywood' with 'pianist'.

'But I never worry about critics,' said Wilford. 'If I worried about critics, I'd never manage anybody. I wouldn't have been able to manage Karajan, if I worried about critics. As the critics said one thing and the orchestra members said another, and managements said another still and audiences came running in because of André's celebrity status, critics just didn't matter at all.'

He did, however, admit: 'There's a time when they can kill a career.' And they did their best to smother André's before it really started.

'I did a terrible thing to him,' Wilford now remembers with a shudder. He put André into the New York promenade concert season with André Kostelanetz at the newly-opened Avery Fisher Hall attached to the Lincoln Centre. As far as the metropolitan press was concerned, it didn't work.

'I realise that the critics had too much to digest – anybody who could conduct, couldn't play that well and anyone who could play that well couldn't conduct. They couldn't accept anyone being so multi-talented. It was like giving children too much to digest. It was

179

the one goof I made in his career.'

That was the final decision to be made about the direction of André's career, the last time for years that he would be booked to conduct and play at the same time. 'We had lots of inquiries from managements asking him to conduct and play, but I told them that he wasn't a pianist. It was very tough. I played it very straight.'

André himself says that he had no doubts that it was the right thing to do. And that goes just as much for the total change in his career that had now been wrought.

'My only regret is that it seems to me I stayed in Hollywood and did what I was doing there for too long. I should have said somewhat earlier that it was time to go and I should have left. But I've never been sorry I played jazz, I've never been sorry I was in films, I've never been sorry for some of the commercial things I was doing.'

He had given up jazz because there was no time for it, but he would have loved it to have continued. He was now giving up films, too, but for different reasons. He was bored with them and didn't want to make the movies the focus of his life any more.

'It might have been nice if I had said earlier that I really should devote myself to more serious music. I didn't because I was successful, I was comfortable and I was having a wonderful time. It took me quite a while before I thought that that was not enough.'

So he was glad he took the risks that Ronald Wilford warned him about. 'I'm going to say,' he told me, 'one of the most loathesome things I'm going to say for this book – it never dawned on me that I wouldn't be a success. It never crossed my mind. Isn't that the most terrible thing to say? Who's to know?'

It was, he admits, all a question of timing.

'My most perfect timing was in leaving Hollywood, for there was to be a ten-year period between when I left and when John Williams came in when there was very little music in Hollywood at all.

'They would hire a rock group, called The Running Sores and they would make an album and then they would kind of shoehorn it into a movie and that was called a movie score. I would have been sacked anyway.

It was a question of early fantasies finally catching up with André – and equally living up to his dreams.

In 1965, he went back to Los Angeles to conduct at the Hollywood Bowl and did so again the following year. Both times, local people found it difficult to accept that their own boy-made-good had changed his allegiances so easily.

Nevertheless, Charles Champlin, the doyen of show business

writers, told his readers in the *Los Angeles Times* in July 1965 about a conversation he had had with a 'nationally-known musicologist'. The man had told him that within ten years, 'I think André Previn's reputation will eclipse Leonard Bernstein's.'

More and more, the two names were being coupled, although not always so flatteringly. Said Mr Champlin: 'It's an imprudent man who looks askance at any prophecy concerning the short but protean Mr Previn.'

The conflicts between what he was doing now and what he had done before still haunted him, although now people were turning their attention to television music, not the work done for the big screen. *Daily Variety* in April 1966 printed a report from Minneapolis headed: 'Nothing Lower Than TV Music – Previn'.

André denied it. He told the paper: 'Some of the TV music I've heard is not only very good but better and more adventurous than anything I've heard in pictures. But, number one, you can hardly hear it, and, two, the sequences seem to be terribly fragmentary, with lots of five-second bridges and plenty of announcer interruptions.'

None of that sort of controversy worried André. When he could record the London Symphony playing Rachmaninov's Second Symphony in 1966 and follow it up the following year with the First Symphony of William Walton – which had already been recorded by the London Philharmonic with Sir Adrian Boult – he was a happy man indeed.

To receive the plaudits of critics, try though he might to say that he takes no notice of any of them, had to be very pleasing indeed – even if it were merely a case of if you're going to get a review anyway, you might just as well try for a good one instead of a bad one.

He may have thought he had wasted so much time in Hollywood, but in the classical field he was still an infant, especially when there were conductors who only seemed to reach maturity in their mid-seventies. It even applied to his piano playing, for although Wilford wasn't selling André as a pianist, there were still a few previously unreleased records hitting the market *after* André had got into his conducting stride.

But he was willing to take the flak because he liked doing the work. That perhaps was good enough reason for André's film commitments to be lessening as he had planned. But they still existed. He was particularly happy with his 1965 picture, *Inside Daisy Clover*, often described as a 'kind of' *A Star is Born*, about a girl going to Hollywood. Natalie Wood and Ruth Gordon starred. One of the happiest features of this movie was the song, 'You're Gonna Hear From Me', which got on to the American charts. He wrote it in collaboration with Dory. All very different from the bus tours with orchestras, the grabbing of snacks between rehearsals. In Hollywood, he was once more treated as a celebrity – but he didn't really want it.

Dory has said that it was one of the most exciting of the assignments she had had with her husband, especially since it enabled them to work on a 1930s-style score. 'You're Gonna Hear From Me' was the most satisfactory part of the lot and she was delighted to hear it danced to by the Rockettes, the dancers at New York's Radio City Music Hall and the group for which she herself had auditioned as a young girl.

In 1966, there was a film with Julie Andrews, now a close friend. *Thoroughly Modern Millie* didn't win him any Oscars, but it did get him a nomination. Such things, he tried to tell himself, were even less important now than they had ever been. But working on the picture provided good money and a certain further relaxation from the conducting he was doing. The film looked fun and *was* fun.

That Previn touch was being recognised where he wanted it to be noticed – on the conductor's podium.

The prejudices could be ignored. 'But,' as Ronald Wilford put it to me, 'whenever you engage a young conductor who is unknown, you get prejudice. But he was very, very experienced.

'Because of that Hollywood experience, he knew how to deal with musicians – who had scores in front of them that they couldn't respect.'

Not that it was all plusses on his part. The Boy From Hollywood still wasn't totally at ease as the Man at Avery Fisher Hall. He didn't know everything.

'He didn't know how to pace himself,' was how Wilford describes it. 'It was a totally different process from what he had done before. Even though the score was in front of him, he had as a conductor to know it better than any of the individual players. So study time in his field is very difficult. You have to become a student.

'It was a change in his whole way of living. He had been used to writing a score and playing it the next day in the studio. Now he was working with scores that everyone knew and had played a hundred times before. So he really had to know what he was doing – and at first he didn't do it. André now says, 'It took me many years, and many mistakes, to achieve a disciplined work ethic.'

'You can look at a score last week and then again this week and see something you didn't see before. So there's an insecurity there and so you listen to a lot of records, study other people. Finding out what you want to do is a very difficult thing.'

But he did find out. As Wilford added: 'I don't know a single case when André wasn't re-engaged.'

The musician who had been used to a quite stationary life in Hollywood was now having to do more travelling than ever – and that old worry about flying was getting to him more than he had expected.

'When you travel to work,' said Ronald Wilford, 'you have to study how you live. You get on an airplane. You get off an airplane. You go to an hotel. It's not your bed. It's not your pillow. Then you have a rehearsal the next day. It's an orchestra you don't know and a repertoire that they've played a lot before you did.'

His manager asked André to go to Toronto to conduct the symphony there. 'Oh dear,' said André, 'that means I've got to fly.'

He said that he would go only if Wilford went with him. 'It was a terrible experience for me,' he remembered. 'André was terribly nervous. He couldn't sleep. He was too nervous. He couldn't study. He was too nervous. That was a serious problem for him. He had to cope with that. He was a nervous wreck. He was nervous whether the plane would ever get off the ground. He was a nervous wreck worrying whether it could ever land safely.'

Wilford tried to offer him the security of his own experience. 'I'd flown all my life. So I tried to show him it would be all right – like you take across the street someone who's afraid to go. It took a lot of discipline from him.'

Dory on the other hand just wouldn't get on an airplane. 'I think Dory became traumatised by it and that made it even worse for him to fly. 'It contributed to the breakdown of their marriage. She wouldn't travel with him.'

He had other things to learn to get used to: When do you rest? When do you study scores? As Ronald Wilford told me: 'You've got to know a score better than any player in the orchestra.'

And, Mr Wilford would have added, concentrate on the 'serious' music alone. André found that a bit more difficult than he had agreed at the beginning. As Dory said at the time: 'If he's played a classical concert and then stops by to hear a jazz pianist, when he comes home he sits down and plays funk for half an hour just to prove he can do it.'

Not only that. He was also composing and conducting. And it was worth it. Within two years of starting this new episode in his career, there was an orchestra that wanted him badly.

The eminent British conductor Sir John Barbirolli wanted to concentrate on his first love, the Hallé. He was lessening his other commitments. One of these was as Principal Conductor of the Houston Symphony Orchestra.

They had featured André once before in their programme as a guest conductor and had enjoyed working with him as much as he liked them. So, with Barbirolli's blessing, an invitation went out to the boy from Hollywood. 'Would you like to be our Principal Conductor? André tried to stifle the immediate reaction that he would willingly have accepted the offer of being Principal Conductor of the Symphony of Outer Mongolia given half the chance, and muttered a 'yes'. Once he had left the Houston Symphony's headquarters, Jones Hall, he could be heard to say something that sounded very much like, 'I've got my own band. My *own* band.'

THIRTEEN

American orchestras depend very largely on the patronage of a group of extraordinarily rich people who take it as a kind of *noblesse oblige* to maintain the cultural foundations of their community. To be able to do so assures them, some think, of a place in the next world. It certainly grants them one in this. With the title of 'Patron of the Symphony' new money becomes old. Shady dealings take on respectability.

In Houston, the respectability of Miss Hogg was never in doubt. The prosperity of the Houston Symphony was in large part due to the efforts of this spinster who was the city symphony's principal benefactor.

André's first night was a professional sensation. Schuyler Chapin remembers going there with his wife to hear him and feeling a glow of pride as strong and as powerful as the shiver that went down his spine when he first saw him conduct.

'He wasn't yet great or wonderful and there were a lot of rough edges, things that he didn't do, but it was a marvellous experience.'

Previn's title was officially Conductor-in-Chief. He would lead ten pairs of concerts plus a three-week tour and two weeks of non-subscription concerts. Ten weeks of the orchestra's season would be put in the hands of guest conductors.

What the job did for him was to put an end to if not all but a great deal of that prejudice about Hollywood. As Ronald Wilford put it to me: 'Certainly it had been there. Managements would say, "Oh, he's a Hollywood musician." I would then tell them, "You're getting a superb conductor, not Hollywood."' He fought it. 'I'm one of these people who only succeed if I believe and I'm a believer. No one could say that André Previn would not succeed as a conductor. No one.'

The first concert, in October 1967, drew various responses. The

Houston *Chronicle's* Ann Holmes said she found 'parts of Brahms
. . . and later Beethoven . . . excessively zealous'.

Newsweek, highly unusually, asked him to comment on that.
'Beethoven's Fifth has more intense rage in it than any other piece in
the history of music and we have to get across at the expense of a
little elegance,' he told them.

The Houston *Post* gave him full marks for his first concert. 'No
complaints', reported the paper.

It was enough for him. He was earning about $50,000 a year from
his Houston contract, but there was plenty of money from all the
other work he had lined up. 'They don't pay for Mahler what they
pay for Debbie Reynolds,' he said. And then, as he told me, he had so
much to be grateful for.

What he wasn't so grateful for was the necessity to play socialite,
or rather to grease the egos of the people who considered themselves
to be Houston society.

He had seen the writing of what was going to be expected of him
during his two-year stint with Houston on the wall at the party given
on the very first night of his first season there – 'my very first night as
music director of anything anywhere'.

The party was given by a man who rejoiced in the title of General
Hirsch. 'He was about a hundred years old and very rich, but he was
very nice to me, perfectly all right, but what he was a general of, I
have no idea; something very obscure, I imagine.'

As he walked in, he was struck by the overwhelming presence of a
centrepiece carved in ice – an ice statue, in fact, of André Previn.

His host, General Hirsch, caught André looking at it, as if he could
do anything else. 'Do you love it?' he asked.

'Yes,' André said, 'I think I can say in all honesty, I love it.'

Houston, however, gave him opportunities to demonstrate his
musical abilities. As Ronald Wilford told other orchestra managements who were interested in taking him as a guest conductor, but
who needed a little convincing: 'Do you think the Houston Symphony is that crazy? How many orchestra conductors could you find
who have a name like André Previn? Try him.'

Not everybody thought it was terribly laudible to give up Hollywood for the world of classical music. Sandy Courage told me that he
was greatly missed in the film town – except, of course, by those for
whom his leaving was seen as opening up vacancies for work that he
would have snapped up.

Walter Scharf, the Hollywood musical director, told me: 'I resent
people like him, foul-mouthing Hollywood long after he's left the

place that fed him.'

Billy Wilder, the director and writer whom André admires so much, put forward the same case, but with the wit of a man who could make it convincing – if difficult – for Jack Lemmon to pretend to be a woman while Marilyn Monroe slides into bed beside him (in *Some Like It Hot*). 'I never understand,' he told me, 'why people who have done very well out of this town treat their time in Hollywood rather as though they have been working in a Shanghai penal colony.'

André says about that: 'If he's saying it's not right to criticise, I find it strange coming from the man who made *Sunset Boulevard* – and so upset the Hollywood establishment that Louis B. Mayer wouldn't talk to him any more.'

But he adds: 'I'm sorry I upset Billy. I'm sorry he feels that way, genuinely sorry, because I don't feel like that at all. My admiration for him is so unchecked and he gave me such support and we had such a good time together. I don't know where he got that idea. It is possible, he may have read an interview or two in which I was asked, "Do you ever miss Hollywood", and I said quite truthfully, that the answer was "No".'

I put the Wilder quote to Blake Edwards: 'Maybe Billy knows something that I don't know, but I don't feel, simply because André goes on to do what he is doing, that that is putting Hollywood down. I've not only not read anything, but I've never heard him *say* anything. I'm the first one to be very derisive about this place, but if anyone were to ask André about how he feels about his beginnings and the talent here, I'd never heard him put it down. If Billy Wilder would in his later life decide to become a second Picasso and go off to Paris and succeed, he would be the first to say not very flattering things about Hollywood.'

An André himself says: 'I had the most wonderful time there and I have nothing but affection for it. Had I really foul-mouthed the place, it would have been nothing less than unforgivable, but I never did.' The only thing he ever complained about in public, he maintains, was that whole business of paid publicity about the Academy Awards.

Nevertheless, in the act of packing up and going, he was causing offence to those for whom the name Hollywood represented their own success. To go was to minimise their own achievements. Again, André says he had no such intention. He had just had enough and wanted to do new things – the things he had always planned on doing since that day he was first able to sight-read a score.

'I felt that the goal I had reached was not so hard to get. And I had stopped being frightened by the work and the only way work is going to be any good is when you're frightened of it. I put in eighteen-hour days very often and was pleased with what I did sometimes. But I was never scared of going into the first day's recording of a new score. I was never scared of the prospect of having to write new music, because I knew I could do it. I might do it rather well sometimes and very poorly at others. And I thought that if I'm going to do some serious music as a musician, I have to do something that scares the shit out of me for the rest of my life. And it's true, it's more and more scary as the years go by.

'The first time you do a Beethoven Ninth, you think, "Oh I know those notes and I can do it." And then you see what's behind those notes and what can go wrong and what does go wrong. It gets worse and worse.' They were the thoughts that stayed with him now that he had made his irrevocable decision. Yet when he did sometimes wonder what he had left behind, he knew that there was just no competition: 'The only thing I could do was stay there – the status quo. And the status quo has never interested me. The other thing, the over-riding thing, is self-evident. I hadn't studied all my life to do that sort of music.'

And then there was that 'tenth-rate' music he talked about having to produce. 'If I wrote it myself,' he answered, 'I'm entitled to call it tenth-rate if I like. If I didn't write it but was involved with someone else's music I was always floored by the expertise involved – either by the composer or by the orchestrator, or the playing of it, whatever.'

Any contempt that he feels for the stuff that he played in the MGM, Twentieth Century Fox or any of the other movie studios, he recognises as seen through lenses labelled 'hindsight'. None of that hindsight, he says, however, results in anything but admiration for his colleagues.

'Of course there were dreadful composers. There sure were. But there were others who were brilliant. The orchestrators were absolute Merlins, selfless chameleons who could make any sound in the world with the most disdainful expertise and ease. They just didn't think it difficult. You'd tell them to make something sound a certain way and they would. I was surrounded by people whose technical prowess was so good, I still don't have it.'

That being so, why did he decide to chuck it all? There was more to it than just being bored by not being scared or by having to stand still.

There was also the very factor of what Hollywood represented. It seemed to live for itself. 'Its dog insularity and the kind of extra-ordinary self-imposed limitations on viewpoint – those are the very things that attract people to it; but I am completely without compre-hension of that. It's a disease of that place, which I can't understand.'

With a degree of disgust, he tells the story of the Hollywood ex-ecutive who was so distressed at the way he was being treated that he told Louis B. Mayer: 'I demand more respect or more money.' André recalls: 'So they gave him a raise.'

He wanted none of that to look forward to.

Blake Edwards re-emphasises his own support for the move made by a man many still see as fairly cold. 'There is a reserve about André. He's a very personal man, which some people interpret as being a cold reserve. It's just that he has a way of weeding out the garbage. Most musicians would say, "I'm content with my Oscars and to live on my money in my big house." Not many have the guts to do what he did. But he was perceived by some people in a somewhat con-descending way. They would say, "Oh isn't that nice, but isn't he being more than a little crazy?"'

'A lot thought it was just an ego trip,' Julie Andrews told me. '"Oh, he wants to conduct!" That sort of thing. God forbid, you should be talented and want to do something about it.'

But Blake himself did wonder. 'The thing that appealed to me was, How could he do that? How could he leave all that sort of thing?'

There was no doubt that he had put his all into film music. And he played it with all the enthusiasm he was now about to extend to con-ducting Mahler's Fourth Symphony or the 'Eroica', which Jack had always regarded as the epitome of great music. André likes to remem-ber Sir Thomas Beecham's love of 'lollipops', light frivolous pieces which he enjoyed including in his repertoire, but which he conducted with all the enthusiasm he would bring to the most complicated symphony.

His contempt was strictly reserved for those who were not doing that job or who resented doing it. 'You have to believe in what you're doing to a certain point. We had a very great pianist, I mean a very seriously great classical pianist, in the orchestra at MGM and he kept complaining that he was wasting his time. However, he was making a lot of money and he had elected to do this job. Even at the time, I remember thinking, No this is wrong. If he had said, "All you people are pitiful and I am quitting because I'd rather starve and play Beeth-oven sonatas," Great! But to sit there in relative comfort and play nothing that ever taxed him and get a lot of money for it, and then make us feel he was doing us a favour, I thought that was dead wrong. I still do.

'If your innermost lack of respect for what you're doing permeates work so that it becomes visible and then audible, you're double-crossing everyone. Including yourself. Particularly yourself.'

Despite what Billy Wilder said, André can add: 'It was never a prison sentence. You *could* always leave.'

That was why he was so much, to coin a phrase, in tune with what Chapin and Wilford had planned for him. 'But I had no right to knock it. I could criticise it, naturally. But to deride it publicly is not on. It's just bad manners.'

Fred Astaire always had the answer to that sort of thing. He once told me: 'You do the job because every Thursday, there's a cheque waiting.' André heard him say something of the kind, too, and applauds the philosophy behind it.

Houston wasn't among the top symphonies, but it wasn't a tank town, either. The period going to those places was, in fact, mercifully short. Houston provided him with his first opportunity to plan programmes as well as to conduct, to host distinguished soloists, to hone a craft that he knew had been his since childhood, to increase his repertoire.

The music, though, was what counted. And as he stood on the Houston podium, he could reflect on what he had come to. He was in the midst of the most perfectly orchestrated career structure known to anyone in his business – or any other for that matter. And he could be tough. There were no compromises with what he thought he needed. After being due to conduct a programme made up of William Schuman's Third Symphony, Benjamin Britten's *Sinfonia Da Requiem* and Stravinsky's *Firebird* Suite at the Westbury Music Fair, cancelled the concert and no-one got paid – because there wasn't room for more than eighty-five of the ninety-six members of the orchestra on the platform and he wasn't going to play without the complete complement of musicians.

He reflects from time to time on what led him to make powerful decisions like that, what it was actually like to be in that position. 'While I can say now with impudence that it never occurred to me that I wouldn't make it, it didn't occur to me, even in fantasies, that I would be a really welcome and well-liked figure in Vienna, in Berlin, in Boston, because these were icons to me, the holy grail. I thought I might wind up as the conductor of the . . . you name it . . . the Cincinatti, the St Louis, one of those orchestras. But I didn't know when. It wasn't that I thought I was so good, it was just an area of thinking that didn't occur to me. It was a case of onward and upward. Maybe not now, maybe later. I never thought it would end in heart-breaking failure.'

Other people who had made it so well, so young – the prestige of the Oscars, the fame of the pictures to which his name was attached, the huge amounts of money he had earned by the time he was in his mid-thirties – might have planned a kind of semi-retirement in which they were going to do what they had always wanted to do most in life. But they would have done so in a relaxed way and ended up feeling very, very content to conduct a second-division but highly respected symphony orchestra in Britain or America.

'I was never going to be satisfied with that,' he confessed. 'But having said that, I had never contemplated getting quite as high (forgive me for saying it; it sounds terrible) as I actually have.'

There had also been the assurance at the back of his mind that, should things not work out, he could go back to Hollywood. 'I only had that for a year. I gave my word that after that year, it would end totally. The memory of people in the film business, or their loyalty, is fiercely short. If you haven't had a great success in the past year, not only can you not get a movie, you can't even get a good table in a restaurant. Once you take two years off, forget it. It's over.'

Was Houston going to be the end of the line? And very happily so? Ambition is always a funny thing, virtually impossible to quantify – or to know when it first struck home. For the moment, he was delighted to have his own band and to wave his stick in front of it.

'When the career kind of took off, I am still even to this day never unaware of the incredible turn of events and amazing luck, combined with a lot of hellish work, I have to say, but still you have to be in the right place at the right time.'

As for being 'brave' at starting all over again, 'bullshit'. He was doing what he wanted to do more than anything else. He had been in the commissary at MGM when the pianist Claudio Arrau and the violinist Michael Rabin, who had recorded the music tracks for the picture, were talking.

He couldn't help overhearing their chatter. He couldn't help either, feeling intensely envious as they traded anecdotes – stupid little things like going up and down the steps at Amsterdam's principal concert hall, or the problems of getting a connection at Zurich Airport for the next flight to Berlin.

'These little anecdotes went on and I thought, "I'll never be able to tell stories like that and I want to do so more than anything else."'

In the early sixties he was building up a collection of *true* stories all of his own.

Contentment is a powerful thing and for the moment he was in its thrall. But it was not true that he did it purely for the fun of the thing. 'I needed the money. Oh, yes. I needed the money.'

But then, his Hollywood experience *had* come in useful, just as he thought it would. It did teach him timing, to make the most and best use of the hours available for rehearsal. As he will say over and over again, 'I lament the fact that I was there too long, but not that I was there at all. It teaches you much more than any conservatory training could.' He is certain that he learnt as much that was of use to him at MGM than he would have done working as an assistant in an opera house.

His recordings continued to mount up. He was anxious for there not to be a particular Previn speciality in these. A very wide range of Previn indeed went on to the black acrylic LP discs. It is also true that he was recording more and more English music and a great deal of the work of his other love, the French composers. He recorded Ravel and Françaix and Ibert and work by Debussy. But he also recorded Bartók and even an excursion into Danish music, through Carl Nielsen's First Symphony. Naturally, he recorded Russian music as well, including Rimsky-Korsakov's *Scheherazade*.

Then there was chamber music. He continued to play it – such a passion could not be abandoned. But he was not recording it. Columbia had indulged him, but had made no money out of doing so and no matter how keen Schuyler Chapin was not to bow totally to the power of the almighty dollar, financial considerations did have to come into play. RCA weren't interested either and, as Ronald Wilford had pointed out, André Previn was a conductor, not a pianist. Sometimes, that sharp division was painful, but Wilford had to see it from a business point of view or not at all.

André took the Houston orchestra on tour, and he could thank MGM for the ability he now had to compose on planes or in hotel rooms.

But he was not just travelling with the Houston orchestra. There was London – always London – conducting the LSO in Rachmaninov's Second Symphony. While in town, he got a message that the Vienna Philharmonic wanted him to conduct Mahler. It was as exciting to receive the invitation as it soon would be to do the concert. Then, when he got back from Vienna, there would be three more concerts with the LSO.

Said Sydney Edwards in the London *Evening Standard*, 'Previn's career is taking a similar direction to that of Leonard Bernstein.' Others *had* noticed.

All the travelling he was doing to London, even to Houston, only continued to drive the wedge that was growing between André and Dory. But he was not going to abandon ambitions that had been with him for so long and were now reaching fruition.

England now started playing a part in that fruition. He loved London and he loved Britain. It offered a serenity, almost a sanity, he didn't find in America. When he came to Britain, he soaked in its very atmosphere. The air he breathed, even though it was mixed with the fumes of the Swinging Sixties, gave him a sense of rejuvenation.

If English music had held an importance for him before, to be able to play it in Britain, and perpetuate that playing on records, was rewarding beyond measure. Again, he did so with the London Symphony, an orchestra with whom the bonds were getting increasingly strong.

Critics were writing that he conducted Walton and Vaughan Williams better than Sir Malcolm Sargent. Better than Sargent? It was like an English conductor coming to America and beating the natives conducting Copland.

André's recordings of the symphonies of William Walton were praised by the composer himself – who became a dear friend in the last years of his life. He, too, said he preferred them to Sargent's. It was known not to please the conductor whose immaculate platform appearance at the Albert Hall Proms, and wherever he appeared, earned him the nickname 'Flash Harry'. (It was a name given to him by Sir Thomas Beecham, who when he heard that Sargent was going to Tokyo remarked, 'Ah, Flash in Japan'.)

When RCA decided to record André conducting all nine of the symphonies of Vaughan Williams, the tongues of the British music establishment started wagging at almost as many revolutions as the 33 on the record players reproducing the discs.

'There is in Mr Previn's approach to modern music,' wrote Robert Layton, the eminent critic of the *Gramophone* magazine, 'an uncommon freshness, urgency and sympathy that makes one feel he is encountering the music for the first time.'

The people left behind in California were having to come to grips with the new Previn. When he returned home to Bel Air between engagements, he found ways of combining his new obligations and his new studying with his remaining Hollywood commitments. He also had to induce his Los Angeles friends to come to terms with what he was doing now.

Julie Andrews told me of the first time she went to the Bel Air house for a dinner given by André and Dory. 'He said, "You won't be able to find it, so I'll meet you at the front gate and take you."'

Now that, as a hundred other people will testify, was almost as brave a thing for André to promise to do as it would have been for him to get on a plane and fly once more to Toronto. His sense of direction hadn't improved with the years, as indeed it hasn't to this day.

Bel Air is, in effect, a huge estate comprising the most valuable real estate anywhere in the world. Street follows street with houses which, planted anywhere else, would be big enough to consist of entire roads themselves. The Bel Air Hotel, quite the most fashionable on the West Coast, is the kind of place that seems to require an entry visa merely to go there for dinner.

All this is locked away from the rest of the world by a series of gateways on the main Sunset Boulevard as it winds its way from Los Angeles to Pacific Palisades. It was at one of these gates that André proceded to demonstrate his knowledge of the geography of Bel Air.

Had Julie not had some idea of André's reputation, she might have found it a little easier to follow him from the gateway to the Previn house. 'I followed him in the dusk – it was really quite dark.

'What was really quite disconcerting was that my headlights were shining on through André's rear window and I could see him waving his arms madly about in front of me. I thought he was quite a lunatic.' She also wondered whether he did know in which direction he was going.

When they arrived at the house, he explained what it had all been about. 'He was so involved in being a conductor that he had tapes on in the car, and he was conducting to the tapes even when he was driving the car.'

Julie and Blake and André and Dory remained close even with his career taking such a totally 180-degree turn. Previn and Edwards had the same sense of humour – 'listening to which, no woman should ever be present', Julie remembered. As she told me: 'There were times when Dory and I would hear them telling stories so black or so blue, we would leave them alone. When the two got together, they were like two boys who find they live on the same block. They're soul mates. Their sense of humour is so irreverent.'

'An almost childlike affection for fun,' is how Blake puts it. 'A guy like that can't be all bad.'

André and Dory, Blake and Julie took trips together. They went on antique-hunting expeditions. 'We would compete just a little. They'd recommend a gallery and we'd tell them about one in return.'

But there was the music, too. Occasionally, André and Julie would combine their two considerable resources, like the Christmas record they made together for the Firestone Corporation.

'It is one of the things I'm most proud of, a joy to do. André and I chose the carols, for the words as well as for the music. But those phenominal orchestrations! He was lovable and patient.'

André wanted to find a way of getting Dory, too, to encounter the music he was making now. It was no good for their work to be as far apart as were the distances he was travelling away from Los Angeles.

The opportunity came when André expanded his Houston conducting repertoire to include Mozart. He was pleased with the result, not only because Mozart had always been his favourite composer, but because it tended to stifle the criticisms that, despite his deliberate eclecticism, he was too restrictive in his work.

When he started *recording* Mozart, he thought that the message would get across loud and clear. André suggested the opera, *The Impresario*, sufficiently short to be contained on a single disc.

Both RCA and Ronald Wilford thought that was a superb idea, but it had to be in English. That was what audiences would want to hear. They needed to know what all the fuss was about, and to get the jokes, which, unfortunately, didn't sound terribly funny in most of the translations that were around.

It was then that André hit on the idea of getting Dory to renew their old songwriting partnership – to write the lyrics, as it were, for Mozart. André would translate the German and she would put the words into singing form. The record flopped miserably, although the libretto by Dory has become something of a standard work. Unfortunately, the pair did not make a habit of this kind of collaboration, good though it was from an artistic point of view. Because he was away from home a very great deal, it meant that life was harder than ever for the two of them.

He hasn't done very much opera work in the years since this first fledgling attempt at recording one. 'I don't think that André really likes the sound of the human voice,' was how Ronald Wilford put it to me. 'I suppose if you don't think that the human voice moves you as much as a piano, violin or oboe you shouldn't do it.'

Towards the end of the 1980s and in 1990, André has done more opera than once he did. 'About two a year.' But the principle, on the whole, held true.

'I suppose he is right,' André confessed. 'The human voice has to be absolutely perfect for me to enjoy it.' The very slight imperfections he might just about tolerate with a violin or even a piano he could not accept from a singer.

His problem now, however, was that there were people in Houston who could not accept André as a conductor. He was with Houston but not of it.

André Previn in Hollywood had taught the André Previn in Houston the value of having studied a score from the time it was an empty sheet of manuscript paper. The conservatory teachers would have told their students that putting a clarinet at a certain position in a score would make it sound very nice. 'You nod your head and say, "Uh, huh." But I wonder if it isn't a lot more graphic to write it wrong and hear it played within hours of your having put it down. So I would sit down all those years with my scores, saying, "This sounds very nice", or "This sounds bloody awful." "This is a mistake", "This would sound very much better if . . ." "This you must never do again."'

As he also says: 'I'm a great believer in empirical knowledge and not enough young conductors learn that way. Conducting is the one thing you can't practise at home.'

He knew – and his musicians knew, too – when to be serious and when to joke. He knew how long and no longer he could keep his musicians at their stands before they wilted and started thinking about the shopping they had to do on the way home or how they were going to get time to wash the car or water the garden. The sensible conductor had the intuitive knowledge when to say 'Thank you – see you tomorrow.'

The people who controlled the money that went into the Houston orchestra were not so easily taught. He wanted to play contemporary music and those people didn't want to hear it. He took the orchestra on tour, and hated the places to which they would go – predicated, he would say, on the cities that had Holiday Inns, not on their willingness to go to concerts. Certainly not a willingness to hear anything new.

It didn't serve to endear him to the city or the work he was now doing.

His enthusiasm for the orchestra was under pressure. The musical gilt was beginning to rub off the Houston gingerbread. There were rows ahead. His marriage was not getting any better either – particularly once he had met a waif-like girl who happened to be married to Frank Sinatra.

FOURTEEN

He couldn't get away from Hollywood. Having broken still more his own connections with the film town with every new concert arrangement and each new symphonic recording, he suddenly got caught up with a young woman who seemed to epitomise the new society that Hollywood now represented.

Mia Farrow had been born *into* the place. Hollywood was engrained in her very personality. Her mother had been an eminent star of the 1930s, Maureen O'Sullivan, the most famous of all Tarzan's Janes, but also a creditable leading lady for Laurence Olivier in *Pride and Prejudice*.

Her father was John Farrow, a film director. She herself had had the kind of career that young girls dream about. Films like *Rosemary's Baby* had caught the attention of movie-goers all over the world.

Hardly irrelevant to it all was the fact that Mia was married to Frank Sinatra, a man not to be trifled with at the best of times. But by the time André and Mia got talking over a drink at a London party – which up to that time both of them wished they had never attended – that was no longer a consideration. The Sinatras were already separated.

Mia was certainly no conventional Hollywood star.

She and André had met before the London party. Dory had seemed to take to her before André did. She had called at their home, Dory was to write in *Bog Trotter*, having come across the patio of their neighbour, the eminent film director Alan Pakula, in order to introduce herself. Dory said her skin was 'translucent – the voice had been gently buffed by good schools and privilege.'

Plainly some of the venom Dory felt was being expressed in her writing, but Mia was young and extraordinarily privileged. She had offered friendship to Dory and Dory had been delighted to accept.

They went to restaurants together and Dory felt threatened by this young thing, barely twenty-four years old. But that wasn't what André felt, she wrote. Mia seemed to irritate him. Dory was very pleased to note that.

Later, when André was away conducting the Houston orchestra and she was married to Sinatra, she invited Dory to her home. She confided that she knew André hated staying alone in hotel rooms, which was why she had tried travelling with him, only going by train instead of plane. But she didn't like trains any more than she could cope with aircraft. Now, she told Mia of her dreaded fear – that André would fall for another woman who 'would hold out a hand to him', which he would accept simply because he was lonely.

Then in London in 1967, Mia and André met again at the party – or, rather, after the party.

'It was a horrendous film party,' André remembered. His brother Steve, who was also working in London at the time, asked him to go along to it. 'I really, truly, genuinely couldn't stand it any more and waved to my brother and went out on to the pavement.'

There, waiting for a car, was Mia. 'I said to her: "You can't take it either?" and she said, "No."'

'Right,' said André, 'let's go and have dinner.'

It was a busy time for André, busy even by his standards, which seemed to leave most people gasping for new dictionary definitions of the term. He was constantly in London now and when I interviewed him for the BBC in 1967 he told me: 'There's something about this place that calls to me.' It was not a typically Previn statement. The man who can trade one-liners with a stand-up comic was unusually poetic, but that was the effect the British capital had on him.

There was something else about London he liked. He certainly had no love affair with the Walthamstow Town Hall, but he was quite crazy about the orchestra with whom he mostly recorded there, the London Symphony Orchestra.

By this time, he had not only recorded with the LSO, he had already taken them on tour. Once in Brighton, he came to their rescue – and they in turn came to his, which was a fairly good sort of relationship to build up between orchestra and conductor. The piano soloist for that evening's concert in the British seaside resort – which had first come to fame when George IV as Prince Regent moved his Court down there – had gone sick and André decided to take over the part himself, conducting from the piano. Ronald Wilford wouldn't have approved, but it was a case of *force majeure* and there seemed little alternative. Besides, secretly, he rather fancied the idea.

As he got to the keyboard for the Mendelssohn first Piano Concerto, he felt very happy indeed. Here was really the best of both worlds – except that during the second movement when there is no orchestra to be heard and it is all up to the soloist, Previn forgot what he was supposed to be playing. In simple terms, he just couldn't remember which note came where.

So he played what he thought sounded like Mendelssohn and hoped no one would notice. The orchestra did notice, of course, but picked up the right cue to come in at the point which their conductor/soloist considered it safe to be rescued. At the end, they applauded. As he said: 'Every orchestra likes to see a conductor in trouble – but they get quite pleased when they see he knows how to get out of that little difficulty.'

Later on, a man in the audience congratulated André on his fine playing, but wanted to know which edition of the score he was using. Mental notes were made that day. André Previn and the LSO seemed to get on very well.

With them, he could not only play his favourite pieces – the English composers, in particular – but he could extend his repertoire and feel as if it were a mutually happy experience. If there is a need for good chemistry between orchestra and conductor, all the formulae were in place and, shaken together, produced the right results for the experiment.

The orchestra's manager – and there is some poignancy about this as we shall see towards the end of this story – Ernest Fleischmann, was particularly nice to André, smoothing out numerous problems that came up in the course of a fairly average season.

It was all auguring very well for their relationship.

In 1967, Roy Plumley who, along with the letters BBC themselves, was a British broadcasting tradition, invited André on to his long-running radio programme, 'Desert Island Discs' (Twenty-four years later and several years after his death, it is still running.)

On the programme in those days – the formula has remained unchanged, although there has been a certain concession since then to late twentieth-century technology – people were invited to imagine themselves shipwrecked on a desert island with nothing but eight records, a gramophone and 'an inexhaustible supply of needles'. Like the other castaways, André was asked to choose his favourite eight records – and then to fantasise perhaps a little more seriously: if someone gave him a magic wand to wave, which orchestra would he most want to have as his own?

'Every conductor worth his salt wants a large orchestra of his own one day,' said the show's compere. 'What's yours? Is it Philadelphia, Berlin, what?'

Without a moment's hesitation, he replied: 'Oh, the LSO. Absolutely no question about it.'

Like the thought of being washed up on some unknown desert island, which was a pipe dream of a different kind – he had to confess that he was the last person to be entrusted with building his own shelter or anything that could be remotely useful to getting away from the island – this was really pie in the sky. Such wishes just never did come true. As he told me, 'It was just as out of the question as would have been Philadelphia or Berlin.'

A few months later, he was in London for the odd concert and a few recordings. He was staying in the Savoy when a call from the hall porter came through to his suite.

The Chairman of the LSO, principal bass Stuart Knussen, accompanied by several other members of this self-governing orchestra, were downstairs and wondered if he could spare them a moment to talk. He invited them up, not knowing what they had in mind. They, on the other hand, wanted to waste no time in coming to the point: how would André like to become their principal director?

Whether this was a direct result of 'Desert Island Discs' no one can be sure, but what was certain was that his dream *was* coming true, perfectly and imminently.

It is important at moments like this not to betray too much enthusiasm. Like a woman receiving the marriage proposal she has wanted more than anything else in the world, there is a game to play – not unlike the way a conductor walks off the platform at the end of a piece; both he and the audience know he is going to come back again.

On this occasion, André made no pretence of requiring more wooing. But he tried manfully not to let his true emotions come to the surface. He managed to splatter out a statement that was as laid back as was humanly possible. 'At least, I hope I sounded that way.'

He said then, he now *thinks*, 'Well I would *quite* like that. Let's talk about it again, gentlemen.'

When they left, the need for being laid back had completely disappeared. 'I think,' he told me, 'I jumped over the furniture and screamed loudly. It was just exactly what I wanted.'

It was the beginning of what would be the longest tenure of any principal conductor the LSO has ever had.

If that proved that the orchestra liked André, it was nothing compared with his feelings at working with them. 'I couldn't believe my luck because musically speaking this was one of the great orchestras of the world. I could indulge my passion for English music which I had had for years – and I could legitimately say I was moving to England. So it was like three bull's-eyes with one shot.

'Again, it showed I have been unspeakably lucky in my timing. When my ambitions drove me out of Hollywood, I was not prescient enough to know that I had got off just in time, let alone to find the LSO wanting me.'

There couldn't have been a more appropriate choice to conduct a London orchestra than this still-young man, short, with a beak nose that had already become a favourite for caricaturists who noticed his arrival, and who – as if to demonstrate his familiarity with the British scene – now also boasted a Beatle haircut.

André Previn may have given up what was most people's idea of show business, he may have been seen now almost as a musical Establishment figure, but there was no reason for him to be old-fashioned. What was important was that he really was leading one of the world's great orchestras. As if anyone doubted it, he would say: 'I've always been an Anglophile.

'I had always wanted to live in London.' Now that he was able to put that into practice, as he said, 'legitimately', his pleasure was beyond bounds. But, he adds, 'It was unexpected to the tenth power.'

The idea of living in England was one of his priorities. 'Suddenly, I could go out and look for a country house.'

He found one in the heart of the Surrey countryside, between Dorking and Reigate, in a village called Leigh, which was pronounced 'Lie' and was more beautiful than either of the two towns. It was also next to the village cricket ground, which put him totally into the English way of things.

It meant a journey into London that could take an hour or two if the traffic were heavy. But the serenity of life was very evident indeed in England's green and pleasant land – quite a bit of which seemed to be at André's sole disposal. He had thirty acres of his own woodland, a swimming pool and a separate guest house. There were rooms where he could work, one with his own grand piano, and rooms where he could entertain.

But he was not going to live there alone now. Mia had come to be with him. In the meantime, they shared a small London flat, close to Harrods, that belonged to the top model of the day, Jean Shrimpton.

Ms Shrimpton was used to facing cameras, but Mia and André were in their focus every time they looked out of their windows. On one occasion, they actually saw a cameraman focusing on their living room from the top branches of a tree. It is fair to say that no conductor of the LSO had ever been such a target of the London gossip columns.

He was still married to Dory but with a home established and a new life mapped out for himself, there would inevitably be changes before long.

With Mia, the house and the new orchestra, life seemed idyllic. The BBC invited him to do a series of TV programmes which very closely resembled what Leonard Bernstein was doing in America. He explained music, the orchestra and some of the hitherto seemingly inpenetrable aspects of them both in laymen's terms to television viewers, many of whom hadn't even realised that they liked music until now.

He started gently by discussing American music and its relationship to jazz. Then he did a programme on film music, which was made-to-measure for the ratings. He moved to the composers – gently, again, beginning with Walton who, as an Englishman could be considered easy to digest. As most of the Americans who knew him at that time would testify, he proved instantly to be a perfect communicator. The figures for the television programmes soared – and, as a result, you could no more buy a ticket for an LSO concert without queueing or booking well in advance than you could get into the current stage sensation, *Hair*.

He made more records with the orchestra than he had ever done before – and they sold like the proverbial cakes newly removed from an oven. It was the perfect partnership.

He seemed to have an equally perfect partnership with other orchestras for whom he was now serving as guest conductor. He went to New York in March 1968, at the invitation of Leopold Stokowski, to conduct the American Symphony Orchestra at Carnegie Hall in a programme of Mozart, Beethoven, Nielsen and Ravel. 'No Gershwin, no Hollywood medley, no jazz, no show tunes,' noted Martin Bernheimer in the *New York Times*.

Hollywood seemed no problem in New York. It was never one with the Berlin Philharmonic. There, no one had even heard of the Academy Awards. But there were, of course, other considerations with Berlin.

That first visit in 1968 to his birthplace had to be traumatic. But with the orchestra, he quickly established a rapport – making the same jokes he made in London and Houston, but now in his native German.

He made one condition about appearing with the Berlin – supreme chutzpah if one couldn't appreciate the irony. He wanted the programme to be identical to the one he had heard at the very first concert he had attended with his father more than thirty years before – the Brahms pieces which had been conducted by Furtwängler, the *Tragic* Overture, the Violin Concerto and the Third Symphony.

Language helped. On a later visit, he met Herbert von Karajan, whom André believed to be the world's greatest conductor. When they met, von Karajan told Ronald Wilford: 'That man Previn is very interesting. Do you realise he speaks German better than I do!'

The first tour was an outstanding success, as have been all those that have followed.

Unlike his friend, the violinist Isaac Stern, who to this day refuses to go to Germany, André felt no such principle was at stake. Once there, he was comfortable enough – although, just as he knew he had wanted to buy a home in England, he was certain he had no desire to live there ever again.

But that wasn't relevant that cold, snowy day in 1968 when he took his nostalgic walk up to the pillar where his concert was being advertised.

'You have to come to grips with it, one way or another. You either have to say, like Isaac Stern, that that country does not exist or you put it out of your head because of the members of the Berlin Philharmonic – I doubt if there's even a handful of them who were around in the war years. You can't really hate everybody who holds a clarinet. That's not possible and they do happen to be one of the world's most amazing orchestras.'

But there were personal dimensions involved in his attitude. 'I live a very insular life that is governed by music,' he stresses. 'If it were not for the music, I wouldn't go to Germany. But if it weren't for the music, I wouldn't go to Holland either.'

Having said that, there are certain places where André is not comfortable in Germany. 'I am perfectly at home in Vienna and Salzburg, even though I know that during Hitler's time, they behaved in many ways – philosophically – even worse than the Germans. The Berliners have something that is very close to the New York sense of humour. I get very worried in Munich – even though it is very pretty – because you can walk down the street and see graffiti that takes you right back. And that's scary. I enjoy Nuremberg because it is quite beautiful, but on the other hand, I stayed in an hotel which is a couple of blocks from where the rallies were held and I did not like it *at all*.'

Ronald Wilford saw the emotions in Berlin. He walked with him along the Innsbrukerstrasse. 'It was hard. I remember we walked in the park where he used to go sledding. He was very introspective. He didn't talk much, but you could see he was in a deeply emotional state. He doesn't show his emotions, but I could tell he was deeply concerned and moved. How would his life have differed had he not moved? There's no question that it would have been very different indeed. I could feel him thinking, "What the hell was that in my life?" Musicians generally, because of their discipline, deal with things under their control – it is, for instance, the only way to play the piano.'

Wilford believes that there was an excorcism about the trip for André. He got his feelings out of his system, even those of a man who seemed to him at times so devoid of emotion. I asked Wilford if he was without temperament, because if he were, maybe that helped.

'Oh no. André is not without temperament. There isn't a man alive who's without temperament. He doesn't show it a lot, though. For him to get angry or to have a confrontation is very hard. He is extremely strong – although at times he is perceived as being weak because he doesn't like those confrontations.'

It would always be a problem for him, dealing with confrontations. He generally asked Wilford to deal with them for him.

'But,' as the manager told me, 'that's one thing a conductor *has* to deal with; how to discipline as well as confront. He is a collaborator with his musicians. He wants them to play better, but you can't scream at them. The days of Toscanini are over, the days when that man could fire an entire woodwind section.

'As a result, André can give in, instead of having a confrontation. But to do that, you can be perceived as weak. If so, then all conductors are weak, they all do it. They have to face entire orchestras, which inevitably contain people they can't get on with. What they all understand is that the music is more important than any one person.'

With every excitement attached to the Berlin Philharmonic and with each guest-conducting session with the orchestras of New York and Chicago, there was one wish that could never be fulfilled – that Jack Previn had still been alive to experience those emotions with him.

But the pleasures for him were immense. Not least, for all his successes with other people's orchestras, was the thrill of having those two 'bands' of his own. Thinking about them did marvels for his self-confidence. Except that things were not quite as smooth as they might have been.

The London orchestra members were impressed that he knew all their names and the instruments they played. He had gathered photographs and a chart and worked it all out before he appeared before them on the first day, rather like policemen on duty at the House of Commons at the start of a new Parliamentary session, who know all the new MPs. But after a few weeks, there were apparent difficulties over repertoire. They were recording a great deal of Vaughan Williams, so he played Vaughan Williams in concert. And there was a lot of Walton, too, mixed with a certain amount of Shostakovich.

But there was the feeling that audiences wanted more Mozart and more Brahms. The critics did, too. Their early reviews were nothing that André would have wanted to paste in his scrapbook - and he had to be grateful for his philosophy about the value of what the critics thought.

There was also that fairly enviable relationship between André and his orchestra members, who enjoyed his jokes in between the more serious instructions as much as did musicians anywhere. When the soccer World Cup games coincided with his concerts, he had arranged for television sets to be installed backstage for the musicians during the interval and for those who weren't playing during the concert itself.

It was not an ignored fact that he played to a full house that night, that people bought tickets and didn't stay home to watch the match during a fever-pitch few weeks when even people normally bored by football became fanatics.

In August 1968, he was back in Los Angeles, but a very different LA from the one he had known for so long. This time, he was conducting a concert of the Los Angeles Philharmonic at the Hollywood Bowl. It was a fairly mixed bill, Walton's *Portsmouth Point* Overture, Bernstein's 'Age of Anxiety' (which he had played so long before in the town) and Beethoven's Fifth Symphony.

Even now he couldn't get over the old tags. 'When André Previn first conducted the Los Angeles Philharmonic Orchestra in a "classical" concert about a year and a half ago,' wrote Winifred Blevins in the city's *Herald Examiner*, 'he was fighting an annoying problem of image . . .' By saying that it no longer existed, Miss Blevins was confirming the very opposite. But she conceded that he did well – better than the orchestra, she said – although 'Previn's approach to Beethoven seemed rooted in the concepts of Furtwängler, yet it had far too much logic to be imitative. Tempos were deliberate . . . The effect was large-scale drama.'

But it was in Houston that he was still spending most of his time while in America. His contract was in force, although he now wished that perhaps it were not. He was beginning to outgrow the Texas city.

'I loved the orchestra, hated the city,' is how he puts it.

Not that he was totally excused from the charm routine with the LSO either – at least, not when he was on tour.

With the London orchestra and Vladimir Ashkenazy as soloist, he toured the United States to a superb response wherever they went. But nothing compared with the trip to Daytona, Florida, an outpost not known for its thirst for musical, or any other kind of culture – except as an adjunct to the social scene.

Ashkenazy 'could not accept,' André recalls, 'the American habit of receptions, as I couldn't either, although he has got more urbane about it in the years since then.'

This particular evening, neither of them could stand the prospect of meeting Daytona society, especially when they approached the entrance to the reception room and saw the hundreds of members of the civic gentry established there – 'men in white jackets and the ladies in silver shoes'.

If it aroused, at the very best, feelings of indifference in André, it was the high point of the Daytona festival – and both the orchestra and the festival management begged the two most prestigious personalities taking part to go, too.

'Vova [Ashkenazy's nickname] took one look at who was going in and said that he would no way be a part of it. 'Forget it,' he said.

'I felt very much the same way.'

Both were tired after a rigorous, if happily rewarding, evening's playing. André, while accepting his friend and colleague's reservations, thought that to attend was important for public relations and not to go could be conceived as bad manners in a part of the world where manners were frequently more important than mere ethics.

'I'll tell you what Vova,' André told him, 'these people were all at the concert, but I'm sure they didn't look. So why don't you be me and I'll be you?'

'You'll never get away with it,' said the Russian.

'Well, let's try it,' André suggested, without thinking too deeply about the consequences of playing games on these far too self-important people. Was an insult better than staying away? André convinced his friend to take the plunge.

With that, he took Ashkenazy's wife on his arm and introduced himself, as they went into the chandelier-lit reception hall, as the Russian pianist. Ashkenazy shook hands with his hosts and said he was Mr Previn.

Not only did André escort Mrs Ashkenazy on his arm, he also affected a superb Russian accent – 'the fact that Vova had the same accent made no difference; no one seemed to care.

'We had the most wonderful time. Nobody – not a single person – twigged.' The orchestra members present had been forewarned and promised not to spoil the joke.

'We stayed about half an hour, trying desperately not to roll over on the floor in laughter, having done our bit for those people who thought we were being extremely charming and never found out.'

It was not only a fun evening, but proved something that André had himself long suspected. 'In America, at least, I very often think that at a festival or the beginning of the season, it is the party which means most. It's just that you have to go to a concert first.'

Of course, even serious orchestras with international reputations like letting off steam. André had by now established his principle of travelling with his fellow musicians in the same plane, lining up with them for coffee in mugs or polystyrene cups. He tells them jokes, laughs at their stories and, with his closest friends among the players, goes out to eat. Sometimes, he will go to their homes.

He likes to enjoy what they enjoy. It's part of what could be called pompously – but which he himself would not call it – the team spirit. He loves, for instance, to tell the story of the time a member of the LSO on tour sloped away from the rest of the ensemble to see an X-rated movie. Had one of his colleagues not seen him do it, no one would have known about it. But he did – and told the rest of the orchestra. When the hapless man left the seedy cinema, there was a welcoming party waiting for him – instruments at the ready playing a fanfare. But these were isolated incidents in the totally serious business of keeping two orchestras going.

His fellow musicians seemed to think he was doing a good job, particularly the soloists.

Dame Janet Baker joined André several times during her own singing career, starting with Houston. She sang the Mozart Mass in C as well as big symphonic pieces. There was a lot of Mahler performed by the orchestra and she and André had hit it off well enough for him to welcome her as one of his favourite sopranos, particularly for the final movement of the Second Symphony. Not that there was not an instant of apprehension for the singer at first.

'I was aware,' she told me, 'of his reputation as a ladies' man. I wondered what he would come on like.'

How he 'came on' was as 'a serious, knowledgable, kind man. He never put a foot wrong. I was a bit wary, but it was one of the most enjoyable human experiences of my career.'

It was a relief because what she knew of him she found 'overwhelming. He had such kudos and power. You wonder what it's going to be like for you. With other conductors, big power means big ego – and often a lot of cruelty. With André, what came was kindness and total respect for what he did. He did his homework. Sometimes you felt for him as a mentor, because he did so well know his stuff. There are some who use their music as a vehicle. With him, it was the music which came first.'

She highlighted something that was extremely relevant to his career and his place in music. André was of a generation of American conductors which was unlike any that had gone before. 'There was Bernstein who had a style all his own and there was Previn, more reserved than Lenny, just as experienced in both popular and classical music, but, unlike Bernstein, anxious to put his popular days behind him.'

On the other hand, Janet Baker's experience had been with maestros like Klemperer and Szell, and we know how Szell treated the young upstart. The Simon Rattles and the Michael Tilson Thomases hadn't been invented yet.

'Here was someone,' she said, 'with a total grasp of music, but with a human quality.' He totally turned round for her the image of the conductor/soloist relationship.

Even at that stage of his career, there was prejudice against him. 'He was suspect,' Dame Janet thinks. And the television series which had helped bridge the gap between music and public worked against him in certain serious-music circles. 'The quality of his performance was unquestionable, but there were those who regarded him as a showman – despite those indescribable performances.'

He joined her at a recital at the Chandler Pavilion in Los Angeles. She sang and he accompanied her. 'For a man of his status to do that was quite remarkable, but he didn't think anything of it.'

But that sort of thing tended to reduce his credibility in some eyes. As Dame Janet also remembers: 'I met some very snobby people in San Francisco and mentioned his name – and they laughed. They couldn't see it.'

But she saw it from the podium, seeing how he played as that accompanist. 'Only great musicians have the ability to anticipate what I'm going to do. He must have anticipated my musical thoughts only a fraction of a moment before I did what I did. But he was aware of what I was thinking – things that had not even been thought about in rehearsal. Now, you need a very experienced and sharp musician to be able to do that.'

She didn't ask him to accompany her. She happened to mention that she was going to Los Angeles. He looked at his schedule and said, 'Would you like me to play for you?' As she says, 'He was self-effacing to a degree. He just put himself at my service. Because he could do that, we felt absolute equals. I thought he would impose – as a conductor, of course, he does. But as an accompanist for me as a singer he let me dictate what I needed.'

There is the possibility that he worked with her so easily because Dame Janet is a woman and a very attractive one at that. 'He understands women,' she concedes. 'Women like him, but feel that he treats them as equals. Some accompanists won't give you space – psychologically, that is. They want to prove they are your equals. André Previn had nothing to prove.'

It was the sort of professional relationship that could only be good for two highly professional people. Not long afterwards, the British writer and historian John Julius Norwich asked Janet Baker to take part in a charity concert he was organising in aid of raising money for 'Venice In Peril'. She thought about the request and said that she would do it if André would accompany her.

André not only agreed to do it, he said he would write something for her. That 'something' turned into a song cycle set to the poems of Philip Larkin – another of the profound English influences of this time on André's life and career. 'I was delighted and honoured,' said Dame Janet. 'It never occurred to me to suggest such a thing. But he was perfect. He didn't fall into the trap of overpowering the words. There's a simplicity about them which allows the poems to speak. They speak because he allows them to – again a question of respect for another artist.'

The British guitarist John Williams felt much the same sort of relationship with André. He met him at Houston in 1968 when he was on an American tour. Williams played the *Rodrigo* Concerto while André conducted. 'We got on wonderfully well,' he told me. 'I liked his style and personality from the moment I met him. I can look at someone like André and say, "There's a real musician!"'

About two or three days later, André came to him with a suggestion: 'Why don't I write a guitar concerto for you?'

Sometimes, the professional relationship became a social one, too, as it did between Janet Baker and André. They met socially on numerous occasions – Dame Janet with her husband/manager Keith Shelly, he with Mia. 'He was so glamorous, but a very private human being. He was one of the people I really loved. There are not many of those in this profession.'

Mia meanwhile was pregnant – with twins.

André was glad that he had bought the house at Leigh. 'It's a great place to bring up a child,' he said before he realised that there would be two children. Mia, who had gone off for a time to her home on Martha's Vineyard off Cape Cod, said that she was announcing the impending birth only to stifle rumour, but she was very happy and was coming over to Britain soon.

Mia's mother went on record saying that she thought the whole business was too personal to discuss. On the other hand, Miss O'Sullivan could understand very little about the way the world was revolving in this new era. She remembered fondly, she told André, how she was taken by limousine the hundred yards from her dressing room to the sound stage. And when her daughter announced that she was making her film with Dustin Hoffman, her remarks of disdain for the man's distinctly unstarlike appearance would – had anyone heard them – have made the gossip columns all over the world, to say nothing of the front pages of *Daily Variety* or the *Hollywood Reporter*.

The relationship with Mia didn't please the people at Houston, who had, in any case, been bristling at some of André's attitudes. He wanted to improve the standard of the orchestra, to turn Houston itself into a centre for the arts.

They wanted another Sir John Barbirolli, who just played the kind of music they had liked to hear and had not wanted the experiments André had in mind. Houston was not the place for experimentation.

FIFTEEN

André was not loving Houston and by nearly all accounts, Houston wasn't loving him. The orchestra members, on the whole, enjoyed the way André conducted, but although he was observing the letter of his contract, the board of management thought that he was concentrating too much on London – both on the LSO and on his personal life in Britain.

Linking his name with Mia Farrow, particularly after the announcement of the pregnancy, only heightened their lack of affection for him. Mia represented the notoriety of the Swinging Sixties and nothing was allowed to swing in the music circles of Houston. Every time Mia got into the newspapers – and she was such hot news at this time, that she could fill the front pages of the tabloids by just stepping off an aircraft – it was reason to complain to their Mr Previn who, unaccountably, took the young lady's part and couldn't see what the fuss was about.

When it was revealed that Dory had tried to fly to London – but was too scared to make the trip once she had got on the plane – the tut-tuts from Houston got louder. The board used every piece of evidence they had to complain about the behaviour of their musical director. When he suggested that the orchestra ought to play in the less well-heeled areas around Houston itself, the noise made by the bosses rivalled the sound of the French horns in rehearsal. The orchestra didn't exist for 'that type of person'.

A quickie divorce was called for and André had two at around the same time – from Dory and from Houston.

The twin boys were born to Mia in February 1970, Matthew Phineas and Sascha Villers. 'We are both terribly happy and terribly proud,' André told newsmen. His divorce followed soon afterwards. 'Irreconcilable differences' were cited as the reason.

211

In September that year, André and Mia were married at a Unitarian church in Hampstead. Both Lotte and Maureen O'Sullivan were present.

Dory, meanwhile, who had written that since André had gone she had been 'cancelled out' by God, tried to unravel her 'cancelling out' by doing more writing – and continued to see the people who had been their mutual friends. Julie Andrews saw her from time to time. 'I think it was very hard for her all the time Mia was around,' she told me.

Running his orchestras and writing more compositions continued to occupy André's time to a degree that others less schooled in the affairs of professional conductors might have thought excessive.

Because it was the heyday of classical recording, the LSO's output was huge, making something like eighteen records a year, 'which for a symphony orchestra is unbelievable. But those times were different.

'I was on television in one guise or another, either in my programmes or conducting the orchestra, for many, many years practically every week. So our records sold well and I'd just ring up EMI and say, "Listen we're doing such-and-such piece in a fortnight's time and it should be good, let's record it" – they'd say, "Fine."

'Today, there isn't a hope in hell of doing the same thing because they're much too concerned to putting it in the computer to see how many copies they'd sell in Azerbaijan. It's just hopeless.'

Ernest Fleischmann was no longer in charge. He had left the orchestra before André's appointment and was replaced by Harold Lawrence. Under his management and with André as principal conductor – there wasn't much difference between that post and the title of music director, which didn't exist in LSO terms – the orchestra had never been busier. Concerts at the Royal Festival Hall, concerts all over Britain, concerts in Europe, concerts on world tours. 'And by that I really do mean world tours. We'd be away for six weeks at a stretch and I didn't even have an assistant along. So the working ties and the personal ties were very tight.'

He enjoyed that principal conductor/musical director role. 'The great advantage of it is that, musically, I can have any soloist I want. If I hear someone who is beautifully gifted, I have the right to give them dates. It's the same with repertoire, I get to choose it.'

In fact, a musical director is responsible for what he likes to call 'the musical welfare' of his orchestra. 'He has to be involved in their comings and goings in their problems, in the direction they are going, what to record, where to tour and mainly in his absence, who's going to be there, what are they going to play. That's the same in Grimsby

– if there's a Grimsby Philharmonic – as it is in Berlin.'

But it took a long time before he did the job properly. In fact, he says he accepts that he was 'lousy' doing it both at Houston and with the LSO. 'I was just too young at the time.'

But it wasn't merely a matter of power and responsibility. 'I went to the LSO and was thrown into the deep end. In America or on the continent, if they do a programme, depending on the size of the orchestra, they do it three, four or five times each. Well, by the time they have rehearsed a piece and then done it five times in a row, it's really locked into your subconscious memory after a while. But with an orchestra in Britain, it isn't like that. They do a programme usually just once. One off. Therefore, in those palmy days of the LSO, it was not unusual for us to do three different programmes *a week*.

'I would study just to keep ahead. I didn't have the trunk of material I have at my disposal today. Nowadays, if I have a new piece to learn of some difficulty, whether it's a new piece to me or just written, it's very easy for me to organise a programme which has within it, Beethoven, Brahms, Schubert, Mozart, Tchaikovsky, Schumann. It's quite easy because I just take them out and relook at them. But in those days, it was just as likely I would have to learn a standard piece as learn a brand new one. It almost drove me crazy, but I kept it up. I got away with it, some good and some bad. But at the same time, I didn't have the discipline to say, "Right, because I haven't learned it, I won't do the piece."'

Actually to tell the orchestra, 'I'd rather not conduct that piece gentlemen, because I need more time to think about it – I didn't have the courage to do it. I did a lot of pieces before I should have done them.'

Perhaps fortunately for him – and for his relations with his orchestra – he didn't either say so or know to say so at the time. 'The reason I know it now is that I take up scores that I marked then and think what a balls-up I made at the time I first did them.'

The Beethoven Fifth Symphony is fairly typical of the change of Previn approach from the late 1960s and early 1970s to today. 'When I looked at it again, I wondered why I had my six-year-old son's copy of this. There was a lot in it which showed I hadn't really examined it.' Suddenly, he found himself in the role of his old tutors at the conservatories, with André Previn as his student.

On the other hand, such memories have advantages. 'Because there was a lot in it that I thought was dumb – just from not really, really, examining it – I take it as rather a good sign that I'm not happy with

213

past performances.'

Sometimes, nevertheless, the situation is reversed. He can listen to recordings his memory told him were terrible, but which don't sound nearly so bad all those years later.

Even André has difficulty sometimes in recognising his own work. He would like to think that he could do so. 'Yeh, probably – but as an appendage there are a lot of pieces that you make up in order to fill in the time, and very often I don't remember having conducted them, much less recorded them. Sometimes, when I hear a piece on the radio and they say that it was me, I have to stop and think and very often say, "I don't remember doing that." I don't usually recognise a piece the way a singer will recognise his own voice.'

But his own judgments on its quality he tends to respect, as he does those of colleagues. What he does not respect is the opinion of record reviewers – any more now in the 1990s than he did in those fledgling days a quarter of a century earlier. 'I am convinced,' he told me '– and if I had nothing else to do, there's a game I'd like to play – that if one sent a pile of records to a group of reviewers and switched the labels around, they wouldn't know any different. It's the impossible dream. One month, I'd like all the reviewers of all the records all over the world to be sent the same records with mixed-up labels and you'd get the biggest cock-up ever. It's so funny. Let's say Giulini makes a record of a Beethoven symphony and nine out of ten reviewers will say, "A typically sunny Italianate version of . . ." Absolute total nonsense. There isn't a syllable of truth in that – or that a German does a German version, an English conductor does a restrained version and an American does a super-rhythmic version. I swear to you that there isn't a musician who doesn't make fun of that. If these people were told the wrong conductors, they wouldn't know what the – they were talking about.'

On the whole, his series of recordings of all the Vaughan Williams symphonies, which began in 1967, got the sort of reviews he would have enjoyed – if he had bothered about such things. Recording the cycle would continue until 1972. They were an ambitious set, which are sometimes criticised for that alone. The 'Sinfonia Antartica', his Seventh Symphony, for instance, had narration by Sir Ralph Richardson, which is held by some to be over the top.

He included in the series 'filler' pieces of other Vaughan Williams works, like the *Three Portraits* from his 'England of Elizabeth' on the same disc as the Ninth Symphony.

Sir William Walton still loved André's work. After a performance of *Belshazzar's Feast* in March 1971, André asked the composer to inscribe his score for him. Walton wrote: 'André, King of Kings.'

The following day was Walton's seventieth birthday. His gift from André and the LSO was to go to watch them recording the *Feast*. To do so, the composer kept Ted Heath waiting. The then Prime Minister had invited him to Downing Street as his own commemoration of the day, but he insisted on going to the studio first.

When André conducted Walton's *Portsmouth Point* and the Vaughan Williams 'London' Symphony with the New York Philharmonic, Harold C. Schonberg noted in the *New York Times*: 'Mr Previn has developed into an important conductor. Certainly, he had the Philharmonic musicians responding to his clear beat and when the Philharmonic boys put out, superb orchestra playing results.'

The same critic hadn't been quite so understanding of André's Mozart at an American Symphony Orchestra concert. He described it as 'heavy-handed'. And when Ashkenazy joined André for an LSO performance at Carnegie Hall, the writer was less than effusive. 'Mr Previn has a mighty fine orchestra with which to work,' he wrote. But as for his conducting: 'Mr Previn, talented though he may be, is still in the process of learning his trade.' There had been some improvement, he thought. 'But Mr Previn as yet has not put his imprint on the music. Right now, he seems to be more concerned with basics and there is not much feeling of personality to his work. [He gave] Ashkenazy a tidy accompaniment in the Beethoven G Major but not good enough to meet with the pianist on equal emotional and intellectual terms.'

In London, the *Observer* would say much the same sort of thing and then its anonymous writer added: 'Being principal conductor of the London Symphony Orchestra is like walking on a hundred razor blades. Previn's lack of authority in large areas of repertoire meant that he often learned things too fast and skated through rehearsals.'

André's rehearsals were, in fact, operated to the same extreme timetable that had been the secret of so much of his success.

'All I ask,' he told Martin Bernheimer in the *New York Times*, 'is that people listen and try to understand. The worst possible reaction is boredom. I prefer boos to polite applause . . . No work is scheduled for shock appeal.'

On the other hand, what André was working on now did provide a few shocks. He had proclaimed to the world that the, as he put it, 'boy wonder thing is over'. But then he announced he was going back into show business. It wasn't quite breaking his word to Ronald Wilford. He wasn't working on a new film and he would not only continue to conduct, it would dominate his life. His schedule was immutable. But in between, he was working on a big lavish Broadway musical – *Coco*.

Late in 1966, André had announced that he and Alan Jay Lerner were going to co-operate on a Broadway show of that name, but the world of theatre goers – as anxious, it would later turn out, to put their money into the box office as a child to buy a bar of chocolate – had to wait until December 1969 before they could see it.

Between those two dates, three years of hilarious anarchy and creation, André sat with Lerner and played the role of partner that had been occupied for so long and so successfully by Fritz Loewe.

The Lerner and Previn collaboration would turn out to be nothing like as durable as the previous one Lerner and Loewe set up. It wouldn't last as long nor be anything like as successful. Yet, just the same, their show would run for a respectable year or more. 'It just wasn't very good,' says André today.

But that is a subjective judgment. A Broadway show that jumps the twelve-month barrier – even the twelve-*day* barrier – had something going for it. What *Coco* had was Katharine Hepburn in the title role and huge advance bookings. It also had a gestation period that neither André nor the other people close to him will quickly forget.

If André's early story could have been crafted by Arthur Miller, this one was a gift for Neil Simon.

The first announcement of the show came in July 1966.

The story of Paris couturier Coco Chanel was to be a combination of elaborate costumes by Cecil Beaton, music by Previn and book and lyrics by Lerner.

My Fair Lady and *Gigi* had proved that he and Lerner would get on now that Fritz Leowe had retired. Beaton was a different matter, although the links between composer and designer were mercifully few. When André and Beaton met soon after work got under way, the older man called over to his colleague, 'André, darling boy, how *are* you?'

'Why, Cecil, are you being so nice to me?' André asked. 'You used to ignore me.'

'Ah,' Beaton replied, 'you weren't famous then.'

Now, however, he most certainly was famous and Lerner and he got on with the job knowing full well it would never have been entrusted to a pair of songwriters who were anything but that.

His relationship with Alan Lerner was quite remarkable. 'If he had said "Let's do the phone book," I'd have considered it.' They began as friends and finished much the same way.

They had, however, an unusual technique. At first, it was difficult to get the two men together. One was working on one thing, the other on something else. André was quoted at the time as saying, 'It seems to me that we wrote *Coco* by screaming at each other as we passed in airports.'

When one of the pair didn't like something the other one had written, he would disarm him with politeness. Their code was to say simply, 'It fits.' As André said, 'That meant, "It's a piece of crap."'

One thing, for certain, that you can't ask André is the familiar question, 'Which comes first the music or . . .' It's such a cliché that professionals don't even like considering it. But in this case, it was the . . .

'He was a pleasure to write with,' says André, 'because his enthusiasm and his veneration of the theatre was so real and was so sweet. But it took him longer to finish a lyric than it took an elephant to have a baby. Alan would finish a song with the exception of two lines and then not hand it in until he had finished those lines – which could be months. Whether that was simply a subconscious attempt to keep the songs to himself, I don't know.' (While *Gigi* was being made, Arthur Freed had actually asked André to take the duplicate key he had managed to get to Lerner's hotel room and go in and fetch out the lyric he knew he had been hiding there for weeks: André refused.)

Lerner himself, in his book, *The Street Where I Live*, tells the story of André's songwriting technique. One day, Previn was sitting down – when his partner played the piano, Lerner said he did so with an expressionless face 'and one has the feeling that someone else's arms are reaching from behind him and doing the playing' – talking to him as they discussed a song they were planning to write. André would talk and appear to doodle as he did so. Part of the time he was joking or telling some anecdote or other – and still doodling. Finally, the conversation came to an end. André stopped doodling and handed the paper on which he had been making those effortless scribbles to his lyricist. In that time and while the laughing and joking proceeded unhindered, André had written a song. 'There would be no point to this story,' wrote Lerner, 'if it were a bad song, but it happened to be a very good one and became one of the highlights of the play.'

André described his working arrangements with Alan Lerner like this: 'He would give me a lyric. I would go into a corner of a room and give him a piece of paper and say, "Here's the song." And then he'd say to me, "Don't you ever need to go to a piano?" When I replied, "No," he said it scared him.'

Lerner, though, could always recognise the strength of the piano part he had been handed, because unlike most lyricists he had a good musical knowledge. One of his favourite games was Identifying the Melody. André would scribble a few bars from a classical piece on a scrap of paper and Lerner would be delighted to be able to call out, 'The Thieving Magpie' or whatever it was. They did that together the way other friends told each other jokes. But then they'd do that, too.

There would be many other highlights of writing the play, a blend of professionalism and sheer fun.

During the time that André was working with Lerner, Dodging The Wife became a serious occupation for them both, with Lerner doing the dodging and Previn playing a rearguard action on his behalf.

'He was the most incredible womaniser,' André remembered. They worked together during the marriage spans of three wives, so he feels happy about telling this story without risking identifying the particular wife about whom he is talking. 'They'll never know to which one it refers,' he says disarmingly.

One morning, while they were sitting around working, André spotted the Mrs Lerner of the day walking towards the house. Quickly, Alan whispered to André: 'You were in Paris for the weekend.'

'Hello, darling,' he then said in his most nonchalant, *My Fair Lady* way.

She returned the greeting and then turned to her guest: 'Hello, André,' she said. 'How was Paris?'

'Oh,' he stammered. 'Fine.'

'Where did you stay?'

'From then on,' he now recalls, 'we went into this most phenomenal fantasy.'

When the woman left, André told his partner: 'Alan, I don't mind. But why didn't you tell me?'

Lerner and Previn were doing a lot of evening work at André's apartment. One night, they worked until about ten o'clock when Alan left, ostensibly to go home.

André read for a short while and then went to sleep. At about three o'clock, the phone rang. From the depth of his slumbers, André heard a woman's voice. 'Hi, I'm Alan's wife. Can I speak to him, please?'

The next few minutes would certainly have pleased Neil Simon. 'I came awake like a shot,' André told me.

'Oh, um,' he stammered – as anyone would at that time of the night, 'you know how it is, we got ourselves in such a bind. You know Alan, he doesn't like the one line he's written and we've been at it for so long, he's gone out for a walk to clear his head. And I'm waiting for him to get back.'

'Gee boys,' she replied, 'you're working so late. Look, I'm up now for the night, have him call me when he gets back.'

She hung up. 'I thought . . . Now what?'

The only thing he could think of was to ring the stage manager of the show and tell him there was an emergency. 'I want you to give me two phone numbers,' he said.

'I was thinking of the two most likely girls.'

The stage manager was totally nonplussed. 'Are you kidding, Mr Previn? It's three-thirty in the morning.'

'Do this for me,' said André. The stage manager showed the requisite amount of sympathy. He gave him two phone numbers. The first one called answered directly. 'I'm sorry to have to do this,' he told the young lady who answered. 'I know it's unbelievable, but please put Alan on for me . . .'

'Alan who?' she asked.

'Don't let's kid around, dear,' he replied. 'You know which Alan I mean. There's no time for this. Trust me. Put him on.'

There was a long, long wait. Then came the voice he had hoped to hear. 'Hello . . .'

'Alan,' said Previn, 'Your wife called half an hour ago. And you're out for a walk because you couldn't find the line to finish the bridge of the song we're working on. Call her when you get back to me.'

The next morning at the theatre, he gave André a hug, which is not the usual greeting for the frequently phlegmatic-looking Previn: 'What do you want?' he asked him. 'A Rolls Royce? My life insurance? Thank you.'

'Alan,' said André. 'I don't mind. But tell me.'

Plainly, they liked each other very much. 'I was terribly fond of Alan. He had a great sense of humour and had tremendous talent.'

But he had his quirks, and quirks that he himself knew all about. Almost on the first day on which they started working on *Coco*, André said: 'Alan, I've got something to tell you, privately, but I'd really appreciate it if you'd keep it a secret.'

'Well, don't tell it to me,' he said quite seriously and very defensively.

'But we're partners,' said André.

'Yes,' said Lerner, 'that's why I don't want you to tell me. It's because I like you, I don't want you to tell me. I absolutely can't keep a secret and if you tell me one I won't be able to wait for you to leave so that I can get on the phone and tell it to everybody.'

'I really can't believe that,' André replied. 'If I tell you that I'm going to tell you something that's really important to me . . .'

'Don't,' he said. 'Trust me.' Trust him, in fact, not to be trusted. And André says he was 'absolutely charmed' by that. 'A dear, dear man – but totally eccentric.'

So eccentric that one day he suggested that he and Previn get hold of a miniature submarine and go exploring – for the missing city of Atlantis.

'Don't laugh,' he told André, 'I'm totally serious.' André laughed.

'Don't laugh,' he said again, 'but I think I have got a pretty good handle as to where Atlantis is.'

'Uh huh,' said André.

'No, hear me out,' he said. 'You know my uncle, the oceanographer who has this laboratory in Florida. Now, we go down there and get one of those two-man submarines that the Navy has and we'll go and look for Atlantis and we can work on the show while we're doing it.'

'W . . . e . . . l . . . l . . . ,' said André, 'OK, but who's driving? You have one eye and can't remember from one second to another what's happening and I can't be trusted behind the wheel of a car. So who's driving this two-man submarine?'

Lerner had to think about that one. 'Well, there are slightly bigger ones. We'll get someone to run it for us.'

That problem out of the way, André Previn, always prepared for the unexpected, like a solo violinist's string breaking in the midst of the Mendelssohn Concerto or a percussionist dropping his cymbal, raised another little matter that could possibly just make a difference to a wonderful plan.

'Let's then take this scenario a little further,' he said. 'It's one which you, as a playwright, will like. We're off writing and rewriting a scene for Katharine Hepburn and suddenly we find Atlantis. By God, we find Atlantis! We turn the sub around and we land in Florida and you get out and you say, "Hi – I'm Alan Lerner. I'm a playwright. I wrote *My Fair Lady* and I've just found Atlantis." They're going to be smuggling you files in cakes for the next twenty years.'

'Oh,' he said, 'you think they won't believe us?'

'No,' said André, 'I'm sure they won't believe *you*.'

'He really hadn't thought that one out. He was wild. But charming and delightful.'

Actually, there could never have been any suggestion of the two men working together as a second Lerner and Loewe. Lerner and Previn wasn't on the cards because of the way Alan liked to work. 'He demanded – and he had a right to demand – total, utter allegience to the theatre, which Fritz Loewe gave him. But I couldn't give him that. Leonard Bernstein, who also worked on a show with him, *1600 Pennsylvania Avenue*, couldn't do it either.'

Lerner expected André to be in the theatre every night during the previews and the out-of-town try-outs and to go to meetings afterwards. 'Every time you go into town, if it's still running, you go in and take copious notes and you correct things. I couldn't do that. Which is probably why he had such huge hits and I didn't.'

The fact that the show didn't do at all badly had little to do with the quality of *Coco*, André believes. 'It wasn't a very good show.' Which was why it never came to England.

It wasn't the *Coco* André told me he envisaged. 'I set out to write that show like a tiny French piece with little chansons in it, like a cabaret. I was hoping to have a seven-piece orchestra. But we ended up with Cecil Beaton, a million dollars-worth of costumes, four turntables and a huge orchestra. The whole thing got out of shape because basically the show isn't about anything except clothes. So I didn't believe in the show.'

It was, he said at the time, 'a Sherman tank with music. All those big guns going off. It got to be quite impossible but I kept my mouth shut and learned a lot.'

For most of the period in which the show was being conceived, written, changed, adapted, playing out of town, André was fitting in other work. He was conducting – sixty concerts had been scheduled for the 1966-7 season – but not what he would call 'all the time'. That is, one has to realise, a relative thought and one that has to be filed under the name 'Previn'. His ideas of hard work make a day's stint as a stevedore seem like a game of tennis. 'I had lots of spare time.'

But there could never have been any doubt about doing it. He may not have really agreed to orchestrate the phone book any more than he would have gone looking for Atlantis, but with Alan asking him, there would have had to be a split-second's consideration. 'And I'll tell you anybody interested in songwriting for the theatre at that point, if Alan Lerner had asked him or her to write a show, he would have done it.'

Perhaps only *Phantom of the Opera*, a generation later, had more pre-opening publicity. 'The advance booking was tremendous and the name Alan Lerner was huge box office. He and I had our names in lights with letters the same size as Hepburn's.'

Commercially, the great success was in getting Hepburn to play Coco, even though at sixty she had never sung a song on stage in her life. Chanel herself approved her choice. It was a tough role for her. Not only had she not sung on stage before – she did a Rex Harrison for the numbers – but she was behind the footlights for all but eighteen minutes of the two-and-a-half-hour show.

'She was very nice to me,' André remembered. 'Like a lot of people who have a reputation for being tough and strong, if she thought you knew what you were doing, she was fine. She was impatient with frauds, and I'm all for that. She was impatient of fans, which I thought was unnecessarily harsh of her.'

He didn't consult her about her tunes. 'Alan Lerner had done so well with Rex Harrison that he knew what to do now.'

Financially, it was a success, without any doubt. But Katharine Hepburn in the title role, reciting the songs, was what did it. She also helped the road company no little bit either by starring in the touring version as well. When she left Broadway, her role was taken over by the French film actress Danielle Darrieux, who was sexy and beautiful and had a delightful singing voice, which Miss Hepburn did not have. 'It was the first time I had heard my songs sung properly in a year,' says André – 'and the show closed.'

But no one thought in terms of closure when the starting date was first announced. Word of what Hepburn would be doing got around before the opening. An advertisement in the Sunday edition of the *New York Times* taking up less than an eighth of a page read simply: 'COCO. Box office opens tomorrow at 10 a.m. for the new musical.' Underneath that in small letters was the name and address of the Mark Hellinger theatre. By seven-thirty the following morning, there were already long lines of people outside the building waiting for tickets. By noon that day, the queue had covered two blocks, stretched far down Broadway and had started doubling back on itself.

Even before that, it had taken $1,500,000 in advance sales from ticket agencies – which was not at all bad considering the fact that it cost $900,000 to put on, a huge amount for November 1969. (André's figure of a million dollars for the costumes is something of an overstatement, but the hyperbole does fit into the overall picture.)

Critical reaction for *Coco* was *Soso*. The anonymous reviewer for *Time* magazine wrote: 'The Lerner script makes a stab at smart-set language, but at heart *Coco* is an old-fashioned musical. It stands or falls on its star and its music. Of the eighteen Lerner-Previn songs, eight are Kate's, full of self-doubt, self-confidence, self-satisfaction and self-recollection. Previn has played a schmaltzy Loewe to Lerner's Lerner.'

His own final reaction: 'The show sank under all those costumes. I kept thinking that Alan must know what he was doing, so I just did what he asked me to do, which was wrong. There were some parts of the score which were very nice.'

On the whole, André did not enjoy the sheer mechanics of writing a show any more than he liked the result of *Coco*. 'It takes too long. I couldn't stay interested. It's my fault. It's a failing in me. It takes X amount of weeks to work on a score for a musical. To work on a piece of light, restrictive music for the best part of a year and keep worrying and nursing it and fixing it, I just got bored with it. Which means I am not really cut out to write for the musical theatre – although I like writing for the theatre, like the atmosphere. I just think it takes too long.'

Nevertheless, it was about this time that Lerner was preparing *Paint Your Wagon*, the hit show he had written with Fritz Loewe, for its movie version and, now that Loewe was no longer available, asked André to write a couple of songs for the picture. The result were two in a distinctly Western mould – which is not bad for the man who says: 'I have done everything in music except, I think, play in a Hillbilly band'. They were 'The Gospel of No Name City', which was a kind of sing-along and 'The Best Things Are', a slightly more romantic number.

He was appearing on television, and recording other composers, like Mendelssohn (the 'Italian' Symphony) and Prokofiev (The Fifth Symphony). The records followed on or coincided with concert programmes that contained the works, prarticularly on an American tour.

Later, with Ashkenazy, he recorded all Rachmaninov's and Prokofiev's concertos and piano compositions. The most critically praised of these were Rachmaninov's First and Second Concertos.

Newsweek magazine had in 1966 described André as 'a fiendish worker' and quoted him saying: 'I like to hear everything that's on the page, plus all the unobvious rhythms – the kind of pulse, especially in music, that doesn't seem obviously rhythmic.

It was much the same case now in the early 1970s. He was doing what he was doing simply because of that management of time. He never wasted it. Yet every sour note was quickly corrected. He wouldn't allow a horn to play a quaver if it was a crotchet that was required.

There are musicians today – and at this time there were more still – who thought of him, in the famous phrase referring to the late British Conservative politician, Iain Macleod – as being too clever by half. They resented still a Hollywood composer who had four Oscars, who was outstanding on television, a highly successful jazz man who had sold a million copies of a show record and who now had two orchestras of his own.

John Williams said he saw it frequently enough. 'I think that one of the reasons is that people find him cold – I certainly don't; I find him a little shy and retiring – and complain about not being able to get close to him. On the other hand, he sometimes over-compensates because his mind works so much faster than most other people's possibly can. He actually finds it difficult to fit everything in at the time.'

There was no question, however, that André would find time for a tour of the Far East and the Soviet Union in the spring of 1970.

In four weeks, the LSO covered Tokyo, Osaka, Nagoya, Seoul and Hong Kong. But it was the earlier part of the trip to the Soviet Union, with concerts in Moscow and Leningrad that made the biggest impression on him. Perhaps because, to date, it was his only tour of Russia – we shall see why later on – he will never forget it.

The LSO took with them two men who were justly regarded as the pride of British music, Sir Benjamin Britten and Sir William Walton, with whom he got on like a stack of sheet music ablaze. Sviatoslav Richter and David Oistrakh joined them for the concerts in Russia.

André met Shostakovich then, too. 'It was a great trip, a wonderful success,' André says of it now. 'Dreams came true.'

Since it was in what was still regarded as the Cold War, the trip was ground-breaking to say the least. It was, indeed, a very different world, one crippled by bureaucracy.

There was the time, for instance, when he and Benjamin Britten met in their hotel lobby and came face to face instantly with that strange Soviet phenomenon.

'They had one of those metal stands with postcards on them, the kind that you twiddle around. We chose about six postcards apiece. May Day was coming up and there was something wonderful, or at least there was in those days, to be able to send postcards of Red Square complete with flags and tanks and things to all your very conservative friends in England. We put them into an envelope and put our money down. The clerk then said, "Postcards go on sale at two o'clock." I said, "Yes, but here's the money," and smiled. He said, "Postcards go on sale at two o'clock. It is now one-thirty." And he pushed the money back, emptied the envelope and put the cards back on their stand. It was hopeless. No dice.'

After the opening-night concert in Moscow, things were even more chaotic. 'After the concert we trooped back to the hotel, all of us – Benjamin Britten, William Walton, all the soloists, the head of the orchestra, me – all that.

'We wanted something to eat. Closed.'

At which point the interpreter said to someone in authority: 'These are important people.' No effect whatever. Impasse.

It was then that Walton – 'ever practical' – decided to take matters into his own hands. 'What is there to buy?' he asked. He was told, 'Chocolates and vodka.' So, André says, 'We bought the chocolates and vodka and stole some rolls and repaired to Walton's room where we had chocolates, vodka and some dry bread. And that was our celebratory dinner. It wasn't that they were difficult. Those were the rules.'

But, as he told me, all this was more than compensated for by the response of the Russian people.

The impresario Lillian Hochauser made the arrangements for the LSO tour to be included as part of a British festival in the Soviet capital.

'There were very few concerts that had that sort of reception,' she told me.

Not only were there standing ovations at the Tchaikovsky Auditorium in Moscow, but the demand for the players to accept the plaudits of the audience came in sounds that seemed to rock the building's foundations.

They played Benjamin Britten's *Peter Grimes Interludes* – 'Britten was probably Shostakovich's best friend outside Russia and was always popular there' – and a newish piece of Walton's, his *Capriccio burlesco*. That didn't work nearly as well. As he told me: 'They greeted it with such apathetic silence that I remember not being able to get off the stage before the applause stopped.

A work by Gustav Holst also 'laid an egg'. Then they played Walton's First Symphony. The composer worried about that. 'What are we going to do?' he asked André. 'It's fifty minutes long, but the other piece was only eight and they hated *that*.'

To quote Previn, the orchestra played that night 'like a thing possessed. And it was such a success that the place erupted and the old man William stood up in the box and wept and it was incredible.'

There were some interesting discoveries that André made on the tour. A word that he uses more often than most to describe his work pattern is 'study'. On the Russian trip, his studies produced some interesting results.

André played in Moscow and Leningrad and it was, he said, as though the audience were listening to the Royal Shakespeare Company performing Hamlet. Nobody worried about the fact that a British orchestra was daring to play 'their' music.

'It is, of course, a very Slavic piece but no one in Russia seemed to have heard it in a long time and people were very moved by it.'

The reaction of standing ovations and the plaudits of audiences were not the appreciation that he remembers most of all about that particular concert, however.

'Something happened which some people have taken as very funny,' he told me. 'I certainly did not.'

It was snowing outside – 'when it snows in Moscow, man it snows' – but people were lining the street all the way from the concert hall to the hotel. At the very end of the queue, outside the hotel, was a woman who said she had a gift for the conductor.

'She had on a *babushka* and spoke to me in Russian of which I speak not a word but she gestured to me that she had this gift and handed me . . . an orange. I was *immensely* touched because it must have cost her money she probably could not afford and she would have had to queue for it.'

It was, I suggested, the Love Of One Orange.

But not everyone was totally uncritical of the performance that night. The Russian conductor, Hevgeny Mravinsky, for one, made a telling point. Why didn't André play the whole piece? Previn had no idea that, once again, the scores in Britain, America, Germany and everywhere else their side of what was still the Iron Curtain had been considerably cut. Ever since then André has conducted the Rachmaninov Second Symphony uncut.

The admiration for the name André Previn had spread considerably further by now than he could have imagined. In Leningrad, a young man approached him with the news that he was the President of the Leningrad Jazz Club.

'Now that sounds like something out of Monty Python, but the man said that he was the president of this club and would I care to come along and hear some Russian jazz?' Plainly, he felt it was an invitation he could not refuse.

'On the Sunday afternoon I took some people from the orchestra along to this club where they served only soft drinks, a very sweet, very sticky kind of squash. The music, which was very well played, was very good '50s jazz.'

They asked him if he would play. Naturally, he said he would. 'After all, how many times do you get to play in a jam session in Leningrad? Right?'

As he went on, he says, 'I could hear the sound of about eighty-seven tape recorders going on. I heard later that there were scores of illegal albums on sale.'

André asked his host on the way back whether that happened often. 'Yes,' said the man, laughing, 'what will happen now is that we'll have the club shut. They'll know that you came, that the club was very crowded.'

'My dear fellow,' said André, 'that's terrible. I can't be responsible for that.'

'It's worth it,' his host replied. 'We'll let a couple of weeks go by and we'll open again somewhere else. Then they'll close us again and we'll open up again somewhere else. It happens all the time.'

André asked if there was anything he could do. 'Yes,' said the club president, 'I would like you to send me some albums.'

When he got back, André did just that. But he knows they never reached their destination.

André discussed the problems of bureaucracy hindering the cultural exchange between East and West – 'It was so tight you couldn't have smuggled Margaret Rutherford into your room' – with the Minister of Culture, Mme Furtzova at a dinner at the Kremlin.

He asked her whether men didn't take women into their rooms in Russia. Quite seriously, she replied: 'Not in hotels.'

André worked as hard as he ever had on that trip but enjoyed the effect of his efforts. He enjoyed it certainly more than another overseas trip he made – to Israel, to conduct the world-famous Israel Philharmonic at the Mann Auditorium in Tel Aviv. Unlike Bernstein who played there every year, André liked neither Israel nor the orchestra.

'I just didn't enjoy working there,' he told me.

What he did quite enjoy was a meeting that he and Leonard Bernstein had at a party given by an Arab to try to foster good cultural relations between his people and the Jews. They were the only two people at the reception who were not Arabs. 'It didn't bother me,' André says now, 'but Lennie got more and more uncomfortable.'

To the extent that Bernstein told his colleague: 'Do you realise we have been here an hour and with the exception of "Hello" no one has come up to talk to us?'

Previn said it hadn't bothered him but suggested that they play a game. 'I'll tell you what,' he said, 'I will be one of the other guests and you'll be yourself and I'll come up and talk to you.'

At that, André joined a little circle which he quickly left and went up to Bernstein as though in greeting. 'Oh,' he said, 'how do you like the house, Jewboy?'

Bernstein said: 'Good Christ!' And they went off to have dinner somewhere else.

Working with the LSO was infinitely more satisfactory. It gave him a chance to meet some people he wouldn't otherwise have come across, like the then British Prime Minister, Edward Heath, who was fitting in a bit of conducting on the side. Before becoming Premier in 1970, Heath had been Chairman of the LSO Trust and had worked with André very closely.

In 1971, he accepted – 'with apprehension,' he later confessed – Andre's invitation to conduct the orchestra himself. It was a gala concert in November that year and André suggested that since Heath was taking over his job, perhaps it would be a fairly good idea if he himself took over the Prime Minister's.

'At least,' he said, 'for the length of the *Cockaigne* Overture.'

They appeared to get on well, although Heath is no longer willing to be interviewed on the subject. He once told writer Edward Greenfield that there was a mystery he couldn't understand: 'How is it that a musician of Russian Jewish origin, of German and American upbringing, finds himself at home in the Surrey countryside and in the music of Walton and of that most English of British composers, Vaughan Williams, all of whose symphonies he has now recorded?'

It was at that Heath concert that John Williams played for the first time the guitar concerto that André had written for him – and pronounced himself well enough pleased. 'Although I think the last of the three movements is the weakest. It's an interesting experiment – he uses a jazz guitar trio as a complementary accompaniment, answering to the accoustic guitar. It's very nice, but you need a very good jazz guitar to do it. Its form is a bit unquiet. It's been a bit disconcerting to the public who don't know how to relate to it. The first two movements are perfect. The first is a sort of scherzo. The slow movement is absolutely rhapsodic, gorgeous.'

It was not a difficult piece, he said. André did it because he thought it was a worthwhile musical project. He wasn't paid for it. Williams has played it a number of times in his native Australia and they did it together once in Holland.

He likes the Previn touch. 'I like his conducting style. It's beautifully direct. A part of his general musical approach that I like a lot is a sort of not taking oneself too seriously. I don't mean that he doesn't take his work seriously. The Western musical tradition is self-indulgent, a post-colonial culture that is turned in on itself.' André, with his jazz background, has never been guilty of being part of that philosophy. He genuinely, instinctively feels and expresses music in this wider sense. Not many classical musicians do.

That was true from the way he mixed with his musicians. No one who knows him ever thought Previn was stuffy – which was why, when John Williams, the Boston pops conductor and film composer, and he took off for Houston Zoo one day in the Texas city, no one was terribly surprised. André has always liked zoos. Maybe it helps him understand his orchestras better.

The pianist Emanuel Ax told me that André wasn't demanding enough. 'I can see that,' said John Williams, the classical guitar virtuoso, 'there are orchestras who like a dominating conductor. It's easier for them. It takes a sense of responsibility away from them. But if you sat down with a jazz group or any group of chamber musicians, you would never dream of saying they don't demand enough. You might later say that some people don't put in enough, but not that. One of the real qualities I like in André and which I find limited in the classical establishment, is how he copes with being good copy always – in reviews or part of culture generally – it's like building up great boxers. It's one person with a hundred musicians and the copy is on how he controls those hundred musicians. The degree to which attention is given to this, I find obsessive. As analysis of what's going on in human terms I find obsessive. What I like about André is that he doesn't fall into that trap. He may do, as often as anyone else, great performances of whatever repertoire he's engaged in, but that comes about in a different way. Not autocratic, but because of his enthusiasm for the music.'

Indeed he conveys all that enthusiasm he feels without being extrovert about it.

Williams accepted that. As he told me: 'He doesn't have to overdo the gestures which may simply mean that the natural flow of the music can do a hell of a lot for you without you having to impose on it. It is not simply a skill that he's got. If the classical world underestimates André, they do themselves a great disservice. He is certainly one of the best and greatest of musicians, perhaps one of the five or six best in the world.'

So André Previn in London was already on first-name terms with the Prime Minister. He was with others, too. Once he and his mother were walking through the streets of Soho, when the female impersonator Danny La Rue stepped out of a stage door almost directly in front of them. Danny smiled and said, 'Hi André' and tripped off on his high heels.

Lotte was a little disturbed that André could know someone like that, someone who was so obviously at home in London's principal sex district. 'Do you know many women like that?' she asked. 'It's not a woman,' he said, 'it's a man.' Lotte was totally mystified – and didn't quite know whether it would have been better if he had been a woman.

London and its adjoining area was very much home for André now. But he was touring more than ever. It was what was expected and when he was invited to guest-conduct some of the world's greatest orchestras, he usually ran. But sometimes he wondered about the cleverness of so doing.

'It sometimes seems to me,' he told me, 'that managements organise a conductor's playing schedule not according to how much he can take or his brain can stand, but according to airline schedules. There's no time to study. When the only place you can get to look over a score is Zurich airport, something is wrong.'

SIXTEEN

It was hard, hard work. But he went on doing it. And mostly loving it – if occasionally, he yearned for the days when conductors of the last century would have long ship cruises in which to travel from the old world to the new and to plan their work. In the 1970s as in the 1980s and 1990s, he could go straight from the airport to a rehearsal or – sometimes without a chance to change or check into the hotel.

But it was a worthwhile price to pay for that ever-expanding career of his.

André now had a new agent – Jasper Parrott. Today, Parrott's international artists' management agency is one of the most prestigious in the country, happy with its cable address of 'Birdsong, London'. But when André met him, he was an executive with another firm.

There was something about the young man that André liked. He was also needing help organising his business affairs, especially since Ronald Wilford had decided that André could use a local manager to look after him in Britain and what he hoped would be his business in Continental Europe. He did find someone but the arrangement wasn't working out. So when André and Parrott met at a party in north London, he thought they might get on.

As Jasper remembered: 'We were playing games, quite respectable games I have to say, the kind where you have to identify quite obscure pieces of music from snatches being played, and I did quite well, which I think impressed André a little.' (It probably impressed him quite a lot. André himself had appeared on a radio programme in London in which he did just that. Easily. Quickly. So quick was he, in fact, at identifying one piece that a fellow panellist, Claire Bloom couldn't believe what she heard. All she could say on air when André came up with the answer was, 'Bloody hell'.)

They got talking and Jasper Parrott offered to drive André to the Savoy where he was staying that night. 'It was a terribly battered old banger, a Morris Minor and André had to hold on to the door every time we stopped at a traffic light,' he told me. 'By the time we got to the Savoy, I think André decided that if he could survive the journey, he might survive me.'

In fact, Parrott was about to open his new agency and since he already had Ashkenazy as a client with his present firm and the pianist was ready to come over when he started up, he was reasonably optimistic. Fortunately for both men, André's own management contract was ending at about the same time, so he decided to take the agency plunge.

Parrott knew the sort of work André wanted to do and proceeded with all the enthusiasm of both his then youth and his knowledge of the business. There was a lot to do, but Parrott had a highly saleable commodity to offer.

He also encouraged Previn the TV Performer. 'I've always thought that as a television personality he was much better than nearly all those who do that and nothing else for a living,' he told me.

That being so, a whole series of programmes was mapped out. André had his own chat show – talking to Ted Heath one week, Dame Janet Baker the next.

There were the music programmes as well. One tried to dispel the long-held theory by millions who never go to a concert – the conductor just stands there waving a stick. 'Who needs A Conductor?' was the title of the show, which André suggested sounded ominous. It brought in a huge mail bag from people who really had never known the answer.

The role of the conductor and why he was there at all worried people on both sides of the Atlantic, incidentally. On his own American show, Leonard Bernstein had dealt with the same question, and had had to find the same answers. Whether or not Bernstein, however, was ever faced with the problem with which André had to deal one day in New York is less certain. He was due to conduct the New York Philharmonic, but when he unpacked he realised that he didn't have a baton. So he went to a very big music store and asked the girl on the information desk where he could buy one. 'A baton?' she asked. 'Yes,' said André. 'Oh,' she came back very brightly, wanting to provide the totally correct information. 'For conducting or for twirling?'

Had that followed the Christmas show that André did for the top British television comedians Morecambe and Wise, it might have seemed almost a reasonable question. Except that the Morecambe and Wise Christmas Show was never seen in America.

Eric Morecambe and Ernie Wise were among the best loved of British entertainers right until Eric's death in 1984 and remain so today in memory and on tape. They were funny without being vulgar, ridiculous without seeming totally nonsensical. In one programme, they would do their own version of *Singin' In the Rain*, with Ernie playing Gene Kelly and Eric the policeman – who landed in a full horsetrough. Or they would share a flat in which Ernie played author and talked about the play 'what I wrote'. Best of all, were the shows where they had guests – guests who were always being thwarted, guests who were known as solid citizens of the world, thrust suddenly into comedy situations not of their own making.

There was Glenda Jackson as Cleopatra showing her legs – only to have the knobbly knees of Eric and Ernie in Roman togas entwined over them, or Shirley Bassey dancing down a Rogers/Astaire-type staircase – in Army boots. Then the former Prime Minister, Harold Wilson, appeared and so did his Chancellor of the Exchequer, Denis Healey.

André – known for ever afterwards, as introduced by Ernie Wise, as 'Mr Andrew Preview' – was there to conduct the Grieg Piano Concerto while Eric was the soloist. He instructed Mr Preview not to conduct too fast – and to bend his head down so that the two men, both resplendent in evening dress, could see each other between the keys and the piano lid.

In that, André revealed new talents – as a comedy actor. 'I told them that I wouldn't do it if it entailed making fun of the music. But if they wanted to make fun of me, that was OK.' The music's integrity, on the whole, was not damaged. The conductor with the Beatle-cut, however, was either proving himself to be an idiot or an even better sport than the men and women of the LSO knew him to be. The reaction of almost everyone proved he had made the right choice. It was quite the most successful of all the shows, which each Christmas Day topped all the TV ratings.

Eric and Ernie met André before the show was recorded and asked him if he had ever done anything like it before.

'Absolutely not,' he replied, but said he wanted to go ahead just the same.

They asked him what comedy shows he enjoyed on British TV, their own apart.

'*Dad's Army*,' said André.

'And what don't you like?'

'*On The Buses*,' replied André, referring to a popular but highly crass Saturday-night show.

'Put it there,' said Eric.

'I absolutely idolised Eric and the first day we actually spent talking. He told me that what would make it funny would be if we never intimate that what we are doing *is* funny. We have to do it straight and it will get funnier. And it turned out exactly like that. It pleased them both very much because one or two guests didn't do that. They kept nudging the audience and saying, "Look how funny I am." I managed not to do that, which is why they improvised so much and it got longer and longer.'

If he ever needed an indication of just how important TV was as a medium, it was that show. The very next day he wandered down to his local pub at Leigh and was everyone's hero. 'It meant nothing that I had already done something like 350 concerts at the Festival Hall. But that show ... everyone saw it.

'Again, it was a question of the most enormous luck. I didn't set out and say, "Right, I think it's time I did a comedy show." It was just that someone came to me and said, "Would you like to do Eric and Ernie?" and I said, "Yes, why not?" I had never done a comedy show and Pop! It's always remembered.

'I seem to come up with these things quite passively and inadvertently every few years. I am sure it enrages some of my colleagues, but I don't look for these things. They just happen.'

He was sure that some other conductors said things like, 'Why does he have to be on a comedy show?' The indignity of it – to their profession?

'No. The success of it really.'

So successful that André was brought back, 'and that wasn't as funny because it was just too difficult to repeat what had happened the first time. It was funny, but not as funny. They tried to persuade me to conduct again and I said, No. In the end they got me on their sofa and tried to convince me that they had the inside track on how they could get me knighted and I finally had to fall for it. It looked very funny on paper and we yelled and howled while we were doing it, but it didn't turn out very funny.'

What was strange was that he could actually achieve all that without prejudicing his conducting career. There were plenty who doubted that he would be able to do so – and others who thought he would increase his following simply because he was an international TV star.

There is undoubtedly truth in the latter. André won't deny it. The suggestions that he was doing too much had about the same sort of effect as all those statements belittling his musical abilities simply because he had worked in Hollywood. He was proving that oil mixed with water and the theorists did not like to see their ideas challenged.

Television introduced him to a much wider audience. People who knew André quite well along with his close friends could testify to his sense of humour and his wit. Now, for the first time, millions of total strangers were able to share that wit, too.

He worked to what was partly his own script and without an auto-cue. Jasper Parrott saw how well he worked and nurtured this side of his career more than ever. His command of the language, even when it was colloquial – even when it came in four-letter colloquialisms – was, of course, outstanding and that helped this side of his activities.

'Of course, André is very careful about language,' Parrott told me. 'He enjoys language, both written and spoken and that is often held to be one of the most successful aspects of his work as a conductor. Therefore, in a way, he likes to be in control of that.

'One of the reasons he is so comfortable in a television studio is because of all his experience. He is in control of that situation. What he doesn't like is a situation in which he is not in control and is pressed to make decisions when he is not ready.'

That was how Parrott himself came in so useful. He could help take off the pressure and get across what he thought Previn needed. Usually, he did that. As the years of television work went by and the programmes continued on the BBC, and were networked overseas, there were constantly more suggestions and more ideas to be processed. He really had done in Britain what Bernstein had done in America.

But he didn't set out to do so. 'Lenny's early shows were really phenomenal. They were imaginative, innovative and he was a very great mass media pedagogue. Mine weren't so geared to teaching. They were much more informal.'

But educational they were, just the same. 'You have no idea how many kids wrote to me and parents who wrote to say that after watching the programmes, their kids went out and bought a Beethoven symphony.'

André's philosophy was simple: 'As long as the actual music making was as serious as you could make it, everything around it could be light-hearted.'

On an American late-night show, André got on to one of his favourite hobby horses of the age: the people who made rock versions of the classics were criminals.

The show's host put it to him that to say that was contradicting all that he had said about introducing people to music. As the man said, 'If they first like the rock version, they'll stay on to appreciate the real thing.'

'No, they won't,' said Previn. 'They'll hear them both and prefer the rock version.' And then came the nub of his case. 'I put it to you, if you went to the Louvre and drew a moustache on the *Mona Lisa*, they'd take you away to jail. Yet they get only rich from painting moustaches on Mozart.'

'Is that what you are advocating, jail?' asked the host.

'No,' said André. 'Jail is county. Try a Federal prison. I think it's disgusting.'

He has always had a blind spot about rock music, anyway. He doesn't understand it and likes it even less. But on his TV programmes, he could talk about the things that *did* interest him. He could convey the essence of the individual styles of the great composers. They were all his own opinions. Previn on Mahler, for instance: 'It's a little cosmic. You can't really listen very carelessly. You have to get into it. I find the most blatant of the sorrow says a little too much about himself. But it can really tear you apart. The Ninth Symphony is most the obvious musical presage of death I know about. It's very difficult to hear, but it's very beautiful.'

It was the sort of language he used on TV and what people wanted to hear. There were key words for him on cards. He just talked 'and told my stories'.

As he says, that would not have been possible in America. 'In America, because of commercials, everything is geared down to a very precise time. But in England, they would ask just for an hour's show – an hour's show could be fifty-five minutes or it could be sixty-five minutes. If it over-ran no one cared.'

It was much the same case with all the shows André did, *Music Night, Sounds Magnificent* and *The Symphony*, all in series of thirteen programmes.

Perhaps most notably, he was the first person ever to take a symphony orchestra out of formal clothes and let them appear on the box as they would be in rehearsal – in sports shirts, sweaters, in whatever they fancied or felt comfortable.

The programmes were so successful that it became more difficult to get a seat for the LSO than it was to get tickets for a West End show. 'When we went North, our concerts would be sold out for months in advance – because of television. So think what more could be done on an ongoing basis. But they got tired of it. So, it not being an educative medium – they think it is but it isn't – they let it go.'

Jasper Parrott thinks he knows why. He says that in the end, André did not put enough into those programmes.

'There came a time when André did not give enough time actually to refresh what he had to say on television. He did not invest enough to break his own mould. That was what he had to do, but it became too easy, a little too predictable. Two days in the studio to produce an attractive middle-ground programme and not enough of André's own programme went into it. Largely because André is a very good delegator, he leaves a lot of things for other people to arrange. The trouble with this is that unless these other people know how to bring out the best of him and know how to bring out the cutting edge in what he is going to say, it could become rather anodyne. And it did.'

On the other hand, André believes that TV has lost the art of showing orchestras at work. 'Who's going to be interested in a close-up of an oboe? It's uninteresting. It's not television. You have to gear programmes to be music that is shown on television instead of just showing a photographed concert. *Live From The Proms?* Deadly boring.'

He deliberately didn't make his programmes the way the BBC had always done them before – with a man in a dinner jacket standing at a lectern and beginning a talk with the ever-engrossing words, "In 1783 . . ."

His ideas were different. Television wasn't the right medium for lectures. 'Here we were going into people's sitting rooms. I didn't believe in haranguing them. I wanted to go to them in an open shirt and make jokes about Vaughan Williams.'

He was, nevertheless, surprised at the programmes' successes. 'Here I was, an American, crazy about English music and talking about it on TV.' Certainly, it wasn't most people's idea of a totally commercial formula.

'I took a lot of ribbing. So what if I did go through a period where there was a lot of *Private Eye* jokes? It was never vicious. I didn't mind.'

He had very definite cut-off points, things that he wouldn't do – just as he wouldn't make fun of the music on the Eric and Ernie show. 'Yet what I would do was considered very different from the norm of the symphony conductor. But I thought it was very good-natured.'

So successful was he that he was handed the supreme accolade – an offer of a series of commercials – for Ferguson television sets.

He never really got round to doing the same sort of serious programmes about music on anything like the same scale in America – except when the idea was taken up by a station in Pittsburgh, who then had their shows networked on public television, about which more later.

He tried to do programmes like them in Los Angeles, 'the capital of the entertainment world. But, no. Not a single show. They offered me one show that I thought was detrimental to the music, full of a lot of pointless non-witty lines and I said No. I told them that whatever they did might be quite fine, but not with me. They would have the wrong guy.'

The LSO meanwhile had decided that they very much had the right guy. There had been a few doubts about his adaptability to England, but they didn't last. In 1972, he did something he had never done before – he signed a new contract with the LSO which was totally open-ended. He could stay for as long as he wanted, so long as he gave two years' notice when he did decide to go.

At first, they wanted to make him conductor for life – an appointment like the one Rudolf Kempe had with the rival Royal Philharmonic. André turned down the offer. 'It's too ominous,' he declared at the time. 'It's as though I have promised not to live too long.'

He continued – despite what Ronald Wilford wanted – to appear, if only occasionally, as a pianist. In May 1973, he was the chief artistic collaborator for London's South Bank Summer Music festival and played works by Ravel and Milhaud. Felix Aprahamian wrote in the *Sunday Times*: 'As pianist . . . he unfolded the sparse and rich textures *con amore*, with the involvement of a true chamber music player in ensemble and a conductor's ear in realising the implications of orchestral colour informing both piano parts.'

The following year, he did it again – or as Peter Heyworth wrote in the *Observer*, 'the ubiquitous André Previn . . . invites a group of sympathetic artists to make music with him in a series of chamber concerts.'

There was also that Previn feel for stage musicals. Despite his blooding with *Coco*, he was anxious to try again. And since *Coco* hadn't made it to London, he was starting in the British capital this time – with a very British story. It was that fact which would prove to be its ultimate downfall.

Having said that, just as *Coco* had been a commercial success on Broadway, so *The Good Companions* did more than well enough in London's Haymarket, where it opened at Her Majesty's Theatre in July 1974 and ran for more than a year.

There was a highly satisfactory partnership at work here, too, with André writing the music to the lyrics of one of America's most respected writers, Johnny Mercer. Mercer knew music as well as he knew words and could even sing them in a voice that was frequently better than those of the people for whom he wrote. (He once told me that he refused to give Bing Crosby a song because he knew he could sing it better himself.)

The J.B. Priestley story of a group of ill-assorted strangers who join a seaside concert party adapted well to the West End stage. André said of his partner: 'Johnny Mercer was wonderful. I admired him absolutely boundlessly.'

Unlike Alan Jay Lerner, who would take months to write a lyric, Mercer could do it in minutes. 'Johnny would walk down Bond Street and by the time we got to the place where we were going to have a sandwich, he had it finished.

'And the show I really liked. But if *Coco* was over-produced, *The Good Companions* was under-produced.'

André had always wanted to write with Mercer and had planned to do a film with him. When that fell through, the lyricist phoned André with his suggestion for this show. He re-read the book and knew, he said, that Mercer was right. It was a very good idea indeed. They took it to Bernard Delfont, then the biggest name in British show business and he immediately said, 'Go ahead.' So they did.

Derek Jewell wrote in *The Sunday Times*: 'André Previn's score is polished, varied and sumptuously orchestrated. But an obvious big show-stopping tune or three it has not . . . Rich as the total score is, not one of those songs carries an obvious 22-carat imprint. Johnny Mercer's lyrics have, as you would expect, zip and dexterity.'

Alexander Cohen, the American producer, came to see the show and told André that he loved it. 'But it is so relentlessly English it would have to be almost totally rewritten for America.' So it never crossed the Atlantic.

André, though, was now being spoken of as being more British than American – which was a mixed blessing to him. Americans chided him that he sounded 'totally British' now, which he manifestly did not, although he did give certain words an English slant (which he would pronounce slarnt).

But there were problems. There was the man who found André's credit card and assumed that anyone so well known couldn't fail to get what he wanted – in this case a gold watch.

Questioned, he produced a whole collection of Previn cards and papers. He protested that he was being insulted by not being instantly recognised as the maestro. The detective apologised, raised his hat and made to leave. 'Oh by the way,' he asked, 'that Vaughan Williams piece you played last week on television. Was that the Seventh or the Eighth?'

'Oh hell,' said the thief – and threw up his arms in resignation. It was a fair cop. If André hadn't been a TV personality, he quite likely would have found himself treating this total stranger to his gold watch – and who knows what beside. But there were some people who still didn't appreciate his success.

On the other hand, there are others who feel bad for *André*. Norman Jewison, fresh from *Jesus Christ, Superstar*, told him about the famous Hollywood composer whom he took to the Festival Hall to hear one of André's concerts. It was Beethoven's Ninth Symphony and as usual it aroused the audience in a way that makes a musician feel that he has not only done his job, but done it pretty well. The warmth inside matches the sweat outside. There were screams and shouts.

Afterwards, as Previn bowed to his standing ovation, the Hollywood composer turned to Jewison and said: 'It's extraordinary how that man has fucked up his career.' Anything outside of Hollywood was no career at all.

He couldn't quite understand the Previn sound, which André told *Time* magazine he had wanted so badly. 'Some critics complain that I'm too facile, too concerned with sound rather than content. That hurts because I work hard, damned hard. But I do enjoy most making an orchestra "sound", making it project and play with the wish to sound beautiful. Do you know, every time I walk through the Festival Hall when it's deserted, I'm moved? I realise I've achieved what I've always wanted. I'm a happy man.'

But he kept on searching for more to do. He was about to make his debut at Covent Garden, conducting Walton's *Troilus and Cressida*. He had a regular column in *Punch*. What you didn't ask André Previn was what he did in his spare time.

There was always that success of the LSO, which would have been formidable even if nothing else worked for him. As someone said, 'Now that the Beatles have gone, the LSO are the biggest musical draw in the country.'

He tried not to lose his sense of perspective either. After one concert, he turned to a friend and said: 'That was a pretty good gig.'

But people did still ask him about Hollywood. As he told *People* magazine in 1974: 'How can anybody still blame me for movies that are fifteen years old? Some critics will forgive you for being an axe-murderer but never for scoring a film.'

One of André's problems was that he was away touring quite a lot and so was Mia, frequently to different places at the same time. But for the moment, she was enjoying her current role as a mother and he certainly played father whenever there was an opportunity to take the children into the woods at the back of the Surrey house or play with them in front of the open log fire. It was the rural life that he wanted, combined with everything he had thought he had needed in the way of a family.

In 1973, Kym Lark – forever afterwards known simply as Lark – came into their lives. She was two months old and very, very small ('I had never seen anything quite so tiny') and they had to go to Paris to collect her. They were told that the plane from Saigon would come sometime in the next twenty-four hours. That was all. 'We ended up waiting in the airport for, I suppose, ten hours.'

The child was handed to them by a small Belgian nun, carrying a basket. She told them, 'Monsieur et Madame Previn, voici votre enfant'.

Soon after the arrival in Leigh of Lark Previn, Mia discovered she was pregnant. The child, if a boy, they had decided they would call Django. But when the blond child was born, André immediately declared he was no Django. They struck on the name Fletcher, who almost from the moment he could talk turned out to be a natural comedian.

But the notion of adopting Oriental children had taken a firm hold. In 1975, they brought two more girls into their lives. One they named Daisy. The other was Soon-Yi, who since she was older than the others – five years old, whereas the others came as babies – kept her original name.

With the children around the house – it was called simply that, 'The House' was inscribed on its doorway – and when both parents were there, the Previns did indeed seem a fairly perfect family. The children went to private schools in Surrey.

What is more, the other children took to them completely. 'Once my son Sascha got pissed off that I called Lark, "Princess" sometimes. He asked: "Why do you call her Princess? She's not a princess."

'Lark turned to him and said, "Well, I might be. You don't know."' Lark used to say that she was the only one of his children who looked exactly like André.

That question about the children's original identity was never allowed to come into discussion. The only person who raised it was an American judge.

Lark and the others were legally adopted in the United Kingdom, but since André was still officially of double residence – in California as well as Britain – he had to have her made an American citizen, too.

This was a lot harder than wading through bureaucracy in Britain and didn't compare terribly well with the postcard sellers of Moscow, either, for that matter.

He had to take Lark to a judge in California in a building opposite the Los Angeles Music Centre. The judge looked through all the papers and declared them to be in order. He then asked their lawyer what he took to be the 64,000-dollar question. 'Now,' he said, 'the parents of this child? I take it they are not living?'

'No,' said the lawyer, 'they are not. She was found in a bombed-out village.'

'Wait a minute,' said the judge. 'You don't know the parents of this baby?'

'No,' said André, 'I do not.'

'Well now,' his inquisitor jumped in, 'has it occurred to you, Mr Previn, that this baby might be *North* Vietnamese?'

'No,' said André, 'it hasn't.'

'Well I suggest you think about that.'

André looked at him. 'Well,' he said, 'I've thought about it.'

'It's a very serious thing,' enjoined the judge.

This was another one of those impasse situations. By now buying that postcard only after two in the afternoon seemed a very reasonable thing to insist upon. 'I didn't know whether at that point to get up and punch him on the nose, but I would have blown it. My lawyer was making terrible gestures at the other end of the room telling me not to do anything like it.' So he decided on a safer course of action. 'Well,' André told him, extraordinarily politely, he believed, 'it doesn't matter.'

To the judge, on the other hand, matter it did. 'Well,' he declared solemnly, 'she will have to sign a loyalty oath.'

That was reasonable – perhaps. 'I wanted to tell the judge that at that moment it was very difficult because as we spoke, she was peeing on me.'

Ultimately, they agreed on a compromise. André said he would sign for her. 'You will do that?' asked the judge. 'Yes,' said André and the clerk was asked to prepare the appropriate document.

'I then signed that this child, who was then aged six months, was not going to overthrow the United States Government.'

'Right,' said the judge, an elected official, 'she's yours.'

When they got outside the building, standing on the steps, André says he did not know whether to burst out laughing – 'or throw up'.

After the success of the first adoption, Julie Andrews and Blake also decided to adopt a Vietnamese child. 'André told us it was a very quick adoption and suggested that we go to the nursery in Saigon, too.'

Their own blood daughter, Emma, meanwhile, worried about that. 'So André and Mia suggested that we bring Emma down to their house in the country and spend the day with them to see how lovely little Lark was. We did. It was a very sunny day and very pretty there and, of course, they could not have been kinder. Emma's fears completely dropped away. She wheeled Lark around the garden and was totally convinced. It made all the difference.'

The Edwards' own child arrived soon afterwards.

It was after that, that the Previns decided to go looking for the second baby, who became Daisy.

The Edwards, meanwhile, decided to have another for themselves as well – the Vietnam war was coming to an end and it would have been unlikely that there would be more who would be available after that. Their second child arrived on the same plane as the Previns' – at the most inconvenient time. Mia was away filming, and André was on tour.

Julie Andrews remembered: 'Both babies arrived in San Francisco at the same time on the same plane and we got a telegram from André and Mia asking if we could possibly collect them both. They also couldn't get a visa for the child to get into Britain in time.' So Julie and Blake said they would collect André's child as well as their own.

There, in their suite at the Beverly Hills Hotel, were the Edwards and three babies – the one they had brought over six months earlier, their new adopted child and the Previns' baby, 'who was very ill – suffering from the worst kind of dysentery,' Julie told me. 'I had never heard a child in such pain.' The baby was taken to hospital, and within days she recovered, the visa situation was sorted out and the child became a happy member of the family.

Nothing, however, was being allowed to stop the relentless progress of the Previn career. A great deal was going for him. He had taken the LSO to Salzburg and the reception he and the orchestra got there, from audiences at what was not infrequently thought of as the temple of musical appreciation, was staggering.

It was perhaps the most glittering proof that the LSO was regarded as one of the world's greatest orchestras it had ever had.

The irony of all that was that when André returned, he found himself not so much fêted by the orchestra's chief administrators as . . . fired.

A new chairman of the orchestra, Howard Snell, had been

appointed and he decided that since he was a new broom, he was going to do some clean sweeping. He brought in, as managing director, John Boyden. They were of one mind. The first thing they intended to sweep away was Mr Previn, whom neither liked, and they enjoyed his music even less.

What they thought would do the trick for them was to appoint the seventy-year-old German Eugen Jochum as 'Conductor Laureate'. He said he warmly welcomed his colleague.

At the same time, they said they wanted to make André 'Chief Guest Conductor'. He meanwhile took it that a sacking is a sacking – 'I don't stay where I'm not wanted.'

But it was not going to be left like that, just the same. 'The managing director made one important tactical error. He said. "You will do me a favour by not discussing it with members of the orchestra because they don't know it yet."'

André said: 'They don't know it yet? Don't they really?'

That was the point that the sacked conductor realised he had possibly not been sacked at all, for the LSO is a self-governing orchestra. The chairman and the managing director didn't tell the people who ultimately make the decisions.

'When the orchestra members heard about it, they got into a total rage and called an extraordinary general meeting, at which they fired *him*.' (The managing director.)

Mr Snell announced he was about to resign and Mr Boyden was ordered to pack his things.

'It was a very acrimonious time. Very bad.'

It would be a totally different set-up thereafter. Boyden was succeeded by Michael Kaye, a man who welcomed André's style. 'It was wonderful to see a conductor who travelled with the orchestra, had coffee and lunches with them and when they travelled together, he carried his own bags. He also made exactly the sort of music the orchestra wanted to play and the public wanted to hear.'

The time the orchestra played a concert in virtual darkness during a power cut illustrated that, he believed. 'Nearly every conductor would have said, "My God, my reputation." André just went ahead and did it, in the semi-darkness with no one able to read the music.'

He had been with the LSO for eight years when the row broke up. He stayed for another three. In the end, he was there for eleven-and-a-half years, more than double the length of service of anyone else in that position. 'I think,' he told me, 'unless you are a von Karajan, after about ten years, it should be enough for anyone.'

SEVENTEEN

No one in Britain had known a man like André Previn before. A conductor with the status of a pop singer. A man who lived for classical music yet didn't mind if a labourer mending a road looked him in the eyes and shouted out, 'Ah, Andrew Preview.'

'He is the most popular musician in Britain,' declared the *New Statesman*, a journal more used to analysing the innards of Britain's political situation. 'Low hooded eyes, the black mop of an untrimmed Beatle and a nose large enough to fence with an armadillo – Previn is instantly recognisable, everywhere.'

In short, he was becoming something of a British institution, which is usually considered a fairly dangerous thing to be, but appeared to give André no worries whatever. The *New Statesman* even suggested that the 'Mickey Mouse conductor' as they somewhat unkindly dubbed him, was all set to become the successor in people's minds to Sir Malcolm Sargent. That was intended as more of a compliment than Previn himself might have accepted it to be.

The LSO musicians seemed to like him for himself – and not for his friends. One member put it like this: 'I'd rather hear him say "Ouch! That F sharp was disgusting" than someone else say, "Don't play *troppo forte*, you celli."'

There was a certain modesty about him that they liked, too. He liked to tell the story of conducting Strauss's *Ein Heldenleben*, with the Philadelphia Orchestra. He was very proud of the performance and thought it was close to being fairly definitive. And then he played it with other orchestras and it was not quite so wonderful. To him that was the revelation of a dreadful secret – it had been good the first time because the Philadelphia musicians themselves were good. He looked for nothing less from his other orchestras now.

The LSO liked André as much as audiences liked the combination of conductor and orchestra.

'I was not really used to the built-in sophistication of an audience that has a local luxury of five concurrent symphony orchestra seasons,' he told the BBC radio programme, *Kaleidoscope*. 'Really nothing surprises them in the way of repertoire.' And there was another difference between concert-goers in Britain and those in America. 'The Americans are not likely to be as polite as a British audience, which will applaud anything. By no means must you mistake that for anything but happiness on my part, but it is quite extraordinary that if you play a new piece in London, whether it is something the audience adores or absolutely loathes, you get a certain amount of signs of approval from them at the end of the piece.'

The audiences were not the only ones who applauded him. People for whom André composed enjoyed being able to have a laugh as he went through his scores – laughing with him, not at his work. Ashkenazy was delighted with his *Pages From A Calendar*, a set of preludes which he had written specially for him.

'I'm happy with everything that he does,' Ashkenazy told me.

He and the soloists for whom he wrote always got on well together, because, again, of his innate musical sense. 'He's the best accompanist I ever had,' Ashkenazy told me. 'He knows every note. I've played with all the best conductors today. Nobody, but nobody, is as good as he. There are others who conduct great symphonies, nobody accompanies the way André does. To accompany in a Rachmaninov concerto is very, very hard. But he is always very marvellous. When we did the three Bartók concertos, I never had a better accompanist. They were all very, very fine. The Concerto Number One is hard because you can't hear what's going on, but André was on top of the job. One conductor said: "I'll never do it again. It's impossible." But André did it brilliantly.'

In 1975, Previn received another one of those offers he hadn't the slightest intention of refusing – to be musical director of the Pittsburgh Symphony Orchestra.

He could run it at the same time as he was looking after that 'musical welfare' of the LSO. He had learned a lot since his days at Houston and he knew he could manage the two comfortably enough.

André couldn't have been more enthusiastic about saying yes to the invitation to come to the city which was best known for being the centre of the American coal and iron and steel industries. He had an infinite respect for the music made by its symphony orchestra. He had first conducted it in 1967, with results that didn't exactly make the management of the ensemble want to hear him again. They didn't think his standard matched their own. In hindsight, André would have agreed. But in the intervening eight years, two things had happened – and both of which Ronald Wilford thought he could use to his advantage: André had improved out of all recognition. Wilford suggested that they think of Previn as their next music director.

He went there as a guest conductor, without realising anything special was afoot. Cy – or Seymour – Rosen, the Pittsburgh manager, drove him to the airport after his last concert in the city and quite directly asked him if he wanted the musical director's job. André says that he would have gone off the road had he been driving himself. He hadn't been as excited about anything since that delegation from the LSO came to see him at the Savoy.

As he said at the time: 'I was on a quite normal guest-conducting stint, conducting there for three weeks between engagements in Chicago and Boston. Before that, I hadn't conducted in Pittsburgh in years.' He said he was 'enormously surprised', but 'the more I thought about it, the more I liked it. For the past eight years I worked in Europe far more than America. I was very flattered.'

He not only liked the orchestra but thought that Heinz Hall where they were based was one of the best auditoria in which he had worked, which was saying a great deal.

He immediately set about becoming part of the orchestra, an integral feature of the very fabric of the outfit – although there were criticisms. Unlike his predecessor, the sick seventy-six-year-old Dr William Steinberg – it was because of his illness that he was having to be replaced – André sought what he liked to think was a 'pure' sound. Steinberg would double up on certain instruments or sections of the orchestra during some pieces, particularly by his favourite German composers. In Brahms or Beethoven, he would have four woodwind instead of the usual two. André wanted none of that. It took time for the orchestra to get used to a new conductor. Some never did.

They found it difficult as an orchestra, which had, as one member put it to me, 'great community feeling', to welcome a virtually total stranger who was being hyped, like it or not, as a media star.

Marshall Turkin, who had taken over as the managing director of the orchestra, didn't get on with him from the word go. 'But others loved him,' Joel Roteman, a Pittsburgh newspaper editor told me.

As Joel Roteman put it: 'There were people who felt piqued that he wouldn't make the so-called obligatory social appearances unless he felt it benefited the orchestra directly.'

He did, however, become a very well-known local figure – for much of the same reason as he had become one in London. On the W QED television station, he did get his own series. It was very similar to the sort of programme he was presenting in London, but with the Pittsburgh orchestra sitting where the LSO sat in the BBC studio.

It worked well, but until it got a showing on public television, was never seen outside of Pittsburgh. One thing that impressed André was the outfit's call sign; the letters QED for an arts station, he thought, was a brilliant idea.

'I told the owner how impressed I was,' he recalled for me. 'The man hadn't a clue what I was talking about. They were just the letters he had been allocated and didn't know they had any significance.'

But he had no illusions about what he was doing. 'I've never thought I was trying to make serious music popular, because it doesn't need my help. But it's true that millions see it on television, that's a hell of a lot of performances packed into one night.' As he said, if out of every ten people who tuned into one of his programmes, six immediately turned of, that still left a hell of a lot of people.

One of his programmes included a talk with Dame Janet Baker – 'one of the finest musicians I know'. He asked her if she had always wanted to be a musician – 'you know, like me. I always knew I would be one. I never wanted to be a fireman or anything.' She confirmed that she had only wanted music for her career.

She also played the piano. But, she said, she had to count every time she sat down, ready to play. 'So do I,' said André, 'but I have no mathematics after five or seven.'

Music and mathematics are supposed to require the same sort of mind and to go together automatically with each other. 'Uh hah,' André told me, shaking his head, 'not with me they don't. I have no mathematical ability at all.' Later in that same conversation we were talking about buying some milk. 'I need two quarts. What's that – a gallon?'

On television, he had the ability to ask questions that others might not have dared to ask – questions that almost everyone else would have wanted to know. Like, 'We all know what happens to boys' voices. Quite seriously, I'd like to know this – does anything similar happen to girls?' Yes, she told him, it did. Something very peculiar happened when I was fifteen,' she said. 'I was told not to sing at all for two years. My voice got deeper.'

They agreed that neither of them liked competitions. It was almost impossible to do one's best in a competition hall – as we had already noted.

He would, before long, find out precisely how unreal competitions were – but from the other side of the fence. He agreed – and he has never agreed since – to judge a piano competition. 'I hate competitions,' he told me, as if I really needed to know how he felt, 'because they falsify people's talents.'

On this particular occasion, the winners had been decided and the prizes already awarded. But one of the competitors, a very pretty girl, told André and his fellow judge that she had played badly because the piece was strange to her. Could she possibly play something else? The competition was over, but they decided to hear her. 'She played something else and played it *very* well indeed. So well, in fact, that although we couldn't award her the prize that day, we decided to give her a special prize.' Her award was the chance to study with a certain, and now unnamed, maestro.

What happened next is, André delights in saying, 'a real locker-room story.'

The girl started taking her lessons and by all accounts was benefiting tremendously by her sessions with the teacher. It was, she wrote home, every bit the rewarding experience she had anticipated – and couldn't have been more grateful to the judges for presenting her with the opportunity. One day, as a means of demonstrating *their* appreciation, the girls' parents came to visit. They arrived to be told that their daughter was with her teacher, in the middle of her instruction. They went into the maestro's room. The only problem was that there they, to quote André, 'found that she was *giving* a lesson, not taking one'.

And, he didn't have to add, the subject was definitely not music. 'As a result, the parents went gunning for me and my fellow judge.' Fortunately, they didn't catch up with either of them – who immediately vowed they would never get involved in that sort of thing again.

More seriously, he also totally dislikes top-rate musicians who give public master classes, particularly on television. 'There's a misplaced ego there,' he told me, 'people saying they have the perfect answer and know everything. They can't possibly – unless Schubert lives at their house.'

Although André doesn't consider himself primarily a teacher – certainly not one in the Bernstein mould – he does occasionally teach at Tanglewood, the summer home of the Boston Symphony. He likes to quote what his colleague, the Japanese conductor Seiji Ozawa, told a student at one of these sessions: 'I can't teach you what to want.' There was a great lesson in that, he thought. 'You can teach a young

249

person to get what he or she wants out of a piece of music – you can't teach them what to want.'

Every time he and Ozawa have their conducting lessons at Tanglewood they give a concert with their pupils at the main theatre there. Only Bernstein was the exception to that rule. He used instead the famous 'Shed' which seats something like 10,000 people.

André and Ozawa once asked the man everyone knew as Lenny, *Why* did he use the Shed? 'I suppose,' said Bernstein in all seriousness, 'it's because more people come to my concerts than to yours.' As André told me: 'You couldn't take exception to that. It was merely stating an established fact – like "You're wearing shoes."'

The *Christian Science Monitor*, reviewing two of André's Tanglewood concerts with the Boston Symphony in 1980, were to note: 'Even under the tight – almost insufficient – rehearsal schedule of Tanglewood, Previn works the sorts of wonders it takes certain favoured guests a good two or three weeks to accomplish.'

Certainly, there were few difficulties about people coming to Previn's concerts, particularly those with his new Pittsburgh orchestra.

The original agreement was that André would be in Pittsburgh for half the subscription season of twenty-eight weeks, while Steinberg would still be honoured with the title of 'Music Director, Emeritus'. As we have seen, names don't bother André very much. He wanted to feel that they wanted him as much as he wanted them, so he insisted on the members of the orchestra confirming his appointment before he took over. This they happily did.

Like the LSO at the Brighton concert, it was the way André coped with a problem that endeared him to the membership.

As before, the crisis happened while André was playing a solo piano part – maybe Wilford had had the right idea when he insisted he only conduct – in the Mozart Piano Concerto in C Minor, while he also conducted from the piano. He found, too late for anything to be done, that the E flat string was broken – one of the most vital in a C minor chord. All André could do was play without using that one important key. When the orchestra realised how he coped, they also decided he was their man.

Emanuel Ax first met him at Pittsburgh. 'He's a real presence, but he put me at ease straight away – because he behaves as though he's completely unconscious of his own importance. While other conductors intimidate people, he doesn't feel as if his ego should be important. He prefers loyalty to command.'

But there was something else about Previn's conducting that made pianists like Ax very 'comfortable'. As he told me: 'It's because he's a pianist himself. He's not just very intensely musical but he understands the craft of piano playing better than anyone.'

Ashkenazy echoed that. 'We were recording some Rachmaninov together on two pianos. My wife heard it and said, "It's so funny to hear a second piano. It's almost as if it is intruding." André said, "That's what I feel." He's so modest.' But he had no reason to be, said the Russian. 'It's amazing. He doesn't need to practise. He can sight-read to perfection. He has marvellous co-ordination. It can be in the brain, but without good hands, it doesn't work. André has terrific hands. It's a challenge to play with him, and yet he has never wanted to play on the highest level.' (Perhaps the man André calls Vova ought to have spoken to Ronald Wilford.)

Certainly, conducting the LSO, guest-conducting the other ensembles and nursing the Pittsburgh took more than enough of his time. He took an apartment in the city and set about keeping home for himself – which was not the easiest thing for a man who didn't know one end of a screwdriver from the other.

He did, however, get to understand what a can opener was. So he occasionally cooked for himself – a can of soup which he emptied into a saucepan together with a solitary sausage. He also had one spoon and one fork. 'I didn't care,' he told me. 'So I was inept, but it didn't worry me.'

He most certainly was not inept with his music, but he *was* noticing things that he hadn't spotted before. Just as when he looked at his previous markings on a score and wondered whether a child had been at the sheets of paper, now he realised that there were gaps in his work and the way he practised it.

Nobody else thought much about it, but as long ago as 1978, he said: 'With any interpretative artist's life, the older you get, the more you do, the more the gaps seem glaring. There was a period when it seemed to me that every guest conductor and all the other orchestras were doing those giant killer Mahler symphonies with a regularity that was *numbing*, so I stayed away from them or did them in other places and now I regret it.'

With Pittsburgh joining London as his own 'band', he was now doing something like one hundred concerts a year – in addition to the records he made and his television appearances. The workload was huge. It meant that he was away from home a great deal, as all conductors are. He couldn't sleep properly. He read before turning out the light at about one or two o'clock in the morning. He got up at seven to make himself a cup of tea, which was an English habit he was never to lose. Frequently, he spent most of the night reading or writing when he couldn't sleep at all. If he managed four hours, he was lucky. None of it had any deleterious effect on his work. He said his ultimate nightmare was to get to rehearsal unprepared and that never happened.

There were those in the American city who felt they didn't know enough about him, for all the media hype. A Pittsburgh music critic, Robert Crone, said of him: 'He was always an elusive private figure.' Carl Cohn of the Pittsburgh *Press* had a different criticism in mind: He didn't show, he said, enough consideration for the senior members of the orchestra. Older musicians, he said, suffered because of 'Previn's near adoration of youth'. But George Anderson, Editor of the 'Lifestyle' section of the Pittsburgh *Post* remembers him only affectionately. 'His finest features were his self-deprecating wit and his wide range of musicianship.' He did not necessarily think of those qualities in that order.

When he wanted to take the orchestra on an overseas tour, there were more sniffs from people who didn't approve of what he was doing. The tour would cost $350,000. 'What for?' asked one board member, 'for the agrandisement of the orchestra, the city – or of André Previn?' The barb was not shielded in any way, but the orchestra went – and it was another huge success.

That word 'success' worried him. 'It has been misapplied. A good teacher, a good plumber is a success,' he told me. 'To define success as money and applause is dumb. Applause and money is representative of the approval of others, not of oneself. Great composers don't get applause and don't get a great deal of money. Is that right? Wayne Newton gets a great deal more money and applause than Mel Powell or John Harbison. Is that right?'

He says it is undeniable that he loves to be on the receiving end of applause. He cites the story of an assistant conductor working with him at Pittsburgh, an Englishman named Michael Lankester.

'He's an absolutely lovely musician, a nice man. We were in Salzburg together when, after a concert, we went to a restaurant across the Square. As we walked through, just like in the movies, the people got up from their tables and applauded. Now half of me was thrilled and half of me embarrassed. Here was Michael, a success in terms of being a sensational assistant conductor, who grinned and said: "I could get used to this."'

On another tour with the Pittsburgh at which Lankester was there to cover for André should it be necessary, Previn asked him whether, secretly, he didn't harbour a hope – that one day he would get hit by a bus. 'No,' he replied almost angrily. André admitted to me: 'I wondered about that. In his position, I think *I* might have.'

There were more personal problems than those picked up by the local critics. He would have liked to have spent more time with his wife and with his children.

But that problem of not seeing his children worried him more and more, particularly the two daughters he had had by Betty. 'I admit there was this guilt thing,' he told me, 'so I tended to over-compensate.' He said he was never happier than when his family were all together at The House. Sometimes, he and Mia entertained the children to a puppet show. Mia adapted *Peter and the Wolf* to the marionettes. She recited the story and André played the piano. But those days were few and the times when both were home together were getting fewer, too.

The trouble in Pittsburgh had been that people didn't quite know what to expect. As one writer put it in the *New York Times*, before a Pittsburgh concert at Avery Fisher Hall, 'He was expected in some circles to act like the jet-set conductor *ne plus ultra*.' So much so, that posters for his Pittsburgh concerts were headed simply 'PREVIN'. 'Expectations of glamour,' wrote the *Times* man, 'sat in the air.'

What didn't sit quite so happily in the Pittsburgh air were the gaps in his own tastes. He couldn't bring himself to say he regretted not sharing the love of other musicians for Wagner. Not that there were any political reasons for having no great affection for the man who was Hitler's favourite composer. As he was to tell me: 'I hear the really astounding genius in it, but I find long stretches where my attention wanders.'

In the late 1980s, he and Vladimir Ashkenazy discussed this missing link in the story of André Previn's musical appreciation. 'With all my admiration for *Parsifal*,' André told his friend, 'it's difficult to sit through. After listening to it, I wonder if Reagan is still President.' These days, he listens and wonders if George Bush is still President.

There were subscribers to the Pittsburgh concerts who worried about his never conducting that composer in his programmes. Joel Roteman remembered for me: 'Many long-time subscribers and older musicians also couldn't understand why he didn't play Bruckner. This brought him into even more conflict with Marshall Turkin and several symphony members.'

But the editor said, there were evident compensations. 'He certainly lifted the morale of the orchestra, particularly after the death of William Steinberg. He improved the quality of the musicianship and he certainly gained national media attention for the Pittsburgh

Symphony, which had long been a quality orchestra but little known outside this area.' His tours with the orchestra were welcomed more than practically anything else he did.

And there was another important feature to his work. He established the office of a composer-in-residence, which went to John Harbison.

'It was the most wonderful break,' Harbison told me. 'It got me going, but it also meant I gained a very valued friend.' Harbison was to go on to become a Pulitzer Prizewinner.

If he really could make a go of Pittsburgh, André's reputation was going to be enhanced in America, possibly to the status it enjoyed in Britain. Yet even now, they were still calling him 'Hollywood's Previn' and it was no still joke. When a *New York Times* writer went into a music store in New York, the same one where André had been asked if he wanted a baton for playing or twirling (he now wishes he had said, 'One with fire at each end,') wanting to be pointed to the latest Previn release, he was directed to the pop counter.

He was rectifying that by recording with Pittsburgh as well as the LSO. Simultaneously, the orchestra was regaining its old caché and he was building on that, too.

And not just Pittsburgh's. He was recording with the Vienna Philharmonic, which gave him more pleasure than almost anything else he did professionally. There were so many orchestras with which he was working as a guest conductor that he was able, like a tailor making a bespoke suit, to choose which sort of music he played with which orchestra. Now, he really could say that yes, he wanted to conduct his beloved Richard Strauss, but it should be with the Vienna orchestra. Walton, Vaughan Williams, Britten and Shostakovich were made for the LSO. Haydn and Mahler? That was Pittsburgh territory at that time; now he records both in Vienna.

He was not only broadening his orchestral repertoire, but also his contact with soloists. Isaac Stern was working with him now. 'I think he is quite the most ideal accompanist,' he told me. 'I have only one fault with him,' he told me. 'I don't work with him often enough.'

One of the reasons why he is such a perfect accompanist is simply that he knows what his soloists want. He marks scores with their initials, so that any particular request they may make at one concert will be remembered for the next – rather the way a luxury hotel notes the requirements of certain prestige guests who hate blue wallpaper and thereafter always put them in a room decorated in green. The wallpaper on his scores was always of the right colour.

All his success at Pittsburgh, though, did not have to mean that he was going to give up his interest in the LSO.

If there were complaints, Michael Kaye told me, it was the old story of his not being demanding enough. 'Some orchestra members are totally masochistic about that. They want more direction than André seemed to give them.'

It wasn't that he was easily satisfied, he would say, but they were giving him what he wanted. Other people thought that the explanation was less pleasing for them. Previn, they said, was cold. He was unable to emote. As Kaye says: 'The conductor/orchestra relationship is always a difficult one. Everything in the caldron boils up. A lot of musicians resent conductors and soloists. Many musicians think that life is unfair – that they could have been conductors or, at the very least, soloists. That sort of thing does lead to tension.'

But on the whole, there were few problems with the LSO. He still regarded it as one of the world's finest orchestras and was glad to be a part of it. What was more, he was still a part of Britain. The house at Leigh might seem to be even further away from London as the number of cars clogging the roads grew steadily higher and he got less and less keen on the alternative of travelling by train – 'because there will always be a notice chalked on a blackboard saying that the eight-thirty has been cancelled and the nine forty-five is half an hour late'. He was willing to put up with it all because it was his home and he liked it that way.

He took the LSO on more East European tours in 1978, going from country to country. He had dreadful back pains during the run and went home half-way through, but he did the front and back ends of the trip, not missing out a single city.

Now, though, he had Pittsburgh to take care of at the same time. One of the most frequently made complaints was that the fourteen weeks he spent with the orchestra were not enough, but it was no more than most orchestras had from most conductors.

It did, however, provide ammunition for those who weren't totally delighted with having him. As Joel Roteman observed: 'Previn's biggest failure here was his perceived lack of leadership.' It was part of a continuing story of his favouring the young at the expense of the old. 'The young musicians loved him and regarded him as their ideal leader, but it enhanced the schism with the older ones. They didn't like the attention he paid to the young people.'

Sumner Erikson, who was eighteen when he was hired by Previn as a tuba player, told me about the reaction of other members of the orchestra when he was chosen at his audition. One man shouted out: 'But he's only eighteen.' 'I don't care how old he is,' said Previn. 'He may only be eighteen, even if he's only eight, he's still my tuba player.'

Erikson added: 'I have nothing but the strongest admiration for André. He's an extraordinarily talented musician, very sincere. He had a very healthy relationship with the musicians. He was always supportive and it didn't matter I was only eighteen.' He particularly liked the fact that he allowed him to be soloist in the Vaughan Williams Concerto for Bass and Tuba. It was only his second season with the Symphony – the kind of trust many conductors didn't offer. Even so, he says, 'He had a great sense of discipline, but he never ever used intimidation. A very genuine person.'

Harold Smolier, a cor anglais player, concurred with that. As he told me: 'He is so intelligent and does things better than any other conductor I know. A nice man who always wanted to be one of the guys.' Once again, it was the appreciation an orchestra member felt for a conductor who travelled and drank coffee with his rank and file. 'But some felt he was too friendly with members and didn't work us hard enough.'

The controversies, however, continued to dog Previn throughout the eight years he was to work with the Pittsburgh orchestra, including one that had absolutely nothing to do with the music he played or the friends he made.

It was simply over the clothes he wore. André had for long found the sleeves of the traditional tail coat or dinner jacket worn by members of his profession as too constricting for one who constantly was waving his arms around, so he had a coat specially made for him – a long jacket which he wore over a dress shirt and his bow tie with the traditional black trousers. The real difference that was immediately evident was that it had no sleeves; it was like a long waistcoat. People didn't like that. It didn't have the elegance or the dignity they thought that their conductor should show. In the end, he agreed to conform and the row was over.

His toughest relations continued with Marshall Turkin, however. Things were so bad that when an offer came up to conduct the San Francisco Symphony, the ensemble which had been dominated for so long by his old mentor Monteux, he decided to accept – only to withdraw his agreement when he heard that Turkin was retiring. Four days later, the managing director announced he was staying, but wouldn't have any detailed contact with his conductor. Instead, a new artistic director was to be appointed as a kind of liaison. But that never happened.

André tried to keep the orchestra and the board of directors away from his arguments with Turkin, which grew stronger all the time.

Turkin didn't want to spend money, he said. Nor did he want to extend the repertoire, which André thought was necessary to put the Pittsburgh in the same class as the orchestras from Boston, Chicago and Cleveland. If it could be taken for granted that every year those ensembles would play in New York and get rapturous responses, why not Pittsburgh? He wanted unusual works performed, like Britten's *War Requiem* and a concert version of *Wozzeck*. The real killer was his relationship with Turkin. He wasn't sure how much longer he could work with him. It wasn't so much that he didn't like the man, he didn't understand him. He couldn't comprehend how he could act secretly about arrangements for concert performances and tours – which, in any case, should have been André's prerogative – without telling him.

When André made a speech to the board of directors complaining about lack of funding, Turkin made one, too – apologising for André's complaints.

Then André made an announcement that he would be running a series of chamber music concerts. Turkin said it couldn't be done. There wasn't the money.

In parallel with all this were the other lives of André Previn, the man who sought privacy more than anything, but who lived a life that was more public than – with the exception of Bernstein's – that of any other conductor either America or Britain had known.

It had always been like that. In 1977, André Previn had got himself into another controversy, this time the one that had him banned from the country that had given him one of his warmest welcomes, the Soviet Union.

EIGHTEEN

Composing has always been part of André's life. He was doing it all the time he was in Hollywood and he has been doing it part of the time ever since he became a 'serious' conductor. But if he knows his true status waving that baton in front of an orchestra – his statements about success are no more than established facts, as true as if Bernstein really had said he was wearing shoes – he is considerably more modest about his composition work.

'I write just because I like to write,' he says. 'I have no illusions about my stuff being played after I'm dead, I just want to hear it played next month.'

One could say that that was why he didn't bother about a swathe of reviews that seemed at one stage to be telling him to take up another profession. But then, he never took much notice of reviews for his conducting or for his records, so what did it matter? And the people for whom he wrote, did, on the whole, like what he did very much.

To that end, he will write almost whenever a respected colleague asks him to do so. He won't write if he is *not* asked to. He needs the push of a commission from an artist whom he respects or at least that of a deadline, even if he has created that deadline for himself. At the Leigh house, he would retreat into the adjoining cottage, lock himself away and produce his music, because he knew that if he didn't do it then, he never would – and then the piece after that would be delayed even further.

There was no better tribute to the musicians with whom he worked at Pittsburgh than a work called 'Principals', which was dedicated, literally, to the principal members of the orchestra and gave every one of them a chance for a solo.

Every Good Boy Deserves Favour wasn't dedicated to anyone in particular, although it involved, in its way, both the Queen of Great Britain and the General Secretary of the Communist Party of the Soviet Union.

The title, taken from the acronym for the E G B D F notes on the lines of the treble clef, was the musical play he and Tom Stoppard wrote for the festival celebrating the Queen's Silver Jubilee in 1977. It had started earlier than that, however.

The two men had been thinking of working together since 1973. That was when they had met at the Greenwich Theatre, where Mia was acting in a play by the Spanish playwright Lorca that had been translated by Stoppard. As Tom remembered: 'He said then, "If you ever need an orchestra, I'm your man."'

So he and his man decided to act on the suggestion. 'We thought of doing something for the Edinburgh Festival of 1976, but it turned out to be just another deadline that we missed.'

It also turned out to be the piece responsible for getting both members of the partnership banned from the Soviet Union. The play was set in one of those Russian psychiatric hospitals to which political prisoners were sent. There, they could not only be brain-washed but incarcerated (and perhaps forgotten) for a totally limitless period.

The story was about one of those prisoners, a fictional character, but it was more about the system itself, one in which a man could share a cell with an inmate who really *was* insane – and who believes that a whole symphony orchestra is in there with them.

That was where André came in – he wrote the music for the symphony orchestra which the poor madman thinks he is hearing, as well as for the doctor in charge of their 'welfare', who just happens to be an amateur violinist.

It was perhaps the perfect demonstration of what happens when those deadlines come creeping up. It was while working on this score – in which the influences of the Russian moderns like Prokofiev and Shostakovich were plain – that André's back problem meant him having to give up some of his concerts on that LSO East European tour.

His back is more than just a problem. It is the site of a chronic condition that resurfaces perhaps only once in ten years. But also between those flare-up times, he is frequently in constant pain – a pain that sometimes can be seen on the podium as the back bends with his arm movements. The symptoms are similar to those of a slipped disc, except that some of his discs have not so much slipped as fused permanently together. As he says, 'They have eroded.'

Just about his most severe outbreak of the trouble came during the time he was working on *EGBDF*. His doctor ordered him on to his back – flat on his back, without any movement. It's a sentence that would have been terrible for almost anyone. But for a conductor? For a composer with a deadline?

For a man who recognises himself to be as technically inept as a fluffy dog falling over his own tail, André himself came up with a solution that ought to have won him some kind of award for initiative. He had an architects board swung from the ceiling – and wrote the score from his prone position. Michelangelo would have been impressed. But, as André told me, his years of conducting experience had never proved more useful. 'I don't think anyone who wasn't so totally used to waving his arms as I am could have done it. At least *they* were pretty strong.'

There was also the compensation of working with Stoppard, by now a close friend. They shared a taste for wit, which can sometimes turn into something more serious. At one of the playwright's garden parties, André, impressed with the guest list, asked him: 'Do you have any friends who are *not* famous?' 'No,' said Stoppard. 'It's easier that way, because it means no one is envious or resentful.'

'I loved working with Tom Stoppard,' André told me. 'We both work at lightning speed and it's all over. With Tom, there isn't time to get bored.' Even so, it still took three to four years from conception to the first staging of the piece.

For André, *EGBDF* turned out to be a convenient way of acceding to the LSO's suggestion that their principal conductor write something specially for the Silver Jubilee.

His original idea was for a piece for narrator and orchestra, of which he thought there was 'lamentably little' to be heard. After *Peter and the Wolf* and *Joan of Arc* and *King David*, what was there?

Tom then had an idea which was, says André, '*absolutely* hilarious – but it was one joke. I went to work on it, but it didn't seem to get us anywhere. It was a one-way street.'

The idea was of a mad millionaire who owned an orchestra. But there was no way to make it work and André was, before long, away conducting and Stoppard was writing his play *Travesties*.

'We spent a lot of our time entertaining each other with gags of one kind or another,' said the writer. 'I know that I was going through a sort of Hoffnung strain at the time.' (Gerard Hoffnung was a cartoonist who also gave one-man performances as a stand-up humourist.)

Said Tom: 'I had this vision of a drummer with two big kettle drums. I thought he would bang the drums and find that the tops of them were only the skins of whatever they were filled with – like porridge or something.' But this and others were just filmic ideas.

There were, he says, 'some hilarious squabbles'. The problem he thought was that he is, to use his own words, 'an ignoramous about music. I can't separate music very well, so if I offered a musical pun it was operating at the most fundamental level of cliché.'

But he got more and more excited about the prospect of working with André. He rang him with an idea for a play which, he confessed, 'is quite a way off what you have in mind. It involves a full symphony orchestra which needs to be on stage.

'I went away,' said Stoppard, 'wrote it and let André see it.' He told him his idea about a Soviet asylum, which while certainly not intentionally totally funny, had a few laughs in it, and was, as he said, way off what André had in mind. But there was reasoning there, too. 'I suddenly thought,' he told him, 'that the idea of a Paul Schofield in a dinner jacket didn't really turn me on very much.'

He sent the opening sketches of what became *EGBDF* 'and,' André says, 'I was absolutely wild about them.' He had to be if he were going to sustain his part of the operation while suffering what he now recalls as 'the worst agony of my life'.

That was when he started pinning the manuscript paper to his architect's board and set to work. Said Stoppard: 'What we did was consecutive rather than concurrent. I didn't know what he had written, really. He could only play me the piano part of it, which didn't mean much to my tin ear. So *he* knew what I had done, but *I* didn't know what he had done until the first rehearsal.'

No one at first had any idea just how well it would work. As André said: 'We always thought of it as a one off.' But from the opening night at the Royal Festival Hall with the LSO and the Royal Shakespeare Company under the direction of Trevor Nunn, it was plain that that wasn't going to be so. 'It was, I suppose,' André told me, 'one of the greatest moments of my life.'

The play went on to New York at the Metropolitan Opera House and has since played in dozens of other countries, among them France, Israel, Switzerland, Sweden and Austria. It has been given more than 300 times 'in every language you can think of. It's playing some place all the time.' And there have not just been professional performances. There have been university productions, too.

The people who came to see it liked lines such as the one from the doctor to the political prisoner: 'You are here because you have delusions that sane people are put in mental hospitals.' But they liked the music, too. André's symphonic compositions had never had a better response.

'Tom was wiped out by it,' recalls Previn, 'because he had never written anything where 3,000-plus people laughed at once, cheered at once, applauded at once. This was more people than he was used to in one theatre, under one roof.

But the success came only after he had tried to talk André into some weird musical ideas, like suggesting that the play ended with the opening bars of Beethoven's Fifth Symphony. André's answer: 'Tom, you once told me that your favourite ending of a play was the last line of *The Front Page*, "The son of a bitch stole my watch." Do you think we can get somebody to say that after Beethoven Five?' "All right," said Tom, "you win."'

Actually, they both won. The play was critically acclaimed from the first performance, even though *Newsweek* did describe it as 'one of the most unwieldly curiosities of our time'.

Schuyler Chapin saw his old protégé's work and said he felt proud. 'It represents the peculiar mix of the talent André has,' he told me.

Among the things it did was to cement the relationship that existed between André and Tom. 'He's so smart,' says André. 'Quite the most intelligent man I know. He says things you wish you had said.'

And to Stoppard, his friend is simply one of those soul mates that André himself seems to collect with the ease of a butterfly hunter in a garden on a summer's day. 'He's one to whom you don't have to explain your jokes, whose references are very similar and the speed of celebration are very similar. He's one of those people you don't have to try with. He's a tremendously literary figure for me. His feelings about literature are not very different from his feelings about music. He has read books that I wish I had read.'

The one thing they don't have in common is music, thanks to Stoppard's self-confessed 'tin ear'. 'I feel very embarrassed about working with him because I think he deserves somebody who knows more,' he told me. 'Because he's got such a wide compass, he knows what *I'm* up to, but I behave very badly because I don't go to his concerts. I don't go to concerts, because they bore me. I don't go, the way I don't go to ice skating. It's shameful really. I just can't whip up an interest, although he goes to my openings, and I feel I *ought* to reciprocate. But I've no interest in classical music. I never know who's playing what, where and when. So in a way, I feel he's wasted on me.'

He was also embarrassed when André did his best to make him welcome into his world. Stoppard and his wife were invited to one of the Previn LSO concerts at the Festival Hall. 'I didn't know what he was playing, typically. But tickets were waiting for us. We sat down.

I'm not sure if I'd been to a concert before then. André came in wearing a nice suit and carrying a little stick, that's all I thought I would notice.

'Just before he started playing, I saw him look out for us and then make some little gesture – and I went all cold. My heart almost stopped. There he was, about to play some dreadfully complicated piece and he looked up at us. That he could do that, even think about it, shocked me. All the blood in my body froze. It was as if you go to see *King Lear* and Lear, before he starts speaking, looks out on to the audience to make sure you are sitting there. I've never felt so honoured in my life. To get a Tony was nothing like that.'

What most people didn't know when *EGBDF* had its première was that it was going to represent something of a symphonic swan song. André had decided to end his job with the LSO. He was going at the end of 1979, eleven and a half years after jumping over the furniture at the Savoy. 'Unless you are a Karajan,' he repeated, 'the time comes to go. Otherwise you become a little too well-known piece of the furniture.'

But the orchestra knew they would miss him – and indeed, almost twelve years later, they still do. 'He turned it into a great European orchestra,' said one player.

To mark their appreciation, they appointed him Conductor Emeritus, while his own role went to Claudio Abbado.

'There was absolutely no rancour,' André remembered when we discussed this.

What he was not happy about were the lack of rehearsal facilities and the poor pay the musicians had to suffer. What was more, 'you could never be sure whether you were going to get three hours for rehearsal or just two, because the musicians might have to go off to do a jingle for dog food, which pays more money.'

If that situation was bad in 1980, ten years later, it would remain unchanged. Altering it has by now become a Previn crusade.

Even without the LSO, there was plenty of other conducting work ahead for him. He still had Pittsburgh and he was appearing on television – advertising fake fur coats as well as going to the changing of the Guard and saying that you saw it best on his make of TV sets. He was also still writing his articles.

But with the advent of 1980, he thought the time had come for a rest. At the age of fifty-one, he announced he was taking a sabbatical.

It came at a time in his life when he needed it. His marriage to Mia had gone from difficult to impossible. She was away from home a great deal filming and it was while working in the South Pacific that the marriage came to an end. Another reason for the break was that she felt she was not made for the English countryside. André, for his part, believed he truly was. He even played cricket at the club next to The House.

As someone said at the time: 'It was a classic case of "When one door closes, another slams shut in your face."'

They agreed that they would have joint custody of the children. But there was to be a new happiness ahead for him – in the form of a woman named Heather.

NINETEEN

Heather is tall, wears glasses, enjoys walking around in jeans and seems as far removed from what some people would deem the glamour worlds in which André Previn has moved for forty-five years as is possible to contemplate. But she has brought him the most happiness he has ever known.

Not that that even seemed a remote possibility the day in 1971 when they first met. The former Heather Sneddon, daughter of a middle-ranking British diplomat, was married to the actor Michael Jayston, who had just had the biggest success of his career, playing the Czar in *Nicholas and Alexandra*. Currently, he was working on a film with Mia, called *Follow Me*, a not terribly successful piece based on the Peter Shaffer play The Private *Ear* and the Public *Eye*, which in the West End had starred Kenneth Williams and Maggie Smith.

The Previn twins were a year old, but Mia still found time to entertain and she invited the Jaystons to The House. Of course, they talked about films.

Because they had been living in Spain for a year, the Jaystons had nowhere to stay now that they were back in Britain. 'So while we were looking, Mia invited us to take the cottage across from the house in Leigh.'

They were there for about eight weeks. But Mia was the Previn they got to appreciate. 'We didn't really know André at all, because all that time he was away with one of his orchestras. Mia was there, looking after her then year-old twins.'

The Jaystons settled into the home that before long they found at Cobham, Surrey. Heather had a baby and Mia, by now one of her close friends, came to visit her in hospital. The Jaystons went to The House for dinner. They got on so well together they became something of a foursome, going out to dinner as two pairs of friends who liked each other and had a certain amount in common. Heather by now had three children, two boys and, like the Previns, a Vietnamese-born adopted daughter, Li-An.

And then the Jaystons divorced. 'It was very hard for me, because I had three little ones. Michael had found someone else. There was nothing acrimonious about it; it was just life, but I had no one else in *my* life.'

What she did still have were the Previns as friends. She would go on her own to them for dinner at Leigh, but only occasionally, and after a time, they seemed to lose touch. Then André rang her – to say that he and Mia were also getting divorced. 'I told him I was sorry and sympathised, but we didn't talk very much after that. He was away a lot in Pittsburgh.'

But then one day he got back from America and phoned her.

Neither of them had thought much about their common situation being anything more than something to talk about, a cause for mutual commiseration and an opportunity to have a laugh. He *always* made her laugh.

But then one day he rang to say that he had two tickets for Wimbledon.

The temptation of the occasion was paramount. What André had on offer was not just two tickets for the world's greatest tennis championship, but two, at the world's greatest tennis championship, for *the royal box*, the box where they served champagne and strawberries and cream with every volley on the centre court below.

'Until then, I'd just thought of André as a nice enough chap,' she recalled for me. After that day, she thought of him in rather more personal terms. 'We had an absolute ball,' she said. 'He made me laugh like a drain.'

The royal box was as far removed as she could imagine from the home where she was then living in the Surrey town of Woking, a nice enough spot on the leaflets put out by the estate agents, but hardly with a reputation for social excitement. That afternoon, she felt her whole existence had been temporarily transformed. She didn't know that the transformation was about to become permanent.

It was the first time they had been together on their own for any length of time. 'I hadn't laughed for years. I had been stuck in Woking. All of my days had been a struggle – getting the kids to school, trying to find the money for their schools.

The day at Wimbledon was the perfect antidote to all her problems. If it were characterised by the laughs, even then they took a long time in coming. 'If you haven't laughed for a long time, it's rather like getting an old creaky engine going. But then it started happening, even if I only seemed to laugh a lot inwardly to begin with.'

A photograph of the pair appeared in the papers the next day, captioned, 'André Previn escorting Françoise Hardy', which showed just how accurate some people in what was still Fleet Street really were.

She didn't see him for several months. He was away with his orchestra and during the school holidays he tried to spend his time with the twins, who went to the same boarding school as her own sons.

Certainly, she didn't think of him as someone she was likely to marry. They both, to use her phrase, had decided to get on with their lives.

All this coincided with André's impending parting of the ways with the LSO. The orchestra decided to give him a present to mark his tenth anniversary with them. What would he like? A baton? No, he said, he fancied some engraved glass. He also knew a glass engraver called Heather.

He is fond of saying now that not only did he take the engraving home with him, but also the engraver. 'That isn't quite true because it hadn't happened yet.'

She was still desperately unhappy. 'And so was he. He had been knocked into a loop over his divorce because of his children. He didn't anticipate any of this happening.'

Before long, it was clear that, despite all her reservations, Heather and André would get married.

They did so in Pittsburgh in January 1982. She gave her occupation as 'making designs in glass'. But she wasn't going to make a profession out of it. 'I don't have that problem about answering the call of talent because I don't have any,' she says modestly.

Immediately after the ceremony, Heather set about making a whole series of telephone calls – calling her parents, her sister, her friends. André sat and watched. 'Aren't you going to call anyone?' she asked him. 'No,' he said, 'I haven't got anyone.' The only person he thought he could call was his mother, but he said, 'I'll have to tell her in person.'

'I know,' said Heather. 'Call Dory.'

'But I haven't spoken to Dory in ten years.'

'Doesn't matter,' she said, 'give her a call.' He did and she was pleased to hear from him.

That could have been a ticklish situation. André knew that Betty would have been easier, although the first contact there was to be in person. Heather first met Betty at a concert given by the Pittsburgh

Symphony in Los Angeles. Heather was there with Lotte, her new mother-in-law. (One of the problems of being the wife of a performer is that she can never sit with her husband. As she told me: 'I'm a grass widow – my old man's up there while I go alone.')

On this occasion, she had the senior Mrs Previn with her. Betty was there too, and Mama jabbed Betty with a long finger and said, "Betsy, I'm here with André's new wife."'

It could have been difficult, except that Betty, now happily married to the jazz guitarist Mundell Lowe, took it in the spirit in which the greeting was intended.

'Betty turned round, stood up and smiled. And she said, "Hi. I'm number one!"'

Heather said, 'Hi! I'm number four.' As she told me, she likes her predecessor immensely.

With Dory, the phone call on his last wedding day changed everything between her and her former husband. 'It seemed to break the spell. It was very hard for her when André had married Mia. Nobody had spoken to her. That one phone call seemed to close a chapter in Dory's life and enabled her to get on with things.'

Heather told André she wanted to meet Dory. So she invited her to meet them. 'She was very nervous, as was I,' Heather told me. 'But we found out there was no need to be so. We both had red hair. We were both stringy birds. She had a sense of humour stretching from here to Hong Kong. I just thought she was a wonderful woman.'

Dory had by then remarried. When she came to London, she called on Heather and they went out together. 'She and André are now great friends. I was pleased to be the instigator of that, because she has become a very good friend.'

Heather comes back again and again to her conception of the role of Mrs Previn, compared with that as seen by the previous holders of that title.

'The mistake he has always made before was in falling in love with women who had careers of their own. I don't really want to do anything apart from enjoying life with my husband.'

André was her ideal partner in that, from the first time she met him, she realised that he liked doing ordinary things if not always with ordinary people. Like Tom Stoppard, he liked to be stimulated by the company he kept, but that did not mean he wanted to be the centre of attraction. Perhaps that accounted for all those people who said he was reserved.

'He's not reserved,' said Heather. 'He's just fiercely private.'

With Heather he went out more than he had for years – to the homes of people like Julie Andrews and Blake Edwards.

What their friends had noted about André now was that he seemed to be smiling more. The slightly hang-dog expression they had got to know in the years before seemed to have gone. The colour on his face looked better.

'André doesn't bitch about going out now on official occasions,' Heather told me. 'And we can poke fun quietly at people we're doing duty for.'

You didn't often see the Previns sitting in theatres, although they would go off to a play when they could. 'I'm condemned, on the whole,' Heather told me, 'to a diet of André's concerts and Tom Stoppard's plays.'

There was no question that she was good for him. He recognised that and when he talked about his previous marriages, he would tell her: 'I did it until I got it right.'

She says that she tries to persuade him to do more composing 'because he's so good at it' and to play the piano in public more than he did. 'But he'd rather sit in the sun.'

He recognises this dimension she has introduced into his life. 'Without her shouting at me, I would never have finished the concerto I've been writing,' he told me in the summer of 1988.

Although he would say he wasn't sure he would know a piece he had conducted when he heard the recording, she is certain that she could. 'You can hear all the notes,' she said. 'Not a wash of sound, he always manages to make everything clear.'

Heather and André took time to get on with each other's children, although it seemed more sensible – and cheaper – in the first years of their marriage for André to go to his six children in America rather than for all six to travel to England. So he would make frequent detours to see them in New York. It wasn't enough, but it was something. The guilt remained. When Heather did see them, they got on well.

Heather's two boys found it more difficult to relate to André, but her daughter Li-An was officially adopted by him and became his daughter every bit as much as the others were.

The life with André turned into something he had not known before. Heather travelled with him when he went away and moved with him to The House, which was not easy since there were constant reminders that it had been Mia's home before it was hers. And in their marriage there was no conflict of careers. Not only was André the one with the talent and the amazing workload, she was happy not to even try to compete.

Heather also enjoyed being with his mother during the final couple of years of her life.

'She was a really wicked lady with a stiletto humour.'

They went to see her in hospital just before she died. 'She was moaning and groaning, complaining about the food.' What she really wanted most of all were 'Koenigsberger klops,' she said. The dumplings of her youth were what she craved, which they thought was a fairly good sign.

'She was a wonderful woman,' recalls Heather. She died soon afterwards.

In 1984, their son Lukas was born. They decided on the name because they liked it and because it had a certain international sound. 'It was kind of worldwide, which wouldn't need explaining anywhere.'

Heather says he has been the high spot of their life. It is not something that visitors to their home need to have proved. One only has to see the boy who looks more and more like Christopher Robin with André to realise the extent to which he has become the apple of his father's eye. He also has the advantage of a father who can spend time with him. Lukas arrived at a time when André could afford to arrange his life so that the child formed part of it. He travelled with his parents and on at least one occasion, after a Sunday afternoon performance, trotted on to the platform to be at the maestro's side. As André has said, as long as the music is treated properly, what goes on around it doesn't matter too much.

When the time came for Lukas to go to school, André said he felt tempted to go and sit in the classroom with him. With no chance of that, he suggested they get a tutor for the boy. Heather vetoed the notion before it got much further than that, a notion.

But it was never a really serious dispute. 'I just think I am one of the luckiest women alive. He is a great husband. He is very thoughtful. He's also great fun. If things go wrong, he can usually overcome practically everything with a laugh.'

She doesn't allow his importance in the world in which they live to take over their lives.

I myself have rung their home to hear Heather answer and say, 'I suppose you want to talk to His Nibs.'

He himself will not draw back on agreeing how good she has been for him. On tour now that Lukas is at school he speaks to them both on the phone every day. When she can, she still joins him overseas.

She loves being with him in Vienna or Salzburg when he conducts the Vienna Philharmonic. She travels with him to Berlin when he fronts the orchestra there. 'He's a totally different person when he's with German-speaking orchestras,' she says.

That's not something that he himself sees. 'I tell the same jokes, only in German.' Yet it is undeniable that he is particularly comfortable with them.

A conductor should be as unwilling to name his favourite orchestra as Fred Astaire used to refuse to reveal the identity of his favourite dancing partner. What he will say is that 'No orchestra plays more beautifully than the Vienna.'

As with all his orchestras, he lines up with them in the corridors outside the gilt-encrusted Musikverein for coffee served in plastic cups and poured from an urn and tells anecdotes to men who are used to standing to attention in the presence of their 'Meister'.

It is a word used often in Vienna when Previn is around. He and I were having dinner at the elegant Imperial Hotel late in 1988 when the pianist in the bar saw him approach. The man, a musician who had not learned to play the piano in the last couple of decades, stood when he saw André approach, bent his head forward and whispered a respectful 'Meister'.

'I wish he hadn't done that,' said André. It was one of those embarrassing results of that word 'success'.

But he was rarely embarrassed when he was in his more accustomed role as a professional. When the camera broke down before a television programme was about to be recorded, he knew that something had to be done to stop the audience becoming restive.

'You have no idea how I admired him for what he did that day,' said Heather. 'André went out and did a stand-up act. I hadn't seen this facet of the multi-faceted man,' she told me.

Actually she was annoyed by it. 'I went back quite outraged that he hadn't let on that he could do it. I've never been more blown away. I suddenly realised that I had not married one man, but several.'

All of those men brought some fairly distinct advantages to her lifestyle, however. Again in Vienna, they will waltz on New Year's Eve at the ball attended by the President of the Republic in the Musikverein. 'It's a remarkable evening, so beautifully choreographed and well dressed it looks like something out of a film by Fellini.'

It is about the only dancing André does.

At other times in Vienna, he is on a firmer footing. His comfort in German is so complete that few suspect he isn't a permanent resident.

He dresses the part – wears a dark green coat and a little hat with a feather in it. He shops with his family in those garments made to measure for the East European winter. Once he, Heather and Lukas bought a few things in a shop in the city centre. Naturally, André, in his faultless German, negotiated the transaction.

Heather and the little boy left, with André staying behind to pay the bill. As he handed the money to the shopkeeper, the woman handed him back a hundred-schilling note. 'And,' she said, 'please bring some more of your clients here.' She thought he was a tour guide.

At home, Heather does the driving. 'André's a horrible driver,' she explained. 'He charges ahead, never indicates. He just leaves a trail of accidents behind him. Fortunately, you never see them!'

It was part of his general failure with things practical. He has never learned how to wire a plug, so should one expect him to be a good driver? She, on the other hand, is very practical. When he worried about travelling from Leigh into London, she said, 'Why don't I learn to fly a helicopter to take you in and out?'

Heather has learned not to be infuriated by having to step in with the screwdriver when it is needed, even by the fact that whenever André is ill, 'He's a dreadful patient.'

One of the things the Previns have in common is a susceptibility to migraine. 'I'll get up and shut up because it won't do me any good to grumble. André, though, will complain long and loud. I'll say I'm not feeling so well, either. André will then complain longer and louder.'

But he has tried to help her – like the time the man she calls 'the most culinarily inept person I've ever met' tried to get her something to eat when she wasn't feeling well. There wasn't a lot he could manage, but her demands weren't great. He thought he could deal with the problem effectively. After all, he had achieved miracles with a saucepan of soup and that little sausage.

'She fancied some jelly or Jel-O, as it's known in the States, so I went down, got out a packet and looked at it and it seemed reasonable enough. It amounted to "Just add water" and I thought I could do that. But then I noticed that on the package it said if you wanted to make it a little more glamorous, you could add fruit.'

He looked around again and found a tin of half peaches. And he opened that. 'I thought it would be great.' He looked at the instructions again and they said, 'Fold in the peach.' Fold in? 'Evidently, it means putting the peach in very gently and then stirring it. But I didn't know that. I tried to think of a way of folding it. So I took half a peach and folded it and put it in and it went – wang – unfolded again. I did it again and the same thing happened. I then looked around and found a toothpick and folded it again, this time using the toothpick to secure it. I thought I could get the picks out later. I got quite a talking to for that.'

Thereafter, he was happy to leave those culinary arts to Heather, particularly when she made chicken. 'It's my favourite food. I like ordinary chicken – not boiled. I don't like chicken that's been mucked around with. Chicken A-la anything. No.'

His tastes were simple, and so were hers. Once every three weeks or so the two of them might have a malt whisky or a glass of vodka, but it was the good old English tea that appealed. Heather very quickly got to know that before they went back to America, a suitcase filled with virtually nothing but tea packets had to be packed along with everything else.

In 1985, she was still travelling with him to Pittsburgh. But that was a destination that was finally removing itself from his travel itinerary. Marshall Turkin ran the orchestra and André felt the place wasn't big enough for both of them. One had to go. The one who went was André Previn. There were two other orchestras waiting in the wings for him, one in America, the other in London. He accepted an offer to become music director of the Los Angeles Philharmonic soon after agreeing the same role with the Royal Philharmonic.

TWENTY

He accepted the offer of the Royal Philharmonic because it was too good an opportunity to let go. It meant he could still look after the musical welfare of a London orchestra without, though, feeling so much part of the furniture.

He went to Los Angeles because an offer was made to him after the departure of Carlo Maria Giulini to take over one of the great orchestras in America. The Royal Philharmonic operated on a virtual shoestring, but they had had an international reputation since they were founded by Sir Thomas Beecham. The Los Angeles Philharmonic, on the other hand, bespoke wealth – from the people who were subscribers, to the salaries paid to its members.

It isn't easy running an Amercian orchestra. The union rules are very tight and when the LA Phil. as everyone knows it, goes on tour, they are not allowed to rehearse while they are away.

The rehearsal problems with London orchestras are of a different order. They are the same with the RPO as with the LSO. André not only never knew how long a rehearsal would last – there was the odd difficulty of the orchestra members going off to play for a TV commercial for washing powders, if not dog food – but also the location of these sessions was sometimes steeped in a mystery that was unfathomable to musicians who had never worked in Britain. The first rehearsal for a particular concert could be in his old recording rooms in Walthamstow and the next in the heart of the East End – or, if he were extremely lucky, on the stage of the Royal Festival Hall itself.

'A catch-as-catch-can situation,' is how he still describes it. 'Everybody is on automatic pilot.' And that is almost never intended as a criticism of his musicians.

'I'm filled with admiration for them,' he told me. 'Why more people don't ask, "Is it too late to learn dentistry?", I don't know.

274

And he added: 'I really cannot think of any other place in the civil-ised musical world where players still get paid by the session and where they are forced to take on more and more work in case there is a fallow period just around the corner.'

It took a great love of both the orchestra and London to accept the situation. 'It really is quite terrible,' he told me. 'The orchestra play beautifully. But it would be even better if the members had enough money to allow them not to take on other work. They would be less rushed, feel more comfortable and more rested. Everyone would benefit.'

It wasn't enough just to say that *Americans* were better paid than their British counterparts in whatever work they did. 'You could just as easily compare London with the North Pole.' The mind con-templates the prospect of the fee scales for an Eskimo orchestra play-ing in a giant igloo. But André is still sure that they would be better paid, if only in herrings, than musicians in London.

It was a battle he began in 1985. He continued it when, after a couple of years, he changed jobs with his old friend and colleague Vladimir Ashkenazy, who had been principal conductor and now took on André's role as music director, and he is continuing to fight it still six years later.

Even after all these years, he still fails to understand the lack of status accorded to serious musicians in the British capital, all so dif-ferent from Vienna, where the snow-swept winter streets, just as much as the sun-drenched pedestrian pathways in summer, seem to echo with the music of the Philharmonic.

'There, the members of the orchestra are the nobility,' André mused. He once went into the city's most fashionable store with one of his instrumentalists. The man wanted to open a charge account. 'As soon as he said he was in the Vienna Philharmonic, he was in. They bowed and they scraped. It wouldn't be like that in England or in America.'

'No, not at all,' said the concert master.

As is quite usual in these things, André's RPO appointment was announced two years before he was due to begin it – if a symphony orchestra hasn't got itself booked up two years ahead, it's in trouble, so it had to know who the conductor was going to be. But once announced, André was itching to get going. He began work with them a year before the contract's starting date – particularly on a TV series on the orchestra. When he was finally able to get going as music director, he had all the Previn guns firing simultaneously: The Festival Hall was the site of a Previn Festival, which became known as 'The André Previn Selection' – not just of RPO music but also of the things that appealed to him – jazz with Oscar Peterson and Buddy Rich. Ravi Shankar, the guru of modern Indian music, with whom André had worked before, performed alongside Ashkenazy, who played André's own Piano Concerto, which he was pleased to see was now firmly fixed in the repertoire of both Emanuel Ax and André Watts. And then there was also Kgung Wha Chung, Yo Yo Ma and the orchestra itself.

The idea of work was burning a hole in his conscience. 'Not long ago,' he told me in 1989, 'Heather and I were talking about travelling. She said she wanted to go to Paris because we hadn't been there for a very long time. All I could think of saying was, "Why? The orchestra there I find very dull." She said, "Not to play, you so-and-so. Just to go there." I do so much travelling that the idea of going somewhere on holiday didn't tempt me at all.'

On the other hand, he has always been very good at resisting temptation. At about the same time as the debate on Paris, he had an invitation he normally would never have dreamed of accepting. To go to Hawaii and play Strauss waltzes on New Year's Eve. He almost laughed the idea out of court. 'Forget it,' he told his manager. 'Wait,' he was advised. 'You take Heather and the family.'

'No,' said André again and a Previn 'no' normally has no room for 'maybe'. But on this occasion, the manager was pressing. 'They'll pay you $100,000,' he said.

Not even a man of Previn's standing and wealth could resist that sort of offer. For one evening, $100,000? Besides, who the hell would know? Or would they?

'Would they want to publicise this?' he asked.

'Yes,' said the manager, 'I think they would.'

Again he said, 'Forget it' and this time there were no 'maybes'.

What he was offering the RPO was not certainty, but the promise of a whole new life after a time in which their financial fortunes had become so low, there were rumours of closure. He was going to change the programming of the orchestra. The man who by now was spoken of as still wearing the last remnants of a Beatle cut known in the business was going at it with as many cannons firing as in his last performance of the *1812* Overture. He had refused to consider the LA Phil. until he had been sure he could accommodate both it and the RPO and his commitment to the London orchestra had to be the first priority, since he had accepted it first.

He was going to be in evidence, and he was going to try what was, for them, new things. 'The safest repertoire in the world has not yet been proven to fill seats,' he explained, 'so you might as well not fill them by playing other music.' That did not mean, however, that he was intending to play a constant stream of world premières, 'just music that isn't always played to death'. As he said, 'It is still possible to surprise an audience with a piece of Tippett.'

It was a promise he was to keep in both his new musical homes. He told me about one of the great moments of serendipity he experienced in Los Angeles. 'I found a symphony by Harold Shapero which had not been played since its première in the 1940s. It was a tremendous hit.' So tremendous that the orchestra recorded it and repeated the performance in Chicago and Boston.

He had a technique for getting to know his 'bands'. He demonstrated it on his first day rehearsing the LA Phil. at the Dorothy Chandler Pavilion. He asked them to play the *Enigma Variations*. He conducted and he listened. Then he told them how he wanted it done in future. If he wasn't sure that there really was a definite Previn sound, this way he could tell what was specifically *not* his sound.

Of one thing he was sure: in Los Angeles, he wouldn't be facing the sort of restrictions with which he was confronted overseas – like still being banned from the Soviet Union. He had plans to record the Brahms *Requiem* with the Dresden Philharmonic, one of the finest East European orchestras. They wouldn't let him in because of *EGBDF*.

But people behind what was still the Iron Curtain heard him just the same, from smuggled records. He was going to make albums with both the RPO and the Los Angeles orchestra now, a fact that, Bernstein and von Karajan apart, would make him arguably the most recorded conductor in history.

He enjoyed making records. If nothing else, it provided extra work for his orchestras and helped him widen his scope with them. With British orchestras, it meant he could get to play programmes more than once. But he never listened to his own records more than once. 'I just like to *have* them,' he told me. He was also glad to know that people went into stores all over the world and bought them. He would still have preferred it if the musicians got more money and worked in better conditions.

'We appreciate his fight for us,' said one member, 'but I don't believe he's going to win. London may have all these different top-class symphony orchestras, but there isn't the respect for serious music to really change matters.'

Neither is André going to change the situation of London's concert halls. He has great fondness for the Royal Festival Hall, the RPO's headquarters. The old Royal Albert Hall is, he says, for window shopping, not for listening. Manchester has the Free Trade Hall, where his Pittsburgh predecessor Sir John Barbirolli ran his Hallé Orchestra for generations, and he likes that. He likes the suburban Fairfield Hall in Croydon, but it's love that keeps him conducting in the British capital.

Los Angeles, on the other hand, has good concert facilities. It would also bring him a host of problems. But in 1985, he looked forward to a long future in the city that gave him both a home and a profession.

'It does strike me that I have led three completely separate lives, details of which are sometimes amusing,' he told me in 1988. 'There was first of all Hollywood, then there was the whole jazz thing and for the last thirty years as a classical conductor. The thing I was good at was knowing when to leave – and get on with the next thing.'

The Los Angeles job provided him with a perfect reason for coming back, a new adventure in a way, a chance to bring the Previn sound to a totally different group of people. Now he would know whether it was simply the work always being better than the musicians or whether the musicians could equal the work.

He insisted on various things as soon as he joined the orchestra, not least of which was bringing John Harbison back in the Previn fold. The man who had been composer-in-residence at Pittsburgh and was a victim of the Previn-Turkin row was now going to have a similar role in LA.

It was to remain a perfect partnership, particularly since Harbison's wife and Heather are great friends and the four enjoy each other's company.

As a professional, Harbison appreciates him even more. 'His film music influence turned him into a very brilliant recording conductor,' Harbison told me. 'He knows what the mike hears.' He also knows what his friend hears. They play music games with each other – in which their tastes noticeably do not coincide.

'He doesn't go for Schoenberg, for instance, or Bach as much as I do – not liking Bach all that much is André's way of getting his own back on his father. He is much happier with German expressionism.'

Harbison says he finds André moody. 'And the more friendly you are, the more moody he is. Only Lukas can bring him out of those moods.'

André and Heather found themselves a house in what he called the less fashionable side of Beverly Hills, but even though he had spent more years in that part of the world than any other, he insisted that a driver be included as one of the conditions of the job – not as a perk, just for convenience.

'I might be all right going straight to the Phil.'s office, but if I suddenly hit a diversion sign, I'd end up in Kansas City. I have no sense of direction whatsoever.' Maybe that was why he didn't feel that going to work in the city of the Angels, LA, was at all a retrogressive move. 'Geographically, I am close to where I used to work in the studios,' he said, 'but it's a world away in reality. I might just as well be in Bordeaux.'

He went there following the entreaties of the man he had missed in London. Ernest Fleischmann left the LSO just before André's arrival with that orchestra and moved to Los Angeles. When he heard Giulini was retiring, he thought Previn would be a worthy successor. So he flew to Vienna where André was conducting that city's orchestra to offer him the job.

Neither knew that before long they would be on a collision course. 'I had first met him twenty years before when I played with the LSO and he was very nice to me in those days. Now that he had resurfaced in my life, I had the typical arrogance of thinking, "Well, now I know how to handle him." And I was one hundred per cent wrong.' How wrong didn't strike him for a little while. When he first got back to California, all he wanted to do was all that he had ever wanted to do – to make music.

Giulini was generous to his successor: 'André Previn,' he said, 'is one of the most important and respected musicians of our day. The close relationships that he has developed with members of great orchestras and the love and respect they have for him make him a very special human being indeed.'

That was what he said in print and his comments were widely publicised. It was doubtless no more than what he really thought. What was not publicised, however, was the fact that the orchestra members discussed the projected appointment at a special meeting that was called while on tour at Richmond Virginia. By a majority vote, the idea of André as their music director was turned down.

'Despite that,' Lorin Levée, the principal clarinetist told me, 'he was imposed on us. A lot of us didn't like it then and we don't like it now.'

On the other hand, there were some who got to like him very much and very quickly, like the personnel manager, Irving Bush. He told me: 'I like him very much and he's been very good for the orchestra because he is such an impeccable musician. He gets involved with us so much – and that sense of humour is tremendous.'

There are some who knew he would be good for the orchestra the moment they heard his name. One such was the first violinist Harold Diktorow, who had been with the LA Phil. for forty-two years when I interviewed him in 1988 and had first played with André at the Hollywood Bowl in 1953.

'Even then, when he was fitting in some classical concerts at the Bowl while working on major movies, I was terribly impressed. When it came to the vote, I was one who said: "How can you say 'No' to him when you haven't even heard him?"'

But the vote went against him although the appointment stayed.

'There are still some people who don't want him,' Diktorow said then. 'They like him but think he is not one of the inspiring conductors. They say he is not exciting enough. He doesn't get the orchestra excited.'

Six months after our talk, those thoughts would come to the surface, but there was not much talk of it after André took up the job in 1985. The orchestra members were handed 'evaluation sheets' and asked to state what they thought of him as a conductor now that he was *in situ*. A vast majority were ready to take back their reservations. He scored a batch of 'As' on his 'Leadership', 'understanding of music' and 'his beat'.

'When he first came here,' said Danny Rothmuiler, the assistant principal cellist, 'André insited on a very democratic way of running the orchestra. People were asked to discuss their thoughts with him. He trusted them.'

People predicted that Previn would bring back pizzazz and glamour to the LA Phil., the kind of aura that had surrounded it during the reign of Zubin Mehta, who had since gone to the New York Philharmonic.

Soon after the Previn arrival – again publicised as though a Hollywood star had just won five Oscars in a single season; the local papers were full of pictures of him holding Academy Awards – Fleishmann announced he was leaving to take over the Paris Opera. He was, however, persuaded to stay. André said he was glad. He was still sure they would be friends – and he was still one hundred percent wrong.

He told one writer: 'I have known Ernest for a long time. We will have a clear division of labour here. We're just beginning to work together, but we get along well. He may be a bit abrasive in some situations, but everyone knows he is all for the music. That's what counts. I have high respect for him and will take all the advice I can get.'

They would be words he would later wish he had eaten. Could the

Pittsburgh experience possibly be repeated? He was sure it couldn't. They had worked all that out.

He was going to have to accept what he always described as his David Niven role again, though, which meant that once more he was in the newspapers. He had been delighted that the days when he and Mia filled the gossip columns were well and truly over, but now everyone in Los Angeles wanted to know what he had had for breakfast. He hoped it would be a situation that would change. He was, after all, as he and Heather kept insisting, a very private person.

Even so, a great deal of time would be spent smiling at society matrons, telling them how much he liked them and trying to find diplomatic ways of not going along with all they said about those nasty people down the road in Hollywood. None of that was required in London – it was the other side of the coin of the terrible conditions in which orchestras laboured.

The Royal Philharmonic seemed to approve of the way they were being looked after. The *Independent* newspaper in September 1987 wrote of André's 'loving and tactful husbandry', a view that seemed to be generally shared by his musicians.

In Los Angeles, he wasn't any more a naturally social animal with crowds of people than he had ever been. Playing tennis with friends wasn't going to be a problem either – there were any number of them with their own courts.

The big problems, if there were to be any at all, would be for his own sorting out – the auditions and eventual final composition of the orchestra and the programmes they played. He would be there for sixteen weeks of the season, including two of them at the Hollywood Bowl, an open-air arena that he had never terribly liked but there was no question that it brought in the people – thousands of them at a time – to hear good music.

There would also be all the tours and recording sessions he could arrange.

He frequently took his courage into his own baton hand. The first time he conducted the *Missa Solemnis* he told Ashkenazy about it. It scared him, he said. His friend said he could always cancel. His answer was something like if he cancelled everything that frightened him, he would still be playing 'Three Blind Mice'. Even now, there was the need for that scary feeling if a thing was to be worthwhile.

But it brought results. In May 1986, the *New York Times*'s Bernard Holland could report: 'The Los Angeles Philharmonic's second New York concert under André Previn showed how quickly its new music director has managed to transfer his tastes and style to a different set of musicians.'

The orchestra played André's own newest composition, *Reflec-tions*, written for horn, cello and orchestra. He also conducted Elgar's *Enigma Variations*, which demonstrated that wherever he was (except perhaps in Vienna or Berlin) he was still going to play the English music he loved. To show, though, that he was not limited, he also gave Prokofiev's Fifth Symphony. It was the Elgar that Mr Hol-land liked. He said it was played 'with great dignity, in a simple, almost deadpan way. That which is held back – left unsaid – often touches us the most and so we sense that behind Elgar's decorum, the quiet good manners, the wit and the bluffness, there is a quivering emotion that can't quite bring itself into the open. Mr Previn seems to understand this and one admired his refusal to use this music's major climaxes histrionically.'

Perhaps more significantly, the writer added: 'His new orchestra has taken on a polish and grooming that becomes it. Carlo Maria Giulini, Mr Previn's predecessor, was never really able to make the Los Angeles into the rich, darkly powerful instrument he wanted, but the Previn connection may match a set of tastes to a corresponding set of abilities.' Had André ever read his reviews, he might have liked that one.

On the whole, he didn't need to read very much about the way his musicians in Los Angeles thought of him. 'I find him approachable, friendly, one of the guys,' said violinist Camille Avellano. Like many others, what she appreciated most were his chamber-music ensem-bles. 'He's one of the guys because he knows how to play, not just to conduct and there's a profound difference. He always makes one feel as if one is on a very equal footing with him. He's always telling funny anecdotes.'

It was part of the Previn philosophy that had worked for more than forty years. 'Previn asked the orchestra to take it easy with him,' recalled Danny Rothmuiler. 'We were all set for nice conventional tempi without realising that he was going to get a lot more exciting than some people thought. He's very self-effacing, almost nice to a fault. A *mensch*.'

Others would agree about those qualities, the last an old Yiddish word that André himself would probably never use and, like most old Yiddish words, is difficult to translate. It means a man, but more than that, an all-rounded man who cares. Rothmuiler agreed: 'Super conductor, super nice all the time – and with a very long fuse.'

Sr. Giulini did not have one, however. 'When André came here after we had been under a task master, things became very much more relaxed.'

The fault they found was the one others had found with him: 'He kind of allows orchestras to do their own thing. An orchestra does like authority, although most of us like the way he does it. The whole atmosphere is more relaxed.'

Even so, right up to the 1990s, there were still comments in Los Angeles about André's Hollywood background, which weren't always favourable. He was afraid there would be. 'I went in some trepidation because if people started calling me, "the ex-Hollywood composer who is now conducting . . ." I'd be doomed. To my relief, it didn't happen.'

In fact, to a limited extent it *did* happen. While everyone else had forgotten it – in England and in most of Europe, people didn't even know about it any more – there remained those in his old home town who thought he still belonged in a studio in Culver City.

Ashkenazy couldn't understand that. When someone told him that Previn was not to be taken seriously because of his Hollywood background, he stormed: 'What the hell has that got to do with it? Doesn't musicianship count?'

Billy Wilder went on record in one of the city's newspapers, saying that André hadn't bothered to look up his former cronies. But Saul Chaplin told me: 'Everyone was just thrilled to have him back.'

Some newspapermen continued to carp. 'André doesn't get the credit he should,' David Raksin says. 'He's so good.' Isaac Stern agrees with that. 'I think he is one of the greatest conductors of our time,' he told me. The RPO seemed equally happy with André, so different in personality, style and programming from his eighty-one-year-old predecessor, Antal Dorati.

People like Stern, Raksin and Chaplin are the ones with whom he enjoys being. He and Itzhak Perlman have been friends since the time he knocked on the door of the Israeli-born violinist's condominium apartment in Daytona Beach, Florida and said: 'Hi, I'm André Previn. How are you?' It was difficult not to take to him after that, Perlman told me.

They mix socially as much as they can. They also mixed professionally with whichever orchestra André happened to be conducting.

'I always enjoy being with him. He's a riot.' Especially when they talk Judaism, into which both were born but about which Perlman is understandably more knowledgeable.

'I'll say to him, "It's Chanucah next week," and he'll say, "What's that?"' They discuss their children. 'I asked him what does a man have to know to be a good father. Then I said, "What the hell do you know?" He's only got, what, about twenty-eight of them?'

What he really has, Perlman accepts, is the ability to switch off from problems, which, as a music director, he was never without. André interviewed Perlman on TV – as he did in a 1989 BBC series with Gene Kelly and Isaac Stern – and instantly put him at ease. He helped him with his jazz recordings, which included some pieces by Scott Joplin.

'He was extremely pessimistic before we recorded the Joplin pieces,' Perlman told me, 'but because he is so nice to work with he became optimistic.

'I called him up with the idea and he said, "What, are you crazy?" And I said, "No. Not crazy" and he suddenly got very funny and very enthusiastic.'

Most of the musicians sitting behind the music stands in his orchestras appear to like him just as much. There have, however, always been those who think that even Previn can be unfair to an orchestra. The people at Pittsburgh used to say that he deliberately scheduled the hardest pieces, like the Berlioz *Requiem* – 'which is like World War Three' – for his return from a period abroad to keep them on their mettle. He thought they got sloppy in his absence. *They* thought he was being presumptive. On the other hand, there is still the continuing fuss made over his being less demanding than other conductors. Musicians were paid their money and took their choice as to which opinion they accepted.

Those who liked him best were the ones who joined him in his first love, chamber music. At Pittsburgh he had formed a piano trio with Herbert Greenberg, the associate concert master and Anne Martin-dale Williams, the principal cellist. Once at Los Angeles, he made it clear that he would do the same or he wouldn't eat. They liked that. (His one big regret about London is that the musicians with whom he works in the orchestra never have time for chamber music.)

He liked talking about the orchestras being families. In some places they were. In Vienna, a get-together with André is like a family reunion.

They like him, though, for his music. Frau Brigitta Grabner, who was the orchestra's administrator, told me in 1989: 'I think his Mozart Piano concerto is the best I have ever heard.' While Prof. Paul Furst, the managing director, put it the way others have done: 'We book him three years in advance because he is such an excellent musician.' That was why, in 1989, he took the orchestra on a tour of Hong Kong, which proved to be all that they hoped it would.

'He always has a human face,' said Professor Furst. Sometimes

that magnificent gilt-encrusted concert hall with its crystal chande-
liers and its organ supported by Grecian columns looks as though it
needs that human face.

'I don't want you should think he is the best conductor in the
world,' said Rainer Küchl, the Vienna concert master. 'He is not. But
he's the friendliest of all the conductors I know and by being so he
gets very good results. I knew he would because I heard him with the
LSO in Salzburg and he was wonderful. His Richard Strauss is the
best.'

He plays chamber music in Vienna with Franz Bartolomey, one of
the principal cellists whose grandfather was a clarinetist when Gustav Mahler conducted the orchestra. His father was a violinist with
the ensemble, too. Now he anxiously hopes his own son will follow
in the family tradition – and still play with André Previn as his conductor. 'He is one of the few conductors,' he told me, 'who doesn't
conduct just the bars and the notes, but the music – and from the
heart.' They liked him in Vienna, too, because he plays Richard
Strauss – 'but also that he likes to play new pieces'.

'There are not many conductors who play Haydn as well as he
does either.' To André, to be invited as he always is into the Bartolomey family, he sees as the greatest honour of all.

He would always tell stories about his own family – and Lukas in
particular – to his orchestra members. Lukas was due to be born just
as the RPO were about to start filming their TV series with André,
Sounds Magnificent.

Every day, they asked for progress reports and for twelve days
there was nothing to say. He finally arrived on André's day off. When
he came in next morning, one of the members called out, 'What a
pro!' It was perhaps one of the nicest things that could be said to him.
But then they knew about him anyway.

He didn't like analysis of the way he himself conducted. 'I think
that an artist can be much more creative if his technique is absolutely
second nature and never gets in the way of his thoughts.'

Seeing Previn in rehearsal, however, is to see Previn thinking. The
clever musicians were the ones who thought they could read his
thoughts. That is another part of his success. Playing in one of his
orchestras is not just to learn but also to be the other side of tele-
pathy. Was there really such a thing as the Previn sound? Even he
would deny it. The music had to talk, but he wanted the instruments
to do so, too. 'I do drive orchestras crazy when it comes to rhythmic
clarity.'

So what sort of rhythmic clarity in Los Angeles? Despite what he had said before about having the right orchestra for the right piece, he wasn't going to allow himself to be pigeon-holed. They thought of him as being obsessed with British music, but although he would play it, he would also conduct the music he chose for London; Mozart and Haydn and some of the modern composers. If, in Vienna, he was doing Strauss and Mahler as well as Mozart – 'They play it better than anyone else' – he would conduct those in Los Angeles, too.

He wasn't going to be condemned by the title, Specialist, even though he would have the rule: 'I won't conduct anything I'm not convinced by.' Sometimes, he agrees, his audiences had to be convinced too. In Vienna he conducted Messiaen's *Turangalîla* Symphony. The audience wasn't sure. 'I got a crouching ovation,' he said.

Some things, however, were always worth repeating. Like his relationship with Tom Stoppard. They remained the closest of friends, particularly after, in 1984, he composed six songs for his play *Rough Crossing*, an adaptation of the Molnar farce *The Play's the Thing*. The original, non-musical play had been set in an Italian castle. Peter Wood, the director, thought it would be good to have some music, and Stoppard couldn't think of anyone better to do the job.

He wrote the lyrics to André's tunes, the best one of which, says Tom, was 'Who Said It Would Be Easy?' In the end, just two songs were left.

'I liked the different André who was writing songs, different from the man composing concerti or conducting symphonies,' said Stoppard. 'One of the attractive things about him is that he doesn't see different versions of himself. He's just André, the least pretentious man in the world. He has the ability to write different kinds of music. He didn't emerge as a precious flower out of some classical music hothouse.'

Working with him, as he had known while working on *EGBDF*, was an important experience in Stoppard's life, he maintains. 'To my generation, André Previn was a jazz piano player. Everyone had his *My Fair Lady* jazz album, just as everyone had Sinatra's *Songs for Swinging Lovers*.

Previn the songwriter was happy about that show, but he had no plans for any more. He has no plans to write standards again either; in the late 1960s, he sent his song *Second Chance* to Perry Como, whom he thought was old enough and right enough to sing this song of new love – to quote the Dory Previn lyric – the second time around. Como turned it down because it might be seen to prejudice his Catholic beliefs about one marriage for life.

He wondered constantly about that word success. 'Two kinds of people are able to talk about success – the very successful and the failures,' André maintains.

He worries about people searching for success in fields to which they are not suited. 'Young conductors come to me with long CVs and tapes of hopeless performances. I don't really know what they want.'

As for himself, 'I find it hard to think of myself as a big success. When I'm shaving, I'm not so sure.' But he wasn't going to take it when a critic set himself up as a judge of one of his performances either in the concert hall or on record. 'I don't need some clown who is a failed musician to tell me how I've done. I *know*.'

His brother once put it in perspective for him. He said: 'You're in that weird, snotty profession where you don't have to care about reviews or reviewers.'

He didn't have to care about much by then. The career was swinging like a metronome and his marriage was as perfect as he could imagine a marriage ever being. So much so that five years after their wedding in Pittsburgh, they slipped into the little local church at Leigh and got married again there. Just the two of them present, with Lukas as an unofficial witness.

No one knew about it then and no-one knew it until now. 'Fortunately,' says Heather, 'nothing about us gets into the papers any more.'

It was true enough in 1987. So different from previous years, André Previn really did seem to be getting the privacy he wanted. If he did get into the papers, it was strictly for professional reasons.

Perhaps the best advantage he has as a conductor is to give the chances he does to soloists. It is something to which he constantly refers. 'I can say "I heard a piece" and if I want to, we'll have to do it. If I hear an outstanding violinist or pianist, I can say we'll have him or her as a soloist. That's the power of a conductor.'

Swapping roles at the Royal Philharmonic – music director becoming principal conductor – with Vladimir Ashkenazy suited them both. 'Vova' had new ideas of what he wanted for the orchestra and André could have the time to spend doing the job in Los Angeles. And there was no difficulty with having two men with important titles fronting the orchestra. They did different things. Everyone knew, like it or not, the music which André was comfortable with. Ashkenazy had his own favourites, like Sibelius, with whom Previn didn't feel quite so happy, the Russian pianist told me.

'It was a good idea,' said André. 'Neither of us does all that much although he takes them on more tours than I do.'

Was André comfortable? By most accounts, yes. In 1987 he merged his two orchestral worlds and took the RPO on a tour of the United States – its first ever. It was a sensational success, in real terms as well as André's terms, since the word 'sensational' is one he enjoys using.

Touring is not easy. When he isn't sitting with his orchestra members, he flies first class – going to guest-conducting venues, he pays his own fares. He stays at first-class hotels and pays for them, too. 'I want to do it as nicely as possible, because I work like a dog,' he explained to me. Certainly, he's conquered that old fear of flying. 'When I'm in a plane at least I know that nobody can ring me.

'But no, I've got used to it. I suppose that if one had to have root-canal treatment every day, you'd get used to that, too. Also, if you liked listening to Schoenberg every day, you'd like that, too.' That fact was appreciated by most of the people with whom he worked. André did not like too much Schoenberg.

In the autumn of 1988, he took the LA Phil. on a tour of Japan. Heather and Lukas went too. Heiichero Ohyama, the principal viola player and assistant conductor, took the family to meet his own parents and presented them with kimonos. It was a gesture to a man he liked. 'He has such humour and sensitivity,' was how Heiichero put it.

If André wanted to get a point across, there was a subtle way of doing so – like telling the story of the French teacher who posed the question about the lowest note of the oboe. 'He was subtly testing me, making it clear I should know about it. A wonderful sensitivity,' Ohyama told me.

At the ancient city of Kyoto the family went to a rock garden tended by Zen Buddhist monks. André respectfully showed interest in the way things were arranged in circles, all with religious significance. He then noticed that there were even circles on the gravel paths – seven concentric circles each perfectly formed. André asked the senior monk if that was of religious significance, too. The monk thought for a moment, politely looked at André and said that he respectfully had to point out that that was not so. 'It's just,' he said, 'that the rake we use has seven teeth.'

Retire an embarrassed André Previn.

He tried to find out as much as he could about the country before going there. He even tried to learn the language. He always likes to try to learn the languages of the countries he was visiting. After all, his German is nothing less than perfect, his French very good. He picked up Italian in a matter of weeks. 'But after trying to wrestle with a couple of Japanese phrases I had to give it up. It's beaten me. I'm just too old.'

Emanuel Ax told me: 'There's always an inter-action with André. When I do something with him, it never goes unnoticed. He really does make an effort in a concert to be aware and not just focus on what I'm doing. He's so willing to accommodate. But sometimes I do wish he'd be more demanding of me. In recording studios, he's not hard enough on the people around him. He is always happy.'

Ax told me, however, about one recording session with which he was not happy.

'I told him, "André, I've got to fix this. I really think we should do it again." "Great," said André. "Who's going to conduct it?" Perhaps it's hard to be a good person as well as a demanding son of a bitch.'

What Ax really likes about Previn is his jazz playing, which by the end of the 1980s seemed to be an increasingly neglected side of his work. Said Ax, 'If I could play jazz like that, I'd give up being a concert pianist. He doesn't understand why I regard it as awesome. It's like a violinist saying to me, "How can you play with both hands at the same time?"'

At the end of 1989 André came out of the jazz closet. He had been reluctant to do so. The previous year he had told me he wouldn't do it seriously again 'because I don't want to give the jazz critics a stick to beat me with'. But he succumbed just the same. Heather told him he ought to get together again with people he liked, doing something he so enjoyed undertaking. 'You don't have to prove anything,' she said. So André joined his old sparring partners, guitarist Joe Pass and bassist Ray Brown and recorded a new album. Within weeks, it had sold 100,000 copies.

'I never expected anything like that,' he says, 'but I must admit I chose Ray and Joe simply because they are the best, my favourites – and there's a lot of insurance in that.'

The album, *After Hours* was regularly heard on the radio, which Previn thought was the biggest tribute of all.

'Heather did a lot of crowing about all that.'

He even liked the recording procedure. 'So very different from making a classical recording.'

It wasn't done in an old warehouse or garage any more, but in a New York recording studio, but the principle was the same. They didn't know what they were going to record till they got into the studio and then did the whole lot in six hours split into two sessions. 'There were never more than two takes – and no inter-cutting.'

All three men were roughly the same age. André showed Ray Brown a picture of Lukas. 'That's your son?' he asked. André said it was. 'Man,' said Ray, '*my* son's forty-three.' The following spring there was another album, this time with Betty's husband Mundell Lowe on guitar. As proof of how well he and Betty got on these days, he wrote the sleeve notes for her own latest album. Mundell now works regularly with Ray and André. 'He's the perfect Trio guitarist.'

Meanwhile André was invited back into the jazz clubs. Ray Brown told him he could get $50,000 a week for an hour a night. 'Is that sufficiently Uptown for you?' he asked.

All André had to decide was whether he really wanted to get into that neighbourhood. 'But what joy!' he said to me, 'I wasn't sure I could still do it – and I was just amazed at how successful the albums were.'

Occasionally, he goes into record shops looking for his old records – old, old ones some of them, ones that he might even get round to playing. But he has had a couple of shocks of late.

In one second-hand store, he picked out a selection of discs – some for $5, some for $7. Finally, in a bin, he dug up a record which had the name 'André Previn' on the sleeve. He was delighted. 'How much for this one?' he asked the man behind the counter. The man looked at it, held it away from him as though it had an unfortunate smell and said, 'Oh that one – you can have it for nothing.'

'I wanted to kill him,' said André. As he did the owner of another store selling one of his records – on the shelf marked 'Nostalgia'.

There was a condition to the idea of going back to professional jazz. He made his partners promise to tell him at the end of the session if they thought it was no good and that what they had recorded would embarrass them – or him. 'They looked at me as if I were insane.'

His classical music is done with considerably more confidence. Jack Renner and James Mallison of the Tel Arc company work with him on both classical and jazz music. 'He works quickly,' said Renner, 'with enormous patience. He uses just a few microphones and controls the balance himself.'

In Vienna, where he was recording Richard Strauss songs with the soprano Arlene Auger, he moved from concert hall to recording booth, listening to every note, checking each nuance. He had a telephone by his side and if the engineers weren't happy, he'd do it all again.

'Very patient and very kind,' Auger told me. 'I think he is very different from most conductors in the consideration he shows.'

'Well,' he told her, 'you make a beautiful noise, my darling.'

But it was, as we have seen, difficult to please everyone all the time. Ronald Wilford told me: 'Sometimes he's a weak administrator. He kind of gives in. Some people would say that was weak. I think doing that can show strength. He also does have a temper. You can't collaborate with musicians the way he has to do without screaming sometimes – particularly when there is no rehearsal time and the first half becomes a rehearsal for the second half.'

But then his repertoire was by now so great he had learned to cope. He conducted music for the soundtrack of the old silent film classic, *Alexander Nevsky*. Wilford was impressed with the way he did that. 'It was the old Hollywood training,' he said. 'That's duck soup to him.'

Composing was never quite that. He still says: 'It surprises me that people like playing my work.' He makes time to do it, sometimes with and sometimes without Heather's bullying. 'I never learned to start composing and then quit. The trouble is I can't do it while I'm roaring around the world and in airports.'

But if he has few delusions about his work being played after his death, he also has none about their popularity. 'I don't think there will ever be the anticipation for new work by contemporary composers the way there was when people waited to hear the latest from Brahms or Puccini. And there's certainly no money in it.'

TWENTY-ONE

'Previn Resignation Stuns Music World', the headline in the London *Daily Telegraph* was repeated virtually word for word all over that music world. In Los Angeles, the city's two newspapers made it their front page splash story. After a series of rows, André had resigned as music director of the Los Angeles Philharmonic. That was the official story, details of which have never been published.

'It has become obvious to me there is no room for a music director,' the board of directors of the orchestra was told. The rows took hours at the Previn office at the Los Angeles Music Centre and at his home on South Bedford Drive.

The real reason he left was that he and Ernest Fleishmann couldn't work together. The pressures of trying to run his orchestra and playing politics brought conflicts that just couldn't be resolved.

As André told me, revealing the details for the first time: 'Soloists were hired. Guest conductors asked to appear. Programmes arranged. Recordings were fixed. Without asking me.'

He fumed about the way he was being treated. 'I'd say, "I think next year, I should like to do the Mahler Two," only to be told, "Oh no – because So-and-So's going to do that."'

Whoever So-and-So was, he didn't like the sound of that. So-and-So might have been a very good conductor, whom André would have welcomed as a guest. 'What do you mean, So-and-So? He's coming here?' No one had told him the man had even been invited. The conductor who saw his job as looking after the musical welfare of his orchestra needed someone to look after his own.

'I told you,' André says Fleishmann told him.

'No you didn't,' said André. '*I* want to do it.'

'Oh, but he's coming. Don't worry about it.'

As he now remembers: 'It all got completely, utterly out of hand. I couldn't make any decision, therefore I couldn't run the orchestra. I could have coped with the office work, even with being David Niven, etc. I couldn't cope with the fact that I was in that building but I was not given the opportunity to be music director.'

It was very much a question of chemistry – or rather the lack of it – between Fleishmann and André, an even less compatible formula than the relationship between him and Marshall Turkin. 'I've got to hand it to Ernest,' he told me, 'even now he's terrific. He manages the orchestra with the kind of self-centred ruthlessness that I guess it takes.

'I told him that he himself was totally incapable of uttering the phrase, "I'll consult the music director."'

Time magazine warned of trouble in the future. The thirty-year-old highly gifted Finnish conductor Esa-Pekka Salonen was appointed in André's stead. 'They said,' André told me, 'exactly what I had been saying: that the new music director now, he will have a great shipboard romance – Utopian love and kisses and after a year or so, he'll say, "I'd rather do . . ." and the dance will start again.

'In fact, I think I was usurped, screwed. Usually when a music director is usurped, he's at least told about it. I was bypassed completely.'

Unwittingly, Esa-Pekka Salonen was at the centre of the row from the start. He didn't realise that when he was appointed principal guest conductor, there would be trouble. But there was – because no one had told Previn. As André now remembers: 'We had a very good meeting and after about an hour in which I told him that I still wanted him to be a guest conductor, he said to me: "It's still all right, isn't it, if I take the orchestra to Japan?" I said, "What? Esa-Pekka, you had better come back and sit down again." I found then for the very first time that no only had he been told he was going to do the Japan trip, he had been contracted to go.'

The Japanese liked the LA Phil. so much that they wanted two tours, the one André himself was going to lead and another one for a conductor he would nominate. Instead, a conductor was nominated by Fleishmann. That was when André acted.

'There was hell to pay. I went to the president of the orchestra, the president went to Ernest and Ernest said, "You're right . . . I did this one very badly."

'When the board heard that, they pulled the rug out from under Ernest. And he never forgave me. It was just a matter of time. But he's very clever. I knew we weren't getting along, but I never saw him coming.'

That was particularly the case because André's contract had another three years to go – and they were obliged to tell him what their precise plans were.

Two weeks before the final, final blow-up, a senior member of the board came to see André – with an offer. 'We have had a meeting of the board,' he had told him, 'and we think you ought to go home and celebrate with your wife. We would like you to sign a new contract and you can do what you like. You can have another three, four or eight years . . .'

Not only was André Previn having his contract extended, he was told, but it was going to be fairly open-ended.

'My goodness,' André asked the messenger of such good tidings, 'does Ernest know about this?'

'What,' the man asked, 'has Ernest got to do with this?' And they wanted Ronald Wilford to write directly to the board and not to Fleishmann. 'I said that was rough, it's never done. He said that it was going to be done then.'

'Is that in the bag?' André asked.

'It's in the bag.'

Not only was he going to get more money, but the billing was going to be different. Instead of concerts being advertised as 'The Los Angeles Philharmonic – Music Director, André Previn', in future they would proclaim: 'André Previn with the Los Angeles Philharmonic.'

That very night, the board met Ernest Fleishmann. Two weeks later, they came back to André and told him that the planned new contract could not now go ahead.

'To this day, I don't know what happened,' André told me. People wrote into the LA *Times* and asked, "What's he got? Dirty pictures of the board?" Nobody knew.'

Previn told the board member that, of course, he wouldn't stay where he was not wanted, but reminded him of the previous conversation, and said that 'unbeknownst to you, my secretary was sitting in the adjoining room with the door open and she heard this.'

The man, says André, 'gave a great answer. He said, "André, I don't doubt for a minute that you thought I said that." I said, "You didn't say it?" And he replied, "No. You thought you heard I said it."'

André announced that he was giving up the post of music director. He did not want a title. The orchestra didn't want a man with a title – 'because they don't know how to cope with it'.

And he adds: 'To be fair, Ernest is a very, very clever man. But he's a man of such inpenetrable ego that he thinks that what he says is earth shattering. The truth of the matter is that you get past Burbank and nobody knows who he is.'

The *Los Angeles Times* reported that Fleishmann always gets what he wants. 'That's exactly what happened.'

He says it was "all a set up I think, everybody felt unbelievably manoeuvered'.

André was also 'very, very hurt by it'. But, as he says: 'Fleishmann wants to do everything – and he hasn't got it in his personality to utter the phrase, "I'll check with the music director."'

The day it was all announced, the members of the orchestra presented André with a cartoon – captioned 'Help Wanted'.

Since the news of the change was announced, André had a series of telephone calls from friends – all of them saying, he maintains, 'I told you so. Didn't I warn you? Don't you remember I told you five years ago, you can't go there, they'll drive you to suicide'.

André was still contracted to appear with the orchestra as guest conductor.

He went back to the orchestra the first time after the row the following September. It was traumatic for him. He didn't know how he was going to be received.

He needn't have worried. He began his first rehearsal with the words, 'Well, so what's new?' The orchestra clapped wildly.

As he stepped out for his first concert – he got a standing ovation from the orchestra. 'After each piece, there was like a circus-like response.' So much so that he told the assistant manager as he walked into the wings: 'Remind me, will you, I ought to quit more often, this is the biggest success I've ever had here.

'And that suits me fine. Now I'm there making music with an orchestra which I get along with great and they like me. We do lovely concerts and make very good records. I quite like that, I come in, we have rehearsals, we have lovely concerts and I go off. In other words, I get on with that which I consider the principal part of my job but which doesn't mean I have to work within that kind of orchestra structure.'

When the wounds were bound and healed, he realised he was as hurt for the players as much as he was for himself. 'There are perhaps fifteen great orchestras in the world, each with about a hundred people in them. That's 1,500 people in the WORLD. Don't you think they are special people who deserve special treatment? Then, when management thinks these people are interchangeable with people on an assembly line in a tuna-packing factory, I don't like it.'

On reflection, as far as he was concerned, he says: 'Los Angeles was not some kind of petulance on my part, not a manoeuvering ploy. There was the unending scheming . . . It was like some John Le Carré novel. I couldn't handle it. It had been going on for many years.'

His orchestra liked the way he behaved at recording sessions. 'No,' he'd call during a recording in the summer of 1990, 'its pum-de-pum-de-pum . . . OK. Let's play pum-de-pum, de-pum.' That part of John Harbison's new symphony had to be rerecorded – André was singing as he conducted.

But as Harold Diktorow told me: 'There are still some who don't like him. You have that with every conductor. There are some who want the Zubin Mehta-Bernstein style. He gets that way himself sometimes, but he's really not that sort of conductor.'

Diktorow's son Maurice is the orchestra's doctor as well as a reserve violinist. 'André keeps the orchestra well,' he told me.

But Lorin Levée, predictably, is glad that Previn is no longer music director. 'He was the wrong man at the wrong time. The views of the orchestra were not passed on and the orchestra paid the price. This city needs excitement. It's a name-orientated city. He had the name from MGM, not as a classical musician.' So even in his own orchestra Hollywood wouldn't go away.

Levée went on: 'It's true he had a good relationship with the orchestra, but that's not the issue. His performances were not stimulating. There was nothing wrong with them, but there was nothing right with them either. He wanted to be everybody's friend. You can't be everybody's friend, you have to be a boss sometimes.'

Danny Rothmuiler put it to me like this: 'André's greatest quality at this time was that he never showed any of the tension of the break-up. He kept a stiff upper lip. But we have to face the fact that those people who liked him before will always like him. Those who don't like him, never will.'

And then there's the bassoon player, Alan Goodman: 'There was a mob psychology involved. People saw how the wind was blowing. People were swept up and said, if there's a fuss there must be something wrong, so lots of people complained that they didn't find him inspiring, musicians close to management told tales. They were looking for God when they had André Previn. And we should appreciate that he is such a friendly warm person, even though that always means that people would take advantage of him. I thought that with him, we had nowhere to go but up.'

Another member of the orchestra, who didn't want to be named, told me: 'It turned out to have been something of a mis-match, like the wrong jockey on a horse. This orchestra is without tradition, without self-discipline, without effective, safe government. A very individualistic band needs a tight rein on it. So there was a sordid, unnecessary scenario taking place before our eyes – information was withheld, there was misinformation, deceit, divisive plotting, personal agendas masquerading as artistic judgment. It all took its toll on André and the orchestra.

'Why did we have to go through all of that? He understands very well the nature of the orchestra although he may not have realised that this orchestra was unchangable, that individual freedom was valued above group identity. It is not the crown jewel of the city's cultural worth. We were all constantly riding shotgun.'

One member of the orchestra, an all-American young man with the all-Scots name of Rob Roy McGregor is so fond of André that he and his wife, who also plays in the orchestra, asked him to be the godfather of their son. He told me: 'Throughout all the events of the year, one person alone conducted himself with class and that person was André. This was most impressive to me because I saw everyone else reduced to a rather base state when things got really tough. This was my first experience with that sort of power struggle which Shakespeare wrote about. André was the one who retained his composure and stature as an honest and gentle person.'

Others shared that view. There was Anne Giles, for instance, the principal flautist (or flute player, 'it depends on how much they want to pay me'). She told me: 'André is a conductor we don't see very often. He has a real sense of chamber music and it's marvellous what he has done for the main orchestra's repertoire. It's so good to have someone who's a real musician.'

Heiichero Ohyama was sorry to see him go. 'He has no secrets from us. From most conductors, we get, "Mind your own business". If André doesn't know something, he'll admit it and say, "I don't know." The problem with the orchestra now is that there are many people who want to take over. We are losing direction – and that's a fatal situation because a dispute in an orchestra becomes a dispute from person to person.'

Trumpet player Boyd Hood liked André's sense of compromise. 'That's not a weakness. It's more a mark of his being a great musician.'

In London, as we have seen, his problems were totally different, caused by what André saw as the lack of concern and consideration shown to the musicians. 'There's just no getting around the fact that a London orchestra in the current impasse set-up of things has no chance of being world competitive. They can play great. They give stunning concerts, but they are not as reliably flawless as the great orchestras because they can't be. If you play rubbish and know it's rubbish before you go in, with or without a conductor, with rehearsal or without rehearsal, the playing gets terrible. Once in a while someone comes and pulls out all the stops and they play great, I'm full of admiration for them.'

He admires the way all the musicians who have worked with him play. He can't understand it, he says, how flute players can make their sounds without having their arms hurt unbearably. It's one of the mysteries of the art.

What never mystifies him is the compulsion to play and for the audiences to listen.

At the end of 1989 he went back again to Berlin, now a city quite suddenly freed, a city suddenly without a Wall. He conducted a concert there with the Berlin Philharmonic, 'it was the most successful concert in my life in terms of music making and reactions from audiences.'

The orchestra were never better and they thought he couldn't be improved, either.

As they were about to leave for London, they found the airport was fogbound and had to drive to Brussels – where they were told that the plane at their disposal could take the musicians reasonably comfortably. There was also room for either their clothes or their instruments. They had the choice – which would they take with them? It wasn't really a question to ask an orchestra, even this one, the most formal ensemble in the world.

So they went to London and played in jeans and sweatshirts – not even the suits they wore for rehearsal – and everyone loved it as much as they had in Berlin. The surprise of seeing an orchestra playing in anything but dinner jackets was so overwhelming that the people at the Festival Hall seemed to enjoy it all the more for the lack of formality.

But that was just one change from what could be regarded as normality. When he went to Britain, André was no longer going home. Leaving Los Angeles turned into a complete switch in the Previns' lifestyle. He not only sold his Beverly Hills house, he sold up The House, too. It wasn't just that he didn't really need to spend so much time in Britain any more, the cottage in Leigh had always been Mia's house and now he wanted something new for Heather.

They bought a brand new, large house standing in eight acres in upstate New York and when he first moved in, André looked like a dog wagging two tails – or perhaps it should be a conductor waving two batons. In addition to the usual reception rooms and bedrooms, there was a study and a library where even Lukas knew he had to be quiet. He did his composing downstairs in a basement – because he knew that if he had somewhere comfortable in which to work, he would continually break off to make tea. He had a guest house and stables and walked for four miles every day. It was very cold in winter and very hot in summer, but it was beautiful, it was near a shopping mall to which he and Heather would go late at night and have a great time.

Besides that, things got done there. He never stops telling people that when Heather's car broke down, the garage apologised for not being able to repair it until that afternoon. 'In London I found that if I went into a shop close to five-thirty, they'd get annoyed.'

More than that, England was no longer the green and pleasant land he had first found more than an quarter of a century before.

'The quality of life has changed and changed for the worse. And I don't want to send my children to school in England. I think the standards of education are terrible.'

His children are his delight more than ever now, particularly since all that old guilt has really gone. He takes them out for dinner at a restaurant and is as proud of them as he has ever been of anything in his life. 'Is this your class?' a waiter asked him recently, eyeing his Oriental daughters. 'My class?' he replied. 'No. They're my kids.'

Lukas hasn't yet started asking questions like that of the man he calls 'Dadda'. Christopher Robin is growing and no matter the problem, he can still make a nasty taste in his father's mouth turn to marshmallow.

Lukas has his own piano teacher, André will no more teach him formally than Jack would have taught him himself. 'I know that when he said, "Let's go out and play," we'd go.' But he has taught him to play tennis – to such an extent that he has gone on to another teacher who thinks he is so good, he may one day play at Wimbledon. Considering that that was where his parents had their first date, it would perhaps be only fitting.

He has fathered his career with perfect devotion, although I saw him in 1990 manfully face a fan at someone else's concert we were attending. 'Hi,' said the man, 'are you Mr Previn?'

'I am,' said André.

'What are you doin' these days?' the man pressed.

'Not much,' said André. 'Just loafing.'

Hardly. He was busier than he had ever been before in his life. But he had it under control. As he told the LA Phil. at a rehearsal: 'Try not to be so relentless.' But relentless he continued to be in pursuing his life in all its varied forms.

The year 1991 was to see André not just continuing his never-ending – or, as he would put it, 'endless' – round of concerts and recording sessions, but in the course of so doing finding new paths to walk and old associations to renew.

It was the Mozart bicentennial year and André was in the throes of marking his favourite composer's occasion suitably.

For German-language TV stations he strode the roads that Mozart had taken on his various world tours, walking the lanes as well as going into the concert halls – all the time making the typical Previn jokes and comments which he thought made the composer's story all the more fascinating without insulting or appearing to make fun of the music that followed his commentary. Then he did the same thing again in English. The American producers liked them a lot more than did the Germans who wanted him to take the whole thing exceedingly seriously. Fine, he told them, but if that was the way they wanted it, they had got the wrong man. The producers decided that they really had got the right man and let him do things his own way.

More significantly to him, he celebrated Mozart by taking the Vienna Philharmonic to Japan. It was again a perfect mix – one of his favourite orchestras in the country he knew he could be guaranteed the kind of reception he craves. It was, to use another Previn phrase, sen-sational. 'To take the Vienna Philharmonic on tour, particularly to Japan, is the closest thing I know to a triumphant entry. The places were so packed, you couldn't get a sardine into any of those halls to hear an orchestra which plays Mozart better than anybody else alive. To be on a tour with them and play nothing but Mozart programmes was one of the great treats of my life.'

He might have had fewer aspirations of triumph when he accepted an invitation to conduct students at the famed Curtis Music Institute in Philadelphia, an academic establishment whose alumni read not so much *like* a Who's Who in Music as actually is a Who's Who In Music.

The invitation had been a long-standing one and André had willingly enough accepted the chance offered him by his old friend Gary Graffman, the eminent American pianist who for the best part of a decade had been heading this prestigious institution, made up of between 160 and 170 youngsters from all over the world who each year win scholarships (none of them could get in there by paying for admission).

It was not an invitation to be treated lightly. As he said: 'You could imagine easily that if you have 170 kids on full scholarship out of all the ambitious youngsters in all the world, they have to be awfully good.' André accepted the invitation to conduct the students' annual concert held at the Philadelphia Academy of Music, the very building at which the Philadelphia Orchestra itself plays.

The date had been arranged a year earlier. There would be no fee, simply expenses, but he would have to work as hard with it as though he were conducting the Los Angeles Philharmonic. There would be no compromises with what he anticipated would be an exceedingly good *student* orchestra. It turned out to be slightly different.

'It was in many ways an eye opener,' he says now. 'One can say under quite a few circumstances, "What a wonderful student orchestra!" and "aren't the kids marvellous?" But I came away from there with, not the impression, but the knowledge that this was, right now, a world-class orchestra.'

From youngsters aged between 14 and 24, many of whom had already appeared as soloists with professional symphony orchestras, he heard music played the way he hears it at every concert with one of the numerous internationally-famed ensembles he conducts all through the year. 'There were absolutely no concessions to be made,' is how he put it to me. 'If you wanted to compare it, you would have to go to the major orchestras in the major cities – and even then you would have to be careful about with whom you compare them because they can play anybody out of house and home.'

It was the sort of awakening – and joy – for André that comes when a teacher discovers a pupil can be taught nothing more. These, though, were not *his* pupils but young people who had a love for music that comes alive in every generation and to which he could relate totally. It was what music was all about. 'They are not all going to wind up in orchestras. Some of them are going to be soloists and some of them, very great soloists at that.' Now, one of the problems with brilliantly gifted students is that they know how gifted they are and tend to relate to other people as though they are doing all the favours. Not the Curtis kids, as he delights in calling them.

'There is not an ounce of cynicism, not a moment of boredom. There's no resentment. No one looks at his watch. No one says, "When is rehearsal over?" They would just as soon work twenty-four hours straight. They are not angelic. I'm not talking about the Vienna Choir Boys. They are not just determined to get good grades. They are not sitting there out of fear. They simply are so passionate about music and what they could contribute to it that it fills their day. The amount of selflessness and effort is just remarkable.'

The experience of playing with them his own work, *Principals* – the one he had written for the Pittsburgh orchestra, which he chose because of the opportunities it provided for a number of soloists – a Mozart piano concerto, which he himself conducted from the keyboard, and the Vaughan Williams No. 2 symphony, the London, which he had been specifically asked to conduct with the Curtis orchestra, was more than just the eye opener he describes. it was a great awakening. 'I hadn't expected to be able to compare them with some of the greatest orchestras in the world'.

He recognised it not so much from what they did right, but how they rectified what they had done wrong. 'There was one violin passage,' he recalled for me, 'which was a mess.'

He told them, 'This is purely technical. I'd like to leave it today and come back to it tomorrow.' The following day, he did return to the passage. The mistakes had not only been rectified, the performance by the violinists was perfect. All the eighteen first violins were spot on. He asked how many of them had taken the work home with them. All eighteen put up their hands and said that they had. 'The terrible and sad thing is that that gets lost. You can't play for a whole lifetime and keep that particular zeal; when they get older and have responsibilities, they want to get home – but the thing that is wonderful is that it renews itself in generations all the time. Those people who have been fashionably pessimistic about the future of symphony orchestras are just wrong. A week like that would make anybody happy about the future of the symphony orchestra. Obviously, they are the best, but there are others at other schools who are probably close, too.'

Almost immediately afterwards, he made arrangements to do a similar concert at Curtis the following year. 'And I can't wait. After a particularly tough season, feeling overworked and wondering how I could get everything done, it was a wonderful refresher course in how we all got into it in the first place.'

As he confesses: 'When the fourth plane in a row has been cancelled and your luggage has been lost, you suddenly ask yourself, "What AM I doing here?" But I came away from Curtis so happy and I was glad to be a musician. I was so proud of the fact that this was a particular discipline that will always renew itself.'

At about this time, André Previn agreed to his own exercise in renewal. He agreed he would go back to his old love, the London Symphony Orchestra in October 1992. The announcement came the day

after he had announced that he was giving up the principal con-
ductorship of the Royal Philharmonic – going out of his way to stress
that he had no quarrels with the RPO and that, contrary to what a lot
of people were alleging, he was, and always will be, a great admirer
of his old friend Vladimir Ashkenazy. Now the LSO could reveal that
he had accepted the title of Conductor Laureate of their orchestra. It
plainly had a sound about it that appealed to him more than that of
'Conductor for Life' which still seemed to indicate that perhaps he
was not going to live very long.

It had been an offer that members of the LSO had been pressing
upon him for a long time. They had pursued him all over the map.
They went to America to try to entreat him over. They had given a
party for him the last time he had been in London – organised by
Clive Gillinson, the managing director, at which all the 'old boys and
girls' he had known so well during his time with the LSO had been
present.

'I enjoyed my work with the RPO a lot,' he told me, 'but there are
both selfish and practical reasons why I now look forward to this.'
The practicalities were obvious to him. For all that he had said about
the Barbican before, he was now satisfied that improvements had
been made to the hall which would make it more to his liking and the
over-riding fact was that the orchestra could regard it as home. There
would be little need for them to go looking for outside rehearsal facilities because they could nearly always rehearse at the Barbican itself.

'For anybody outside of England, stating that fact would seem like
an insane remark, but it isn't in Britain because all the other orchestras do have to look for other places in which to rehearse.'

Just as significant was the fact that both private patrons and the
City of London, to say nothing of the Arts Council, had managed to
raise enough money for the LSO for the musicians not to have to go
looking for more dog food commercials. 'It sounds so callous to cas-
tigate the other orchestras for not paying their musicians enough so
that they don't have to do outside things, but I'm getting to an age
where my time with one orchestra is limited every year and I would
like that time to be spent doing things under conditions closer to the
optimum than other orchestras are able to give.'

Not only were the LSO members spared what he calls 'demeaning'
work, but they had time to perform chamber music. As he recalls:
'The guys in the RPO always said, "Oh, chamber music! Wouldn't it
be wonderful!" But they not only didn't have the time, they couldn't
count on that time remaining open if they did have it. It's a fact that
in all the years in which I have been working and with all the orches-

tras I have conducted, the RPO is the only one with whom I have never played chamber music.'

The LSO, which constantly commissions new music and has a composer in residence, planned to inaugurate a chamber music season, which was a delight for him to hear. 'The other thing is that they have a pretty imposing stable of committed conductors who will keep the standards of that orchestra as high as possible. Unlike most London orchestras who are forced to have almost anybody who is available that many times a year, the LSO has made a series of commitments to a lot of very good people.'

Clive Gillinson is certainly glad to have André aboard again. 'The thing about him,' is that he is a conductor who cares for his musicians. We appreciate that, even the little things like travelling with members of the orchestra and having snacks with them.'

There were also, for Previn himself, the sentimental reasons. 'I started my career in England with the LSO and was with them for eleven years and I owe them. It's more than just for sentimental reasons. We made over 200 records and I took them round the world, it seems to me, twice a week.'

He was going to make more records with them in the future. He could also be sure that those records would not then be duplicated by the same orchestra very soon afterwards under a new conductor – which happens with other outfits and, as he says, kills both records before they have a chance of getting into the shops.

'I cannot tell you how many times I have made records with the RPO which they have *instantly* duplicated by playing the same work with other conductors.

But there was more to do with the RPO. He was still going to take them on a tour of Japan before he took up his LSO position in the autumn of 1992 and would make some records with them, but he was looking forward to his 'new old' orchestra immensely. As he told me: 'How many times in your life do you get the opportunity to complete a circle?'

In a way, he was still completing his jazz circle, enjoying every recording gig in a sophisticated studio just as much as he ever had in the Los Angeles garage. In the late spring of 1991, he spent a week in New York recording jazz with his old sparring partners Ray Brown and Mundell Lowe. But this time with the seemingly unlikely addition of the soprano Dame Kiri Te Kanawa, perhaps currently the best known classical female singer in the world.

André and Dame Kiri had already proved themselves to be a heady combination. Five months earlier, they had recorded *Der Fleider-*

maus in London. To quote André, they had got on 'so famously' that they were about to do a lieder recital together at the Vienna Festival and were to do another Strauss opera, *Capricio* in San Francisco.

It was her idea to do – 'that loathsome word – a cross-over record,' he says. Backstage at Covent Gardent that December when they recorded *Der Fleidermaus*, he had tinkered with some tunes which he thought she might enjoy and she did.

'It is endlessly amusing for me these days to step back and see Ray Brown and Mundell Lowe cooking away and there among them, by God, is Dame Kiri. And she's wonderful, singing a lot of pretty, upthings.' 'Upthings' like 'Too Marvellous For Words' and 'It Could Happen To You', 'the sort of thing you could find on any record by Peggy Lee. I don't think we will go and open at Ronnie Scott's, but I would if they wanted us to. She is absolutely marvellous.'

There was also more work with other sopranos. He had been commissioned by Carnegie Hall to compose for their centenery celebrations. He chose a five-song cycle written especially for Kathleen Battle with orchestra and words by Tony Morrison. Both the singer and Carnegie Hall were delighted with the results.

There were plans for recording a number of operas in Vienna – most of his old reticence had by now gone – and he was enjoying the results of another new composition which had been enthusiastically received – a set of variations for solo piano especially for his friend Emmanuel Ax.

And then there's Heather, who has made the man now sixty-two years old feel thirty years younger. She still says he's naughty. 'He's wicked, actually. But I think I'd had it if he ever stopped.'

People see it watching him on the podium, making sweet music. They'd hate it if he ever stopped.

INDEX